THE
Tapestry

MARYANN MINATRA

HARVEST HOUSE PUBLISHERS
Eugene, Oregon 97402

THE TAPESTRY

Copyright © 1993 by Harvest House Publishers
Eugene, Oregon 97402

Library of Congress Cataloging-in-Publication Data

Minatra, MaryAnn, 1959-
   The tapestry / MaryAnn Minatra.
      p.   cm.
   ISBN 1-56507-037-2
   I. Title.
PS3563.I4634T36   1993   92-20866
813'.54—dc20   CIP

Although my name is on the cover... without your continual encouragement and faith, I could never have written this book. That is why The Tapestry *is lovingly dedicated to you, my beloved.*

Acknowledgments

Sincere thanks to Harvest House for their enthusiastic response to *The Tapestry*.

Deep thanks to my family and friends for their enthusiasm and encouragement in my writing.

To my sister-in-law Beck, thanks again for being my makeup artist; I needed it!

To Susannah, Sam, Meg, Rebecca, and little Emily... I am fully convinced there aren't five better kids anywhere on earth. Having this book published is indeed a special highlight of my life, but ya'll are really what makes me rich.

And finally, to Him who blesses abundantly, thank You for this gift.

Pennsylvania, 1828

♦♦ ♦♦ ♦♦

The woman had been upset for days. She ate and slept very little. Her husband, when he was home, took no notice of her distress. He had more pressing concerns—like scratching enough money together to buy more whiskey. When she had become his bride five years earlier, there had been more money. But it, like his business, had been gambled and drunk away.

So the woman sat in her cane-backed rocker for hours at a time and waited—and prayed. She didn't bother to light a candle or lamp, but simply let the fireplace provide her light. When her eyes were not closed in prayer, they rested on the little form sleeping fitfully in the narrow bed. When the child became restless or cried out, she eagerly scooped him up, drew closer to the fire and rocked him. In those long hours she reflected on the last few years, and wondered at how her life had changed so much.

The tension had been present from the beginning—a reality before the minister had even finished the wedding ceremony. How could she have been so blind to her husband's true nature? She ceased to ask herself that question—there was no answer. Yet the tension had grown until she even feared for her young son's life. Four nights ago her husband had returned after a two-week absence, roaring and belligerent, cursing and violent. This time she could not restrain or calm him. He abused her verbally and finally raged out against his own flesh, shoving his two-year-old son so roughly the child had fallen, breaking an arm.

Now the boy lay feverish, his arm tightly bandaged. The doctor had said it was not a serious break and the boy would recover with little problem. But what did the future hold? she wondered. Surely there would be more abuse. The woman feared for her son not only physically, but emotionally and spiritually as well, for wasn't an earthly father supposed to model the heavenly Father's love? What, then, was her little boy learning to expect from God? What hope was there? She had been praying for her husband three long years—with no apparent effect.

The next day the child was the same, and with reluctance the woman left him in care of a neighbor and went to church meeting. Perhaps here, in a group of fellow believers, she would find an answer to her problem. She would also see her sister and brother-in-law. They, with their infant daughter, were moving west, drawn irresistibly by the alluring Missouri territory. It crushed the woman to think of their leaving; they were her only living family.

The meeting room was crowded by the time she arrived and she could only smile a greeting at her sister, who was tightly wedged in close to the speaker's platform. The woman sat with bowed head, thinking. She wept and prayed, and before the minister had closed his message, she had an answer. The answer left her cold and terribly sad—but determined.

The next night, the little boy drifted off into peaceful, fever-less sleep. The woman took a square of blue homespun and placed her son's few clothes and one other small object in the center and tied it carefully. She leaned down over him, smelling his hair and skin, breathing deeply, so she wouldn't forget. She studied the smooth curve of his baby cheek. Her tears flowed down on the covers, yet she knew in her heart she was doing what was best. Finally she took him in her lap, holding him carefully—minding his arm—and sang, then whispered, then prayed for him. She never slept that long night.

"Do you know how much I love you, my son?" she murmured. "I'll pray for you every day! You'll be a man of God!" she finished in a breaking, passionate whisper.

Sunrise came too soon. She picked up the child and carried him through the woods to her sister's house. The woman kissed her son a final time then passed him and his little bundle to the arms of her tearful sister, sitting beside her husband in the loaded wagon. The two women held each other and the parting sister spoke needed words of love and encouragement. Giving up a son was difficult enough, but in this year of 1825, leaving a husband, however abusive, was almost unthinkable.

"I'll write you as much as I can. I know we'll be together again, someday. Don't worry about Henri," the sister said, glancing down at the child and gently stroking his face.

The woman smiled a trembling smile and waved as she watched the wagon join the line of other wagons rolling west.

Chapter 9

Kentucky, 1829

He was just over six feet, broad-shouldered, dark-haired—and frowning. His arms were crossed and he shifted irritably from one foot to the other. He couldn't dance, didn't like dances, didn't want to be at this one. He had only come to please his cousin. He hoped they could leave soon. He was made even more uncomfortable by the many open stares he was receiving. Sullen though he might be, he was also quite handsome. His dark hair was thick and wavy, his blue-green eyes were set in an olive-skinned face, his chin was strong and square. His cousin nudged him.

"Will, you're not even trying to have a good time! Look, the gals are practically... Well, I just wish I were in your boots!"

The room in which they stood boomed with the rhythm of feet scooting across a puncheon floor. Candles in sconces flickered along the walls and a bright kerosene lamp hung from the center of the ceiling. There was dancing, laughter, music and food.

"Who is she, Bart?" the dark-haired man asked suddenly, pointing across the crowded room.

"Who?"

"That woman there, in the gray silk, with the dark-brown hair."

"Ah... So, you *have* picked one out, eh?" Bart O'Dell was laughing.

Will frowned. "Now, tell me. Who is she?"

"That, my dear cousin, is Rebecca Cash, oldest daughter of John and Violet Cash. Sister to that beauty there," Bart said, pointing at a younger, lighter-haired woman nearby. "Her name is Elizabeth."

Will never even glanced at the younger sister. He had noticed the auburn-haired woman the moment she had entered the room on the arm of a tall blond fellow. She was immediately swept into the circle of dancers, while her escort retreated to the perimeter of the dance floor. Will could see the creamy smoothness of her skin and craned his neck this way and that, frustrated that he couldn't see the color of her eyes. He noticed she smiled a great deal. His eyes were riveted on her and it surprised him to suddenly realize that he had no intention of giving up his scrutiny.

"Is the man that she came in with her beau?" he asked Bart.

"Now, Will—"

"Is he?" he demanded.

"I don't know if—" Bart stopped, amused at Will's sudden change in behavior.

"Listen, Will," Bart resumed, "Rebecca Cash isn't for you. She's..."

"She's what?" Will asked, still not drawing his eyes away from her.

"Well, she's peculiar for one thing."

"Peculiar? How?"

"Independent type. Picky about men. Snobbish if you ask me. She—"

"Turned you down, eh?" Will chuckled as his cousin turned red.

"I'm telling you, Will," Bart insisted, "she's strange. Different ideas. Besides, if it's looks you're after, her sister is much more of a beauty."

"I think Rebecca Cash is the most beautiful woman I've ever seen," Will said, stubbornly.

"Be sensible, Will."

But William O'Dell gave no sign of hearing his cousin's warning. He left Bart's side and made his way across the dance floor. Many eyes followed him, curious to see what suddenly motivated the handsome stranger who had stood stone-faced all evening, dancing with no one.

She was taller than any other woman there. Her chestnut-hued hair fell in rich folds down her back and it made him think of silk as she turned to look at him. The music ended and before it could begin again, he spoke to her.

"Good evening, Miss Cash." He bowed slightly.

"Good evening, sir," she returned in a low voice.

"My name is William O'Dell and I'm from Illinois and—"

"Yes, I know," she said smiling.

"You know?"

"Of course. Your arrival is a big event to my little man-starved town."

Will felt supremely embarrassed. He cleared his throat awkwardly.

"I'm pleased to meet you, Mr. O'Dell," she said, extending her hand. Her smile was teasing, but friendly.

"Shall we dance?" he asked, leading her out onto the floor.

They danced a few minutes in silence as he forced himself to focus on things just past her shoulder. It was very difficult not to look at her closely, now that he had the chance.

He was not the most skilled partner she had ever danced with, but she could sense stability and strength emanating from him.

"My cousin said two interesting things about you, Miss Cash," he said, finally.

"Oh?"

"He said you were . . . peculiar."

She laughed heartily and he slightly tightened his grip on her arm.

"Thank you! And what other compliment did he bestow, dare I ask?"

"He said you weren't the loveliest woman here."

"Your cousin will turn my head with such flattery!" she said, laughing again. "And did such odd credits appeal to you, Mr. O'Dell?"

He said nothing for such a long time that she was forced to look into his face. She was surprised to see his eyes and mouth had become serious. His voice was intense, barely above a whisper as he leaned down toward her. Without realizing it, they had stopped dancing.

"My cousin doesn't understand me and has no idea what I want . . . in a woman. And he has absolutely no judgment on real beauty."

She faltered, a bit nervous now. "Mr. O'Dell, I'm hardly a flighty young woman easily taken in by such compliments. I—"

"I wasn't complimenting you, Miss Cash. I was merely stating the truth."

She couldn't laugh, or even smile now. He hadn't let go of her hand and was gazing at her with obvious, intense interest. Suddenly, someone was at Will's elbow and Rebecca managed to wrench her eyes away from him. Will turned to find the blond man at his side. He was scowling. Across the room, Bart O'Dell was chuckling at his cousin.

"Isaiah," Rebecca said in a voice that was still shaky, "this is Mr. William O'Dell from Illinois. The most ... interesting dance partner I've ever had."

Will could sense it would be a wasted effort to even extend his hand to the silent man. There was something about him ... but Will would puzzle it over another time.

"I think I'm ready to leave," Rebecca said presently, regaining her composure. "I wore my most elegant shoes, Mr. O'Dell—and my tightest ones, also! Mother worries I haven't a shred of natural vanity, but I do!" She laughed, the easiness had returned to her voice. She was back in control of herself.

"Thank you, Isaiah," she said, as the blond-haired man slipped a shawl around her shoulders. "Thank you for the dance, Mr. O'Dell." She gave him her hand.

He held it lightly and took a deep breath.

"My business is finished here and I'd planned to leave in the morning. But ... Can I call on you tomorrow, Miss Cash?"

"Tomorrow?"

"Yes," he said. The look which passed between them was a long one.

The door to the Cash house was opened by a girl Will estimated at fourteen years of age. He noted she had the same blue eyes that Rebecca had, but there were no other similarities. She openly gawked at him without saying a word. He removed his hat.

"Is Miss Cash in?" he asked.

"I'm Miss Cash, Rebecca's Miss Cash and Elizabeth is Miss Cash," she replied saucily. "Which one do you want?"

Will squirmed. "Miss Rebecca Cash."

"She's in," the girl said, assuming a pout and saying nothing more.

"May I see her please?"

"Who are you?" came the tart reply.

Will twisted his hatband angrily behind his back. "William O'Dell," he said, striving to keep his voice polite.

"How do you know Rebecca?"

"May I step in please?" Will asked through gritted teeth.

"Suit yourself." She grudgingly opened the door wider. Giving him a final impish stare, she flounced down the hallway to a set of closed double doors. Will could hear someone's voice coming through the door, reading aloud.

"Oh, Miss Cash, you have a caller!" said the girl, sliding back the panels. She ran off, giggling. Rebecca looked up from where she was sitting, and Will couldn't fail to notice the flush of color that came to Rebecca's face when she saw him. She was sitting on the sofa—and the blond-haired man was lying beside her, his head in her lap. Seeing Will, he swung up abruptly, and Rebecca stood more slowly, laying the book beside her on the sofa.

"Mr. O'Dell! hello," she said.

"I'm sorry, I didn't know you weren't alone," Will muttered awkwardly. He began backing up.

"It's fine," she urged. "Please come in and sit down."

Reluctantly he perched on the edge of the nearest chair, never having felt so out-of-place in all his life. He could feel himself beginning to sweat.

"I...I stayed another day because of you, Miss Cash," he blurted, shocked at the loudness of his voice in the still room.

His mind was reeling. What a ridiculous thing to say, O'Dell, he scolded himself, even if it is true! The woman's beau is in the room!

The blond-haired man grabbed the book on the sofa and closed it loudly. Will focused on him, since he couldn't look at Rebecca. What was it about this fellow? Was he a mute? Was her attraction to him the reason Bart had said Rebecca was odd?

Rebecca had been tracing a pattern on the arm of the couch and now looked up.

"You are very direct, Mr. O'Dell. I would imagine you're a good businessman."

"Actually, I don't like this part of my business very much at all. The selling, I mean." Before he could stop it, his eyes rolled upward in embarrassment. What a thing to say, he chided himself.

"What do you like about your work then?" she asked, graciously ignoring the implications of his remark.

"Growing apples. Well, that is, the Lord grows 'em, I just harvest 'em. Working with the trees, helping them grow. That's what I like."

She nodded her head thoughtfully. What was it about this stranger that made her think of strength and boyishness together? She could imagine him at nine or ten twisting his cap in the presence of a girl. The thought made her smile.

The blond-haired man stood up.

"We'll finish later, Isaiah—all right?" Rebecca asked, laying a hand on his arm. He nodded silently, caught up his cap and gave Will one final sharp look before striding past him, out of the room. The parlor was quiet again. Will still felt uncomfortable and Rebecca's eyes twinkled with amusement.

"Your family is all back in Illinois?" she ventured finally.

"No, I haven't any family in Illinois anymore. I'm an only child and my folks died ten years ago."

Silence again.

"You were reading that volume there." He nodded toward the thick black book at her side. She smiled and smoothed the cover. Will could see it was a Bible.

"Yes, Mr. O'Dell, it's a favorite of Isaiah's and mine. A collection of all our favorite authors."

Will smiled, finally relaxing to Rebecca's subtle humor. Their eyes met again—and the panel doors slid open loudly.

A woman in her late forties fluffed into the room. Will had never seen anyone so ... flamboyant in appearance. Violet Cash made every possible effort to cling to her fading youth and beauty. Her efforts were quite remarkable and, just a few neighbors whispered, somewhat theatrical."

"Why, Rebecca!" she cried in an animated voice, "We had no *idea* you had a *caller*! Gracious *me*!" She turned the full force of her eyes on Will and extended a plump hand.

"Mr. O'Dell, this is my mother, Mrs. John Cash."

"Violet," she insisted sweetly.

"Ma'am."

"So pleased to meet you, Mr. O'Dell. Why didn't you tell us, Rebecca?"

From the corner of his eye Will could see Rebecca stiffen. She made no answer.

"What brings you to Harristown, Mr. O'Dell?" Violet queried.

Will explained as briefly as possible. Rebecca watched him closely.

"Apples—how quaint. Where did you meet my daughter?"

"At the dance last night, Mother," Rebecca interrupted.

"Ah... Tell me, Mr. O'Dell... Do you find Kentucky girls as pretty as those in your state? After all, Illinois is rather primitive—barely in the Union."

Mercifully, Will was saved from answering by the entrance of two men.

"John, look. Rebecca has a caller! Mr. O'Dell from Illinois."

Will was really sweating now. The older man glowered at him a moment.

"Fine. Now, let's eat," he muttered, and stalked away.

Rebecca turned three shades of red and thought she might pass out.

"This is my son, James." The two shook hands briefly, then James followed his father.

"Now, you'll stay and dine with us," Violet Cash said, firmly.

"Oh, no! I mean—thank you, but I really need to be going."

"Nonsense! You came to see Rebecca and you must stay and dine with us." She linked her arm through his. Will sighed, realizing there was no escape.

In the dining room, Isaiah pulled out Rebecca's chair for her.

"Mr. O'Dell, this is my oldest brother, Isaiah," Rebecca said, proudly.

Isaiah gave Will a slight nod. So! Will thought. He turned his attention back to Rebecca's mother. He would not give the young woman the satisfaction of seeing his surprise.

The meal was memorable for Will, less for the food—which was delicious—then for the steady stream of chatter which Violet Cash maintained through the entire meal. He had never been questioned so in his entire life. He noticed Rebecca would not look at him, and seemed to be suffering from frequent bouts of stifled laughter.

When the meal was finally over, he made ready his flight.

"No, really I must go now," he replied to the inevitable entreaties. "Thank you for the meal."

"But you and Rebecca have hardly had any time alone," Violet Cash protested.

"Mother, I think Mr. O'Dell really needs to leave," agreed Rebecca.

She handed him his hat and showed him to the door.

"I'm... sorry," she said.

"Why?" he asked.

"Well..." She began to laugh behind her hand. "Really, it's me. I can't help it; they were really in grand form." And she went off into a helpless peal of laughter.

"I'll be back in the morning. Ten sharp," he said, suddenly.

Her laughter stopped instantly.

"What? Mr. O'Dell, really—"

"Until tomorrow, Miss Cash," he said firmly. He put on his hat and left.

He was at her door at ten sharp—just as she knew he would be. She was on the front porch as he rode up.

"Good morning, Miss Cash!"

"Good morning, Mr. O'Dell."

He dismounted and walked up to her, handing her a small bunch of wildflowers.

"I saw them as I rode over," he explained, "and I thought... Well, I thought you might like them."

He had pulled off his hat and was smiling at her. She couldn't say anything for a moment, feeling overwhelmed by his gesture and his magnetism.

She is so beautiful, he thought. "Lovely morning," he stammered.

She looked at him and took him prisoner with her eyes.

"Yes," she answered, simply.

"Shall we go for a walk, Miss Cash?" he said, offering his arm.

She nodded, rising. Leaving the porch, she chose a path away from the house. They walked for several minutes. Finally, they stopped.

"I'm awfully partial to my Illinois," he said, "but Kentucky has plenty of right to boast, too."

"You stayed another day after your business was finished," she observed.

He nodded. "Yes, and I do need to be starting back. But... You're my business now too."

Her hands went to her hips. "Mr. O'Dell!" she scolded.

"You could call me Will."

"Mr. O'Dell, I am *not* a part of your business! You've gotten a strange fancy into your head and—" His persistent smile was almost irritating her—almost. "You're probably used to getting your own way."

"Yes," he drawled. "You know what they say about only—children."

"Now—"

"Excuse me, but may I ask how old you are, Miss Cash?"

She burst out laughing, in spite of herself. "What a question! You are so...so direct, Mr. O'Dell!"

"I was just curious about your age."

"I'm twenty-six," she said with a challenging toss of her head.

"I'll be thirty next month," he replied.

"Fine. Now—"

"Can I call you Rebecca?"

"You are so infernally persistent!"

He shrugged, grinning.

They both laughed this time. She was standing close enough to him to see every line of his face. He was so...so very...

"I came to Harristown, Kentucky on business—and no other purpose," he began to explain, slowly. He paced to and fro in front of her. She was smiling inside.

"I went to the dance the other night because my cousin Bart urged me."

"And you were the belle of the ball!" she said with mock seriousness.

He considered her words a moment. Ignoring her jest, he went on. "I'm going back to Illinois and—you're making it darned difficult!" he said impatiently.

"Me?" she stammered. "Now listen to me, Mr. O'Dell—"

He took her hands. "Rebecca Cash—I'm asking you to go back to my home with me."

"Mr. O'Dell, I hardly think my father will approve of abduction! I know he seemed absent-minded but—"

"Miss Cash, I'm not talking about abduction and you know it!"

Now she became serious, pulling her hands from his.

"Don't say anything else. You'd better leave." She turned away.

"You've got me all upset inside!" Will protested. "I don't want to carry you off like a heathen. I want to marry you!"

"Don't—"

"Now, please, Miss Cash, you have to listen! Give me a chance. I...don't have much to offer you, I admit. I have land and a home...not a lot of money. I love God and I try to follow His ways. I would be a good husband to you. I would...I would cherish you, Rebecca!"

Still she would not allow herself to look at him.

"I know I haven't said, 'I love you.' Well, I don't...just yet. I mean I *like* you an awful lot and I admire you very much. I feel you're a good Christian woman and that's been my highest requirement all these years. You don't even have to cook! I tell you, Miss Cash, you are the most beautiful—"

"Stop! Just...Just stop!"

"I can't stop, don't you see!" he persisted. "If I feel all this now when we're just beginning, just think how much I could grow to love you!"

She was crying softly, now, and he took her by the shoulders.

"I didn't mean to make you cry," he said. "I...know I'm not too good at proposing."

"I can't marry you, Mr. O'Dell."

"Why not?"

Then Isaiah was there beside them, coming as silently and as suddenly as a shadow. He placed a threatening hand on Will's arm.

"Isaiah!" Rebecca touched his arm. He looked very angry.

"I wasn't hurting your sister, Isaiah," Will said.

"I'm fine, Isaiah, really." Rebecca patted her brother's arm reassuringly.

The silent man reached out and touched a tear on his sister's cheek. "We are just talking," Rebecca insisted. "Would you mind waiting for us over there?" she finished calmly.

"He's very faithful to you," Will said gently, as Isaiah moved away.

"Yes." She squared her shoulders, and Will could see the determination—and the pain—in her eyes.

"I was in love...once. Then he left unexpectedly, and I decided then and there I wouldn't become involved with anyone, ever again."

"One louse bites you and you throw us all out forever?"

"It would just be best I think," she said, firmly.

"Why?"

"I have plans.'

"Plans? May I ask what they are?"

"You've met my family," she explained. "You see how ... how harsh they can be. I'm surprised you came back."

"Are you really?"

Now she had to smile. "You are *so* very persistent! ... No, I suppose I'm not terribly surprised." Then she sobered again. "My family cares precious little for my brother, Mr. O'Dell. You can see that he has problems. The man—the one that said he loved me—he despised Isaiah, too. He left, and I'm glad. I intend to take care of my brother and let him take care of me. I love him; I always have. I plan to get a house where we can live peaceably. My family tires of my spinsterhood and Isaiah's impairment does not honor the Cash name—or so they think. We're rather alike, he and I."

Will kicked at some loose stones, thinking hard.

"I'm the answer to your situation, Miss Cash," he announced at last.

"You're impossible!" she cried.

"No, just direct and persistent," he corrected. "Now ..." He reclaimed her hands. "Could you possibly ... learn to care for me someday?"

Her mind whirled. Why was this man, whom she'd known less than forty-eight hours, so captivating? She thought of his words earlier: *I would cherish you, Rebecca.* Could she grow to cherish him? He wasn't smiling and because he waited, so obviously overwrought, she had to smile.

He took her smile for encouragement.

"Marry me, Miss Cash," he pressed. "Come home with me to Illinois. You *and* your brother. We can all have a good life together."

She looked past him a moment, then back into his eyes. "Yes, I'll marry you, Mr. O'Dell."

"You can call me Will."

Two days later, Harristown, Kentucky saw the departure of one of its daughters. Rebecca Cash married the apple merchant from Illinois. Perched on the seat of a wagon, she waved goodbye to her rather amazed family.

Isaiah did not travel with them. He had taken Will aside the day before they left.

"You an' 'Becca go on," the blond-haired man said in his slow, thick-tongued voice.

"Yes, Isaiah," Will replied, "after the ceremony tomorrow, we'll all leave."

"No." Isaiah shook his head stubbornly.

"No?"

"'Saiah folla behind you. You two together. She you wife now."

Suddenly, Will deciphered his meaning. Isaiah wanted his sister and her new husband to be alone. He would follow them, but at a distance which would not intrude upon the privacy of the newlyweds.

"All right, Isaiah. You follow us," Will smiled.

Rebecca, overhearing, instantly protested. Will held up his hands, placatingly.

"Now, Miss Cash! I imagine he'll have little trouble following us. He's wise in his own way." The two men smiled at each other. Isaiah nodded at his sister.

That first night, they camped by a quiet, lazy river. Will took care of the horses while Rebecca cooked their meal over the open fire.

After a few bites he exclaimed, "Brains, beauty, and can she cook!"

Before the firelight faded, he drew out his Bible and they read and prayed together.

"It's how we should begin our beginning," he said, simply.

The fire dwindled and the stars came out. Will helped Rebecca up into the wagon where, he found, she had made a soft bed of quilts for them. She pulled out the combs from her hair, watching him. He smiled and took her in a close embrace.

"Mr. O'Dell, you are so very direct!"

"Yes, and I rather think you like it!" he smiled, and kissed her gently.

Their laughter floated out on the night air.

Several days later, they crested a hill that overlooked Will's land.

"We're home, my gal!"

She squeezed his hand.

Two days later, Isaiah casually rode in. His face was tanned and Rebecca had never seen him look happier. They were all home. In Illinois.

Part I

Threads in the Hands of the Master

Chapter 1

Christmas Eve,
1842

◆◆ ◆◆ ◆◆

*P*eppercreek, Illinois was a sensible, unpretentious place which aimed at being nothing more than a quiet, friendly little hamlet. It did not publish its own tabloid, but relied on the news from Springfield—fifteen miles to the east—or Salem, eight miles south. Some years in the future it would try its hand at publishing, but that effort would fade away—like the town itself. Just after the turn of the century the town would be remembered only by old timers and antiquated maps, the site marked by nothing more than a meandering farm road and a grain elevator.

The main street of Peppercreek boasted a blacksmith and livery, the doctor's home and office, a carpenter's shop, a seamstress, and three private homes. The white clapboard church and schoolhouse stood at the west end of town, centered in a pasture that frequently accommodated picnics and summer revivals. The only imposing structure in Peppercreek was Baily's General Mercantile, a two-story building of gray weathered wood and countless narrow windows.

It was a clear winter night in Peppercreek—a night so cuttingly cold it could hurt your lungs to inhale. Hundreds of stars were scattered across the dark sky. Within the hour, the wind had shifted and a gauzy veil of clouds stretched over the landscape—innocent looking, yet heavy with snow.

On the O'Dell farm, a furlong or so distant from the cluster of buildings which marked the town, night and cold had settled on all creatures, human and animal alike. The white rock house, its sentinel line of slender aspens in the front and sturdy oaks in the back, was dark save for a single light burning in a lower window. It was a handsome, well-built house—made from Peppercreek's native rock—with green shutters at each window and a long, broad front porch. Three dormers jutted from the tin roof above the porch. Behind the house were stock pens and a large barn. Beyond that stretched a fifteen-acre apple orchard, gaining a growing reputation as producing Illinois' finest apples. Locals considered it the most prime property in Sangamon county. An apiary and a horse-breeding operation rounded out the enterprise. It was a farm that had known the blood, toil and pride of three generations of O'Dells.

In a darkened upstairs room, the young occupants were not yet asleep. After all, it was Christmas Eve. The windows were icy as three eager little faces pressed themselves to the glass. They had been put to bed with an admonition for quiet and immediate slumber, but they had disobeyed and now stood shivering in their flannel nightgowns.

The oldest was a slim girl of nearly ten, with serious blue-green eyes and a sleek auburn braid down her back. Her skin was olive, like her father's. She had been reluctant to disobey her parents, but felt drawn to the window like a pin to a magnet. She recognized the change in the wind—a beautiful, unique drama was unfolding outside. Tonight she had just gotten her feet warm in the folds of the log-cabin quilt when she heard that special, almost-silent sweep of the wind.

"Don't sneeze on me, Libby!" This came from the middle child, a vocal, energetic girl of eight. She had followed her sister out of the warm bed, groaning. If Wyeth, the oldest, was going to be naughty, it must be all right. She was nearly as tall as her sister, but "fleshier," as her plainspoken grandmother said. Her hair hung in two braids, thick cords of honey yellow. Her face was fair, like her mother's. She was cheerful, easy going, not overly tolerant of anything serious. Her name was Louisa.

The youngest sister, who had received the warning about her itchy nose, stood on a stool, stretching her five-year-old frame to see the grand thing her older sister was in awe about. She, like Wyeth, was the image of her father: dark-skinned and green-eyed, but with a cap of very dark curling hair that touched her shoulders.

"Can't see, can't see," she complained.

"It's just snowing," said Louisa snappily. "Hush up, now."

"There is no 'just' about a snowfall, Lou," responded Wyeth, seriously. "It's a . . . quiet, wonderful melody." She had that dream-like tone in her voice that practical Louisa knew well. When

Wyeth spoke like that, you knew she was in her own world. Louisa didn't necessarily understand everything her older sis said, but there was an unspoken respect for this vision of another world that Wyeth seemed to have.

"Look! It's like we're the only ones in the whole world! It's so quiet and peaceful!" Wyeth exclaimed.

"Can't see!" whined Libby again.

Louisa hoisted her up in her strong arms and all three were silent for a few moments, spellbound by the magic of the snowfall.

"The trees are dipped in frosting," murmured Wyeth.

A sneeze erupted from Libby again, showering the glass with tiny droplets. Louisa was disgusted. "Libby! Cover your nose! Where's your hanky?" she scolded. She turned to her older sister. "It's cold, Wyeth. Let's go back to bed," pleaded the now-shivering Louisa.

Wyeth drew away reluctantly. The three hopped back in bed, the two older girls on each side, Libby in the middle. They quietly discussed their hopes for the next day. Then the door opened and their mother's face was under-lit by the flickering light of the single candle she held.

Looking at their expectant faces, Rebecca had to smile. "Wyeth, how do you manage to get any sleep with these two rowdy sisters of yours?"

Louisa and Libby snickered. Wyeth thought a moment.

"Well . . . it *is* a sore trial." She was completely serious and Rebecca was glad Wyeth couldn't see her smile. She knew Wyeth had taken the expression from her grandmother.

"It's snowing, Mama," piped up Libby.

"Oh? How do you know that, daughter of mine?"

"We were—" She halted in guilty silence and they all burst out giggling.

"The snow is so beautiful, Mama. It . . . almost makes me cry," said Wyeth.

"Cry?" Louisa sounded scornful.

"Yes, it is lovely tonight," agreed Rebecca. "Still—how about settling down and going to sleep?"

"Is there anything in our stockings yet?" asked Louisa slyly.

"I doubt it. Too many little girls still awake."

"Mama, I just want to know ... Did they have snow in Jesus's time, on his birthday night?"

"Now, that is a good question, Libby, but I just don't know."

"Merry Christmas, Mama!" cheered Wyeth.

Rebecca went to the bed and gave them all a quick hug. She was stopped at the door by Libby's voice.

"Mama, I just want to know. Did you have the Bible when you were a little girl like us?"

Rebecca turned her face to the darkened hallway a moment.

"She's not that ancient, Libby!" Wyeth said, highly exasperated.

"What's 'anchin'?" Libby asked.

"It's 'ancient'!" scolded Louisa. "Don't you know anything?"

"Easy now, Louisa," Rebecca soothed. "Yes, we had the Bible when I was a little girl. Now, then ... goodnight, girls."

Back in the living room, Rebecca O'Dell found Will dozing on the sofa. She smiled, sat beside him, and kissed him on the cheek.

"Hum? Oh ... Were the girls asleep?" he asked sleepily.

"Not quite. They were awake enough to ask me if it snowed on Jesus's birthday and if the Bible was around when I was a little girl."

Will chuckled, taking her hand in his.

"Am I looking that old, Will?" she asked, a tiny edge of worry in her voice.

He laughed again at her seriousness.

"Well ... I was thinking awhile ago—" he began.

"You were sleeping," she teased.

"Well, before that. I was ... thinking of something I said to you years ago. I was wondering if I had kept my word."

It was her turn to be surprised at his sudden seriousness. His hand still held hers as he traced her slender fingers.

"What was it you were thinking about, Mr. O'Dell?" she asked gently, using the name they always used in the tenderest moments to honor their first meeting.

"Remember when I was asking you to marry me and I said we could have a good life together?" He paused to look into her eyes. "Have we, gal?"

There was vulnerability in his voice and she knew why. Her tall, strong husband had a sensitive soul that never failed to amaze her.

"After thirteen years of loving you," she said pulling his head down close to hers, "you know very well that for me, any life apart from you would have been no life at all."

"But," he persisted, "the hard times, gal. Our sons... The fire... When I almost lost you..."

Her fingers went lightly across his lips. "And the good times. Three healthy girls, wonderful, blessed girls. My health, Isaiah, Grandmother, our friends, our home..."

He laid her hand against his cheek, "Your hands are still beautiful, but not so soft as they were when you became my bride. There's been such hard work for you."

"And such love," she answered, dismissing his concern.

He pulled her closer and she rested against his strong chest. "No regrets?" he whispered.

"No regrets."

He smiled to himself. "Merry Christmas, Mrs. O'Dell."

"Merry Christmas, Mr. O'Dell."

Alice Tufts was a tart-tongued widow lady full of vim and vigor who could boast (and did) of being from one of Peppercreek's first families. Will and Rebecca had asked her to be their children's grandmother. They had seen beyond her frank manners to her kind, devoted heart. She was alone and needed someone—they had a family without a matriarch and needed her. It was a simple arrangement that had worked beautifully.

She maintained her independence by living in town, but was a regular participant in all the goings-on at the O'Dell place. Her importance was well evident in the simple fact she was so often quoted. "Well, Grandmother says..."

On this Christmas day she sat with the family after the dinner was over, the paper litter scattered about in testimony that gifts had been exchanged. Libby was tucked in the crook on her arm, and the old lady stroked the soft curls absently.

"Pa, tell us about Long Knife O'Dell," asked Wyeth, perching on his chair.

"Wyeth, you've heard that story a dozen times or more," Will protested.

"Please, Pa, please," Louisa and Libby joined in.

"Well, all right." The girls drew closer to their father, ready to hear again the vintage story—a true family drama that always seemed to thrill them.

"About sixty-four years ago—"

"1778," supplied Wyeth.

Will nodded, smiling. This oldest daughter of his could tell the story flawlessly. "That's right, Wyeth," he smiled. "Anyway, like I was saying, George Rogers Clark led one hundred and seventy riflemen up into this territory to fight the British."

"But if they carried rifles, why were they called Long Knives?" asked Libby. The sisters smiled indulgently, she always asked that same question.

"Because," Will replied as he always did, "they also carried long, sharp knives—"

"That was their trademark, in a way," interrupted Wyeth.

"Why?" asked Libby.

"Well, Libby," Will continued, "back then this place didn't look just as it does now. It was much wilder. Bears and panthers roamed about as freely as cottontails and squirrels do now. The land was also thick with trees and scratchy underbrush. Long knives could hack away at that."

"Indians?" asked Libby.

"Yes—some friendly, some not. So these frontiersmen were very skilled with these long knives, and by winter they had fought the Brits and run them out. The government rewarded each of them with three hundred free acres of land. One of the Long Knives was Joshua O'Dell."

"Joshua *William* O'Dell," Wyeth corrected.

"That's right," said Will, "my grandfather. A big fellow who could hunt bears with a switch."

"Has fiction just replaced fact?" Rebecca asked coyly from her chair.

Will ignored her. "So he returned to his Kentucky home, then came back to Illinois to claim his land. He carried little more than his rifle, an ax, and a skillet. And he carried something else, something very important to him—"

"Apple trees!" sang out Louisa.

"Seedlings," corrected Wyeth.

"That's right. Apple tree seedlings. One hundred and fifty of them. He carried them in a canvas bag that he kept moist from his canteens. Well, he walked and rode a long time. He wanted to find just the right three hundred acres. He got lost after a few weeks of tramping over the country. There were just a few scattered settlements back then, you see. He ran out of food and water. Winter was coming on and game was scarce. Oh, I forgot another important part of the story. Now what was it... Hmmm..."

The girls all laughed and chorused together. "Pepper!"

"Pepper? Oh that's right. He had some pepper for his food, and—"

"Pa!"

"Now I remember! His only companion was a black hound named—"

"Pepper!" the girls sang again.

"Excellent memories these girls have, Rebecca," their father smiled.

"What kind of dog was he?" asked Libby.

"Uncertain ancestry, I'm afraid, Lib. Just a good ol' dog. So here was Joshua O'Dell becoming very weak with hunger and thirst. His diary shows that he thought this wild Illinois territory would be his burial ground. His dreams of the first apple orchard in Illinois would die with him. He fell down on the ground unable to go on. Then..."

"Pa! Go on" they urged.

"Then the little dog started barking and Joshua crawled after him. There was a creek, full of fish and water; life for the man. He named the creek Pepper Creek right then and there. He claimed the land all around it and planted his precious apple trees. Ten years later, the settlement of Peppercreek was founded."

"How did he get a wife if Pepper was all he had?" asked Libby.

"At forty-five years of age he went back to Kentucky for a bride...as only a truly wise man will do," he said, winking at Rebecca.

"And the first doctor of Peppercreek was Dr. Marcus Tufts," added Wyeth, as an epilogue.

Grandmother nodded, pleased her own family history had been remembered and woven into the tale.

"My father delivered Joshua O'Dell's son, William," she said, "and William's son—"

"Pa!" the little girls said, clapping their hands.

Will gazed around the room—this warm home, so filled with love..."What special gifts on Christmas day, my girls! God has given us so many good gifts."

The sky was a dull and icy blue. The wind chopped at her dress but Rebecca didn't really notice it. She stood inside the white picket-fenced plot on the brow of the hill behind the house, drawn into her own world. She inhaled the cold, sharp air and refocused on the markers at her feet. When she had come to this farm thirteen years ago, there had been only four gray stones in the plot—Will's parents and grandparents. But now there were six—two smaller stones, like little stone lozenges.

The words "John William O'Dell" were carved into one of them. He had been a fair-skinned baby with blond curls and fathomless blue eyes. A sudden fever had claimed his young life when he was only two months old. Rebecca closed her eyes, feeling afresh the wave of shock that told her he was gone—even if it had happened twelve years ago. She looked at the other stone. Robert William O'Dell was born and died on the same Christmas Day a year after the death of his brother. The tears came as they always did. A part of her and Will was buried here.

She heard laughter and turned to see the girls running to the barn to help their father with the evening chores. Three wonderful girls. She sighed as she closed the gate. The vigil to this place was always painful.

Summer, 1843

The year turned toward spring, then summer. Late summer was a time of dry heat and crickets fiddling in the still evening, of corn ripening in amber waves in the fields. Late summer was the schoolhouse newly full of restless children eager to be back outside, swimming in the creek.

Wyeth and Louisa had not reached the crossroads yet where they always met their friends on the way to school. It was the first day of the term. They walked holding hands, their dinner pails swinging at their sides.

Louisa released a melancholy sigh.

"I wish I could stay at home like Libby. I wish Miss Madison would just leave off the book part of school. I wish we could just have art and music and dinnertime."

"Books are like wings, Lou," Wyeth admonished. "They take you places you'll never get to go in any other way."

"You know school is more than reading," Louisa responded. "It's geography and history and sums and that awful penmanship. I do wish Pa and Ma would see reason and not make me go. Who cares where Poland is, anyway?"

"Louisa, this is only your second term! Why... You're going to grow up into a perfect dunce! You'll be ignorance personified!" Wyeth loved the feel of big words rolling off her tongue. She loved books and school, while Louisa had a passion only for fun.

"A dunce?" mused Louisa. "Well, I'll be a pretty dunce then," she said, smoothing her blue calico. She had overheard a few compliments on her looks over the years and a tiny seedling of vanity had sprouted in her pretty little head. "Besides, what have books to do with getting married?" she said.

Wyeth burst out laughing and stopped in the road.

"Married? Louisa that's... decades away!"

"How long is a decade?"

"Ten years."

"Well, I'm eight now, nearly nine, and a decade is ten, so... Eight plus ten is... is..."

"Eighteen. See? You can't even add." Wyeth was scornful.

Louisa shrugged. "Eighteen. I imagine I'll already be married for a couple of years at eighteen. So, I have less than one decade to wait, so there!"

Wyeth shook her head. "You're only eight years old and thinking of marriage. You're a goose, Louisa. You think of boys too much."

Louisa haughtily swung a braid over her shoulder.

"That *is* one good thing about school—boys. But, it's not me thinking of *them* that matters, Sis; it's getting them to think about *me*! There's Jane and Molly," she said, pointing. "Look at their pretty ribbons!"

Chapter 2

Illinois, 1844

◆◆ ◆◆ ◆◆

*R*ebecca believed life often turned not on grand events, but on seemingly insignificant points—like an ordinary country dance. A particular spring morning in May seemed so routine, but by the time the clock struck midnight, the date would be forever etched in O'Dell family history.

It was late afternoon and Will and Wyeth were returning from Springfield. The day that had been so calm and sunny suddenly turned dark and threatening. Dark clouds were rolling in and rain began pelting down. Just five miles from home the rain came down in earnest and resounding peals of thunder split the sky. The air was much cooler and the sun was completely blotted out. Then the lightning flashed and Wyeth saw it—movement near a line of trees off the road. It was so dim and uncertain; rain and wind were slapping at her face and her father was busy keeping the horses steady. There—she saw it again!

"Pa!"

"What is it, gal?" asked Will tensely, fearing Wyeth had spotted a dreaded funnel cloud.

"Pa, there...look! Something is moving in that brush."

At first, Will thought Wyeth was imagining things in her fear.

"There, see!" she pointed.

Will did see, and in an instant he had brought the horses to a standstill and was out of the wagon. He turned to Wyeth and shouted, "Keep 'em steady. That's a girl, you can do it."

He ran through the slashing rain and wind to the bushes and knelt down. Wyeth was amazed to see him pick up a body. He came up to the wagon with the limp figure in his arms. It was a ragged looking boy.

"Is...he...dead?" Wyeth asked her father.

"No, but he might be if we don't get him home quick. Unroll the tarp, my girl." Will leapt to the wagon seat, slapping the horses and shouting, "Beauty, Cinnamon, home!"

At home, the lamps were already burning, sending a beckoning glow from each front window. Libby's face was pressed to the glass.

"They're home!" she shouted.

Rebecca's mending basket flew from her lap. "Louisa, go check the tea. They'll be wet through."

Will had swung the wagon into the barn. He lifted Wyeth down and found Isaiah silently at his side.

"Isaiah, saddle Moss for me. I need to ride for the doctor." He lifted the tarp. "We found him by the road."

Isaiah moved away quickly.

Inside the house, everyone gasped when Will unrolled the canvas.

"Who is he?"

"What happened?"

"Is he dead?"

Recovering from her initial shock, Rebecca resumed her natural efficiency. She sent Wyeth to change into dry clothes and the other girls to prepare the spare room by the kitchen. They moved the boy in there when it was ready. He lay so pale and lifeless in Will's arms. Rebecca sent the girls away and closed the door. Will began to peel off the wet rags. Rebecca cried out involuntarily. "Oh, Will . . . he . . ."

The sight was pitiful. The boy seemed no older than seven or eight and was terribly malnourished. His skin was taut over his ribs and two bright spots of fever burned on his cheeks.

"He's starving," Will agreed. He looked up at Rebecca who had started to cry and pulled her into his arms.

"He's going to be all right. I think we found him in time. I'm going for Doc Noble now."

The boy did not stir while Will was gone and Rebecca and Isaiah sat at his side. She studied him from head to toe, a thousand questions filling her mind. Presently Will returned with the doctor, and his examination was brief.

"He has a fever from exposure," Doc Noble pronounced. "This draught I'm leaving will take care of that. He shows signs of severe neglect. Malnutrition."

"Who can he be?" wondered Rebecca.

The doctor shook his head. "Haven't heard anything of a missing boy. I'll drop in at the sheriff's when I get back to town. Maybe he's heard something."

"Might not be from these parts at all—may be a runaway," mused Will.

"What he needs is to be kept warm and to rest and eat lots of good food," Noble said. "I know he'll get that here." He paused as he put on his hat. "Prayer wouldn't hurt, either. I'll be back tomorrow."

The room was still after he left and Will and Rebecca pulled up chairs to the bedside—almost mesmerized by the little form beneath the covers. Rebecca's hand crept into Will's. Prayer, the doctor had said. Yes, that was all they could do for now.

The little patient slept through the night with Will, Rebecca or Isaiah alternately at his side. Then morning came and he stirred, mumbling something inaudible. A soft hand rested lightly on his forehead and he opened his eyes slowly, tiredly. He felt so weak.

"I'll see if his fever is down," said the voice. "Why, good morning!"

He was finally able to focus and found a woman with a gentle smile leaning over him. He pulled away weakly from her touch and his eyes were wide with fear.

"Will, he's afraid!"

Now a man came into view. "Don't be afraid, son," he said, speaking slowly. "We're not going to hurt you. We're going to help you get well. You need to eat and rest." He touched the boy's forehead, "Yes, his fever is down."

The boy saw the woman's eyes close and her lips move silently. Hadn't he seen his own mother do that so many times? Perhaps this woman and this man with the gentle voice did not need to be feared.

Rebecca helped him to a drink and Will perched carefully on his bed.

"Now, I can imagine you might be a bit afraid waking up in a strange bed like this. I know I would." His voice was so calm that the boy stopped trembling, thinking that he could not imagine this strong-looking man being afraid of anything. His eyes latched on Will's face. "My name's Will O'Dell and this is my wife Rebecca. My oldest daughter and I found you yesterday during a storm not far from here." He wanted to reach out and touch the dark-haired little boy.

"Can you tell us your name?" Rebecca asked gently.

He turned his eyes away from them at this and they knew he would not answer. In a moment, he heard the door close and he knew they had left him.

He knew he had nothing to fear from them, but those long months of being alone had left him tense and suspicious. It would take time to get over that.

In the hall, Rebecca struggled against tears. "Will, he's so thin and afraid. What are we going to do?"

"Just what we've been doing, gal."

"But can you imagine how terrified his family must be, with their little boy missing?"

His hands rested on her shoulders. "We'll trust the Lord to care for them as He is caring for us here."

They came into the kitchen where the girls and Isaiah sat waiting. Isaiah was the only one without an expectant face. The barrage of questions began.

"How is he?"

"Who is he?"

"Where's he from?"

"How old is he?"

"Where's his fam—"

Will held up his hand. "We don't know any of that yet. He's weak and afraid. His fever is down—that's all we know."

"But—" began Louisa.

"We are going to have to be patient. All of us," he finished with a warning glance at each girl.

"I just know we're going to be best friends," said Libby as she studied the ends of her braids.

The next few days passed with Will and Rebecca quietly caring for the strange little guest. They said very little, except to explain what day it was and what they were going to do for him. He continued to accept these ministrations silently, his eyes wide and fixed. Sometimes he could hear the sounds of cooking and smell the delicious aromas coming under the door. He also could hear muted voices and laughter—which intrigued and frightened him.

Mellow sunshine poured in the window one morning as he waited for his breakfast. He hoped the woman named Rebecca would be bringing it soon, for he was hungry. Finally the door opened and she came in bearing a tray. "Good morning! I'm sorry I'm a bit late with your breakfast, but there's some excitement about, you see. A new colt was born—just at dawn."

She raised him up and gave his face a quick wash. He did not mind that, really; she was so brisk and gentle about it. In any case, he couldn't have resisted. He was so very weak.

"Thank you," he said softly. They were his first words since coming here.

She hesitated and he could sense her excitement.

"I knew you'd speak one of these days, but...I don't know what to do, now that you have! Are you hungry this morning?"

"Yes, ma'am."

Her smile broadened.

The boy was just finishing the last bit of oatmeal when Will stepped into the room. He came up to the bed and the boy's questioning gaze met Will's friendly one.

"You look better this morning, lad," he said, smiling.

"His fever is gone and he ate all his breakfast," Rebecca said proudly. The boy's thoughts were all in a tumble, but one thing was clear to him: It took very little to make these people smile.

"It's a grand morning, then." Will scooped the featherweight body up in his arms before the boy had time to be afraid. He carried him to the open window where the curtains fluttered in a spring-scented breeze. From the window the boy could see the big barn and a corner section of the orchard, awash in a profusion of pink and white blossoms.

The boy drew an audible breath and his arms tightened around Will's neck.

"Beautiful, aren't they?" Will said, looking proudly at the trees. "Every spring, they put on the same grand show—and it never ceases to thrill me. As soon as you're strong enough to be up, I'll take you for a walk. Would you like that?"

The boy looked at Rebecca, then back to Will. He nodded. Will laid him gently back in bed.

"You know," Will said, "you have me at a bit of a disadvantage. You know my name, but I don't know yours yet."

The boy picked nervously at the quilt a moment, then his eyes lifted to theirs.

"Ethan. My name's Ethan."

"Ethan... What a nice name," Rebecca's voice was barely above a whisper.

"Ethan, do you have a last name?" Will prompted gently.

The boy hesitated and they could see a shadow of reluctance pass over his face. They would learn to recognize that look. Will cleared his throat in the silence, vowing to himself not to press the boy too quickly.

"Can you tell us how old you are?" he asked, quietly.

"I'm... eight."

"'Bout what we figured."

"Ethan," Rebecca said, venturing to take his hand in hers, "you are welcome in our home as long as you're here. But we must get word to your family. They must be sick with worry."

He drew his hand slowly from hers. "I don't have... any family." He didn't miss the looks they exchanged.

"Well... We'll let you rest now," said Will, rising. "Do you suppose you would feel up to meeting the rest of the family this evening? They're pretty anxious to meet you."

The shadow came again and Rebecca spoke up quickly.

"They're just our girls and their uncle."

"How many?" he asked timidly.

They both laughed at this. "Just three, though I can imagine through the walls they've sounded like a dozen or more."

The boy pulled at the hair above his ear and thought a moment.

"All right... I guess so."

The girls, particularly Libby, were excited. They had not seen the guest who had already changed the life of their family so much, not since that rainy afternoon five days ago. Libby even brushed her hair for the occasion.

"So... He's eight!" she said to her mirror. "Eight! Just two years older than me. We'll be good friends... forever."

Louisa laughed. "You make it sound like he's going to stay here."

Libby whirled around, her face instantly sober. "Well, of course he is."

"He has a family somewhere, dodo. Soon as he's well he'll go back to them."

"Nope, he's staying here with us."

"Oh?" Louisa surveyed her little sister with patronizing amusement.

"Yes, he is. I know it."

"How?"

"Just . . . a dream. We were big and . . . he was like our brother."

After supper, Rebecca and Will led the girls, followed by Isaiah, into Ethan's room. Ethan became nervous at the sight of them—their eyes were round at the sight of him. Will had warned them in the kitchen to try not to stare and bombard him with questions.

"He's so pale!" Libby blurted out as she entered the room. Will frowned.

"That's the monkey that you've probably heard through the wall," said Louisa. "Her name is Libby, and I'm Louisa."

Libby stuck her tongue out at her older sister.

Rebecca spoke up, "Ethan, these are our girls. This is Wyeth." The slender, dark-haired girl gave Ethan a quick, shy smile. "And this is my brother. The girls call him Uncle Isaiah."

Ethan had been so absorbed in studying the three lively girls, he hadn't noticed the tall figure that still stood in the shadow of the doorway. Ethan could see in a glance that the man was taller than Will. His hair was cropped short and so blond it was almost white. His impassive, mild face was unlined, his eyes were pale blue. He neither spoke nor smiled, but nodded his greeting to Ethan. He drew his eyes away and back to the girls who had seated themselves around his bed.

"Where are you from, Ethan?" Louisa asked with unusual gentleness.

"I'm from Ohio," Ethan answered without hesitation.

"Ohio! Well, how did you get all the way to Illinois?" asked Libby, sitting herself comfortably and somewhat possessively on his bed.

"I . . . walked."

Will and Rebecca exchanged glances.

"You walked? All the way?" Libby was incredulous.

"I walked a lot . . . of the way. Rode in wagons some. When . . . I crossed into Illinois I rode on a ferry."

"That would be the Illinois River," Will furnished.

Ethan nodded, but his eyes stayed on Libby. They were talking to each other as if the others were not there.

"But your family—you left them," Libby continued.

"Elizabeth, we did not bring you in here to question Ethan, just to meet him," Rebecca interrupted.

"Ma, you know Lib has a bad case of chatter-mouth. It doesn't even close when she chews!" said Louisa, and everyone laughed.

"Well," countered Libby, "Louisa is Miss Primp. You know what her favorite picture is, Ethan? Her mirror!"

"Girls!" admonished Will.

"What about your family, Ethan?" asked Wyeth, gently.

"I don't have any brothers or sisters, and . . . my . . ." He fumbled for words, and the shadow returned to his face. Will began to regret he had brought the girls in so soon; the boy was still like a scared rabbit. Libby reached out and lay her hand on top of his.

"It's all right, Ethan," whispered Libby.

He brought his eyes back to her and Rebecca could see him relax. She felt an odd and sudden intuition as she looked at the two of them. It seemed a bond was forming before her eyes between her youngest daughter and the little stranger. Libby seemed to have reached through his remoteness in a way she or Will could not. She became concerned—Libby would be terribly sad when their guest had to leave.

"My father left a long, long time ago," Ethan was saying. "It was just my Ma . . . and me. She died awhile back."

Silence enfolded the room.

"Why did you come to Illinois?" asked Louisa.

"I was going west."

Will stepped closer. "West?"

Ethan nodded. "Just . . . west. I had . . . heard things about out west. I didn't know what else to do." He dropped his eyes back to the quilt.

The silence came again.

"You were going to walk west by yourself?" Libby managed, finally.

He nodded.

"But you're just eight! You are the bravest boy I've ever heard of!" Libby enthused, clutching his hand warmly.

Will and Rebecca didn't miss the tug of a smile that came to Ethan's mouth. It was the first they had seen. It drove the haunted, serious look momentarily from his eyes and Rebecca's suspicion was confirmed—he was a handsome little boy. She heard his amazing story, which she never doubted as true, and longed to gather him up in her arms. Will spoke up.

"All right, girls, say goodnight to Ethan."

They all did, but Libby lingered a moment, leaning over him confidentially.

"You'll soon be able to get up and I can't wait! We're going to be good friends. You belong here, Ethan!" She squeezed his hand.

He drifted off to sleep with her words still in his ears: "You belong here, Ethan..."

Will and Rebecca sat with the boy as he ate his evening meal. They were pleased to see that in a week's time his fever was gone, his color improved, his appetite now hearty. The fearful cast in his eyes came less often, his speech was no longer so stilted. They knew a large part of his ease was because of the affectionate welcome their daughters had shown him.

Will was telling Ethan about the frisky new colt out in the stock pen, noticing the eager expression on the boy's face. Then he leaned forward, thinking hard about just how to place his words.

"Ethan, Mrs. O'Dell and I have been talking about your plans. Doc Noble says in another day or so, you'll be able to get up, eat your meals at the table, and such."

"All very slowly while you get your strength back," Rebecca interrupted.

Will nodded. "Do you still want to go west, son?"

It had been a long time since anyone had called him son, and it warmed the little boy's heart. He had given some thought about what he should do now. It was a heavy responsibility for one so young.

"Well... I'm not sure what to do..." He dropped his eyes, feeling suddenly as if he might cry.

"You know, going west is a difficult trip, even for the hardiest pioneer," Will said gently. "It's especially difficult when you don't have an exact destination, or even any family waiting for you."

Still, Ethan didn't raise his eyes.

"We all think you did awfully well to get as far as you got!" Will said.

"You do?" Ethan asked shyly.

"We sure do. A very brave thing, like Libby said. Now," Will broke out in a broad smile, "folks back east think of Illinois as west, so I think it would be truthful to say you did make it west, Ethan."

Ethan looked carefully at them, a slight smile pulling at his mouth.

Rebecca took his hand. "Ethan we want you to stay here with us. We—" Ethan could sense she was trying not to cry. "We want you to be a part of our family."

"Isaiah and I are outnumbered by females here," grinned Will, "I could sure use your help with 'em."

"Will you stay?" Rebecca asked.

Close to tears, Ethan could only nod.

Within a month, everyone—the girls especially—felt Ethan had been there always. Will came into the kitchen one morning. Rebecca met him at the door.

"You're frowning," she said.

"Am I?" He pulled off his hat and ran his hand through the raven-colored waves of his hair, still dark but marbled with gray as well. "I suppose I'm just amazed. I've shown Ethan the barn, the orchard—all over the place, really. He follows me around and seems to understand everything I say, and remembers it. He pointed out a tree in the lower pasture that needed pruning— one I had missed. You saw that mess of fish that he and Isaiah caught. He caught over half of those. Thought I'd take him hunting as soon as I can. Imagine he'll be a good shot." He took a long drink from the glass Rebecca handed him. "He's very responsible for a boy his age."

"He's talking and laughing more too. Look out there!" she said, pointing out a window. "He and Libby are playing tag again.

I heard him this morning with the girls, teasing them as . . . well, as brothers and sisters will do."

Will set his glass down and took Rebecca's hands. He looked long into her eyes. She smiled back at him, loving him with her gaze.

"Tell me," he said softly. "What is it?"

Her smile deepened. He knew her so well!

"I've been troubled about Ethan since he came," she said finally, "concerned about us keeping him. Doing the right thing, you know. Last night I woke up and came down to check on him. He woke up and asked for a drink. I got him one and he said 'Thank you, ma'am,' and fell back asleep. Will . . . I watched him for awhile. Do you know I've memorized every line of his face? . . . I know how his hair curls on the back of his neck . . . How his eyes crinkle when he smiles. I've gone foolish over an eight-year-old boy." She gave a nervous little laugh. "Then I got up and went to the window. The orchard was in moonlight. I can't explain it exactly. It wasn't a clear voice, yet, it came to me . . . the Lord saying, 'He is your son now, Rebecca. It's all right.'"

Will pulled her closer. "What a loving God, Rebecca! He has given us back a son!"

Rebecca O'Dell had made peace with her losses years ago. She had accepted the death of two infant sons. She had not grown bitter—and now, it seemed, God had rewarded her in a unique and wonderful way.

Chapter 3

Missouri, 1844

◆◆ ◆◆ ◆◆

*A*nne Mullins was a joyful woman. It was not uncommon to hear her deep laughter float out from her cabin anytime of the day. There were a few who mumbled Anne Mullins was *too* joyful—it must be a sin to be so happy, they implied. Hadn't sickness claimed the life of her husband? Hadn't two straight years of poor crops left her nearly destitute? Yet, whatever they felt about her joy, their respect for her was undiminished. And no one in the county could match her for cooking, quilting or midwifery. There was no sickness too severe or contagious to keep her from being at a bedside.

At forty-two, she had lived a full life: love, marriage, childbirth, the adventure of moving into an unsettled land and planting a home there, the death of Caleb—her husband—the love of God, the love of her neighbors. Now spring again brought beauty to her, she reflected, looking at the rose bushes her Caleb had planted years ago. Standing in the doorway of the house they had built together, she thought of him: so strong, so quiet . . . Her thoughts were interrupted as a brown mare, prancing and lively, swung into the yard.

"Annie girl!" called the rider. "Ma, can't you hurry her up?" the young horseman complained to Anne. "We're going to be late and she's in there fussin' over her hair. Changin' ribbons or something!"

"Now Henri . . ." Anne admonished from the doorway.

"It's true, Ma! She's going to see Leman Harrison, not to hear Reverend Cartwright! I'm leaving, Annie!" he threatened , calling again toward the house.

Anne smiled. Her tall Henri, so full of life and energy, all aflame to hear the mighty Methodist preacher.

Then a girl of sixteen brushed past, giving her a quick peck on the cheek.

"Ma, you sure you can't come?" asked Annie, her daughter.

"No, I told Mary I'd come sit with Sim while she goes to hear Reverend Cartwright."

45

"Do I look all right, Ma?" the girl asked, concern wrinkling her pretty forehead.

"Lovely—"

"Annie, come on!" cried Henri, impatiently.

"You might even listen to Reverend Cartwright a little, dear," Anne said, walking down the path with her daughter.

"Oh Ma, I will! I'll tell you the text he uses," she said, laughing.

"Swing up, sis—we've got to hurry," said Henri.

"You're not going to ride wildly, Henri Mullins! Tell him not to, Ma! He'll mess my hair!"

"Which you've spent all these hours fussin' over," teased Henri.

"It's a disgrace to have to ride behind you like this!" Annie complained. "I do wish the wagon wasn't broken," she said as she settled behind her brother on the mare's wide back.

"Hope Peter Cartwright doesn't preach on vanity this evening, Annie!" Henri laughed. "Bye, Ma!"

"Goodbye, Ma," called Annie as the horse cantered out of the yard.

Henri slowed at the curve in the road, as his mother knew he would, and raised his hat to wave back at her. Then it was quiet again at this little cabin in the valley, the bird song in the trees the only sound.

But Anne did not hurry in to change her apron and begin the short walk to her neighbor's. Instead, she stood still, leaning against the doorway, ignoring the cat that weaved around her legs. Henri's goodbye still lingered in her ears.

If there was one shadow in Anne Mullins' life, it concerned her beloved Henri. How she loved him—and Annie! They both could make her laugh so! Then the face of Rachel, her sister, came into her mind. She remembered that morning some sixteen years ago . . . The anguish and the courage in her sister's face as she handed her little son over to Anne Mullins' care. Tears came to her then, along with the memories.

There seemed to be no other way to keep the boy safe from his father. He could have been injured again—or worse. They had agreed to keep in touch through letters until Henri could come home to his mother or she could join him, out west.

The trip to Missouri had been made without incident. As soon as possible, Anne had sent the letter back to her sister. Yet, there had never been a reply to Anne's first letter—or the second, or the third. One year passed silently into the second, the third... and still no word from Rachel.

By now, young Henri had come to call Anne "Ma." Then, one autumn, the stress and worry about her sister got the better of Anne. She became depressed and listless. One evening, Caleb pulled her into his lap and showed her a little leather bag of coins containing their meager savings. He would return to Pennsylvania to look for Rachel.

And so, Caleb undertook the long trip, with Anne remaining on the farm with Henri and little Annie. But his search proved fruitless. It was as if Anne's sister had vanished completely. No one could provide a clue. It seemed that Rachel and her husband had left several years previously, during the dark of night. Caleb extended his search until the money was nearly gone, then wearily returned home.

Anne's faith sustained her in the disappointment. One night shortly after Caleb's return, she dreamed of her sister. All she could remember of the dream was Rachel's smiling face. Peace settled over Anne. "She's in His care," Anne thought upon waking. "One day I'll see her again!"

The little boy Henri grew tall. He had the blue eyes of his mother and Anne loved him as deeply as if he were her own flesh. They were the only parents he knew, and in all the years, in their uncertainty, Caleb and Anne had not told him the truth.

Anne changed her apron and headed down the path. He was eighteen now—yes, she decided, old enough to be told the full story.

Peppercreek, Illinois

"A miracle has happened here, and that much is plain," Grandmother stated with typical bluntness. She and Rebecca were crocheting on the front porch.

Rebecca looked up, smiling, and followed the direction of the old woman's gaze toward the front yard. Ethan was pushing Libby in the wooden swing from the big oak tree, their clear, young laughter easily reaching the two women's ears.

"How long has he been here? Six weeks? And look, he's like a different boy," continued Grandmother.

Rebecca nodded. It did seem that all Ethan needed to thrive was the proper environment. That, and lots of good food, joyous play and hard work. Yet Rebecca knew there was more to it than that. Ethan needed the constant, warm attention of a loving family. He needed the devotion and encouragement of a man. He had become like Will's shadow.

They all felt he had grown at least an inch or two and the thin arms were beginning to fill out. His cap of black, curly hair had a healthy shine now, and his eyes sparkled with good humor. He talked without reservation, constantly laughing and teasing with the girls. His gaze was frank, curious and friendly.

"He'll be a tall boy," Grandmother said, her fingers nimbly working the crochet needle in and out of the pattern.

"Yes, I think you're right," agreed Rebecca. "By the time school begins, he may need longer pants!"

"Has he ever said how much schoolin' he's had?" Grandmother asked.

"No, he doesn't like to talk about his past, but he can read and do sums all right."

"Glad he didn't put up a fuss about going to school."

Rebecca laughed, "I admit I thought of that, since he likes to be with Will so much. But Libby and Wyeth have done a good deal of persuading, so I think he'll go out of curiousity, if nothing else." She smiled. "I think he'd do anything Will asked him to do."

"You didn't say Louisa was in on the persuading," Grandmother observed.

Rebecca sighed, "The boys at school are about the only drawing for Miss Louisa, I'm afraid."

"Hmm . . . more interested in boys than books," the old lady said, shaking her gray head. "She's after me to tat her a new lace collar, but perhaps I'll tell her I need to see her term grades first, before I throw a stitch."

Rebecca laughed at the older woman's shrewdness. Then they both looked up as Ethan left Libby at the swing. He had seen Will pass into the barn, a pitchfork over his shoulders. Will had not given Ethan a glance, but Ethan had seen him and was after him in a flash.

"Have you mentioned adoption to Ethan yet?" Grandmother queried.

"No," Rebecca replied slowly, "Will wants to give him more time."

Grandmother watched Ethan till he was out of sight.

"You know, with his dark hair and build...I think Ethan could pass for Will's own son."

Rebecca glanced at Grandmother, feeling as if the older woman had read her thoughts. "You do?"

Grandmother nodded.

Rebecca said nothing. Though she felt silly mentioning it to anyone, she had noticed the similarity herself. She brushed back some straying hair, glancing over at the white fenced plot— thinking of Grandmother's words when she had seen Ethan for the first time: "The Lord does work in strange and marvelous ways."

"You're not...nervous are you, Ethan?" Libby asked as they walked along the road into town.

He smiled back at her, "No, are you?"

"Well, it's our first day of school and...we should have left earlier with Wyeth and Louisa. We're gonna be late!"

Just then, the schoolbell's final toll rang clear in the morning air. They broke into a trot.

Peppercreek's young scholars were finding their seats when Libby and Ethan arrived breathless at the front of the schoolhouse. In the entrance, Libby pointed out the benches where they were to leave their dinner pails. Excited talk and laughter ended when Miss Madison rapped on her desk with a ruler.

"Students! Students! The bell has sounded... Now, Peppercreek school, fall term 1844, will come to order. Let us stand for the—" she now saw Ethan and Libby at the end of the aisle. Libby glanced up at him, proud to have such a fine, sturdy-looking boy at her side.

"You're new," Miss Madison said simply as Ethan walked forward.

"Yes, Ma'am. My name is Ethan Alcott," he answered clearly.

"He lives with us," piped up Libby.

The teacher's smile was pleasant—she had heard about Ethan. Everyone had—Peppercreek was, after all, a very small town.

"We all welcome you to Peppercreek School, Ethan. And good morning to you too, Elizabeth." Miss Madison inclined her head in an admonitory gesture. "Let's remember to be prompt tomorrow morning, all right?"

"Yes, Ma'am," Libby replied softly.

"Elizabeth, your place is beside Sara James."

Libby was beaming at this; Sara was her best friend.

"And Ethan, do you know what reader you might be in?"

"Well, Wyeth has been helping me along in the third one."

"Fine. Let's put you here, by Roy James."

Ethan slid onto the bench beside the boy Miss Madison had indicated. The boy was clearly younger, but Ethan suffered no embarrassment from being a seatmate with a boy in the second reader, even though by age he should have been in the third. The boy gave him a shy smile and Ethan returned it.

While the teacher continued talking, Ethan glanced around with interest at the first formal schoolroom he had ever occupied. Peppercreek's fathers had taken more than a casual concern in their children's education. They had built and established a simple but well-supplied schoolhouse. It was one room, currently educating nineteen pupils.

At the first morning recess Ethan was introduced to more of the traditions of school life. He had fully expected Libby to stay with him, but he soon discovered that boys and girls generally stayed apart, even outside the schoolroom. The older girls grouped together in the shade and the younger gathered in another spot. Boys drifted to the other side and typically played tag or some other physical activity. Ethan walked up to the boys' group, his hands in his pockets, his head slightly cocked with curiousity. There were nine boys in the Peppercreek school that session, ranging in age from six to fourteen. They instantly crowded around him, full of friendly questions. Ethan had a temporary sinking feeling in the pit of his stomach. He did not like to talk about himself. Perhaps if he parried the questions quickly and casually their interest would be soon satisfied.

Louisa put her arm around Ethan as Wyeth and Libby walked home just ahead of them at the end of that first day.

"Did you like school?" she asked.

He shrugged. "It was all right, I guess."

She sighed. "That's how I feel—something to be endured. What did you think of Timothy Foster?"

"Who?"

"Timothy Foster. I'm sure you met him. He's eleven and sooo cute."

Ethan shrugged again, "I couldn't see if he was cute or not, Louisa," he answered soberly.

All three girls burst out laughing at this, and Ethan smiled, glad he had made them laugh.

Gradually school and studies became a routine to Ethan—he who had never known routine before. He had plenty of tutors to help him with his studies. Socially, he needed no help at all. Popularity replaced novelty for Ethan in the schoolyard. He was well-liked. The other boys found him fair and easygoing. The fact that he proved to be the fastest and best thrower among the younger boys did not turn his head; he was able to enjoy their wins, also. But Ethan's emerging popularity did not come entirely without cost, for every schoolyard is governed by a self-elected leader. And, of course, this leader will have some loyalists under him. Peppercreek School was no different.

Jip Denham was twelve years old, a lumpy, long-limbed youth who had taken an instant dislike to the new boy. As one who is unfair and unfriendly will do, he did not trust Ethan's fairness and friendliness. Jip was accustomed to maintaining unchallenged rule over his peers, obtained by athletic prowess and bullying. In this, he was the image of his belligerent father before him. He had brought the first flush of embarrassment—and a little anger—to Ethan on the last day of the first week.

The boys were finishing their lunches when Jip leveled a sneering look at Ethan.

"Hey, Alcott! If your ma died, where's your pa?"

The other boys turned to Ethan with curiousity.

"Don't know," Ethan mumbled. "He just . . . left . . . a long time ago. Wasn't around much."

Jip let the subject drop until a couple of weeks later. By now, Ethan knew—for no reason he could imagine—this boy did not like him. Jip's open hostility was the one shadow in the otherwise happy school days.

School was out and Ethan, along with Roy and a couple of other boys, was walking home. Jip came up behind them soundlessly.

"Hey, Alcott! If you don't know where your pa is . . . What did that make your ma?"

Ethan whirled around, clean-minded enough not to understand the implication, but sensing an insult in Jip's tone. He was tired of Jip's taunts.

"Take that back," Ethan growled in a low and trembling voice. The blood was pounding in his ears.

"I'm twelve and you're a pup, Alcott!" Jip laughed.

Ethan flung himself at the larger boy while Jip was still smiling. It was a short fight with alot of dust flying, feet kicking and scratching. Neither got in any decent blows. They parted mutually, Ethan livid that Jip had torn his shirt and Jip surprised that a boy smaller than he had fought without giving in. It did not change Jip's attitude one bit. If anything it whetted his appetite for more.

Roy tried to console Ethan—they were good friends in the making.

"You hurt, Ethan?" he asked anxiously.

"No . . . He didn't hurt me. Look what he did to my shirt, though."

Will and Rebecca said little about the fight, and Rebecca mended the torn shirt. But the trouble between Ethan and Jip could not be mended as easily as a shirt. As weeks passed Ethan's popularity and Jip's animosity were well established. The conflict between them seemed inevitable. One thing was certain—Ethan was not afraid of Jip.

Will, Isaiah and Ethan sat comfortably in the barn late one evening. October winds thudded against the strong walls. They were sorting through the baskets of apples, preparing them for the wagonmaster who would come in a few days to ship them to all parts of the state and beyond. Ethan was proud Will had let him stay up after the girls had gone off to bed, thrilled to be a part of the harvest. He had been here six months and his life was as happy and content as any boy's could be.

"Storm blowin' in," Will remarked.

"Maybe it pick da appas fo' us," said Isaiah slowly, his head bent over his work.

Will nodded, "Just as long as the wind's pickin' isn't too rough."

Ethan looked at Isaiah, already understanding the guttural language that the man spoke. He had finally grown comfortable around him. Isaiah's silence had unnerved him at first, but Libby had given him assurances.

"Don't be afraid of him, Ethan."

"I'm not afraid of him exactly . . . I don't know."

"He loves you, Ethan."

"How do you know that?"

"I know him. He loves everbody."

He had come to really like Isaiah, working beside him in silence, grateful when by gesture Isaiah had led him to the creek to fish.

"Ethan, it's gettin' late. You ought to head in to bed."

"There's no school tomorrow," Ethan reminded Will, eagerly.

Will glanced at him and chuckled. Ethan had done admirably in his studies for having had such little formal education. However, he was showing that his real interest lay in working, fishing and hunting.

"Any trouble with Jip, lately?" Will asked.

Ethan shook his head. "I try to stay clear of him."

"Good idea."

They worked in silence while Will turned over in his mind how to broach an important subject with Ethan.

"Ethan, Rebecca and I talked to a lawyer in Springfield last week."

Ethan looked surprised.

"We . . . talked to him about legally adopting you."

Ethan looked at the pile of scarlet fruit at his feet. It seemed to him that the hearty, sweet smell of apples was in his skin. He loved the smell already. He looked Will in the eye, his heart racing.

"We don't want to rush you, Ethan, but we would like you to be our son—legally."

"Would it... change my name?" he asked cautiously.

"Change your name? Well... yes, I guess you'd be Ethan O'Dell."

Ethan looked at his feet again. He did not want to hurt Will's feelings, but...

"Ethan?" asked Will cautiously. "Is there a problem with changing your name?"

"Well... my ma, she always told me Alcott was a good name ... a name to take pride in. She said her father and grandfather had been ministers. She wanted..." He didn't know how to explain, and he hated sounding ungrateful.

"You want to keep your name for your mother's sake?" Will asked.

"I know O'Dell is a good name too," Ethan said hurriedly.

Will laughed. "I think honoring your ma is a fine thing, son. Will you let us adopt you if you can keep Alcott?"

"Could I? Would you?" Ethan asked, holding his breath.

Will bent down to him, eye level.

"A name won't change the way we feel about you, Ethan. You'll be Ethan Alcott, our son! God sent you to us!"

Four months later the legalities were concluded, and a celebration was held in the O'Dell house. Grandmother Tufts brought a huge basket of her lemon cookies and the girls bought Ethan a new fishing pole. It was cold outside, but inside there was warmth, love and laughter—Ethan had a family. A real family.

The complexion of fall was the bright orange of pumpkins, the crimson of apples, and the gold, bronze and scarlet of leaves in scattered rainbow heaps on the ground. Fall was frost like fine, frigid lace over every blade of grass—a delicate prophecy of the season soon to follow. Then the snows came, mounds and blankets and drifts of dazzling white, the coconut-white flakes falling ever so slowly and quietly.

Spring came, bringing with it the mellow sun and planting time. Ethan had now passed a year with his new family. He had become one of them, sharing in joys and labors, growing in body, mind and spirit. Sometimes, late at night and alone in bed, he thought of those early years—so dim and distant—as if he had been another boy, a different Ethan. He had brought only his name from the past.

Ethan loved his new family. The girls, in particular, were the delights of his young heart. He never failed to be amazed at how easily and openly they had accepted him. Wyeth, being the oldest, was someone to look up to, and he enjoyed the easy, undemanding relationship they had. Louisa made him laugh and brought out his best teasing skills. She was so frank and unassuming—there was no place for gloom in her presence. And of course, he and Libby had a special relationship, knit together from the first. They loved to take long walks in the woods around Peppercreek. Ethan did not mind when Libby's friend Sara James tagged along. Strangely, it was because of her that Ethan had his worst fight that first year.

It was a Friday evening social at the schoolhouse. It was a time of games, spelling bees, socializing and refreshments for parents and students—an evening to break the monotony of the long winter nights. It was a very crisp February night and a group of boys and girls talked and laughed in the circle of light that fell through the open schoolhouse doors. Their parents lingered in the entryway. Ethan noticed Jip and his cronies pestering Libby and her friends. Standing with Roy James, he paid only slight attention to what Roy was saying. He sensed that Jip's crowd was being unusually obnoxious. They were grabbing the girls' hats and running with them, delighting in the wild screams of protest from their victims. Then a boy made a dash at Sara James's hat and ran off with it, laughing. Sara, Roy's sister, was a slim, lithe girl about Libby's age, with large cornflower-blue eyes and braids of silky blonde. She was Libby's devoted friend, still somewhat shy around Ethan, whom she regarded as a celebrity to be treated with awe. Sara, who was herself fleet of foot, sprang after the thief.

Then—clearly, so Roy and Ethan might see—Jip stuck his foot out in Sara's path. She fell on the hard-packed schoolyard. She came up, trying very hard not to cry over the painful cut on her chin. Jip's cronies laughed heartily—but not Jip. Instead, he was watching Ethan and Roy with narrowed eyes. Libby was furious; her arm around Sara, she called Jip everything from "fat bullying beast" to "ugly, mean lumphead." Jip was unmoved. Roy cleared his throat nervously and stepped over to the circle.

"You all right, Sara?"

"Is she all right?" Libby blazed. "Just look at her chin! Jip tripped her."

Ethan stood by Roy's side, outwardly casual, kicking at the dirt—inwardly, tense and angry.

"He . . . did it on purpose, Roy," said Sara through her tears.

"You tripped my sister," Roy said shakily. He was a quiet, passive boy, at least three inches shorter and forty pounds lighter than the beefy Jip.

"Reckon she didn't see my foot. Needs glasses, maybe," Jip said insolently. Jip's friends laughed at this.

"Reckon you should apologize for havin' your big foot in the way," Ethan said slowly.

There was a terrible silence in the clear night air. Libby glanced up, half wishing the adults would come out and half wishing Ethan's fist would remove Jip's sneer.

"It doesn't matter, Ethan. I'm all right, really," Sara said hurriedly, rightly sensing the schoolyard teapot was about to boil over.

Ethan gave her a quick look and smile, then refocused on Jip.

"No one tells me to apologize," Jip said in his best threatening voice and was on top of Ethan in an instant, relishing the advantage of surprise.

Ethan scrambled out from under him quickly—he did not want to fight this kind of scrappy scuffle. He wanted to get in some respectable punches.

When the horrified parents pulled the two apart moments later, Ethan had bleeding knuckles and Jip a dreadfully black eye. Both boys were sternly forbidden to attend any more Friday night socials. Ethan's victory was tainted by the disappointment he could see in Miss Madison's eyes.

He did not know what to expect of Will and Rebecca's reaction. To his relief, they responded calmly, feeling this was part of having a healthy son—and hoping both boys would soon outgrow the feud.

The next months slipped by as beads on a necklace—days of joy and laughter, fewer days of sadness and pain. Days well mixed with work, play and rest—routine and uneventful days.

On the last day of 1845, Grandmother Tufts celebrated her sixty-fifth birthday. The girls orchestrated a lavish family party for her. She pretended to rue the attention and fuss, but inwardly she enjoyed it immensely. Will had toasted her with spicy, hot cider.

"You're getting better each year, Grandmother, and that's a fact!"

A tinge of blush could be seen under the wrinkled skin.

"There, Will O'Dell . . . You know better than that! Why, the only thing that improves with age is cheese!"

In years to come, Will would often think back on these years, as a golden time in his family's history. Blessings were abundant, and no one lifted up more grateful hearts than he and Rebecca. Those early years of pain, loss, struggle and sorrow seemed dim and distant.

Chapter 4

Missouri, 1846

♦♦ ♦♦ ♦♦

*H*enri Mullins sat, chin in hand, gazing pensively into the fire. He had arrived early that morning, expecting a loving welcome from his mother—expecting good food for a few days, instead of his own flat cooking. He had expected to relax and share with her the exciting things that had happened to him in the nearly six months he had been gone from home.

Henri was an ordained minister, riding the preaching circuit in Missouri and parts of Kentucky for nearly two years now. There was much to tell, much to laugh about, much to thank the Lord for. He wanted that special encouragement that only she could give him. He wanted her to pray for him before he left again, to ask a blessing on his work. But Anne Mullins was dead—two weeks in her grave.

Henri went to his sister's cabin when, upon his return, he found his mother's cabin cold and empty. When he rode up and Annie saw him, she flew into his arms and sobbed—and he knew his mother was gone. She had been nursing a sick neighbor, his sister related, and had taken the illness herself. It had happened very quickly.

Now he sat alone, holding a letter and small bundle that his mother had left for him. He placed another log on the fire and opened the letter.

My dearest Henri,

For days it has been on my mind to write you. It's been a persistent thought, and because of that, I know it must be from the Lord. Perhaps it will be better this way, while out on the trail. Alone, you can read this and pray over it and when you come home we will talk it all over.

There is a chilling wind about tonight and Jumper is curled up here beside me, twitching after those fleet-footed rabbits you used to hunt. I wonder where you are tonight? Are you warm, son?

I should have told you this long ago, but no time seemed just right and uncertain things are always easier to put off. Your father and I didn't want to be cowards or deceptive.

Henri, no mother could love a son more than I have loved you, even though you are a son not of my body, but of my heart.

Henri stopped reading, a shocked expression on his face. He looked into the fire a long moment, then reread the sentence.

I know this will come as such a surprise to you. Can you understand?

Years ago, a young girl who was the beauty of her small village fell in love with a dashing older man. The man was not a believer—in fact, he scorned the things of God. Yet, he had captured the girl's heart and she married him. He left her for long periods of time and when he came back he showed himself to be a man of strong temper and given to drink. For three years, there were no children born to this mismatched couple. During all that time, she felt she could surely change the man through the strength of her own faith. Finally, a son was born to them, and for a time the man came home and they were happy. But when the boy was two years old, the man became violent—so much so that he would even strike the baby boy. One terrible night, during one of his rages, the father broke the little boy's arm. His mother knew she must do something to keep her little one safe, so when her sister went west, she gave him into her keeping, always hoping they would be reunited.

This is your story Henri, and I am your mother's sister. We tried to find her but never could. My Henri, can you forgive me for not telling you sooner? Will it cause a shadow between us? I pray fervently that it will not. I love you so much, son.

Henri finished the letter, reading the names of his real mother and father and the date and place of his birth. He folded the missive slowly, then looked at the bundle which, according to Anne's letter, was the parcel that his mother had sent with him eighteen years ago. He looked back into the flames, lost in a million thoughts... Then he turned the kerosene lamp down and, bowing his head, cried softly in the quiet cabin. Did Anne have any idea how he appreciated her? Had he told her enough times how much he loved her, this woman he knew—whom he would always remember—as mother?

Peppercreek, Illinois

It was a perfect day for a July Fourth celebration. Clouds were scattered, high and fluffy across an expanse of piercing blue. As the noon hour drew close, wagons of Peppercreek families assembled at the meadow where all outdoor gatherings were held. Pepper Creek, clear and cool, curved only a few hundred yards away—a shallow stretch, perfect for wading. The program of the day was pleasantly familiar to the families of Peppercreek.

Colorful quilts were spread for families to sit on and one wagon was drawn into the center of the meadow to function as a serving table for the feast. The wagon's boards groaned with the delicious bounty of the farming families: fried chicken and ham, a bushel basket of roasted corn, crocks of beans and slaw and beets, a dozen different varieties of pickles and a mouth-watering array of pies and cakes.

After the dinner there would be games of tag and horseshoes and all kinds of races. As evening approached there would be enthusiastic singing of patriotic and religious songs. A small fireworks display, the highlight of the day for the children, would usually finish off the celebration. Then, everything would be gathered up for the trip home—sticky, dirty children, exhausted mothers and fathers—all wending their way home to the accompaniment of impatient milk cows, bawling at the gates. The pasture would be left quiet again, and the field mice would come out in the still darkness to do their own feasting.

Late in the afternoon, Ethan and Roy sauntered down to the creek. They waded awhile—until Ethan grew bored.

"Let's go down to the cave, Roy."

"Reckon we should go so far? Better go tell my ma."

"Aw come on," Ethan urged, "she knows we're about somewhere, playin'."

Roy agreed and the two headed down the creekbank. A quarter-mile distant was the cave they called their "secret place." So far, they had managed to keep its existence a secret from the probing ways of their two tag-along sisters. Roy James, a year younger than Ethan, rarely disputed Ethan's suggestions. Ethan, for his part, relished Roy's comradeship and loyalty. They had formed a close friendship in the past two years.

Soon they were stretched out in front of the cave's entrance, a portrait of companionship. Ethan was fishing and Roy was gazing dreamy-eyed into the clear water. The cave was a cleft of rock, ten feet up from the creekbank, accessible only by climbing. The opening was partly screened by a profuse growth of leafy bushes and weeds. The boys had stocked their hiding place with an old horseblanket, a dented, rusty tobacco tin filled with nuts, a box of fishing lures and line, a tin cup and plate for impromptu meals of freshly caught fish and a tattered, dog-eared copy of *Ivanhoe*.

After an hour of leisure, Ethan became hungry.

"You watch my line, Roy. I'm going to run back to the meadow and get us some cookies."

Roy yawned and nodded. "Don't let the girls see ya."

Back at the picnic grounds, Ethan was shocked—people were preparing to leave. And it was still so early! His mother called him from the O'Dell family wagonbed, where she was busily packing away the remains of the picnic food.

"Ethan! It's time to head home."

"But it's early yet and . . . What about the fireworks?"

"There's a cloud coming up," Rebecca replied, pointing toward the curdled western horizon. "Looks like a storm."

"But—"

"Climb up, son," Will said, coming up to the wagon and beckoning Ethan.

"But it looks fine to me," Ethan protested. "Maybe just some rain. That won't hurt," Ethan said, full of disappointment. Will looked at him curiously. He had never heard that tone from his adopted son before.

"Maybe just rain... Maybe worse," Will cautioned. "Let's head home, anyway."

"Where's Libby?" Ethan asked, thinking quickly of another tactic.

"She's riding with the Jameses. They'll drop her at the crossroads," said Rebecca.

"Can I ride with them too?"

"All right," Rebecca said after a silent conference with Will, "but straight home."

Libby called out to Ethan from the Jameses' wagon, across the meadow from the O'Dells'. Suddenly an idea formed in Ethan's head... an impulse, a temptation. He glanced up. Will and Rebecca were already riding off.

"Roy and I will ride home with Pa!" he called to Libby, and she nodded.

In the gathering gloom and wind, in the hurry to be home, no one noticed Ethan slip back toward the creek. He walked quickly, taking little concern for the sudden rise in the wind or the sudden coolness in the air.

Back at the cave, Roy was chattering about something, but Ethan wasn't listening. This was the very first time he had lied to Will and Rebecca. He wondered what the punishment might be if he was caught. He could already see Rebecca's disappointed face in his mind. What would Will do? Yet, it was done, he decided, despite an odd feeling forming in the pit of his stomach.

On the road home, Will's and four other wagons were driving as quickly as possible. By now, the wind was rising into an angry tempest. Then, as suddenly as it had come up, the gale quit. All the wagons stopped at the crossroads.

"There's no wind. Feel how calm it is," said Rebecca in a worried tone. Wyeth looked anxiously at her mother.

A woman screamed and all eyes swiveled to the left. Everyone present felt a moment of pure, blanching fear. The choppy, gray clouds were gone, replaced by something far more ominous than a summer storm. The sky to the west was a solid black curtain—and a wide, black twitching snake of cloud dropped from the curtain. Already visible was the spray of destruction where its fury touched the ground. A screaming rumble could be heard, like the progress of a freight train.

In that instant, before women's screams and children's panicky crying began, Will stood up, the roar of the wind forcing him
to shout.

"Hold on, folks! We're closer to my place and we can all make
it if we keep calm." He began shouting instructions, and one by
one, the wagons turned, the drivers urging their teams into a
desperate gallop toward the O'Dell farm.

The ride to the O'Dell's was furious and no one in any of the
wagons ever forgot it. As they swept into the yard, tree branches
were already bending in frenzy and loose objects flew through
the air like dangerous missiles.

"What about the horses?" Wyeth screamed as they all jumped
down and ran for the cellar. Isaiah was there, leaning with all his
weight to keep the heavy wooden door open in the roaring wind.
Will was the last one to dive into the cellar, his face gray and filled
with regret that he could do nothing for the horses. The thick
door came down with a thud and for a moment there was silence
in the damp, dusty darkness.

Then a lamp was lit, illuminating the tense and frightened
faces of the twenty-two people huddled in the O'Dells' cellar.

"Let's pray, folks," Will said, quietly.

Outside, a fury was being unleashed, and, though underground, the shrieking wind was not entirely muzzled. There were
bangs and thumps and—once—the awful, piercing scream of a
horse. Wyeth bowed her head and sobbed.

"It sounds like the end of the world," Lem Tucker moaned.

"Well, if it is, He'll find us praying, and that would be best,"
Will replied. "A person shouldn't wait till a time like this to get
right with the Lord, but it is better than not at all. Is there
anyone—"

"That's enough of your religous talk, Will O'Dell!" snapped
Jeremiah James. "I'll not be converted in your apple cellar!"

Another man spoke up from the shadows in a corner. "Where,
then, Jeremiah? Where would be best for you?"

James' blush was invisible, but his silence was eloquent
enough.

"Where's Ethan and Roy?" Libby asked, suddenly.

"Aren't they in here?" Will asked, holding the lamp up to light
all corners of the underground room.

"They were supposed to be in your wagon," said Mrs. James, tersely.

Will looked worriedly at Rebecca. "Ethan said they would ride with the Jameses," she said in a low, fearful voice.

"Oh, my poor boy!" wailed Mrs. James, collapsing against her husband.

Libby and Sara turned pale, clutched hands and began to cry. Will tightened his arm around Rebecca.

"I'm sure he's safe, gal. He would have seen the storm coming and taken cover. It'll be all right." But his lips formed a silent, fervent prayer.

The wind was still howling like a tortured beast. Will closed his eyes. There was no way to know what destruction and loss they would find when they opened the big door. Then, finally, there was total silence...

Ethan and Roy watched in horror as the water below their rock perch suddenly churned into an ugly green.

"Look Ethan... What makes the water that color?" Roy asked in a whisper.

"I... don't know..."

"Let's go back to the picnic," Roy pleaded, his eyes huge with fright.

"We can't, Roy! Don't you hear that wind? Besides—they'll have already left."

Roy's teeth chattered. He looked to Ethan for comfort, but found nothing but fear in the older boy's eyes. From where they sat, they could see beech trees bending to the ground on the opposite bank.

"Oh Ethan! I'm so scared!"

Ethan knew Roy had wet his pants and felt sorry for him despite his own fear. It was all he could do to keep from trembling violently. Then a sudden blast of wind shredded the trees, sending a maelstrom of branches hurling through the air. The sharp fragment of a tree limb stabbed into Ethan's leg. With a cry, he pulled it out and tied his handkerchief around the bleeding wound.

"Ethan, look at the water!" Roy screamed.

The creek was swirling up to the edge of the rock.

"We're gonna drown!" Roy whimpered.

They pushed themselves as far back into the rock cave as possible, curling tightly into balls. Ethan put his arms around Roy, thinking that he would die, regretting that he would never be able to apologize to Will and Rebecca for lying.

A wall of storm-driven water roared into the cave, drenching the boys. Before Ethan could catch his breath, a blast of creek-bottom mud exploded over them, covering them, filling their ears and mouths. Just as suddenly, the water sucked out—then total silence.

At first, they were too terrified to move.

"You alive, Roy?" Ethan whispered hoarsely, when he could clear enough of the foul mud from his mouth.

Roy looked up, his face chalk white, his nose bleeding.

"Yes, but... I'm awful... c-cold."

"Come on, I think it's over," Ethan said, helping Roy to his feet.

They peered down from their rock shelf. The creek was calm and back to normal level. They looked at each other in alarm—the surface was littered with hundreds of dead fish. Wordlessly, they wriggled down the bank and began walking toward the picnic meadow. They came to the picnic spot and stopped. It looked exactly as if nothing had happened—except that a baby's bonnet dangled peacefully from the top of a huge oak.

"It's so quiet," Roy said, still frightened. "Do you think they made it home all right, Ethan?"

"Sure, they left long before it hit."

They began walking shakily down the road, too frightened to talk, their mud-caked clothes plastered to their skin. Ethan stopped to readjust the improvised bandage on his leg.

"Does it hurt much?"

"A little."

"Ethan, you sure our folks will be all right?" He sounded like he might cry again.

Ethan put his arm around his friend. "It's my fault, Roy. I lied to your folks and mine, and I'm awful sorry. I think they'll be all right."

"It's all right, Ethan. I ain't sore at ya."

They came to the turnoff toward Roy's house. After a final parting wave, Roy began to run. Ethan continued home with a painful limp and a heavy heart. All around him was destruction; twisted, splintered tree trunks and torn limbs were everywhere. It seemed the closer he got to home, the worse it became.

What if something had happened to them? he thought. What if they had not made it to the cellar? He began to run, ignoring the piercing pain in his leg. A fear, more powerful and urgent than any he'd ever felt in his life, propelled him forward.

Turning into the lane that led home, he stopped short. In the broad green pasture lay four of his father's cows, sprawled dead on the ground. He moved forward numbly, blanching at the sight. The poor beasts had been killed instantly when their stomachs had blown open. A section of the formerly neat picket fence had been mangled into a splintered ball. He was crying aloud now, his lungs screaming with the effort. Then, suddenly, his father was there.

"Ethan!" Will was shocked by the boy's appearance. His face was stark white, caked in mud, blood was soaking through the crude bandage on his leg. Sobbing, Ethan ran into his open arms.

"Oh Pa! Pa! You're alive ... Oh, Pa!" he clutched at Will like a drowning man clutches a lifeline.

"I'm all right son ... and you're all right, too." He stroked his son's head. "You're safe ..."

"Pa, is Ma all right? And the girls? Are they?"

"Yes, son, they're fine. Now, let me look at your leg ..."

"Oh Pa, I lied," the boy sobbed. "I never ever will again!" He threw his arms around Will once more, and they stood there in the road until Ethan grew calm.

"Let's go home, son ... Your Ma's waitin'."

Ethan had held tightly to Rebecca's neck as he told her the story of what had happened to him. She stayed calm as she cleaned and bandaged his leg, letting her tears spill out later, alone in her room. The next morning he was up early, riding with Will to the James farm. His apology to Roy's parents was sincere and brief.

"Mr. and Mrs. James, I'm very sorry I lied yesterday. I could have gotten Roy killed. I hope you'll forgive me."

Mrs. James immediately embraced him and he and Roy shook hands solemnly. Sara gave him a shy smile as she stood chewing on the end of one pigtail. Only Jeremiah James stood with folded arms, not speaking.

And so, life returned to normal, with cleanup and setbacks and fears to get over. The girls grieved for the lost cows and colts. Yet Will and Rebecca shined even in their loss—for the first time, and forever, Ethan had called them Ma and Pa.

Returning home from a walk to the creek one morning, Wyeth found a male guest at her house. She hurried into the kitchen where she found her mother and Louisa busy with dinner preparations.

"Who is that man with Pa?" she asked.

"Don't know, but he's a lawyer and he's staying to dinner and if you're not too tired from your walk, I saved setting the table for you." Louisa was plainly irritated.

"Thank you, Miss O'Dell," Wyeth returned pertly. "I will set the table while you go give your tresses the required one hundred strokes before receiving company."

"Girls," Rebecca warned from the pantry.

Libby peered out the window.

"Whoever he is, he sure is skinny. Look how he's makin' Pa laugh."

"His horse doesn't carry much more weight than he does, poor thing," Wyeth said in a glance.

The stranger drove a rattletrap of a buggy, pulled by a raw-boned, balky-looking horse. The tall man in the black woolen frock coat looked just about as dusty and unkempt as his horse. The O'Dells could not know from appearances that they were about to entertain—and be entertained by—the county's foremost young attorney.

The table was laid, and the attorney, Abraham Lincoln by name, took his place among them. There was nothing impressive about his features: a long nose, bony chin, deep-set eyes, large,

fleshy ears. Libby decided he had a kind face and liked him
instantly. Louisa liked his smile but thought him homely. Wyeth
enjoyed his voice, but firmly decided his hair was barbaric. His
face was mobile, changing constantly with the stories he told.
And he told a good many.

Over dessert, Wyeth and Louisa excused themselves, but
Libby and Ethan remained at the table, fascinated at the man's
ability to weave a story from anything. Then the conversation
turned political, though Will was not a man to take much interest
in politics. He read the papers, but was never one to lean over the
fence and gab with a neighbor or debate over at Baily's with the
old men.

The subject turned to slavery—Will wanted the country
lawyer's thoughts on the subject. Illinois was a free state, but the
issue was coming up frequently in the papers, though still mainly
back page copy. They all noticed Mr. Lincoln's face become
shadowed when he spoke of it. He laced his fingers behind his
head as he leaned back in his chair. There was something about
this home that seemed to relax him, make him feel as if he had
known these folks for a long time.

He drew a deep breath. Years later, Ethan would still recall
his words.

"Although volume upon volume has been written to prove
slavery is a good institution . . . we never hear of a man who
wishes to take the good of it by being a slave himself."

Will nodded. Mr. Lincoln had expressed his feelings quite
succinctly.

"Another slice of pie, Mr. Lincoln?" Rebecca asked.

"Thank you, but no, Mrs. O'Dell," the homespun attorney
replied. "I need to hitch up old Buck and be on my way. I told my
little wife I'd be home by sunset."

He unfolded his long legs and extended his hand to Will.

"I'm grateful to Buck for throwin' that shoe, Mr. O'Dell! I've
enjoyed the meal very much. You have a fine family."

"Please come back anytime," Rebecca invited.

"And bring more stories!" Libby piped up. Lincoln laughed.

"I'm just a wholesaler in stories, Miss Libby, nothing original."

Libby and Ethan helped to clear the table after he had left.
"He's a nice man—but so skinny!"

"Libby," Rebecca admonished with a smile.

"Well, he is. As grandmother would say, a knittin' needle casts more of a shadow than that Mr. Lincoln!"

Chapter 5

Spring, 1848

♦♦ ♦♦ ♦♦

*T*he geraniums were a bright red riot in Wyeth's garden when Henri Mullins rode up to the O'Dell house, Ethan riding double behind him. Ethan slid off the horse, hurrying into the house. "I'll be back in a minute," he tossed over his shoulder.

Henri dismounted, stretched, and lazily flipped the reins over a picket in the fence. He looked at the big white house with an appreciative eye. It was spring, the loveliest time in these parts, and a multitude of colors were in profusion. He pushed his hat back from his sweaty forehead. This was just about the finest house he had seen in a very long time, he decided. Though Henri Mullins was no trained artist, he possessed an artist's eye for beauty, symmetry and order. He wandered along the fence until he came to the garden that was planted next to the house. His eyes widened.

Late May found the flowers and herbs in Wyeth's garden proudly rearing their heads with splendid, natural arrogance. Henri was amazed. He had not expected to find such a manicured garden, such a palette of color in this rustic Illinois valley.

Suddenly, a girl dressed in very soiled trousers and a torn old shirt, popped up from the grasses not more than four feet from him. "Oh!" was all she could manage in the surprise of finding a young man leaning on her garden fence.

Henri was surprised too. "I'm sorry! I didn't know anyone was there. Sorry if I frightened you, Miss."

Wyeth said nothing, being acutely embarrassed by her appearance.

"You see, I was admiring your garden," Henri explained. "I don't think I've seen such a fine one before."

Still Wyeth said nothing.

"My mother used to grow that," Henri said pointing at a slender plant. "But I can't remember the name of it."

"Lavender," Wyeth replied in a low voice.

"Lavender, yes, that's it. Does it still smell as sweet?"

She broke off a piece and handed it to him.

70

"Hmm... Yes. Makes me think of my ma..." He seemed lost in thought, talking more to himself than to Wyeth. "Funny how strongly the smell of something can bring back a memory."

Wyeth was marveling over this easy-going stranger, still heartily wishing she could drop back to her knees and disappear.

"Say, I'm sorry!" Henri said a moment later. "What a clod I am, not introducing myself! My name's Henri Mullins. I gave Ethan a ride home."

He swept off his hat and Wyeth was further amazed. He was treating her like she was a grown woman—not a little girl!

Henri noted the quick rise of blush up her slender neck. She finally lifted her eyes. "I'm Ethan's sister."

"Pleased to meet you, Miss...?" he prompted again with a smile.

Wyeth had never felt so foolish in all her fifteen years. Here she was, dressed in boy's clothing with dirt on her hands, and a stranger was practically paying her court. She would later be horrified, up in her room, to find a smudge of dirt under her nose. How could she possibly face the stranger again?

But Henri saw less of the boy's clothing than he did of the young girl with long chestnut-colored hair and amazingly green eyes. Her face was flushed with work. Wyeth reminded Henri of a shy young colt. But he still didn't know her name.

"This garden—have you done all the work by yourself?" he asked.

"No... I mean, yes... I mean, my ma helps, sometimes."

"It's taken a lot of work—I can see that. It's the prettiest garden I've ever seen, Miss—"

There was an awkward silence while Wyeth tried to untie her tongue. She gestured about nervously, after wiping her hands on the soiled trousers. "I started it when I was eight years old."

"Well," Henri persisted, "I've remembered the name of this lavender here, but I don't know yours yet."

He has a nice smile, Wyeth thought. "My name is Wyeth," she said finally.

"Wyeth..." It seemed to her that he tasted her name as he considered it. "I travel quite a bit and I've never come across 'Wyeth' before. Well, it suits you, like the lavender."

Now it was Henri's turn to become embarrassed as he felt the full strength of Wyeth's gaze on him. He heard voices from around the corner of the house.

"Here he is!" Ethan called out. "He's a preacher and he gave me a ride home and this is his dog and he goes everywhere with him, right there on the back of the saddle! Guess what his name is, Ma! Guess!"

Rebecca and Will had returned with Ethan and now stood chuckling at their son's excitement.

"Let's see, a dog that jumps, you say? How about 'Jack'?" Rebecca guessed.

"Oh Ma..." Ethan said disgustedly.

"Well, tell us, son," said Will.

"Jumper! His name is Jumper!" They all laughed.

The multicolored hound was circling their legs in joy at the obvious attention. Will strode toward the young man, holding out his hand.

"I'm Will O'Dell and this is my wife, Rebecca. We've been introduced to your fine canine companion, but—"

"I'm Henri Mullins, sir." They shook hands. Will looked down at Ethan.

"Son, did you take a tumble from Mr. Mullins' horse?"

"Sir?"

"Your shirt is torn and there's a rip in the knee of your britches. Not to mention the bump on your cheek and the scratches on your knuckles."

Ethan gazed at the ground, his face growing red.

"I ran into Jip and his crowd," he murmured.

"Oh, Ethan..." Rebecca groaned.

"Looks like you ran into him pretty good. That's another torn shirt for your ma to mend."

"I tried not to fight, honest, Pa! Jip tried to break my pole."

"All right, we'll talk later," Will said. "Go get cleaned up, son."

Henri waited until Ethan was gone before he spoke. "I can vouch for your son's words, Mr. O'Dell. I happened upon the situation quite by accident and was unobserved for a few moments. Your son seemed to just want to go on his way, but both boys jumped on him. One was considerably bigger than your boy."

"Both boys were on Ethan?" Rebecca asked, her voice shocked.

"Yes, ma'am. I think he would have looked worse if I hadn't come along. He was using his fists pretty good, though."

"Yes, he can use his fists, all right," Will said with a slight smile.

"Will, I think this trouble between Jip and Ethan has gone on long enough. Perhaps it's time to talk with Jip's father." Rebecca looked worried.

Will rubbed his chin thoughtfully, "Maybe so." Then he looked at Henri and smiled. "Seems like you've gotten introduced to my family real quick, Mr. Mullins."

They all laughed.

"Ethan did manage to tell us you're a minister of the Gospel," said Rebecca.

"Yes ma'am, I ride the circuit. I was on my way up to Logan County to see Mr. Peter Cartwright and it looks like I got myself lost. This is my first trip to Illinois."

"Welcome to Illinois, then!" said Will heartily. "Where you from originally, Mr. Mullins?"

"Please call me Henri. I'm from Missouri."

"You know, you're not so far off from Cartwright's, but it's a good day's ride and your horse looks pretty winded. Why don't you spend the night with us, or even a day or so? Christ is the head of this house, and you're more than welcome here."

There was something about the tall slim young man that Will immediately liked. Perhaps it was his easy smile.

"Yes, please stay," Rebecca coaxed. "Supper's ready soon."

"My wife's fried chicken will sure beat anything that you have in your saddlebag there," tempted Will.

Henri smiled broadly. "Your wife's dishwater would beat anything *I* can cook!"

In later days, Henri often thought of that first meal at the O'Dells. Everyone was so friendly—even Wyeth, after she had gotten over her initial embarrassment. The meal looked even better than Will had advertised. Henri tried his best to refrain from taking seconds of the good fried chicken, but succumbed when they pressed him. He had that youthful slenderness that no amount of eating could seem to affect, and he couldn't help noticing Rebecca's pleasure at watching his enthusiastic enjoyment of her good cooking.

Of course he could not be wholly absorbed in his food, since Ethan and Libby were firing questions at him nearly nonstop. He did not seem to mind at all, and seeing his good-natured smile so often, Will and Rebecca did not try to rein them in.

"Have you come across Indians, Mr. Mullins?" Ethan asked, leaning forward in his chair. Will and Rebecca exchanged a smile.

Henri finished his bite. "It's got to be 'Henri' between us, Ethan, or I can't think properly. I'd never know who you were talking to."

"All right," said Ethan laughing. "It's 'Henri,' then."

"I'm afraid the Indians are being pushed farther west all the time, Ethan, so I don't come across that many. Now, the first circuit riders did, years ago. That was a big part of their ministry, besides bringing the Gospel to the pioneers. I have met a few Indians. Some were willing to listen to the story of Christ and others weren't. I found them no better and no worse than any white man. They are a proud people, and rightly so. They aren't always savages, as they've been painted. One Indian brave was used by God to save my life, once." He stopped at this critical juncture, as a gifted storyteller will do, to take a few bites.

"What happened?" Libby asked, wide-eyed.

"Libby, let Mr.— Let Henri eat," Rebecca chided gently.

"That's right, Libby, you must let me get stoked up for the next story," Henri replied, chuckling. "Well, anyway... It was about the second year I was on the trail, and one night I became sick—some sort of fever. I lay like that for two days, with very little food or water. No one was expecting me, so there was no one out looking for me."

"Did you think you were going to die?" asked Louisa.

"Yes... I did. I prayed and felt as if I were ready to go if the Lord was ready to take me. Then, about sunrise of the third morning, I woke up and there was something blocking the sunlight in my face. I thought maybe it was my horse, Barnabas. But it was a man, and when my eyes adjusted I could see it was a brown-skinned man.

"He was just like every picture in your mind of what an Indian looks like: animal skin around his waist, long straight black hair, bow and arrows tied around his back, feathers in his hair. I could tell he looked at me a long time, and I was just too sick to even speak. Then, there was water at my lips. He ripped a part of my shirt and made a cool compress for my head. Then, there was food. I don't know how many days he helped me, but when I finally could get up, he was gone. Barnabas was tied to a tree nearby with a pile of fresh-pulled grass in his reach. When I got to the nearest settlement, I was told Indians hadn't been seen in those parts for over fifteen years."

Everyone was silent a moment. Wyeth watched Henri's face and instinctively knew it was a very personal thing for him to share, not just another story.

"He was an angel," said Libby finally. "An Indian angel."

Henri smiled tenderly. "That's about the conclusion I've reached, Libby."

"Do you always sleep out?" Louisa queried.

"Oh no. If I'm near a town I may put up in the tavern or inn. Often a family will invite me into their home, like you folks have done."

"They let you preach in a tavern?" Will asked, incredulous.

Henri chuckled. "A few have. Some of those people have been much more open to me than some believers in the area. Sometimes I'll just talk with a few men, sometimes not even bringing up the Gospel if it doesn't seem the best time. Sometimes I sit with just one man and after he puts aside what I am and realizes that I'll listen ... well, he opens up."

"Do taverns take good care of Barnabas?" Ethan asked.

"That reminds me of a little story about that very subject," Henri grinned.

Will smiled down into his teacup, amused that this guest had such a capacity for storytelling and that his family was enjoying it so.

"A minister was applying for lodging at a tavern," Henri began, "when the innkeeper said to him, 'Sir, I perceive that you are a minister. Please let me know if you are a Methodist or Presbyterian.'

" 'Why do you ask?' responded the preacher.

" 'Because I wish to please my guests. I have determined that a Presbyterian minister is very particular about his food and bed, while a Methodist minister cares more about the care and feeding of his horse.'

" 'Very well,' said the preacher. 'I am a Presbyterian and my horse is a Methodist!' "

Wyeth had trouble falling asleep that night. She moved restlessly in her bed as she remembered meeting Henri Mullins in the garden. It was a new sensation to her to be treated so politely, like a grown-up. Certainly none of the boys in her group ever treated her that way. Henri seemed so much older than her, yet ... Just before they had all turned in for bed, she, Ethan and Henri had lingered on the front porch, watching the stars come out like diamonds studding the night sky. Then, the trees began to move in a wind seemingly stirred up by the moonlight, a soft, sighing wind. No one had spoken for a long time in the cool, fragrant, purple shadows of the porch. Then the tempo of the wind picked up, creating a different pitch in the trees.

"Sounds like a storm is coming up," Ethan finally said.

Henri nodded absently, thinking for a moment how grateful he was to have a comfortable bed in which to pass the night.

Wyeth loved this kind of weather and hated to go in. She could sense the same reluctance in their guest. This wasn't the type of weather to be afraid of. It was thrilling.

"The wind is playing a wild melody tonight," Henri said quietly.

"That sounds like something Wyeth would say," commented Ethan, smiling.

They turned toward the door, and Wyeth caught Henri's smile in the dimness—he understood how she felt.

Wyeth was on the threshold of young womanhood, and her thoughts were often on her future. An avid reader, she had dreams of romance with some dashing hero—like those in her beloved novels. She kept these daydreams tightly to herself, not daring to share them even with her close friends—certainly not with the boisterous Louisa. Louisa thought Wyeth's sense of romance was as undeveloped as her slender figure. But Louisa was very wrong.

When Henri had suddenly appeared outside her garden, Wyeth had been inwardly thrilled—after her first rush of embarrassment. Yet, as she secretly studied him across from her at the table that evening, she felt a slight pang of disappointment. He was tall—one of her mental requirements—but he was too slender. There seemed no real muscle to him. His hair was brown and straight, but his eyes were as blue as hers were green. She had dreamed of a dark brown-eyed man. But his smile, she conceded, was very nice. Wyeth liked him, he would be a good friend.

Henri Mullins stayed two days with the O'Dells, yet there was more to his prolonged visit than just convenience and good food. It was the family itself. They pressed him to stay even longer, and when the time came to say goodbye and ride off, he was shocked at how lonely he felt. He chided himself sternly. This was not good at all for a man who was claimed by the trail-riding ministry. He had been on the circuit for more than three years, with only occasional visits to his sister and her little family. Home for Henri Mullins was a night spent in a rustic tavern or on the floor of a believer's cabin, but most often it was the leafy canopy of a tree, with the starry sky as his vaulted roof. Home was his own rather primitive cooking and the few personal belongings kept in his saddlebags. Home was Barnabas, his big chesnut gelding, and the wiry hound, Jumper.

But something within the fabric of the O'Dell family beckoned to something within him. He knew he must leave, but—strangely—found himself reluctant to do so.

At last, he said goodbye, with the promise that he would return when he was in the valley again. It was a promise he knew he wanted to keep. After he left them, he often reviewed the visit in his mind. It made the miles to Peter Cartwright's pass quicker.

Fall, 1850

The woods were carpeted in wet, muddy leaves, but Ethan decided to cut through them instead of going along the New Salem road that would have been quicker. He liked the deep feeling, the cool, wet silence of this forest cathederal. Jumper rambled along beside him, his new and constant hunting companion. On Henri's most recent visit they had all agreed the hound was becoming too arthritic for the long travels. Ethan accepted responsibility for the dog with pride.

He heard the rumble of a wagon going down the stretch of the New Salem road that ran parallel to the woods. It was soon lost to his sight. Then there were horses, three that he could see. Strangely, they seemed to be going slowly—almost covertly. It dawned on him that the horsemen were following the wagon that had passed moments before.

He kept walking until he heard raised voices, angry voices. He jogged quietly along now, full of curiosity, still well concealed by the trees and brush. Sliding down an embankment even with the road, he crouched behind some bushes. He lay his finger across his lips to silence Jumper. At first he couldn't see the riders, only their horses. His heart thumped in agitation when they finally came into view—the Denham brothers. He watched as one tossed an empty bottle into the trees.

Ethan took in the situation quickly. Jip and his two older brothers, Tyler and Saul, had blocked the wagon from passing down the road that led to Peppercreek. All three wore sullen expressions and Ethan could tell Tyler had been drinking. He glanced quickly at the wagon. It was a well-made wagon driven by a middle-aged man. A younger black man sat on the seat beside him.

"I say that nigger is a slave, fat man!" Tyler said arrogantly, jerking a thumb toward the young black man.

"He's a free man," the wagon driver returned calmly. Still, Ethan could sense the tense anger in the man. "Besides, it certainly is none of your business, one way or another."

"Aw, sure it is, fat man. I'm makin' it my business. Now, I say you're sneakin' runaway slaves into Illinois. I say he's probably wanted down South." Tyler laid a hand on the off horse's harness.

"Let go of my horses." There was acid in the man's voice now.

Tyler spit on the wagon and reshifted in his saddle, giving a wink to Saul who held the other horse's bit. Jip sat quietly.

"Get up there, nigger," Tyler said, pointing his whip at the silent black man. The black man's head was lowered, as if he had not even been spoken to.

Ethan placed his trembling hand on Jumper's neck to soothe the dog's low growl.

"You deaf, nigger?" Tyler asked, and Jip and Saul laughed evilly.

Tyler stood in his stirrups and skillfully cracked the black-snake whip within a foot of the black man's head.

"Does that help your hearin' any? Now I said get up there and do me a little dance."

The older man made a gesture to the man at his side and the black man stepped over into the wagon bed and began a feeble shuffle.

"Is this the way Illinois treats strangers?" the man asked angrily. "You've had your fun, now move on!"

Tyler ignored him.

"I plan to report you to the authorities in the next town." The man's voice was hissing now.

Tyler flipped his whip around and with the handle struck the older man hard across the mouth. "Hush up, fat man. Now dance faster, nigger!"

The man pulled out a handkerchief for his bleeding mouth, his eyes blazing. All three Denhams were laughing loudly now and Tyler continued to crack the whip just inches above the black man's head.

Ethan shifted nervously, glancing up and down the road, hoping that there might be someone coming to end this ugly scene. But there was no one. He felt panicky. He knew where the Denham's kind of fun could end. He felt his mouth go dry and his heart was thudding in his ears. He crept closer, unobserved.

The whip cracked again, "I don't much like your hair, nigger. Let's take a little off and clean you up a bit!"

The whip started down again, but this time there was another cracking sound from the underbrush, and the whip flew through the air. All the horses jittered. Ethan slid down the embankment and walked slowly toward the the wagon, his squirrel gun aimed at Tyler Denham's chest.

Tyler cursed violently. "You could have shot my thumb off!" he screamed.

Ethan kept the squirrel gun leveled on him.

"I'd have shot your ol' thumb off... if I'd been aimin' too," Ethan replied evenly.

"Alcott," Jip growled through clenched teeth.

"Who is this—?" Tyler snapped.

"Ethan Alcott, O'Dell's boy," Jip spat out.

"This the varmit you had all the trouble with at school?" piped up Saul.

"He didn't give me no trouble," Jip said evenly.

"Move on, Alcott. This ain't none of your affair," Tyler said fiercely. He leaned down for his whip.

Ethan cleared his throat, trying desperately to clear away the nervousness in it. "No, Denham, it's time for you to move on... and you'll have to leave your whip here."

There was a tense silence as Ethan met Tyler eye to eye. Then, Tyler's lip curled up in an ugly snarl.

"Reckon you oughta know you've just made some real trouble for yourself, boy." He motioned to Saul and Jip to start down the road. "You'll be hearin' from the Denhams, Alcott. Be sure about that."

Ethan did not lower the rifle till they were out of sight. Then, he leaned against the wagon, suddenly feeling light-headed and faint. His legs trembled so he thought he would surely fall down. He finally had been part of an "adventure," but he certainly felt less than heroic. He had forgotten the men in the wagon until a voice was at his shoulder. The older man had climbed down and stood beside him.

"Here." He held out a canteen, but Ethan didn't seem to see it.

"It's just water. Get yourself a drink," the man insisted.

Ethan took a short drink. "Thanks."

Ethan finally looked at him, surprised that the man seemed so cool and calm.

The man extended his hand. "J.A. Packer."

"Ethan. Ethan Alcott."

"Alcott," the man said to himself. "You all right?"

Ethan just nodded. He wanted to go home.

"How old are you, Alcott?"

"Nearly fifteen, sir."

"Live close?"

"Couple of miles. Peppercreek Orchard."

"I was on my way to Springfield. Am I on the right road?"

"Yes, sir."

The man stretched. "Let's get going, Amos," he said, climbing back up into the wagon.

Ethan started to move off, but the man's intent gaze held him. It's like he's trying to look right through me, thought Ethan.

"Were...those the town toughs?"

"Yes, sir. I...guess so."

"They'll keep their promise? They'll make trouble for you?"

Ethan did not say anything.

"Well...I'm grateful to you, Ethan Alcott."

The horses moved off, stirring up little dust. Ethan watched as the young black man turned around and raised a hesitant hand.

All the family was gathered around the dining table and only the slow, steady clock could be heard in the room. The girls looked frightened (though Libby was very proud of Ethan), and Rebecca was pale. Will gazed out the window.

Ethan had come home, obviously upset, unable to speak for a few moments. The noon meal waited in the kitchen as Rebecca persuaded Ethan to sit and try to tell them what had happened.

"Is that all, son?" Will asked, when Ethan's tale was finally out.

"Yes, sir."

Louisa spoke up quickly. "Did you leave his whip laying there in the road? Because if you did, that wasn't very smart and I—"

"I picked it up and dropped it in the creek," Ethan said tiredly.

"Ethan, what if you had hit Tyler's hand? It could have been a serious injury and they could have Sherriff Tanbee out here." Will's voice was curt.

Ethan said nothing, staring at the clean white smoothness of the tablecloth.

"Son, you've jumped into another man's fight...and that's hard business," Will warned. "Now you have the whole Denham clan as your enemies."

Tyler and Saul Denham, both in their mid-twenties, had the dubious distinction of being Peppercreek's most shiftless rowdies. With their hard, unkempt appearances and frequent drinking binges they kept their reputations well intact.

"What will they do to Ethan?" Libby asked, but no one answered her and Ethan gave her a slight smile across the table. He was truly sorry he had upset her and the whole family.

"Did you think of the consequences of what you were about to do before you did it, son?"

"No, Pa. I didn't think."

"Well, one of these days actin' without thinking is going to get you into serious trouble, Ethan." Will hadn't meant to sound hard, but it came out that way.

"Will, please . . ." Rebecca said nervously.

Will rubbed his forehead. The headache he had nursed would hardly be helped by this new crisis. He sighed deeply.

Ethan had never felt so frustrated in his entire life.

"Pa . . . I didn't think, but all I knew was that if somebody didn't do something soon . . . Well, that colored fella was going to be hurt bad. The other man didn't have a gun or anything to defend himself with and I know the Denhams . . . Did I do wrong?"

Rebecca came around the table and put her arms around Ethan. Will's eyes went from the pleading gaze of his wife to the open, confused expression on his son's face.

"Son, you did right," Will said, slowly.

It was a long time before the O'Dell family found out why the Denhams took no immediate revenge against Ethan. They would not know for some years that the violence had been restrained, strangely enough, because of Grandmother Tufts. She did not tell them what she had done, believing it was best not to "hang all her laundry on the line." But she gained a measure of quiet satisfaction that she had been able to help Will and Rebecca's boy.

Libby, of course, had flown to her the next day to tell her of Ethan's heroics and the Denham threat. Grandmother said very little in return and Libby was disappointed. After she left, however, Grandmother put on her hat, her shawl and her grimmest expression.

She went promptly to the squalid house where the Denhams lived and faced Jonas Denham with hands on her hips. As grizzled and profane as Jonas was, Grandmother was still a formidable sight with her jutting chin and snapping gray eyes. Her words were simple and to the point. If she heard one word of trouble coming to Ethan Alcott from any of the Denham boys, the right of way across her land that the Denhams had enjoyed for years would be quite unceremoniously closed. Jonas Denham grew very red of face and very angry, indicating by the curtest of nods that he would abide by her words. When she left, the air was filled with his curses.

"Bide your time, boys... Bide your time," he told his sons bitterly. "A better time will come—one that Alice Tufts can't stop."

He would be in his grave when those words came true.

Ethan didn't even tell Roy of the event, and Will and Rebecca forbade the girls from gossiping about it. Tyler Denham, sensing that only his brothers knew of the episode, had no public pride to defend. He could just as easily move on to other hates.

But Jip had seen his brothers humiliated—and he would not forget.

Part II

Masterweaving

Chapter 1

Peppercreek, Illinois
Christmas day, 1852

◆◆ ◆◆ ◆◆

*W*ill O'Dell had never spent a Christmas day in bed before, and he did not like it. Doc Noble had said besides the short walk from the bed to the dining table for the Christmas feast, he was to lay flat on his back for at least another five days. Ten days ago, he had tripped on the cellar steps, breaking his left foot and cracking three ribs. He had been rather sullen about this convalescence—inside he felt embarrassed, clumsy and just a little old. He thought he might have heard Rebecca mumble something about pride going before a fall, but he wasn't sure. He did know she didn't mind telling anybody and everybody he was the worst patient she'd ever nursed.

He frowned when he thought of the extra work his injury caused for everyone, especially Isaiah and Ethan. He was truly grateful Henri was here and would be until the end of January. Besides the good conversation, laughter and stories that he brought, Henri Mullins was not one to shirk work.

Since their first meeting, Henri's relationship with the family had strengthened. He had become like a son to Will and Rebecca, and a cheerful older brother to Ethan and the girls. When his work brought him up into Illinois, he would come to Peppercreek. He knew each welcome he'd receive would be as warm and as generous as the first one was.

He came at intervals, sometimes as long as six months between, with a tanned face, hungry, ready to work alongside them, full of enthusiasm, full of new stories.

The bedroom door opened and Rebecca came in, bearing the tea tray.

"Ready for tea?"

"I'm not sure I can hold it . . . after that meal. Not being able to get up and move around. Just lay here like a log . . ." His voice was petulant.

Rebecca always had trouble not laughing outright at Will's pouting. Still strong and tall, but now supine and helpless—it was unusual for her to have him almost completely at her mercy. Will stubbornly suspected his wife was enjoying all this.

He took his cup. "Girls getting ready. I can tell by the flying footsteps overhead."

Rebecca nodded. The gifts exchanged, the meal over now on the crystal clear and cold day, the younger members of the family were bundling up to go ice skating at Miller's pond.

"Henri and Ethan are getting the sleigh ready," Rebecca added.

"Want to go with them, Mrs. O'Dell? You are looking pretty spritely this afternoon."

"No thank you, sir. Quiet and comfort suit me just now. Besides, I never skate without my gallant skating partner at my side."

She drank her tea to cover her smiling. Will gave her a sour grin and returned to his farm journal. Will was a notoriously inept skater.

Several minutes passed, until Rebecca sighed significantly. From behind his paper Will offered a mere "Um?"

That was all Rebecca needed. "I've been sitting here thinking . . . about Libby. Remembering when I realized I was carrying her."

Will put the paper down and looked at his wife.

"I never told you, but I wasn't terribly happy about it at first. I just wasn't sure. I thought about . . . about John and Robert. Of course, as she started growing, and I felt that first movement . . . Well, then I was so glad. But today, I'm especially thankful for her."

"As for them all."

"Well, yes. Yet, Libby will be here longer after the others have gone. It won't be quiet and empty so suddenly."

"After the others are gone? Where are they going, Mrs. O'Dell?"

"Will, you don't suppose our girls will be spinsters, do you? They'll marry and have homes of their own. Not far from us, I hope. And Ethan—"

"Marry! Rebecca, that's so far off! What would even make you think like that?"

Rebecca laughed. "Oh, Will! Far off? Wyeth is nineteen next month and you see what a pretty young woman she's becoming."

"They're all pretty," he grumped, sinking back into his journal.

"A lot of girls are married at nineteen and you know it, Will," Rebecca persisted. "We'll do well to harness Louisa in till she's that age, you know."

"Are you bringing up this disagreeable subject because I'm bedridden? You're giving me indigestion."

"Will, don't you want your daughters and son to marry? Has your own marriage been so disagreeable?" she asked coyly. "You won't discourage their little love affairs will you?" Her voice was tender.

He shook out his paper angrily. "I won't discourage them ... but I certainly won't encourage them!"

They had come into Will and Rebecca's bedroom to say goodbye and to receive their parents' cautions. "Don't get too cold or too tired; watch for thin ice; keep the horses properly blanketed; and be home before dark." Now their laughter and eager young voices were gone and the house was silent in the winter afternoon. Will tossed his paper aside. "You know, the house is awfully quiet. Besides Isaiah napping, we are alone, Mrs. O'Dell."

Rebecca looked up innocently. "Yes, the quiet is pleasant, isn't it?"

"Um ..." he said, as his eyes studied his still beautiful bride. "I have some ideas of my own ... about my recuperation."

Rebecca stifled a smile with great difficulty. "Oh? Well, I certainly think you should share them with Dr. Noble tomorrow when he comes to check you."

"No ... no, Mrs. O'Dell, I think not."

Their eyes met in complete understanding and they both burst out laughing.

"You're looking tired, gal—"

"Just awhile ago you said I looked spritely."

Will ignored her. "You look tired now," he said as he patted the bed beside him. "I'm lonely over here, Rebecca."

She stood up, coming to him with a smile. "Some things never change—do they, Mr. O'Dell?"

Wyeth and Henri were standing on the snowy edge of Miller's pond. It was a glorious day for skating, for being out in the cold, raw sunshine. Henri and Ethan and some other men, when they first arrived, had dragged up limbs for the huge warming bonfire. A black cauldron of bubbling and steamy apple cider was suspended above it.

Ice skating on Christmas day at Miller's pond had become a Sangamon County tradition, now going on fifteen years. It was an enjoyable way to work off heavy Christmas dinners and for families and friends to exchange Christmas greetings. The young people in the crowd considered it a very important social event. This day at least sixty people were gliding across the bluish sheen or grouped along the snowy perimeter.

Wyeth, taking a break from the skating, stretched her hands out to the fire. Mr. Clampitt, who presided over the cider, handed her a cup with a courtly bow. Dear Mr. Clampitt, she thought. A bachelor now in his mid thirties, he was the scorn of most single girls. Wyeth had not been immune to his attentions. And he did not inspire her...

"Careful! It's mighty hot," he warned.

"Thank you," replied Wyeth as she and Henri moved away from the fire.

She took a tentative sip.

"Mr. Clampitt is very solicitous over you, Wyeth, offering to help you with your skates," Henri observed dryly.

Wyeth rolled her eyes at him. "He also offered to help about six other girls, so I won't take it too personal." She smiled, "I do wish someone would marry that man."

Henri laughed and they turned back to watch the skaters. Libby's high-pitched scream could be heard above the rest. Roy and Sara James, along with Libby, had joined hands and were being "snaked" across the ice by Ethan.

"Libby might consider the opera with a voice like that," Henri said, chuckling.

"Why is it Christmas day seems like a day you actually feel?" Wyeth asked. She knew this was the sort of question she could ask Henri without being laughed at. He would understand.

He had been a part of their family now for over four years and he and Wyeth had a friendship distinct from that shared with the rest of the family. They talked about books and poetry—though with life on the circuit being what it was, Henri had little time for reading anymore. Wyeth would share with him the things she had read while he was gone.

Henri talked about sunsets and the changing seasons and moonlight, about pastures thick in wildflowers and craggy mountain ranges colored in a thousand shades, and streams and rivers like ribbons of silver. He painted word pictures about the rustic homes he had visited across Kentucky and Missouri. Wyeth felt she really knew the pioneer wife with flour on her arms and three children clinging to her skirts, or the tow-headed blind boy whose best friend was the brindle-colored calf. She felt their tiredness and their hopes. She could see the fatigue fall away like a garment when they danced at the barn raisings. In her mind, she saw the inner radiance that flooded their work-weary faces when Henri led them in worship. When he told her the story of the Kentucky girl in faded homespun who had given him a delicate bird's nest in gratitude for his bringing the gospel to her home, Wyeth felt she understood the girl's heart.

They seemed able to talk on a level that Wyeth could not use with anyone else. She had found a rare friend in Henri, and while never verbalizing it, she was very grateful.

"I suppose Christmas day is a day you feel because it's so full of good will. You know, there doesn't seem any place for hard feelings on Christmas day. It's something deeper than mere tradition that makes us feel happy. Christmas has . . . an authority, or claim to it, inspires an instinct to feel loving and happy and content. I . . ." he hesitated and Wyeth looked into his face.

"What?"

"Well, I like to think too, it's a part of our innermost spirit celebrating His birth, the very greatness of God toward us."

Wyeth looked past the pond to consider his words. Yes, Henri had put it right again.

"Look there at Louisa," he said in a moment. "She's got that look in her eye," Henri said jokingly.

Louisa and a young man were coming off the ice. They could hear her bell-like laughter and see her shrug her shoulders and toss her golden mane of hair.

"Yes, she has on her battle gear," Wyeth returned. "That's a boy from Alton. He'll be her next victim. We'll hear all about him on the trip home." There was no envy in her voice.

"You know, if you and Lib were like Louisa I'd imagine your folks would pretty well have their hands full," he said, laughing. "It's a good thing you're so sensible, Wyeth."

Ethan called out for Wyeth to join him. She handed Henri her cup.

"Yes . . . that's me, ol' sensible Wyeth."

But there was no laughter in her voice now, no smile in her eyes. Then she was gone.

Henri stood there, surprised at Wyeth's tone. He thought of what he'd just said and realized it had not come out as he had intended. Perhaps Wyeth had thought he meant all the beauty in the family was with bubbly, outgoing Louisa. He frowned—he had not meant that at all—and it bothered him that Wyeth might think so.

Then, surprised that his mind had preserved it, he remembered a conversation of some years earlier. Ethan had been talking. He was put out with Louisa over something, but defending Wyeth.

"Louisa's nothing but fluff and ribbons sometimes, you know," he said scornfully. His arm went around Wyeth's shoulders. "Wyeth is . . ." He was searching for an illustration.

"Louisa is silk, Ethan, and I'm dependable brown calico," Wyeth said with a trembling smile.

Henri winced inside himself, startled that for all his closeness to Wyeth he had never detected this feeling before. He realized there were depths to her that he did not know.

An hour later, the skating crowd began to break up. The sun was slipping behind gray, frosty clouds and the temperature was dropping. Ethan hurried to ready the horses and sleigh.

Libby plodded to the sleigh ahead of Wyeth and Henri. Henri took Wyeth's skates as she pulled up her muffler.

"Henri, I can carry my skates."

"I know you can."

"You're carrying Lib and Louisa's. Don't be silly."

"Indulge me in a bit of gallantry, won't you?"

She laughed and he was pleased to see her good spirits had returned. He looked down at her, her face pink and glowing from the chill and exertion. She surely had no idea how appealing she looked.

"Have you had a good time, Wyeth?" he asked, his voice low.

She looked up, smiling. "Oh yes, I love to skate. It's the closest I come to flying!"

His eyes were smiling and friendly upon her. It was quiet, and for a moment Wyeth enjoyed the feel of Henri's look. She wasn't embarrassed or uncomfortable—for this was Henri.

"You know, your mother is a beautiful woman," he said suddenly.

Her smile broadened. "Yes."

His eyes held her again. "You're like her, you know... You have the best of your mother and father in you," he said.

He grimaced inwardly. He had wanted to compliment her, to assure her—but here he was, stumbling around!

"Louisa is the beauty of the family," she said without envy.

"She is pretty," he agreed. She didn't notice the distinction he made.

"I'm nineteen and... slender and boyish and..."

Henri stopped walking. "Wyeth, do you not like your looks?"

Wyeth frowned, "Well..."

A nerve twitched in Henri's jaw.

"Henri, is something the matter?"

He dropped the skates and took her shoulders in his hands. "Wyeth, you are the most graceful, loveliest girl I know. You're..."

He stopped and stepped back from her. A feeling, vague and fleeting, passed between them—like a flame quickly snuffed out. Now, they were both embarrassed. They turned without saying more, going to join the others.

"Thank you for saying that," Wyeth said finally, as they came up to the sleigh.

"I meant it," he said quietly.

Spring, 1853

Wyeth hurried into the kitchen, but stopped short when she found her parents sitting at the table. She knew they had been talking by the sudden quiet when she entered. Her mother sat with a passive face and folded hands. Wyeth could see a slight smile tugging at the corners of her father's mouth.

"What is it? What's the matter?" she asked breathlessly. Tendrils of chestnut-colored hair had escaped from her bun and now clung to her warm, flushed face. Her green eyes were sparkling and Will thought he had never seen his oldest daughter look lovelier.

She had been to the pasture beyond the orchard, picking wildflowers. Everyone in the family knew that when Wyeth worked in her garden or gathered flowers from a walk, she was in her own private world. Sometimes it concerned Rebecca, the way she withdrew into herself so much. Then, Wyeth would give her mother a big smile and Rebecca would know her daughter was happy.

Besides liking so much to help things grow, Wyeth had begun a little "ministry" all her own. She took her flower arrangements and pressed-flower pictures to sick folks around Peppercreek. When she couldn't find someone sick, she took them to the elderly or those that lived alone. It was something she had just begun one day. It gave her a measure of quiet, personal pleasure. She loved to sit on a front porch and hear the old stories that her neighbors could tell her. Tales of coming west in a Conestoga, or of family that had fought in the Revolution or come over from Europe as immigrants.

It also gave her a wealth of experiences to share at the evening table with her family. "They had twelve cats—just in the front room!" she had told them the night before.

At this, Louisa had paused in mid-bite and frowned. "Well, I do hope you didn't sit on the furniture! Can you imagine what the back of your skirt would look like?"

Now Wyeth put down the basket of flowers and faced her mother and father.

"Miss Robb . . . was just here," Rebecca said.

"Oh," Wyeth's voice was flat. Old Flame-and-Fury is enough to bother anyone's day, she thought to herself. Wyeth was a very tolerant girl, but Amanda Robb had never been a family favorite.

"She was a bit upset," Rebecca continued.

Wyeth looked at her father then rolled her eyes. Miss Robb lived in a chronic state of upset.

Wyeth gave a dramatic sigh. "Miss Robb—upset?"

"She... was upset about you, Wyeth," Rebecca said, lowering her eyes to the table.

"Me?"

"Well, not just you," Will amended.

"What have I done this time? Let's see... She didn't like the way I wore my hair to church Sunday? Too European? Or—what's her word? Unseemly. Or, was it I sang too loudly at church, and she thought that was being unspiritual? Maybe she thought it meant I was glad the service was almost over," Wyeth said, laughing.

Will drank his tea noisily.

"No, Wyeth, she was upset about you and... Henri," Rebecca said quietly.

"Henri and me!" Wyeth's voice had definitely inched upward.

"She was out taking Bessie for a walk along the creek road last Friday..."

Wyeth could feel the blush begin to creep up her neck.

"...And she saw you and Henri wading together. She said his pants were rolled up and... and you had your stockings off."

"She was very adamant about those stockings," Will said in a low voice.

Rebecca shot him a warning look. A thick silence filled the kitchen. Then Wyeth exploded.

"Why, that old biddy! That—"

"Now, Wyeth! No name calling," Rebecca warned.

Wyeth had begun pacing, her face aflame, her arms flung out.

"Oh Mother, please don't defend her! You know she is a complaining, bitter, self-righteous—"

"Wyeth, lower your voice." Rebecca's voice was unmistakably firm.

Will folded his arms across his chest and leaned his chair back to properly watch his daughter's theatrics.

"Yes, daughter, lower your voice," he agreed. Miss Robb might be back at the door," Will said calmly.

"Will, please!"

"I wish she were! I just wish she were!" said Wyeth, stalking toward the kitchen door.

"Wyeth, I will not allow you to abuse her—either to her face or behind her back... Imagine, ranting so about a poor old woman!"

"Mother! She's your age!"

Will took another noisy sip of tea.

"My age?" Rebecca exclaimed. "She is certainly much older than me, Wyeth!" She narrowed her eyes at Will. "She's really closer to your father's age."

"Besides, Mother, she's not poor. She's just tight! And—"

"Wyeth," Rebecca interrupted, "we are not going to talk about Miss Robb any more. We need to discuss what she told me when she came over."

Four parental eyes focused on Wyeth. She swung around to the counter, tracing aimless figures with her finger.

What a relief that Henri was not here to witness this... this outrage! Wyeth fumed inwardly. An outrage, to be questioned like this! At last she had felt one of those passionate emotions— like her novels' heroines felt. Yes, that at least was a small consolation to this—this tragedy! Her face reddened at the thought of Henri hearing about this romantic insinuation from Amanda Robb. And it seemed her parents had taken it up as well.

But Henri was on his way to Missouri and would be gone for months. He need never know of this episode.

Rebecca's voice broke the silence. "I told Amanda that I was sure you behaved entirely properly and not to worry."

Wyeth turned around, her voice controlled. "Yes, we were wading. I did have my stockings off. I couldn't see ruining a good pair."

"Do you think that was a good conduct for you to assume with a preacher?"

Will had been out working when Amanda Robb had paid her visit. Rebecca had taken alone the onslaught of the woman's tirade. It had left her feeling out of sorts and uncertain. Perhaps she should not have even mentioned it to Wyeth, she thought...

"I don't know what was wrong with my conduct!" Wyeth insisted testily. "We were just talking, and happened to be wading at the same time. Henri is our family friend. He's... like an older brother," she said carefully.

Rebecca suddenly felt very tired. "Actually she blames Henri more than you. She says she doesn't know if she can worship with him again."

"Ma, I assure you nothing was wrong. Nothing was meant by it."

"I know Wyeth, I know that. It's . . . I'm sorry, Wyeth."

"Do I have to talk about this any more?"

Rebecca hated the hurt she heard in her daughter's voice. She shook her head.

Will stood up, his voice now serious for the first time. "Let's get on with what *was* a nice day."

Wyeth sat alone at her little desk in the dormer of her bedroom. She had to be alone. The walk with Henri three days ago along Peppercreek had been such a lovely time—now she felt the day had been brought to trial. It had been a lovely day, she reflected, because of the weather and because there was nothing to threaten her happiness just then. Sometimes she and Henri had talked, sometimes they hadn't. If she wanted to sit in silence and daydream, Henri made a good and understanding companion, he had his own daydreams to spin.

Wyeth shook her head at the memory. Miss Robb was so absurd . . . Then, a reluctant memory framed itself in her thoughts. Wyeth recalled the ice skating party, months earlier. She remembered Henri's face as he had looked at her and told her she was pretty. For a moment, Wyeth had imagined she saw something more than just friendship in his kind, blue eyes. He looked at her . . . She ran her hands through her hair, thinking. Had he looked at her with the interest a man shows an attractive woman? She had never been looked at like that before. It had given her a sudden rush of warm feelings. He looked at me like I was a painting, she thought. A piece of art—something to appreciate.

Wyeth shook her head again. You're letting your imagination run wild with you, she told herself. Henri is like an older brother. He's eight years older than you. Yet the thought continued to nag. How do you account for his look? she asked herself. How do you account for how much you like him looking at you that way?

Amanda Robb could not conceal her shock at finding Wyeth on her porch a few days later. She was not a woman that neighbors felt inclined to come and visit or even borrow from. Amanda knew that the few visits were strictly courtesy. She knew invitations to quilting circles or sewing for a new baby were extended only grudgingly.

Wyeth had brought bouquets from her garden to her and her sister, Bessie. She had evidently taken much time in preparing them.

Amanda Robb had heard of Wyeth O'Dell's "flower ministry." She never did expect to receive one, however. It did nothing to curb her tart tongue.

"Neither I nor my sister is ill, Wyeth."

"I . . . I know. I just brought them to visit."

It was a strained visit, at best. Wyeth offered an apology for her behavior, which Miss Robb accepted stingily. Wyeth rode off, feeling she had accomplished nothing. Still, she did not see Amanda Robb linger on her porch, brushing the flowers against her weathered cheek. Nor did she see the tears in Amanda Robb's eyes.

Spring, 1854

♦♦ ♦♦ ♦♦

*L*ouisa and Wyeth sat in their bedroom, sewing. Rebecca enjoyed passing by the open doorway, hearing their girlish laughter and teasing. Then she would grow somber, feeling a heaviness come over her. Her children were growing up. The girls were young women now—Wyeth twenty-one and Louisa nineteen. Ethan, at eighteen, was as tall and broad-shouldered as Will. Only Libby seemed reluctant to mature, drawing out her childhood for all it was worth. Rebecca shook her head. She and Will knew Louisa would be the first to leave—and soon. There was no ignoring the strength of her romance with Joe Morgan, the boy from Alton she had met two years before. He was a fine lad, a young doctor who would take Doc Noble's practice someday. Will and Rebecca had no complaint against him—except that he would take their daughter away.

Wyeth had finished telling Louisa the plot to a story she'd read in the recent *Ladies Home Journal*. Louisa preferred hearing stories to reading them herself. She stabbed at her linen awhile, then turned her blue eyes upon Wyeth. They were full of concern.

"Wyeth, Amos Andrews is all right for looks, but goodness, he's so...bookish!" Louisa was always blunt in matters of romance.

"Lou, we don't always discuss books!" Wyeth said laughing.

"Oh?...Well, has he kissed you?"

"Louisa!"

"Oh, don't look so shocked! Your novel heroes kiss, don't they? Good grief! He hasn't even kissed you yet, has he?" Louisa could not be more shocked or disgusted. "What about Moon Face?"

"Lou! You shouldn't call Tom Robbins that! You're awful!"

"Well, has he kissed you or not?"

"Stop!" Wyeth said, choking with giggles, feeling she should be very shocked with her younger sister.

Louisa smoothed out her fabric, a dimpled smile lighting her face.

"I have been kissed by four different boys and liked it each time! Well, with Stanley it *was* a bit oniony."

Both girls fell on the bed, laughing. Then Louisa rolled over and peered worriedly into her sister's eyes.

"Who could you marry—or even kiss, Wyeth? If I didn't love you so much I wouldn't be so concerned."

Wyeth smiled. Her sister was generous, wanting the same happiness for her that she had found with Joe Morgan.

"I could kiss Amos ... if he'd ever work up the nerve, I suppose."

"Could you love him?"

"I ... don't know, Lou. Maybe."

"Oh Wyeth, it's fearful! You have no ideas about what you like in a man. How will you ever get one?"

Wyeth rolled over and stared at the ceiling a moment. She knew her sister was well-meaning, but candor was so hard for Wyeth. That meant sharing her inner, most vulnerable self. She could see that Louisa was not going to drop this subject easily.

"You're wrong about me not knowing what I ... like ... in a man, Lou."

"All right, tell me." Louisa hopped off the bed and closed the door. "Come on, Wyeth! I'm not going to laugh or tell. I promise."

Wyeth rolled back over so she could say it without facing Louisa.

"I would like a man who is ... gentle. Someone who loves God. A man who could make me laugh, who was kind ... and strong and handsome," she finished quickly.

Louisa sat up, smoothing her dress, her mind racing. Wyeth stood up and went to the window.

"That doesn't sound like Amos Andrews ... or even Tom Robbins," Louisa said pointedly.

Wyeth didn't disagree with her.

There was no teasing in Louisa's voice now. "Wyeth, that description sounds like ... Henri Mullins to me."

Wyeth spun around. "Louisa, don't say that!"

"Why?" Louisa's feminine mind had caught the truth before Wyeth could admit it to herself. "Everything you said—'loves God, makes you laugh, is kind and gentle.' Henri is handsome, too."

"Louisa, he's like family. I'm like a little sister to him."

Louisa raised an eyebrow. "Maybe, maybe not. You forgot 'quotes poetry'. I've heard him recite poems just like Amos does."

Wyeth shook her head, not realizing her thoughts were even vocal.

"Amos quotes poetry out of books. Henri... speaks poetry from his heart..."

Wyeth pressed her hands against her cheeks as the truth dawned on her. Her voice was barely above a whisper. "I *do* love him, Louisa!"

Silent tears began to track down her face. Louisa rushed over to her.

"What's the matter, Wyeth? Why are you upset that you love Henri?"

"I feel silly somehow," Wyeth sniffled. "I told you—he thinks of me like a sister."

"You don't know how he feels about you anymore than he knows how you feel about him. I think it's perfectly wonderful!"

Wyeth sunk down on the bed. "You don't understand, Lou."

Louisa took her by the shoulders. "I understand that you're being a goose. Listen, he's supposed to be here by the end of the month. So—"

"So what? Am I going to just walk right up to him and—"

"No, but we'll watch him very closely and he's sure to give away some feeling, and—"

"He never has before."

"Well, maybe you can drop a hint."

"Drop a hint?" Wyeth jumped up and began pacing. "I'll drop dead before I say a word! Louisa you mustn't say a word either, no matter how tempted you are." Wyeth stopped and looked at her severely.

"Oh Wyeth, I think you're exaggerating."

"Promise me, Lou. I've never meddled in your affairs."

"You've never needed to... Oh, all right."

"I don't want you to even mention this conversation again— please."

Wyeth fled out of the house and to the orchard, fully convinced in her young heart that she would regret her confession to Louisa.

The following week passed slowly for Wyeth. Every knock on the door, every horse coming down the lane caused her to jump. She was moody and irritable; laughing one moment, on the verge of tears the next. Nothing pleased her. She dearly wished that she had gone with Grandmother Tufts and Louisa to Springfield for the week.

Everyone noticed her conduct. Even patient Will became exasperated with her a few times. Rebecca was concerned and hoped Wyeth would talk to her. One afternoon Ethan stalked angrily into the kitchen where his parents were having tea.

"Girls!" he exclaimed, slamming his hat down on the counter.

Will and Rebecca exchanged amused looks.

"What is Wyeth's problem?" Ethan demanded angrily. "Is she sick? She just about bit my head off! All I said was her hair looked different!"

Rebecca looked at her son. "Libby tells me you are . . . not immune to girls, Ethan."

"Libby talks too much," Ethan said, blushing. "But they'd sure drive me crazy if they acted like Wyeth."

"Then you better swear off them, son, because girls become women and that's all we've got to marry," Will said, laughingly.

"Oh, I don't plan to marry."

"May I write that down?" Rebecca teased.

Ethan grabbed a teacake and strode into the hall, shaking his head.

"What is the matter with our eldest?" Will asked.

Rebecca shrugged and rolled her eyes, "Girls!"

Henri did not come in a week, but a letter from him did. The family gathered on the front porch as Rebecca read.

> *Dear family,*
>
> *I'm afraid I haven't much time, so this letter will have to be brief. I know you were expecting me to be*

with you by now. I too, was looking forward to being there. But upon my arrival, I found Mr. Cartwright very concerned about the welfare of several missionaries he had commisioned to establish churches in California. Not being in the best of health, he has asked me to go to California in his stead. ("California!" gasped Libby.) *It is, of course, an adventure that I am excited about, but the sorrow in my heart remains that I will be so long away from this family whom I have grown to cherish. I leave in the morning to join a wagon train leaving from Chicago. I will be gone a year or more.* ("A year!" moaned Louisa.) *I have no idea how long it takes for mail to cross the country, but I will write you. Pray for me as I see the west and bring His good news! You will be forever in my thoughts and prayers,*

Henri

Everyone went about the rest of the day wrapped in private disappointment. Louisa could not meet Wyeth's eyes. She felt crushed—she knew Wyeth well enough to know her sister would fold up her secret feeling and bury it in her heart.

Wyeth lay awake that night, trying to navigate her thoughts and bring some control to her emotions. It had been a rush of feeling she reasoned to herself, that confession about Henri—a natural thing toward this man who seemed to know her so well. He's only a good friend. She thought of him now, his boyish face eager for his Western adventure. Then she thought of his eagerness, his willingness to work hard. Suppose he overextended himself out there? What if he became ill, or, worse, was attacked by wagon-train pirates? There were a hundred things to threaten a pioneer across the vast plains; canyons, mountains... A new thought clutched at her. What if... What if he didn't come back? No... No, he would come back. He had always come back.

She rolled over. Through the open window she could hear the rustling and shimmering of the aspen leaves in the night wind. It was a soft sound, comforting and relaxing. Music, Henri would call it. Henri. She sighed—a year was a long time. The flame of feeling would burn brighter or—burn out.

By 1854, the circuit-riding preacher had nearly become a relic of the past, like candles for lighting and men in knee-breeches and powdered wigs. Henri Mullins had joined the tail-end of the movement ten years earlier. Now that the frontier was fully opened up and churches were being established, the preacher on horseback with a gun on his hip and a Bible in his saddlebag was less needed. The associations that had sponsored them, paid them and sent them out were dissolving. The men who had ridden long and hard and lived a spartan lifestyle were now settling down to sedate church work or farming. Most, of course, were bachelors; now, perhaps, there was time to establish families. But these rugged men who had faced measureless challenges and seen measureless miracles had their memories to revel in.

Henri had his. In the long, tedious hours across the plains, he shaded his eyes against the sun, and remembered...

It was one of his first meetings. He had been nervous at first, disappointed at the low turn-out. But he knew, at the very least, his voice would carry in the cabin. He had valued Mr. Cartwright's words, but somehow he simply couldn't "boom" like the man encouraged him. It was an unspoken measure of a preacher as to just how loud the man could deliver. What he actually said was secondary; it was how fiery and dramatic he was that counted. That's what drew the crowds. Yet he couldn't be like that. It felt unnatural. He would do his best, that was all there was to it.

But Henri had underestimated how he'd been blessed. He didn't need a booming voice or a performer's theatrics. Folks were drawn to this tall, slim, young man, who smiled, who spoke carefully, who spoke like he was talking to them personally. When they leaned forward to catch his words, he had them hooked. He drew from simple, everyday experiences that they could understand.

One of those first meetings had been down in southern Missouri. He could still see it clearly, as if it had been yesterday, not years ago. He had worn a new white shirt and a black string tie. It had been hard not to continually run a finger around the collar where it scratched him. He felt so stiff—"like an Egyptian mummy!" he had muttered to Barnabas.

There were fifteen people crowded into the Webber's common room that autumn night. Only six of them were adults—and one of those adults was very nearly deaf. Even with such a small turnout, Henri quickly determined he would still preach to them what he considered his best and longest sermon.

It was a difficult night for Henri, with only one teenage girl attempting to threaten eight children into reasonable quiet. It was also hard for him to retain his train of thought with Mrs. Webber hopping up every few seconds to swat a child. Even when she wasn't swatting, Henri was distracted by the things she could do with her eyebrows. Midway through the sermon, he noticed Miles Johnson become rather fidgety. Still, Henri was undaunted— he still had two very important points to make. Deaf Miss Tyler nodded at everything he said, then politely drifted off into a pre-bedtime nap.

At last, the meeting was over and Henri was glad. His new shirt stuck to his sweaty back. They all shook his hand and told him he had done a fine, fine job. He walked home with Johnson, who was to board him for the night. He was exhausted, yet tense. He asked for a word of helpful criticism.

"Wal..." the farmer drawled reluctantly.

"Please, go ahead, tell me."

"I reckon you did all right."

"All right?" Henri tangled a moment with his ego. "You're not too enthusiastic about my sermon, I can see that."

"Wal, son, it's like this. When I go out with the feed wagon and only three of my heifers show up, I don't pitch off my whole load." He revolved his tobacco wad and gave Henri a friendly slap.

It was a kaleidoscope of experiences from those years on the trail; vivid still, for this had been his whole life.

One experience gave him sweaty palms even now, just thinking about it. He had heard of it happening to other circuit preachers, but he never dreamed it would happen to him. He had come upon a solitary, isolated cabin in the dense woods of Kentucky. It was the first cabin he had come across in two days. No hound dog barked a greeting. He heard something in the stillness as he slid off Barnabas. It was a moan, a human sound of pain. Tensely he stepped into the cabin. A woman, whose husband was out hunting, was trying to deliver her baby. With only a short greeting, Henri had rolled up his sleeves and become a midwife. He would never forget that day.

There were homes where he visited that he enjoyed simple but delicious cooking. There were other homes where sharing a meal was a real trial. The severest test was the home that served a meal of fricasseed canine. Meetings were held in homes, taverns, and open fields. Henri enjoyed the outdoor settings best for bringing the gospel.

But what he thought about most was not just the experiences, nor the beautiful, stirring country he had seen. It was the people; separate families and faces that were still vivid. People who had touched his life, made him laugh or moved his soul. In his mind, he called them "my people." A secret dream of Henri Mullins was to some day write about his people.

One of his favorite families had been the Martins in Kentucky... It had been a very warm spring day, when Henri first rode onto the Martins' property. He was bone-tired and in need of good food and a bath. Barnabas and Jumper needed rest also. He hoped he would find all of that and more at this home. Old Tom Martin, with his wife and grandson, lived on the outskirts of the little settlement. Mrs. Martin had invited him home after his first meeting in this area four years earlier. From then on, he had a standing invitation to stay with them.

Tom Martin was a man in his late eighties who had made his livelihood in the trade and selling of other people's castoffs. Besides the handkerchief-sized flower garden that his wife kept, there was no beauty in this homestead. The yard in front of the cabin overflowed with Martin's treasures—rusted plows, milk cans, crates of chipped crockery, broken clocks and warped butter churns, three-legged chairs and broken harnesses, and bags of quilt scraps.

Now, as he grew older and somewhat arthritic, Tom Martin sat more often by the cabin window, trading tales with his neighbors and musing with himself about his life. While being a rather irascible old fellow, enjoying an occasional shocking or suggestive story, he had developed a deep affection and respect for the young preacher. He looked forward to his coming and always pressed him to stay longer.

The visit in the Martin home that Henri liked best to recall had happened two years ago. James, Martin's grandson, eagerly greeted Henri just before he turned the bend onto the Martin property. His face was anxious.

"Didn't want you to say nothin', Reverend Mullins."

"Well, hello, James. Get on down, there, Jumper! What's the matter, James?"

"I was afraid that you might embarrass Pappy. He don't mind braggin' on it to other folks, but I think he would feel ashamed for a preacher to know."

"Know about what, James?" Henri slipped off Barnabas and walked beside the slim teenager.

"Well, you know how Pappy likes to go to the tavern nearly every day?"

"Yes, he's told me he goes there to play dominoes."

James nodded eagerly. "Pappy loves to play, enjoys the playin' and not to bet. Guess he's purty near the best in the county. Well, last week Newt Jones brought his cousin with him to play. That cousin got sore that Pappy was winnin' so much and accused Pappy of cheatin'!"

"Uh oh," Henri said with a low whistle. He knew Tom Martin well enough to know that a temper still could flare up in the feisty old man.

"Pappy would never cheat and that's the worst thing a man could call him! Well, he jumped right up, grabbed the little chair he was sittin' in and broke it over the man's head!"

Henri burst out laughing. James clutched at Henri's arm as they came into the yard.

"Sssh, ssh! Reverend Mullins! If Pappy knew, he'd be most upset. I just told you because he's got a gash on his head."

"Did the other man strike back at your grandfather?"

"No, Pappy got the gash when the chair flew apart. I guess Newt's cousin won't be callin' Pappy a cheat no more."

Henri chuckled. "No, and I rather imagine he won't engage him in another game of dominoes."

They tied Barnabas to the rail and began to unsaddle him. Henri's nose told him Mrs. Martin was about to serve up another one of her delectable feasts. Knowing the company he was about to keep and the meal he was to enjoy, he felt the fatigue melting away.

"Your grandfather is indeed a character, James."

Dinner was just as he had expected. The small oak table was covered in a clean white cloth and blue willow dishes. A jar of daisies reigned as centerpiece. There was a platter of roast, creamed potatoes, summer squash with cascades of fresh butter down its sides, a plate of thick-sliced tomatoes and a heap of steamy rolls.

"Good thing ya come when ya' did, Henri," Tom said with his mouth full. Henri winked at Mrs. Martin and James, for they all knew what the next words would be. " 'Cause when you come is 'bout the only time James and I get a decent meal!" Mrs. Martin dimpled and gave her husband a playful shove.

After the meal, Henri and Tom sat alone on the porch steps. Tom settled his wad of tobacco comfortably and leaned back. Henri leaned back also, waiting for the old gentlemen's predictable dialogue. They talked of crops and weather and he repeated for Henri the relative merits of each of the well-loved hounds that came wagging up to sniff at their feet. Then he became silent and Henri closed his eyes. Henri jolted awake a few minutes later, shocked with himself that he had fallen asleep. Sunset was lowering its misty curtain and he glanced over at the man at his side. He expected to find him napping as well.

But Tom Martin was not napping. He sat with his head bowed, tears slowly coursing down his leather-like cheeks. They were slow tears—like a child's.

"Mr. Martin? Tom? Are you all right, sir?" Henri asked gently.

The man gave a moan, "My old soul . . . My mean old soul . . ."

Henri leaned over and patted him, but the old man kept his head lowered. "God gave me a good Christian woman over sixty years ago . . . He's been powerful good to us; we've never been hungry or without no roof over our heads . . ." He sighed deeply. "I've outlived all my children; they're gone. Only got my wife and grandson. That James, he's such a fine boy, ain't he?"

"That's the truth, Mr. Martin," Henri agreed.

"I was a wild young 'un, preacher, truly was. Drank a shot of my daddy's whiskey once and was sure I'd swallowed a drop of hellfire. Never touched any again . . . Tried to be a good daddy and a good man to my wife." He paused as he drew out a faded handkerchief to wipe his eyes. "All that goodness to me, Henri, and I never thanked Him . . . Never thanked Him with my life, I mean. I been thinkin' about Him a lot lately."

"What have you been thinking about Him, sir?"

"Do you suppose . . . he could love an old sinner like me?"

Henri felt his love for the old man grow. "Thousands of years ago, He walked down a dusty road," Henri replied gently. "He was deeply tired and sad and hurting. Some soldiers stretched Him out and nailed his hands and feet on a wooden cross. As He hung there dying, His great heart was beating with love for a man named . . . Tom Martin."

"I want Him as my Saviour and Lord," the old man wept. They prayed and when Henri left their home two days later, he was convinced this had been a highlight of his ministry.

Of course, not every frontiersman welcomed Henri warmly or embraced the message he brought. There was blatant rejection, unfriendliness, apathy. When Henri remembered those tough times or seemingly fruitless meetings, he invariably thought of Dan Tell. Mentally he called Dan "the man who enjoyed his sin."

Dan Tell was a wealthy lawyer that Henri had come across when he conducted meetings in Jonesboro, Missouri. He was a flamboyant, loud man who shadowed Henri his entire time in the village. The believers had already privately told Henri this man was blatantly ungodly. Henri did not need to be told this—the man articulated this well enough through his foul language and leering manner. What puzzled Henri was that Dan kept a strict attendance at each meeting and dogged his steps between meetings. He realized that the man reveled in any shock he could give the young preacher. It came to a climax the night before the last meeting, at a barn-raising dance.

They stood beside a wagon, watching the dancers; Henri grateful the man had finally ceased his constant banter. Then Dan Tell turned and perused Henri with an amused, arrogant, critical eye.

"Guess your convictions keep you from dancing," Dan said with a sneer.

Henri chuckled. "No, actually I don't care to have any of these young ladies angry with me for breaking their toes. Barnabas and I don't have much time to take dance lessons."

Dan lit his pipe, his eyes daring. "I have my wife over there and another one just past the state line, besides the gal I keep in the next county. I drink until I'm good and drunk. I swear, using every ugly word I care to. I cheat and steal and do what I blasted well please." He laughed up in Henri's face.

"How long do these dances usually last, Dan? I'm gettin' pretty tired and am supposed to stay with the Johnsons, but they look like they'll go till the crack of dawn." He could not supress a yawn.

Dan looked at him with a mixture of disappointment and suspicion.

"You don't act shocked."

"Shocked at what you said? No, not particularly. Kind of scares me though."

Dan was pleased. "You mean you're fearin' for my eternal soul?" he laughed.

"No . . . not that."

"What then?" the lawyer snapped.

"Well, what you just said reminds me of something that I haven't thought of in years, something that scared me when I was a boy."

"Tell me," Dan said, irritable but curious.

"When I was ten or so, my Ma sent me over to a neighbor with some soup. The old lady was taken sick and my Ma was nursing her. So, I got to her cabin and the door was open and I became afraid."

"Why?"

"Because it was so quiet, unnaturally quiet. I looked into that dim cabin and called out her name. There was no fire; it was cold and dark. I was sure nervous." Henri stopped and watched the dancers a moment.

"Go on, go on," Dan urged.

"Hmm? . . . Oh, anyway . . . I crossed over to the bed and there she was. Her skin was so white . . . I reached out my hand and touched her and her skin was like ice." He readjusted his hat. "I saw death up close that day for the first time. It wasn't particularly pretty. I look at you, Dan Tell, and it scares me to think I'm standing by a man as dead in the soul as that woman was in body." Henri turned his gaze full on the lawyer. "It's a strange feeling, talking to a dead man."

Henri's eyes were blazing. A surge of red spread up Dan's thick neck as he tried to control his rage.

"I'd like to hit you, preacher boy! Lay you out flat, right here!" Dan hissed.

Henri's face was amiable and calm again. "Yes, I can see that you would. It would make another interesting boast for your list, eh Dan?"

Dan's fists clenched and his breathing was jerky. He spit at Henri's boots and stalked off.

Henri was very surprised to see Dan Tell in his usual place on the back row the next evening. Yet, there was definitely a difference in the man—he was not his usual rowdy, boasting, brash self. Instead he sat mute and stone-faced. His arms were folded, his eyes riveted on Henri. He could see Dan's contempt for him was running strong. Henri turned to the simple pulpit with a sigh, bothered that he now apparently had a dedicated enemy. Perhaps last night's words, fueled by a touch of temper, had been too impulsive. He had not expected to have much of an impact on the reprobate Dan Tell, and, while not particularly liking the man, had not actually wanted to alienate him.

Henri opened the meeting with prayer and then there was an hour of singing. Not seeing Dan's face clearly, Henri began to forget the man was there—but that did not last past the first sentence of the sermon. Dan coughed loudly, choked repeatedly, thumped his chair up and down, and exited and reentered the building every few minutes. He made a great display of swatting at a fly that tickled the believers sitting nearest him. Henri now knew how the man planned to take his revenge. Henri preached— but he also prayed.

Dan's performance had become so loud and disruptive, the congregation began to cast him severe looks. He sneered back at them. Henri wondered how long before a believer would jump up and try to bodily remove Dan. Henri was really sweating now.

The meeting was coming to a close and Henri was glad. Then a shy young girl stepped out into the aisle and came up to Henri as he gave the invitation. She was the only one who came, and with trembling joy she began to explain why she had come forward. Henri and the believers were rejoicing. Then, in the silence of her small voice, Dan Tell belched very loudly. A deathly silence fell over the crowd and the young girl turned very red and teary-eyed.

Some in the meeting had said Henri suddenly grew taller. His eyes were smoldering with an anger he was fighting desperately to control. His voice was loud enough to make Peter Cartwright proud as he reached out his long arm and pointed at Dan.

"In the name of the Lord, I command Satan and all his demons to leave Dan Tell!"

The smile on Dan's face fell away, wiped off like a rag cleans a slate. His eyes grew wide and horror-filled. He clutched at his throat, then pitched forward. Someone in the crowd screamed.

Henri and others quickly gathered around him and stretched him on the rough plank floor.

"He's dead!" a hysterical woman wailed. "Dan Tell, killed by a preacher!"

Some days later Henri could laugh over that, but now his voice still sounded grim. "No, he's just passed out. Someone get some water for him," Henri said as he loosened the big man's collar.

Finally, Dan slowly opened his eyes and they sat him up. He was still shaking and his skin was white and pasty.

"I don't want to be a dead man! I don't!" he moaned.

"Dan, you're not dead. You just passed out," a woman corrected sourly. "And, I might add, not a bit too soon, 'cause my man was about to come over and thump you up 'side the head!"

"I don't want to be a dead man," Dan groaned again. Only Henri understood what he meant.

They helped him back up on the bench where he sat, hunched over and weeping.

"Never thought I'd see the day when ol' Dan Tell was blubberin' like a baby," someone mumbled in the crowd.

Henri's face was sober, his voice barely above a whisper. "Anyone who would like to leave may do so now, for the meeting is officially over. But for those who stay, I ask that we pray now. Pray for Dan Tell."

No one moved—and it wasn't entirely a spiritual commitment. There hadn't been a drama like this in the little town for quite a while. So they prayed for many quiet minutes. Then, Dan's crying ceased and he opened his eyes and staightened up. There was a sense of expectation in the air.

"Are you all right now, Dan?" Henri asked gently.

He did not answer but walked to the front of the church, turned, and faced them. His face was tear-streaked but calm, his voice steady, all mockery gone.

"Folks, I'm sorry for the way I've been actin' during meeting tonight, causing a ruckus. I was hating Henri, and wanted to get back at him. I'm sorry, Amy Smithe for interrupting you. Will you forgive me?"

The young girl smiled and nodded.

"You've been born into the kingdom today, Amy...and so have I," Dan said humbly.

"Amen!" shouted the congregation.

"I tell you that I will from this night forward be faithful to my wife. I'll not drink another drop of liquor or swear...Well, I'll try hard not to. Any of you that I've cheated—I'll repay you. The land that you wanted to buy from me for two years to build a church, I give to you."

There were more shouts and hallelujahs, and many came to embrace Dan. Henri stayed two days longer than he had planned because of Dan Tell's urging him to do so. They spent the days and evenings talking, praying and reading Scripture. Henri had never seen such a change in a man as he found in Dan.

That had been over two years ago, Henri reflected. On each visit back to Jonesboro, Henri found Dan Tell established and growing in the faith. If it had not been for his failing health, he would have accompanied Henri on the long trip west. Dan Tell, Henri smiled to himself, the man who loved sin no longer.

Henri's thick letters came to Peppercreek as the long months passed. No one in the O'Dell household had been farther west than the western edge of Sangamon County. So the letters opened up new vistas to them—like reading a travelogue, Wyeth said. The letters brought them the endless miles of prairie, "...like a waving, silent ocean under the bluest sky you can imagine..." Henri described the rugged, snow-crowned Rocky Mountains. "No other natural wonder has stirred awe in me like these have. Gigantic, proud, shadowed in purple and ice-blue..." "The shimmering heat waves" around the Great Salt Lake. The desert: "It seems to go on forever and ever, a flat brown expanse...desperate heat..."

By the fall of 1854, Henri had reached California. He had seen the booming gold fields, sprawling and rowdy San Francisco, and the vast blue ocean. "How can I describe the ocean to you? Or the pungent, salty breezes that come across the waves ... or the gulls that scold and scream overhead ... The Pacific ocean is a living jewel, a sapphire and pearl-colored jewel ... My travels have declared the handiwork of a very creative God ..."

The letters were read carefully, then reread. It was Libby who voiced a thought they had all had.

"He's so taken with California. You don't suppose he would stay there forever, do you?"

Chapter 3

Sierraville, California, 1854

♦♦ ♦♦ ♦♦

*7*he whale-oil lamps were cheap, giving off a musky, flickering light in the little cafe, but Henri really didn't notice the odor tonight. He was absorbed in the newspaper spread out on the table before him. He had come here, as he did for every meal, because "The Tin Chicken" did not attract the rough and rowdy mining crowd—and because the food was very good. But tonight, unnoticed by him, his food grew cold, sitting on the table. It didn't matter; he was riveted to the grim stories in the paper.

Sam Longhorn, the owner and cook, came to refill Henri's tea cup, but, instead went back to the kitchen, shaking his head. He had glanced over Henri's shoulder and seen the black masthead, *Cincinnati Recorder*. Each man had a right to his own interests, of course, but Longhorn had no concern at all for the affairs back east. Those were "the States" and this was California and plainly, to the big cook, entirely separate and unequal. Hundreds of miles of desert and mountain range, canyon and prairie divided the east and west. It was just as well to think of the states as another continent. A good meal was about to go unappreciated, just because the young preacher was captivated by a foolish eastern newspaper. Sam was plainly irritated.

For no explainable reason he'd taken a fancy to the preacher from back east. Sam's friends marveled at this, since the big, gruff man would usually barely serve an eastener, much less be friendly to one. Still, the two had struck up an easy companionship almost immediately.

"So, you're a preacher, eh?" the beefy-faced Sam had queried, on that day when they had met.

"That's right," Henri answered, smiling.

"Well, reckon' I won't hold that against ya."

Henri could not decipher the reason he had been drawn to the robust man. He suspected there was a very kind heart buried beneath all the gruffness and sarcasm. The man's past had left him with an emptiness that bitterness had filled by default. He had told Henri about his coming to California after Henri had made only a few visits to the cafe. In so doing, Sam had shocked himself, for he had never spoken of it to anyone else in the ten years he had been here.

"We came out here for a new start, us and thousands of others. All wantin' a new beginning and puttin' away the past. I just got tired of being abused about my skin, 'bout my eyes. See, my mama was white, but my daddy was full-blood Chinese. So, we came out here, all high hopes. Such a long, rugged way . . . Take me all night to tell ya the sights we seen and things we went through. We buried my brother Peck the other side of the Rockies and . . . my wife Maggie died two days from the California border. The way was just too long and too hard . . . Got here with five dollars in my blue jeans, one chicken still livin' and Maggie's tin pie plate. That was all I started with."

"That's where your cafe gets its name," Henri offered.

"Yep, one tin, one chicken."

"I think you've done very, very well from such a difficult start. This is the best place in town. I'm sure Maggie and Peck would have been proud of what you've done."

Sam looked down at his greasy apron, overwhelmed at Henri's words of praise. From any other man he would not have allowed it, but from this man he knew it was sincere.

"California needs strong, honest men like you, Sam," Henri continued. "I know that firsthand from the men I have to bunk with and try to minister to. California is big and brassy and drawing men by the hundreds. Good men can make a foundation for this to become a state that will be a pride to the Union."

Coming back from the kitchen, Sam pulled up a chair beside Henri's and began to pick his teeth. He was courteous enough to let Henri fold his paper, say grace and eat a few bites before he began talking. It wasn't hard for the big man to do since Henri was now giving appropriate attention to the good food. He waited.

"Great dumplin's, Sam," Henri enthused.

Sam nodded as if this were common knowledge.

"Dumplin's are an art and make no mistake. Can't have a heavy hand with 'em or you end up with 'em tastin' like a gunny sack full of chicken feathers ... So ... I reckon you might say the mail boat seduced ya." Sam gestured to the newspaper.

Henri chuckled at the expression and nodded. "Everyone was talking about the news, so I bought a paper."

"Uh huh ... And now you're all fluffed up and agitated."

"Now, Sam, I am giving credit to your culinary skills, aren't I?" Yet Henri's smile faded as he pushed back from the table.

"Yes, I guess I am agitated, as you say," the minister admitted. "Kansas is only a day's ride from where I grew up. My sister and her family still live there. I know folks in Kansas ... I've preached there. This ..."

"I ain't plannin' on readin' that rag myself, so you just go ahead and tell me the particulars," Sam returned, dryly.

"Well, it seems that this Senator Douglas from Illinois proposed a bill in Congress that would allow the two new territories of Kansas and Nebraska to decide for themselves if they want to be slave or free. President Pierce supported it and now the bill is law."

"Uh huh. And don't I recall a certain compromise of 1820 that prevented extention of slavery any further West?" Sam asked. Henri smiled briefly. For all his distaste for "back East," this big burly man was not ignorant about what went on there.

"Yes, but this new bill makes that one null and void," Henri replied.

"Convenient," Sam grunted.

"The paper is full of all the fighting going on between proslavery and anti-slavery men. The territory is filled with violence. Men are killing their own neighbors. Thirty men have died there in the last two months ..." He shook his head, his voice filled with sadness. "Neighbors are burning each other's barns and crops. Innocent folks are getting caught up in it. The papers are calling it, 'Bleeding Kansas'."

Sam poured himself some tea and tried to think of something to say.

But Henri was miles away in his thoughts. He thought of the hotel room he shared with three other men, all miners. He had come to this little mountain town six weeks previous, the last mission that Peter Cartwright had directed he should check on. He had found the pastor nearly broken with exhaustion and stress. Ministering in a rough mining town was no easy task. So Henri had cheerfully taken over the man's duties while he recovered. He would never forget the look of gratitude in the man's eyes.

Now the pastor was ready to resume his work and had reminded Henri a wagon train was leaving in two days, headed east. He must join up with that one if he expected to reach the midwest before the snow fell. Henri had reluctantly agreed. He wanted to make certain all the work the Lord had planned for him in California was over. Sam broke into his thoughts, dragging him back to reality.

"I wonder where such fightin' will end."

Henri's face was clouded. "I don't think it will end for a while, yet."

"Well, preacher, you see precisely and to the point why I'm rooted here in California. California is free and we won't have any slavin' trouble here. Too much trouble back East... I shook the dust off my feet ten years ago, and you should too, Henri Mullins." He gave Henri a big grin. "As you said yourself, California needs good men."

Henri's smile was wistful. "No, Sam, I have to go back, no matter what becomes of this fight. Those are my people..." Suddenly, in his mind he could see the Peppercreek orchard in full bloom. "I'm going home, Sam. I have family there."

Peppercreek, Illinois, New Years Eve, 1854

Because of their laughter they did not hear the footsteps on the porch or the opening of the front door. It was the sudden rush of cold air that caused them all to look up. Wyeth stood in the hallway, her escort helping her off with her coat.

Henri looked up and was shocked—in eighteen months, Wyeth had grown even lovelier. She wore a pine-green dress that drew out the highlights in her eyes. She had pinned her hair up in a fashionable pompadour, and wisps of auburn hair had floated loose, framing her face with the delicacy of an artist's brush. She stopped whatever she had been saying to the young man at her side as her eyes fell upon Henri, across the room.

Libby rushed up to her, her mouth full of scones, "Look Wyeth! Henri! He's back! He's come home!"

For a moment, Henri forgot Wyeth as he heard Libby's words. Home. It had come to her so naturally to make him a part of the family! How good it sounded to him. The long months of loneliness seemed to dissolve in his memory.

He stood up awkwardly, his cup of cider rattling on his plate. "Hello, Wyeth... You've grown up!"

Rebecca had been in the kitchen when Wyeth had come in, and coming up behind them, she was unseen for a moment. There was something about Henri's sudden look at Wyeth— something about Wyeth suddenly blushing when her eyes met Henri's. Rebecca began to wonder... Such looks, particularly Henri's, were hard to counterfeit.

"Hello... Henri..." was all Wyeth could manage. She felt as rattled as he apparently did. The same friendly, boyish face, now framed in a trim gold-brown beard, the sun-chapped cheeks and steel-blue eyes, still so slender. The same Henri, Wyeth thought, but looking at me with such intensity. She was glad when he finally shook his head and turned back to Libby, beside him.

Wyeth shifted uncertainly, grateful her family was in such a vocal mood.

"You've missed all the good parts about California, Wyeth," Ethan said eagerly. She smiled. Her brother looked like he was about to explode with happiness.

"Did you have a nice evening, Wyeth?" Rebecca asked as she came up beside them.

"Yes mother, a very nice time."

Will stood up, beckoning to the young man who had come in with Wyeth. "Come on in and join our little celebration, George. This is Henri Mullins, just returned from California, and we're rejoicing to have him back."

"He was gone over a year!" Libby informed the young man proudly.

It had been a long time since Wyeth had seen her family in such high spirits. Henri came forward then, his hand extended.

"Hello, I'm Henri Mullins."

"George Lance," said Wyeth's escort, his eyes giving Henri a quick scrutiny.

"You're limping," Wyeth blurted out, instantly embarrassed.

Libby flew between them to provide the explanation, her eyes as round as saucers. "He's getting over a terrible case of frostbite on his left toes. He—"

"A blizzard caught him in a pass in the Rockies," Ethan interrupted.

"He almost died!" Libby added, not wanting Ethan to tell all the important and dramatic details.

Wyeth looked down at the floor then turned to George who stood turning his expensive hat in his hands.

"I better be going, Wyeth," he said uncomfortably.

"I'll see you to the door," Wyeth said, barely above a whisper.

"Goodnight, George, goodnight!" Will and Rebecca called, then everyone turned their attention back to Henri.

Wyeth felt embarrassed in the entryway. She imagined they were all straining to hear what was going on. Of course that was silly, since she could hear their voices and laughter. They had already forgotten her, she thought, forgotten her coming home from a big party on the arm of the dashing young George Lance. To them, George Lance was pale and unimportant, compared to Henri's return.

George took her hand confidently in his gloved one.

"I had a very nice time tonight, thank you," Wyeth said.

He only smiled. Hesitating only a minute, he cast a quick glance toward the living room, then pulled Wyeth farther into the shadows.

"Goodnight, my little Wyeth." His kiss was more peremptory than passionate. He was gone quickly and Wyeth leaned against the doorway, with just a little breathless feeling. She looked over at the staircase, almost wishing she could slip up it unnoticed. That was impossible, not to mention rude, she told herself. After all, she should be happy like the rest of the family—he had been gone so long. It was reason to celebrate.

Yet for some reason, she just didn't want to face him tonight. This night at the party had been so...special—such a rare experience for a country girl like herself. She wanted time to think back over every detail and savor it. She wanted the quiet darkness of her bedroom to sort things out in her mind. Now it seemed, Henri's arrival had eclipsed all that. Her family would not be very impressed with her stories of the glittery affair.

With a sigh she entered the room, grateful she did not have to meet Louisa's suggestive looks or gestures. That conversation had been so long ago...Henri did not look up when Wyeth reentered, though he certainly knew she was there. Wyeth slipped beside her mother, blushing furiously at the kissing noises Ethan made in her direction.

Though Rebecca lay still, she was wide awake. Will was slowly drifting off to sleep, despite the excitement of the evening. How great it had been to open the front door and find Henri there, with such a broad smile on his face. Will felt as if a son had come home.

"Isn't it wonderful...to have Henri...home..." he murmured against Rebecca's neck.

"Um..." Rebecca replied.

Will yawned deeply. "He seems older somehow, more mature or..."

"Wasn't Wyeth looking beautiful when she came in?" Rebecca asked.

"Beautiful, yes...I just don't know about George..." Will grumbled.

"Now Will, don't get started on George Lance. You're as bad as Ethan and Libby."

"Well..." He was almost asleep when Rebecca's words threw him wide awake.

"Henri's in love with her," Rebecca said calmly.

"What?"

"Henri's in love with our Wyeth," she stated simply.

Will propped up on one elbow. "What are you talking about, Rebecca? You sound like Louisa!"

Rebecca said nothing and Will could tell she was smiling.

"He just got here. How can you judge a thing like that so fast?"

"I just know."

Will pulled his wife of almost thirty years into his arms. "And how do you know this? Tell me, please."

"I know a man in love when I see one." She traced the line of his jaw with her finger, and tenderly placed a kiss on his lips. Will held her closer.

"From personal experience, is that it?" he teased.

"You were particularly transparent, my Illinois apple merchant!"

"And vulnerable to a Kentucky beauty," he finished as they laughed together.

"And your eldest? Is she feeling the same way? Henri is like a brother to her, after all. Not to mention he's eight years older. Could she take Mr. Mullins seriously?"

"Only the Lord knows that, Mr. O'Dell..."

Everyone had finished breakfast when Wyeth entered the kitchen the next morning. There was so much to talk about, not only Henri's adventure in California, but things that had happened in their lives and in Peppercreek—like Louisa's marriage, back in the summer.

"It does seem quieter around here," Henri had commented and they had all laughed.

Wyeth had already decided to act perfectly natural. There was no reason to be nervous around Henri Mullins. And she would ignore Ethan and Libby's teasing. She drew a deep breath.

"Sorry I'm so late this morning, Mother," Wyeth said.

Rebecca smiled. "Don't fret. Libby applied herself quite well."

"We tried to save more for you, but Henri's back, after all," Will said, chuckling.

"I could tell some real stories about my cooking efforts, but that might ruin Wyeth's appetite," Henri confessed. Everyone laughed and Wyeth began eating.

"Tell us about the big hoedown at the Lance mansion last

night, Wyeth," Will asked. "We didn't get any details when you came in."

"Pa, it is *not* a mansion," Wyeth replied.

"Well, all I know is it's bigger than a barn and has columns in front and a circular drive. That's a mansion to me."

"And slaves," Libby added, mischievously.

"Libby! Stop it! Those people are not slaves. Slavery is not allowed in Illinois and you know it! They are paid servants."

"But what color are they?" Libby said with sixteen-year-old persistence.

"They are black, but they are paid servants. Besides... they're like family to the Lances."

"You don't pay family," Ethan said pointedly as he fixed himself another hotcake.

Wyeth reddened and Will cleared his throat.

"Well, I want to hear about the time you had."

Wyeth cast a threatening look in the direction of Libby and Ethan, wanting them to understand the splendor of the evening and not make silly, irrelevant interruptions.

"It was like nothing I've ever been to before," she began, her voice dreamlike. Ethan and Libby looked at each other and rolled their eyes. Will and Rebecca cast each other a quick glance and smile.

"When we got out of the carriage, there was even a butler to help me out, and—"

"Why did he help you out? Couldn't you get out by yourself?" Libby interjected.

"Well of course! It's just the thing that butlers are supposed to do!" Wyeth said, irritated. "Anyway, there was light and music pouring out of all the windows. There were probably twenty-five carriages in the drive."

"Twenty-five!" Will exclaimed, keeping to himself the surprised observation that George Lance, Sr. had that many friends.

"Well, perhaps not quite that many...I don't know, there were a lot anyway. But they all had drivers in polished liveries. They were all standing around—"

"Good grief! I can't understand why a person would hire someone else to drive him around!" Ethan put in. "If I had horses and a fine carriage, I'd sure drive it myself. Having a driver sounds silly to me," Ethan said scornfully.

"Ethan," Wyeth said in a tone of strained patience, "if you have lots of money you pay people to do all sorts of things for you, so you...can do what you like."

No one said anything. Wyeth was feeling increasingly uncomfortable. Her parents exchanged another look over their cups. Libby broke the silence.

"Does Emily Lance have a personal maid? You know—to dress her and brush her hair?"

"I don't know..." Wyeth conceded slowly, frustrated over the silly details her family seemed to be thrilling over.

"What was there to eat?" Ethan demanded.

"To eat? I don't know, really. I was too excited to eat."

Henri looked down at his plate and smiled. Wyeth had experienced a Cinderella night.

"What did the really rich ladies wear?" Libby asked again.

"Oh there were silks and satins of every color."

"Did you dance?" Ethan asked.

"Of course," Wyeth answered, her voice dropping just a few tones.

"Who with?" Libby pestered.

"George." Wyeth was beginning to wish her family would go off and begin their day. This narrative of the night before was not going off as she had planned.

Libby leaned forward, her eyes mischievous. "Did you dance with anyone besides George?"

"Oh...some of George's friends."

Wyeth looked at Henri and found a smile tugging at the corners of his mouth. Was he making fun of her, too?

"I bet you were the prettiest gal there!" Will said as he stood up to stretch.

Wyeth began clearing off the table, a clear message that last night had been dissected enough. As her family left the kitchen, she washed the dishes, her thoughts still lingering over the night before. She had not told them of George's strong cologne—that would have made Ethan and her father snort in disgust—or how immodestly some ladies were dressed, or the separate punch bowl reserved for the older men. She didn't tell them that George's kiss in the entryway was tame compared to the kisses he had attempted in the shadows at the party. No, she could not tell them everything.

February was just as frigid and stormy as January had been. And Henri was still with them. His career as a circuit-riding preacher was over. Now he was in search of new work, as a church pastor or with some mission. While he helped in the usual chores of the farm, he also spent time in prayer to discern what the next ministry in his life should be. He had never been happier, as he lived and worked with the O'Dells. Ethan was teaching him the art of ice fishing. Together they would tramp the snowy woods and come home with pink and glowing faces. Rebecca would smile when she knew they were coming home. Their laughter always preceded them.

Though Will or Rebecca would not admit it, the pleasant winter evenings were different now that George Lance was a part of them. When he came over, there was a palpable tension, though no one could define why. He talked with Will and Ethan, but they had little common ground with him. With Henri he seemed aloof. Rebecca had never used her eyebrows and subtle headshakes as much as she did now, trying to keep Libby in line. Libby was just as likely to call George Lance "ridiculous and arrogant" to his face as she was to ask him the time of day. Even Wyeth could never truly relax when her family and her beau were together.

It seemed that Wyeth had taken a particular fancy to the elegant George Lance as she had never done before with any young man. For once, and most astonishingly, Louisa was conspicuously silent. With her husband, she was quite the opposite.

Grandmother Tufts was quite blunt when she confronted Rebecca one clear, cold afternoon as they took their tea in the kitchen.

"The house is mighty quiet, Rebeccy," Grandmother said without preamble.

"They've all gone sledding over on Bishop's hill," Rebecca replied.

"Even Wyeth?" Grandmother asked pointedly.

Rebecca smiled, she knew precisely why Alice Tufts had braved the cold drive to Peppercreek orchard—and it was not just for a cup of tea. "Wyeth is in town shopping for fabric. She wants to make herself a new dress."

Grandmother shook her head and frowned, as if dressmaking boded nothing but evil.

"Libby gave me an earful yesterday," she said.

Rebecca laughed.

"It was not glad tidings she told me, Rebecca!" Grandmother scolded.

"I know. It's just that Louisa and Libby are born gabbers."

"Well?" Grandmother demanded.

Rebecca poured the tea with a sigh. "What did Libby tell you?"

"About Wyeth and George Lance! I tell you I'm positively horrified."

Rebecca stirred her tea placidly.

"Is it true Rebeccy? Is he courting her?"

"Yes. They seem . . . in earnest."

Grandmother drew a long noisy drink. "Where has the child's good sense gone? I'm so floundered by this my cream could curdle."

It was difficult for Rebecca to contain herself. Will would relish this later.

"Well, they are courting, that's true. But I'm not alarmed. I—"

"Alarmed? Gracious Rebecca, if a snake had wrapped itself around Wyeth it could be no worse!"

"Grandmother! Really, that's awful. You know the Lance family and—"

"Indeed I do. I haven't lived here all my years not to know a thing or two about folks in these parts, and—"

"But aren't the . . . stories about the Lances just rumors, really?"

"Pshaw, Rebecca. I've said it before, you and Will are too trusting and naive."

"Well—"

"Rumor is for folks who don't know the facts," Grandmother said tartly.

"Will and I hope this . . . infatuation will pass soon. George seems nice enough."

"Hmpf!"

"We must remember that Wyeth is a woman now. We can't dictate whom she courts. I mean . . ." Rebecca suddenly felt very tired.

"Lances have always gotten what they wanted," Grandmother said.

"But, George may not really . . . want our Wyeth."

"Hmm. May just want to break her heart, eh? Still, Lances never waste anything—time, words or money. Everything has a purpose."

That the Lances were the wealthiest family in Sangamon and surrounding counties carried no weight with Alice Tufts. It was her frank opinion their wealth was an uneasy wealth—gotten by less than honest means.

"Grandmother, you're going to frighten me with talk like this," Rebecca appealed.

"I lost considerable sleep over it myself last night, my dear. Louisa's romances were purely entertainment compared to this. My aged bones just can't take too much. And of course there is still Libby and Ethan to go."

"Let's hope that isn't going to be for awhile yet," Rebecca said with a smile, and the tension was eased.

"Well, I have heard that Ethan is not a monk himself."

Rebecca burst out laughing and Grandmother allowed a slight chuckle at herself.

"Let's just . . . hope that Wyeth shows the good sense she always has in the past," Rebecca said.

Grandmother nodded her gray head vigorously. "Yes indeed . . . We'll hope that the apple doesn't fall too far from the tree."

George Lance sat stiffly on the sofa, trying to join in the laughter around him. He couldn't though—he didn't see the humor, so he took another mouthful of popcorn and another sip of cider and wished he could be alone with Wyeth. Her parents had gone on to bed, as her silent, stone-faced uncle had. There was something unnerving to George about Isaiah. He seemed to feel the nearly colorless eyes continually upon him. He didn't like that—so he didn't like the man himself. He was grateful, though, that Wyeth's little sister—who tested his patience like no one ever had—was spending the night with some friend. Now, if only her brother and this preacher would leave them alone. However, that wasn't very likely, George noted grimly, as Ethan poured himself more cider and Henri added a log to the fire.

George glanced over at Wyeth. Her face was pink and her eyes were sparkling from laughter. George looked back at Henri and frowned. He considered Henri a buffoon. He couldn't understand why Wyeth found the preacher so funny. He tried to telegraph Wyeth with his eyes to try to find a way to be alone with him. But she didn't know him well enough to understand him. He pulled his thoughts irritably back to the conversation.

"Well, the almanac says snow till the end of March," Ethan was saying.

"I certainly hope the almanac is wrong," George said confidently. "Snow isn't good for business and, frankly, I'm sick of it."

There was a strained silence and George wondered what he had said to cause it. He did not know Ethan, Wyeth and Henri were all snow lovers—even March snow. He felt a fresh wave of irritation. There seemed an intimacy here that he could not penetrate. He would be glad when spring came and he could take Wyeth out for drives in his fine carriage. He stood up abruptly.

"I need to be going now, Wyeth dear."

Wyeth blushed, though she tried desperately not to. "Wyeth dear" was fine when they were alone, but in front of Henri and Ethan she felt terribly embarrassed. George saw the blush and was pleased—Wyeth O'Dell really was very lovely.

He said goodnight to Ethan and Henri in a clipped voice, then Wyeth led him to the entryway for his hat and coat. Henri stood up and stretched, poking at some embers with his boot. His thoughts were racing as fast as his heart.

Ethan looked toward the hallway and shook his head. What could his oldest sister possibly see in this George Lance? Wyeth had always been so... He yawned deeply, then said his goodnights. Since Henri was the last one up it fell to him to bank the fire and turn down the lamps before he retreated to his room. Henri did not mind—it gave him a comfortable sense of belonging.

When Wyeth reentered the room she felt a definite difference. The lamps were lower, the fire was crumbling in a warm but muted golden light. It was perfectly quiet. Now the room felt

. . . intimate. Henri looked up, and their eyes met. Suddenly Wyeth remembered that snowy afternoon nearly three years before when Henri had looked at her with such intensity. Neither could say a word. Henri seemed pale to Wyeth, though he stood so near the heat.

"Henri, is something wrong?" Wyeth asked, shocked that her voice was quivering.

He shook his head. She felt a sudden confusion now. Henri was no longer smiling, telling tales or laughing. Wyeth didn't know what to do, so she went to the window and pulled back the curtain. A fine, soft snow had just begun to fall. Though she was captivated by it, she knew that out in the cold darkness, George was riding home, and was very irritated. Then, Henri was standing behind her. She could sense his eyes on the back of her neck. She felt nervous now—nervous with Henri!

Actually, Henri was not gazing on the white smoothness of her neck. He was wholly absorbed in the copper highlights of her hair. Henri felt a light had suddenly blazed bright, or a door had swung open somewhere inside him. In that instant, he knew that he was deeply in love with Wyeth O'Dell. Their age difference, their friendship, even George Lance—nothing else mattered. He knew he loved her, perhaps with a love that had been there from that first meeting over the garden fence, nearly seven years before.

"It's beginning to snow," Wyeth whispered, completely unaware of the passion of Henri's thoughts.

Knowing her love of poetry, Henri finally found his voice.

> "I feel the years' slow beating heart,
> The sky's chill prophecy I know;
> And welcome the consummate art,
> Which weaves this spotless shroud of snow."

Wyeth turned around. Henri stood a mere two feet from her. She couldn't resist the pull of his eyes any longer. And, strangely, he wasn't smiling. With a trembling hand, he reached out and touched a silky tendril of her hair. It was even softer than he had imagined. His throat tightened and he felt lightheaded. His hand dropped back to his side. He pushed aside, with the greatest effort, the longing to pull her into his arms. It seemed to him such

a natural and right thing to do. But no, he couldn't do that.
Perhaps that would frighten her. She had made no move, said no
words. Her face seemed expressionless to him—he couldn't
discern her thoughts.

He had to get out of the room! It was too warm and he felt
suffocated. He would go for a walk, past the barn, out into the
orchard. The cold and snow didn't matter at all.

Wyeth felt sure Henri could hear her pounding heart. She was
stunned with his intimate gesture. She fully expected him to lean
down and kiss her. She waited. Then, as wordlessly and silently as
the snow, he was gone.

Chapter 4

Spring, 1855

♦♦ ♦♦ ♦♦

Slavery tension and the problems in the South still dominated the newspapers and were vigorously debated, along with crops and weather at Baily's general mercantile. Yet all that became secondary when Peppercreek folk learned that Wyeth O'Dell had accepted a marriage proposal from George Lance.

It was a warm spring evening, perfect for an outdoor church social. The meal was over and now families lingered around the lawn before starting home. Henri took a deep breath and walked purposefully up to Wyeth.

"Wyeth, can I speak to you a moment?"

She turned around to him, slightly annoyed. "Yes?"

"No, I mean privately... somewhere."

She looked across the lawn at George who was talking with her father and another man.

"Well, can it wait till we get home?"

Henri hesitated, not wanting to force her.

He shook his head. "No, it can't wait." He took her arm and steered her around the church. He led her to a huge oak tree where filtered sunset made rose hued patterns on the ground.

"What is it, Henri?"

"Well..." he broke off and looked uncertainly at the ground. He looked so sad she almost felt frightened.

"Henri? I'm sure George will be looking for me."

"George." Henri's voice was perfectly flat. "Your folks told me about your engagement this afternoon."

He was looking at her directly now.

"Yes... Well, it's true."

Suddenly there came a rush of memories into Wyeth's mind— when they first met over her herb garden fence and she had been so shy; walking together and talking about books. She could see Henri's face in her mind as he had looked at her that day they had been ice skating. He was looking very much like that now.

131

Wyeth was only vaguely aware of Henri's feelings for her. It was too confusing and—dangerous, to think of now. It was easier to push them to the back of her mind. She felt as if she had some small power over him—and it was such a new sensation. It pleased her. And then, too, there was George Lance, unquestionably the most sought-after single man for miles around. He was captivated by her. Wyeth could not think clearly. Things were happening so fast.

"But why?" Henri asked pleadingly.

"Why what?" Wyeth returned, with just an edge of defiance in her tone.

"Why... are you marrying George Lance?"

"Henri, what a silly question!"

"Is it?" He took one small step closer to her.

"Yes, of course it is. Besides it's... none of your business!"

"But... Do you love him?" Henri persisted.

"Henri, I need to be getting back to... George now. I'm sure he is looking for me."

But George was not able to look for Wyeth even if he had noticed her absence from the picnic. Will had seen what George had not, and now continued talking, to keep the young man occupied. George was astute enough to realize walking off from a future father-in-law was not something that should be done.

"Wyeth, do you love George Lance?" Henri asked.

He knew he was pushing her, but he felt desperate.

"This is none of your business, Henri!" Wyeth did not care who heard her raised voice now. She was frightened by his intensity. They... they were only supposed to be good friends.

"Wyeth, please! Tell me why you're marrying this man!"

"Henri, why are you doing this?" Wyeth summoned anger into her voice now.

He stepped back. "You don't know?" his voice was barely above a whisper.

Wyeth turned around and hurried back to George and her father, forcing a smile on her face and swallowing the tears she felt inside.

Henri sat hunched over in front of his small stove, heedless that it needed wood. He had tried to read, but that had been impossible. He could not seem to focus on the words. He tossed the Bible commentary across his bed in frustration, and withdrew the letter from his shirt pocket. It had come in the morning mail and Henri could not help but feel it was heaven-sent. A Dr. Hawthorn in Chicago, whom he had met years previous, was urging him to become a part of his mission team in that growing city. It seemed the answer to his prayers about his work. Now, he had a legitimate reason for leaving.

Henri was leaving the next day, and everyone in the O'Dell house felt Chicago was as far off as California had been. Wyeth climbed the stairs to Henri's room with a stack of his clean clothes and found Libby sitting on Henri's bed beside his open suitcase. Her little sister was hunched over and frowning.

"Well, here's the last of his clothes. Are you packing for him, Lib?"

"Yes, I am." Libby's voice was distinctly hostile.

"What's the matter with you?"

"What's the matter with you?" she returned tartly.

Wyeth shook her head and turned to leave.

"We all know why Henri is really leaving," Libby said calmly.

Wyeth felt her irritation rising. "Oh, you do? Well, I'm glad your hearing was functioning when Henri explained it this morning."

Libby looked smug. "Is that really why he's leaving...Mrs. Lance-to-be?"

"You... You are being an insufferable little brat this morning, Libby O'Dell!" Wyeth stormed.

"Is that why he's leaving, Wyeth?" Libby demanded.

"You heard what he said. He has an opportunity for work. Why are you acting like such a ridiculous—"

"Say, you two aren't fighting over me, are you?" Henri stood in the doorway, knowing nothing about the argument, only that he had heard his name and had intended to make a joke.

Wyeth whirled around, terribly embarrassed. "We certainly

would not fight over you!" Her voice was scathing as she hurried past him.

Henri had felt relieved and just a bit excited, now that he had made a decision and was leaving. As much as he would miss them all, it would be healing to leave now. When he returned, Wyeth would be Mrs. George Lance.

They prayed for him that night and said their goodbyes. When Wyeth's time had come she had extended her hand quickly. Almost shyly.

"Goodbye, Henri . . . I know you will do well in Chicago."

"Thank you, Wyeth."

When Wyeth found the note, Henri had been gone nearly three weeks. She had wandered out to the barn, aimless and restless. She had looked over her herb garden fence, feeling strange, almost frightened that she might be moving before it was in full bloom. In the workshop of the barn she found her father busy at a shelf he was making for her mother's upcoming birthday. She sat on the steps near him without speaking. He looked up, then back down to his work—his daughter did not look like a happy, soon-to-be-wed young woman. It gnawed at him, this worry for her. His one consolation was that she had set no formal date for the wedding. It was always, "Sometime this summer." Lacking any admiration of George, Will nevertheless wondered how Wyeth could keep the young man satisfied with such vagueness.

"It's so peaceful out here," Wyeth finally said.

Will nodded. "One of my favorite places, of course. How does this look?" he asked, holding up the shelf.

"Perfect. How do you keep Mother from finding out?"

Will grinned. "Oh, she knows I'm working on something so she makes a great racket when she comes out here . . . Thoughtful woman, your Ma."

"I can remember when you made the sleigh for her."

"Yes, years ago . . ."

"She cried when she saw it."

Will stood up and stretched. "Yes, she did . . ." His face became thoughtful and Wyeth rightly suspected he was thinking of her mother. She rested her chin in her hands, wondering . . . What would it be like to have such a strong and loving marriage after the passage of years? Could she possibly have that with George Lance?

On an impulse, she scampered up the narrow steps to Henri's room. She opened the door. It was chilly and quiet in the small room. The place was tidy, everything in order, except . . . On the small oak table, propped against a coal-oil lamp, was a white envelope. Wyeth's name was written across it in careful script.

She opened it slowly, feeling almost as if Henri's eyes were upon her.

> *Wyeth,*
>
> *Last night I remembered that I had never thanked you for the flowers you left in my room that first day, months ago. It made the room just right. It made me think of my mother. She always grew them and had a big crock of them on the table.*

Wyeth stopped reading a moment. It was only a simple, friendly letter, certainly nothing that should be making her heart race!

> *Also Wyeth, I wanted to tell you that I was sorry for the way I acted at the social. I hope you will forgive me. I do value our friendship. By the time I return to Peppercreek you will be married. I wish you much happiness.*
>
> *Henri*

Wyeth folded the letter blindly. She could not stop her tears. "Oh how I've hurt him! . . . All he did was . . . love me," she said to the empty room. She felt stabbed in her spirit, angry that she had pushed the truth away for so long. Truth. Why did I deny it so long? she wondered.

George's face rose accusingly in her mind. He was preparing to marry her. And of course, she did not love him. The awfulness of the situation washed over her; she felt totally alone and frightened. It seemed to her too horrible to even try to approach her parents with the truth. She was engaged to a man she did not love.

Wyeth hung her head and sobbed, broken-hearted that she had been so foolish and broken-hearted that she had hurt the man that truly loved her. She had sent him away, just as Libby had accused.

June

Henri's letters came regularly to Peppercreek, as did George Lance. The family withdrew when George came, and Wyeth was not bitter about it. Her parents were pleasant, Libby had bridled her tongue and Ethan gave George fewer dark scowls. When Rebecca broached the subject of making wedding plans, Wyeth became evasive. Will and Rebecca felt helpless. Wyeth had withdrawn into her misery. She became pale with dread at what she must do to George. Her sensitivity recoiled at the idea of hurting anyone—even the brazen, confident George Lance. She could not forget that she had hurt Henri so deeply, a man who had been nothing but a very good and faithful friend to her.

George was a persistent lover. Masking his irritation, he pressed Wyeth to set an official wedding date. She steeled herself and vowed she would tell him the truth the next time they were alone together.

Rebecca stopped her in the hall one afternoon, her face reflecting the concern she felt.

"Are you all right, Wyeth? You're so pale."

"Just . . . pray for me, Mother," Wyeth said as she hurried out.

"I am Wyeth, I am," her mother murmured after her.

"You are very lovely tonight, my dear," George said, smiling at Wyeth.

Wyeth studied his face a moment, wondering how she had ever really found him handsome. They were on the way to a literary at the schoolhouse. These Friday night socials were the highlight of the week to many simple country folk—a chance to broaden their horizons, hear good literature, think on things beyond their routine and glamourless lives. While George found them boring and countrified, Wyeth thoroughly enjoyed them.

George was talking, but Wyeth was not really listening. She found she could pray while he talked.

"Your family seemed quite jovial tonight, Wyeth."

"We had a letter from Henri this afternoon."

George frowned to himself. "Oh." He snapped the reins. "You know, we could just skip the social tonight and keep driving. It's so mild out and Dancer seems amiable. Would you like to?"

Wyeth hesitated, the time had come. "Yes..."

"Warm enough?"

"Yes... No... I mean..."

George laughed, "What is it, Wyeth?"

"You misundertand... George."

"Misunderstand what?"

"We can't keep going... I'm sorry."

George saw the tension in her face and pulled the buggy to the side of the road.

"Dear, what are you talking about?"

Wyeth took a deep breath. "Us. We can't marry." Wyeth felt such a relief to have finally said the words.

"What? Why?"

"Because I don't think... it's what the Lord wants. I've been praying a lot about us."

George felt like cursing. "The Lord wants? What are you talking about, Wyeth?" He was distinctly irritated—this was a night made for courting, not religious talk.

"George, I don't love you. I'm sorry."

George Lance had a mammoth-sized ego for a man his age. He stared ahead several moments without speaking.

"George?" Wyeth asked gently.

"What has caused this... change of heart?" he snapped. Wyeth was amazed at the hard glint in his eyes—where only minutes before there had been passion.

"I... told you, I've been praying and think—"

"Praying? That sounds like stuff from that Henri Mullins!"

"Praying about something so important as marriage? Yes, Henri might say that... but then, my father and mother would, also."

"So you think the O'Dells of Peppercreek are... superior or something?"

Wyeth's stomach knotted, and a lump rose in her throat—George was going to get nasty.

"Of course I don't think that."

"My father tried to warn me about your kind," George said in his best arrogant tone.

Wyeth looked at him directly. "Why didn't you listen to him, then?"

George colored angrily. "You are sounding very much like that grandmother of yours!"

"I . . . think you should take me home now, George. Please," Wyeth returned calmly.

George gave the reins a vicious snap and the horse bolted forward in surprise. Minutes later, they drove up to Wyeth's house. They sat there silent a moment—each wrapped in their own anger and hurt. Wyeth wanted to cry, to get in the house and forget this whole horrible experience. She fingered her shawl nervously.

"George, please don't be angry. I am sorry that this went on so long. We are just two different types of people. We couldn't have made each other happy."

He turned to her. "Are you really breaking off our engagement, Wyeth?"

"Yes, George."

"No one turns down a Lance!" he said, drawing himself up to his full height.

Wyeth lowered herself down out of the carriage. "Goodbye, George."

She walked slowly up to the front porch, her head down, her shoulders sagging. She felt completely exhausted from the spent emotions. She would not know for several days, until Libby indignantly brought the news, that the rumor was that George Lance had dropped Wyeth O'Dell. The relief that the relationship was over made public opinion meaningless to Wyeth.

Wyeth did not see her father at his bedroom window. He had come to look out when he had heard the carriage careen to a stop.

"Who is it?" Rebecca called from their bed.

"Your eldest."

"Home so soon? They just left a little while ago. Something must be wrong."

Even in the twilight Will could see Wyeth's dejected posture. "No, Mrs. O'Dell, I think something is very right—at last!"

Chapter 5

Summer, 1855

◆◆ ◆◆ ◆◆

*W*yeth and Libby were folding clothes one afternoon, when Wyeth abruptly broke the silence.

"Lib, do you still blame me...that Henri left? You were so angry with me then."

Libby, with her easygoing nature, had forgotten about her anger at her sister. "No, I don't blame you, Wyeth. I was just upset that he was leaving. I thought it was because of you he was going."

Wyeth hesitated, uncertain that she wanted to press the issue.

"But Lib, he's a grown man, able to make his own decisions. What made you think I had anything to do with it?"

"He's a grown man and you're a grown woman," she answered simply.

Wyeth laughed, vaguely nervous now. She shifted the conversation.

"You're pleased I'm not engaged to George Lance anymore."

Libby nodded her head vigorously. "Ecstatically happy! He was all wrong for you... He was all wrong for anybody!"

"Libby!" Then Wyeth's smile faded. "I'm not getting younger, Lib. Louisa's already married."

"Henri's getting older and he's not married either," she returned with a sauciness that Alice Tufts would have admired.

Wyeth blushed deeply. "You keep coming back to Henri."

"I thought you hurt him," Libby said soberly. "I thought he left because he loved you...and you wouldn't love him back."

"Why do you think he loved...me?" Wyeth's voice was trembling now.

"Because of the way he looked at you. Didn't you notice?"

Wyeth began to cry. Breaking off with George had been painful, even if it had been the right thing to do. Yet hurting someone that truly loved her...and finding out she truly loved him, that was even worse.

Libby reached out and squeezed her hand.

"Oh, Libby, what have I done? He did love me . . . And I do love Henri!"

"You do? Oh Wyeth, I'm so glad! Now you can both be happy again."

"Libby, have you forgotten? He's in Chicago now. And I hurt him!"

"So tell him, Wyeth. Just tell him."

"Libby, it's too late."

"Pa says it's never too late for good, Wyeth. Remember?"

"But Libby, this is different!"

"Write him. Tell him how you feel and he'll come back and you'll have each other!"

Wyeth stood up impatiently. "You're too young to understand, Lib. It's not that easy."

Libby rolled her eyes. "If you made it wrong, Wyeth, only you can make it right."

Wyeth thought it over, her face softening. "Perhaps you're right little sister . . . perhaps you're right."

On the road toward Peppercreek, Wyeth slowed the horses to a walk. There was time to get to Baily's and mail Henri's package. Right now, Wyeth must give proper notice to the lovely summer day. Summer had not yet burned and wilted the lush growth that the spring rains encouraged. The orchard at home was still a heady, extravagant display of pink and white blossoms. Thick honeysuckle, a tangle of green, white and yellow, curled up the trellis.

Wyeth thought of the orchard at home, how pleasant it was to walk there in the early dew of morning or the cool shadow of evening. A romantic place, she thought, an orchard in blossom. At least that's what the novels always said. Romance . . . Well, for some, perhaps . . . But not for me, she decided. I'll live at home. Teach school, perhaps. Be a spinster—like Amanda Robb . . . She grimaced. Would she really turn out as sour as that old lady?

She turned away from those unpleasant thoughts and imagined herself in the orchard, leaning against a tree, explaining everything to Henri. He would smile and forgive her. He would tell her she was lovelier than the apple blossoms . . .

"Wyeth! Wyeth O'Dell!"

She gave up her daydreaming reluctantly and squinted into the bright sunshine. She had absently rounded the corner in the road and only by means of old Bess's steady good sense had she avoided hitting a buggy coming toward her.

"Wyeth, are you all right?"

"Hello, MaryBeth! I'm fine. Sorry about my reckless driving," she said laughing.

"I called you twice. Didn't you hear me?"

Wyeth shook her head, still smiling. "How was Springfield?" The girls steered their buggys beside each other.

MaryBeth immediately unfurled her new parasol.

"Muddy. Springfield was muddy. Rained nearly every day we were there. Springfield is so provincial, you know."

Wyeth smiled. "Did you shop much? Other than for your pretty new parasol?"

"Oh, just bits and pieces, bits and pieces. But Wyeth, really . . . Who wants to gab about me? I'm just thrilled I ran into you—"

"Literally," Wyeth joked.

"I'm not fully over the shock of what Mother told me when I walked through the door!"

It was not difficult for Wyeth to imagine Mrs. Chase blurting out the "news" as soon as her daughter stepped in the house. Mother and daughter were very much alike. Wyeth had prepared herself for this inevitable confrontation. This was her first trip to town since her broken engagement. She knew she would encounter the small town's hushed assault of whispers and raised eyebrows.

"You could have blown me over with a feather when I heard!" MaryBeth continued and Wyeth was grateful her little sister and Ethan were at home. As it was, she had trouble stifling a smile over her friend's seriousness.

"Is it true, Wyeth?"

"Well, you haven't told me what your mother told you. Was it that my mother and Libby have been sick or that we have ten new colts and two of them are blind or—"

"Wyeth O'Dell! You know perfectly what I'm talking about! You and George, is it true?" Her voice carried a note of awe.

"Yes, George and I are not engaged any longer."

MaryBeth's plump face registered fresh shock.

"Oh Wyeth, what happened? Did he leave you for another girl? Who? Who?"

"No, I just didn't feel it was right for us to marry."

"What? You mean you broke up with George?"

"Yes."

"I'm amazed, Wyeth, totally amazed! You seemed so happy ... He was ... George! I mean ..." MaryBeth was speechless only for a moment. "Was he ... improper?"

Wyeth fidgeted, ready to move on. "No. We just weren't right for each other."

MaryBeth still had one final question. "Was he devastated? How did he take it?"

"He took it fine. Well, I better go, I've a package to mail."

Wyeth rode on with MaryBeth looking after her, incredulous that normally honest Wyeth O'Dell had twisted the truth about the break-up. For everyone knew—no one turned down a Lance.

Wyeth wondered just how many curious looks she would receive as she entered Baily's. Thanks to MaryBeth, she had no doubt Peppercreek would be further enlightened on the Lance-O'Dell breakup. She sighed as she moved along the counter—the novels neglected to tell about the frustrations of a broken romance. Baily greeted her.

"Ah! A May flower in my dingy ol' store!" He bowed deeply.

"Good morning, Baily."

A myriad of colors and smells greeted the shopper who came into Baily's Mercantile. Besides the usual dry goods, there were barrels of crackers and wedges of tangy cheese. Children loved Baily's for its generous candy counter, boasting horehound, marzipan, peppermints and taffy. A stroll down this counter could send your taste buds into flood stage and your appetite into a riot.

Women were drawn to the long shelves of fabric—muslin, calico and corduroy. Men found seed and plows, rifles and rope, harnesses and feed. But the very center of the store, its heart, was a checkerboard, much used and reverenced. It always lay open and waiting for a game between opponents in dusty overalls. Here loafers, shoppers and gossips could spend an idle hour or so.

Yet the essence of Baily's was the owner himself. A grizzled, ramrod-straight, iron-gray-haired gentleman of inestimable years, he was a loquacious man who felt the thrill and the power of this personal kingdom of his. Generous and loyal, old Jedediah Baily, known simply as "Baily" by the whole community, was the most affectionately respected man in Peppercreek.

"And how's the family, Wyeth?" he asked her. "Heard they were down with colds."

Wyeth smiled. The small town grapevine never ceased to amaze her. Then she noticed two girls, a bit younger than herself, at the fabric counter, casting furtive glances her direction. Baily jerked his head toward them. "Been here for over an hour, lookin' at fabric. Don't intend to buy a thing—just lookin' and gigglin'. Sort of gets on my nerves." He looked over Wyeth's short list, lowered his voice and leaned forward conspiratorially. "Hmm... Glad there ain't any silks or laces on here... No weddin' finery."

"You're not the only one who's relieved, Baily," Wyeth replied. "It'll be awhile before Libby needs such things."

"Libby? Well... there *are* other bucks in the pasture, Wyeth," the old man assured her.

Wyeth looked down at the counter, her eyes suddenly filling with tears. "Yes... I suppose so." She had left home this morning and encountered the sting of romance at every turn. Baily felt awkward at Wyeth's sudden emotion. He cleared his throat, angry with himself.

"You tie up your package and I'll get your other things," he said gently.

Wyeth looked one final time into the package to see that the contents were arranged just right. The letter was thick. She hadn't read what the others in her family had written to Henri. She began to close the box, when Libby's words came back to her.

"It's never too late to do right. Only you can make it right."

Only me. Yet how can I begin to make it right? She had asked herself that dozens of times. His note to her had reaffirmed their friendship—nothing more—and expressed hope for her happiness with George Lance. She didn't know for certain, but surely someone in her family had written Henri and told him about her broken engagement. She smiled to herself. If Libby had written it, it would probably be scrawled in capitals.

He had left for Chicago, and any love he had for her may have died out by now. Perhaps she should just leave it at that.

"Is it ready to go yet?" Baily asked as he passed her.

"Yes . . . almost . . ." Wyeth impulsively snatched up a scrap of brown paper from the counter and wrote quickly: "Please come home." She unfolded the letter, put the scrap in, sealed it and tied up the package. It was ready to go to Henri now. She knew doubts and feelings of foolishness would assail her on the way home.

Chicago, Illinois, September, 1855

Up in his small room, Henri quickly pulled off his boots, propped open his window and sat down on his bed. The package was open and he looked over the contents with a smile. Taking a handful of the lemon tarts, he stretched out to read the letter. Just lying down made him feel his weariness again and he closed his eyes a moment. A breeze fluttered the muslin curtain, and lifted a scrap of brown paper from the letter and floated it to the floor. Henri never saw it. He opened his eyes, yawned, and began to read.

Lake Michigan, Illinois Spring, 1856

Henri had a special friendship with Dr. Hawthorne's widowed Indian daughter-in-law. They could talk easily, and he appreciated her insights into the mission work. They sat together one sultry afternoon by the shores of the lake, trying to catch a breeze. The city was sweltering in oppressive heat.

Lucy was speaking softly about the young husband she had lost.

"He was so kind. He loved me . . . for who, for what I was. My brown skin . . . it did not make difficulty for my Joseph."

Henri was silent a moment. The feelings of loneliness he always tried to keep at bay filled him now.

"I can see how you would miss that kind...of love."

She turned now, facing him, studying his face without embarrassment. "Everyone, do they not need that kind of love, like my Joseph gave me?"

Henri nodded.

"You, Henri?"

He laughed, "Yes, I have my family."

"I have my father. He is a good man. Still, it is not the same. You have no wife, Henri."

"Nope, none hidden away anywhere. I'll be a bachelor all my days."

"You have not loved one as you would a wife?" Lucy persisted.

Henri breathed deeply and ran his hand through his hair. Suddenly it was all right to talk about it. Lucy would understand.

"Yes," he began slowly, "yes, I did love someone enough to want her as my wife."

"And?"

"And she married, or was to marry this past summer...We were just friends."

"She did not marry?"

"No...I don't know the details, but the marriage didn't come off."

"Did she know your feelings for her?"

That was a question Henri had turned over in his mind often.

"I don't know, Lucy...I haven't had much experience with gals. I didn't tell her plain enough, I suppose. But it didn't matter, because I was just a family friend. We knew each other for years. I wasn't..."

"Yes?"

"Well, a woman has ideas about the man she wants to marry. Her ideal, her dream. Well, I wasn't it—not for her."

"This is Wyeth, in your family at Pepper's Creek?"

Henri was shocked. "Well, yes. How did you know that, Lucy?"

"There is a look that comes in your eyes when you speak of your family, when you read me their letters. When she is spoken of, I can see."

Henri's laugh was shaky. "You're too perceptive, Lucy."

"My father's words agree with you. She does not write you in these long letters?"

"No, never a word. Why should she? I misunderstood... Maybe I misunderstood my own feelings."

Lucy was silent so long, Henri decided she must have wanted to change the conversation. He did not notice the almost sad note in her voice, when she spoke again.

"I think..."

"What?" Henri asked leaning forward.

"I think your heart still holds... your Wyeth."

"I don't know, Lucy... I want to get over her and put it all in the past."

For the remainder of their time at the lakeside, they were both silent.

Chapter 6

On the Chicago-
Peoria Railroad, Illinois

◆◆ ◆◆ ◆◆

*T*he ride from Chicago to Springfield was beautiful. The tracks curved through forests blazing in scarlet, gold and copper. Corn fields were bare from harvesting and vast prairies trembled in saffron and sorrel waves. The skies were clear with an intense autumn blue. Yet Henri scarcely noticed the beauty. He felt disoriented, aware of his destination one minute, uncertain the next.

Henri was going home to Peppercreek. After being confined to his bed for two weeks with exhaustion and a racking cough, Dr. Hawthorne had insisted he return home to recover fully. He agreed reluctantly, his disappointment robbing him of any strength. The gladness at going home was eclipsed by weakness and fatigue. The headache he'd been troubled with was a constant dull, debilitating throb. When the train stopped for fuel or passengers, he remained hunched over in his seat. All he wanted was to drift off into a long, healing sleep. In his confusion, he never considered that soon he would be seeing Wyeth.

Springfield

"Ever seen such a beautiful October 'afore?" the old station master asked.

Henri broke into a violent spasm of coughing before he could answer. "Yes . . . it is lovely."

"Kind of mean-sounding hack ya got there."

"Yes, it is."

"And don't mind me sayin', but ya look a little green around the gills," the old man continued.

Henri ignored this. He just wanted to get home. This weakness and headache was beginning to frighten him—he couldn't seem to shake them. "So as far as you know there's no coach going to Peppercreek this afternoon?" Henri queried again.

"There's Noah Sloane."

"Do you suppose he'd give me a lift?"

The old man rubbed his grizzled chin thoughtfully. "Wal, ya see it's Noah . . . and . . ."

Henri felt dizzy. "What's the matter with him?"

"Wal, just that Noah tends to celebrate over anything, ya see? Been celebratin' his new nephew for over a month or more. Don't know just what kinda shape he's in for drivin'."

"Where can I find him?" Henri asked impatiently.

"Aw, 'hind the feed store, I reckon. Likes to nap back there."

Henri started at once.

If Henri had ever been more miserable, he could not remember when. Perched on the hard seat of Noah Sloane's wagon, he felt absolutely wretched. It was a mild fall day, with only a gentle breeze, but Henri had become chilled. Sloane seemed drawn like a magnet to every bump and hole in the dirt road as the rickety wagon swayed and jerked along. He clutched at Sloane's sleeve.

"Would it be all right if I climbed back in the bed and lay down? I . . . have to get out of this wind," Henri said.

Sloane raised a prickly eyebrow in suspicion. There was no wind. Perhaps he shouldn't have given the fella a lift, after all. That's what came of always trying to be sociable. Maybe this young fella had something that was contagious.

"Suit yourself," he replied blandly.

Henri climbed over. He was truly desperate—for he had earlier seen the condition of the wagonbed. This just might rate as the worst place he had ever laid his head. There was definite evidence Sloane had been recently transporting animals in the wagon.

Henri lay down, pulling the canvas over him, saying, "You'll wake me when we get to Peppercreek . . . Won't you?"

But his voice was too weak for Noah Sloane to hear. Henri fell into a deep sleep—a journey of terrible and confusing dreams.

When Noah Sloane rattled into Peppercreek two hours later, the thin little bottle he kept in his coat pocket was nearly empty.

His songs to the nag that pulled his wagon had become a bit slurred. He stopped and looked around. Just across the street was Baily's. Well now, he didn't suppose he really needed to stop in the little town. If he kept on, he could reach his sister's in time for supper. That was a pleasing thought. His passenger thoroughly forgotten, he prepared to drive on.

He started to geehaw the horse—but wait! What was it? His fuzzy mind was trying to work something out. Wasn't there some reason he was supposed to stop in Peppercreek? He yawned and scratched his head and came up without a clue. Might as well move on.

Then his eye fell on the bottle by his side. Hmmm . . . Lizzie was sure to smell it on his breath. His little sister Lizzie was a teetotaler. He shook his head mournfully. If Lizzie smelled even a whiff there would be no holding the baby, no sir. Women . . . He gazed back over at the general store. Might as well go buy something to munch on and cover his breath. Maybe an apple. He heard apples were famous in these parts and it was harvest time. Unsteadily, he climbed down.

Rebecca glanced apprehensively out a window of Baily's Mercantile. Even through the dusty panes, she could see a storm was brewing. The sky was a canvas of thick, massive clouds, churning with purple undersides.

Wyeth's laughter filled the big store and Rebecca smiled to herself. It was good to hear Wyeth laugh like that, good to see her smile. That painful experience with George Lance and the months of depression that followed seemed to have fled—Wyeth was herself again, peaceful, busy, content.

Since Rebecca and Wyeth were Baily's only patrons, the old man had them exclusively to himself. He was regaling Wyeth with another story, his payment her young laughter.

Rebecca touched Wyeth on the arm, "I think we'd better start home. A storm is coming up and your father will be concerned."

"Aw, Rebeccy, the almanac says we won't have rain till the end of the month," Baily protested.

"And we both know almanacs can be incorrect," Rebecca said, giving him a prize smile.

"Well, that's true—"

The door jingled and a man sauntered in.

"Wyeth, dear, would you go check the mail, and then we'll be going."

"Well, well, Noah Sloane! Haven't seen you in these parts in quite a while," Baily greeted.

Sloane hiccuped. "Afternoon ... there, Baily."

Baily spoke bluntly, his face twisted in a grimace. "Aw, Sloane, better not get around a flame. That breath of yours could start a fire!"

"Now, Baily ..."

Wyeth had stepped into the little cubicle that served as Peppercreek's mailroom. The O'Dell box was empty. Wyeth sighed with disappointment. There had been no letter from Henri in over two months. His letters had, at the very least, brought him somewhat closer to them. Now he had become a distant part of their lives, all because she had sent him away. She swallowed the lump in her throat. He had never answered her message. It had been over a year, but even buried pain can still hurt.

Noah Sloane was out the door with his bag of apples as Wyeth came up to her mother.

"Ready to go?" her mother asked.

"Yes, I'm ready, I—"

But Wyeth stopped in midsentence and what happened next was never forgotten. She was suddenly lightheaded, her heart racing.

"Wyeth ... are you all right?"

"Yes ... I ..." She turned without another word and hurried across the store. She was trembling with excitement.

"Wyeth?" Rebecca called after her, but Wyeth was out the door.

It was chilly outside and Wyeth drew a deep breath. She looked up and down the main street of Peppercreek. It was empty. The only sign of life—was the man across the street. He was placidly munching an apple while his mare finished hers. Wyeth went to him, uncertain, yet ...

Noah Sloane started to speak, but the young woman had such a strange look on her face that he just stared. Wyeth felt a moment of foolishness. What was she doing out here?

Then, Rebecca was beside her. "Wyeth, what's the matter?"

Wyeth leaned over the wagon bed. Only one trouser leg could be seen under the filthy tarp. She closed her eyes and felt herself sway. Rebecca caught her.

"It's Henri," Wyeth whispered.

He was so white, so thin, so burning with fever that Wyeth was terrified. She felt totally exhausted. It all happened so suddenly. Now Henri lay in Ethan's room—and Wyeth sensed he was fighting for his very life. She lay across her bed and cried until she heard her mother pass down the hall.

"Mother, what did Dr. Noble say?"

Rebecca's face was tense and pale. Wyeth looked so tragic. No, she could not tell her the doctor's exact words, not yet.

He had looked at Will and Rebecca, then down at the still form in the bed. "He's a very, very sick young man. I haven't seen such a case of influenza before. It's a wonder he's not already gone."

Will had pulled Rebecca closer to him. "It's not a wonder, Doc. He's in the Lord's care," Will said softly.

The doctor readjusted his spectacles and gave Will a wry smile.

"Well, yes, then pray, Will, because I don't think he can make it. His lungs are full of fluid. Prepare for the worst."

"Now, Doc," Will said, regaining some of his usual humor, "you and I have had many discussions along these lines before. But I must tell you, if by the worst you mean death for Henri, then no, that's not the worst for a believer at all . . . Ah, but we would . . . miss the boy." Will could not say more, and the doctor placed an affectionate arm around his good friend.

"Wyeth," Rebecca said finally, "Henri is very sick. He has influenza." Rebecca took her daughter's cold hands in her own.

"Mother . . . Will he be all right?" Libby asked, as she came up beside them. Her face was tear-streaked. Rebecca looked at

Wyeth. There was no hiding, no denying now what she saw there. Wyeth loved Henri.

"We must pray very hard," Rebecca said at last.

"I never thought of Henri as a fighter, but that's what he must be," Will said to Rebecca one evening as they sat by his bed. She nodded. It seemed incredible that one so racked with fever and illness could survive as long as Henri had. Still, here it was November, and Henri survived. For six weeks now he had lain so still, his breathing like a vapor. They fed him, cooled him with cloths, and sat beside him day and night.

Wyeth and Libby helped their mother so that the burden of nursing did not fall on her alone. Louisa and Grandmother Tufts came from town and helped as well. Will, Ethan, and Isaiah sat beside him at night. Morning came and still he breathed—they all silently thanked God for another day. Wyeth sat beside him as often as she could, gazing at him with a tenderness that would have amazed Henri if he had waked to see it.

Then, one afternoon, he opened his eyes and pushed away the rag on his forehead.

"Is it snowing?" he croaked. Libby, who was sitting beside the bed, jumped in startlement. They were his first words. "Hello ...Libby." She ran from the room, calling her family. Then Doc Noble came and examined Henri. Finally, his tired, lined face broke out in a smile.

"The fever's gone." He listened to Henri's lungs. "Yes indeed, much better."

Everyone was crying, and Henri gave them a wobbly smile.

It was a slow recovery. He was bedridden for months. At first, he spoke very little. To Wyeth, he said the least. She didn't know it, but he followed her with his eyes. Healing, he whispered to himself, was just to be able to look at her.

Then he was strong enough to sit up in his bed and he began talking at greater length. Will had summed it up with a smile to Rebecca. "The boy's getting better. He just told me a story!"

One afternoon, Wyeth slipped into his room to check on him. He was asleep, but instead of turning to go, she quietly sat down.

She chewed her lip, a bit embarrassed at her motives—she
wanted just to look at him. She studied his face—the way, even so
thin, it still looked boyish. His covers had slipped down to his
waist and his nightshirt was open. She closed her eyes, imagining
what it would be like to feel his chest under her fingers—or to
rest against him.

Henri coughed, then mumbled something. Wyeth's eyes flew
open and she hurried across to him.

"Henri? It's me, Wyeth. Are you all right? Do you need
something?"

"Do...you... Do you suppose..." he mumbled.

She leaned closer. "Do you need some water?"

"Wyeth?" His eyes seemed unfocused.

Her heart was pounding. Was he having a setback, like Doc
Noble had warned about?

"Henri, I'm here."

"Do you suppose if...you kissed me, I mean really kissed
me, I would get better faster?"

Wyeth straightened up in shock, but Henri had grabbed her
hand. It was not the weakened grasp of a sick man. His eyes were
sparkling.

"If you will kiss me, Wyeth, I think I'll surely get better."

"Henri!" Wyeth was never so flushed.

"And not a grandmotherly peck on the cheek, either!" He
would not turn loose of her hand, though she pulled hard.

"You're delirious!" she exclaimed.

"Do you think so? Better call your ma, then." He was smiling
at her. "When I first came here, all I did was sleep. Now, I can't
sleep at nights for thinking about you... To wake up and find you
caring for me... I thought I was dreaming."

He pulled her down to sit on the edge of his bed beside him.
She could feel herself blushing furiously from the nearness of
him.

"Wyeth, your ma told me about how you found me."

She felt confused. Those long months of not hearing from
him...the way they had parted...George Lance...

"The first time I saw you, Wyeth, you were in your garden.
That was nine years ago. The sunlight was all reflected around
you, and at first I thought you were older than you were. You were
so beautiful, even then."

"Henri..."

"I came to love you as a sister, a friend, for those first few years. I have to tell you, Wyeth, I should have told you plainly a year ago. I've tried to put you out of my thoughts, think of you...as another man's wife. To stop loving you. But I can't stop." His eyes searched her face. He pulled himself up closer to her. "Wyeth, do you know how much I love you?"

Wyeth had not spoken.

"Wyeth, why didn't you marry George Lance?"

Finally her eyes met his and she smiled. "I couldn't. I didn't love him." She looked down at his slender hand holding hers, and brought it to her cheek. "I love a man who loves God. A man who is gentle and makes me laugh. A man who made me think the wind in the aspens was music, just for me; that stars had been hung out in the night sky by a loving God just for me to see. A man who hears a symphony in a snowfall."

"Wyeth, do you—"

"Yes, Henri. I love the brown-haired, blue-eyed man of my dreams. You."

One night, Henri found Wyeth alone in the living room. He could not help but think of that other night over a year ago. She was staring into the fire and his presence startled her.

"Do you feel all right, Henri?"

"I'm fine. I just couldn't sleep. Why are you up?"

"I couldn't sleep either."

There was an awkward silence. They both felt their alone-ness in the dimly lighted room. It gave them a sort of headiness after being parted so long. Henri crossed the room to her.

"You look almost afraid of me, Wyeth," he said.

Her laugh was shaky, "Suddenly we're together...and we love each other. I feel afraid of how much...I want you to hold me...and kiss me."

She slipped her arms around his neck and they kissed. Finally, when they pulled apart, Henri's voice was trembling, "I think I feel weaker than I did when I was sick."

She traced the line of his smile with her finger. "You are beautiful to me, Henri Mullins."

"Me? I'm just a poor, plain preacher," his voice was teasing.

She placed her arms back around his neck. "Preacher, yes. Plain, never. Poor? No Henri, you're rich—rich for the love of God in you."

"And rich for your love." He kissed her eyes, and ears, her neck. "Does this mean you'll marry me, Wyeth?"

Her face did not register the thrill she felt.

"Does this mean you're asking me?" she returned.

"Will you be my wife?"

"Yes, I will marry you, Henri."

He pulled a ring from his pocket and slid it on her finger.

"This was my mother's ring. She wanted me to have it for my bride."

"It's beautiful," Wyeth said, her voice trembling now.

"When, Wyeth? When will you marry me?" he persisted.

She thought a moment. He still needed time to fully recover. She tilted her head back to gaze up into his eyes. She felt Henri Mullins was the most handsome man she had ever seen.

"When the orchard is in blossom, then we'll stand beneath the trees and become man and wife."

"You are my beloved, my treasure, Wyeth."

"And you are mine, Henri."

Peppercreek folk came out to the O'Dell orchard one sunny afternoon in May to see Henri Mullins and Wyeth O'Dell married. Some graybeards weren't sure it was entirely proper to marry outdoors. It might be just a bit heathenish. Yet, it was such a beautiful day, their protests were short-lived.

Everyone who attended was in agreement that Wyeth was radiant. Old Baily's eyes grew moist when he looked on her fresh and glowing youth. Grandmother Tufts was not her usual vocal self. She could not trust her voice for happiness. Ethan was beaming. His sister could not be marrying a better man, he thought. Yet it was a bittersweet happiness to all of them, for Henri was going back to Chicago. And this time, Wyeth would be at his side.

It was irrepressible, smiling, self-satisfied Louisa who had the final word to Wyeth. She took her by the arm and whispered, "I told you so."

Chapter 7

1857

◆◆ ◆◆ ◆◆

*T*he trip happened because of a book. Everyone had heard about it, everyone was talking about it, but it was Ethan who sent off for it from a bookseller in Springfield. He brought it home and gave it to his father to read aloud to all of them in the evenings. It took only four nights of reading to finish it. When Will read the last line, the room was perfectly still. It wasn't light reading—no, not at all. Finally Libby broke the silence.

"Do you suppose it's really, truly like that, down there?"

Ethan was staring into the fireplace, saying nothing. Rebecca sat knitting, as mute as Isaiah beside her.

"Well Lib, the Southerners say it isn't true," Will replied.

"Of course they would!" she returned hotly.

"The North is saying it's a masterpiece of truth," Will continued. "That men could behave that way . . . because of a person's skin color . . ." Will was shaking his head.

"Was there slavery in Kentucky, when you were a girl there, Mama?" Libby asked.

She nodded. "Some folks had slaves, yes. Not many, though. You had to travel farther south to find very much slavery."

"Why must there be slavery anyway, Papa? We get along without slaves up North. Why can't they?"

Will sighed. "That's not easy to explain, Lib. There were slaves in New England when our country began. Gradually, it took root down South and became a way of life for them. It's a very difficult thing to change. Tobacco and cotton are the main exports from the southern states and they use slaves to work the fields. They feel if they didn't have slave labor, their entire economic system would collapse."

"But we don't need slaves to harvest our apples," Libby persisted. "We hire men if we must."

"I think we have a daughter bound for the legislature, Rebecca," Will said with a wink.

"She'd set them on their ear for certain," Rebecca agreed.

"I sure would! I'd simply make it illegal to own slaves. I'd set them all free. Why can't President Buchanan do that?"

"There are Southerners in the Congress, Libby, don't forget that," Ethan said finally. "The President can't make laws by himself. And besides, the President may not really mind slavery. Another thing, Lib. The North isn't innocent in all of this either. Think of the Lances and their big household of servants. They aren't called slaves, but that's what they are. You've seen how some folks treat Negroes. They don't treat them a whole lot different than a Southerner does. Remember the story? Legree, the Northerner, is the bad guy and St. Clare, the Southerner is the good guy." This was a long speech for Ethan, but he had been turning this problem over in his mind a great deal these days.

The family drifted off to bed with only Ethan remaining up. He looked down at the thin volume that lay on his knee. *Uncle Tom's Cabin*. Such an inoffensive title, but the book was causing a whirlwind of controversy across the country. The papers reported Southern senators denouncing it from the floor of the Senate. Copies were being publicly burned in Atlanta, Charleston, and Savannah. The North proclaimed it an accurate picture of slavery down South. Ignited by people of both persuasions—pro-slavery and abolitionist—a fire of hatred was being fanned into life. And the fire surely couldn't be contained much longer.

Ethan was deeply troubled by the book. Of course, he had never believed in slavery, but on reading the book he realized his feelings had been vague. Slavery was miles away; how could it affect him here in Illinois? This was a free state, after all. Yet the book had stirred his sense of right and wrong. Could there possibly be men like Simon Legree? It was too heinous to believe.

The trip was Rebecca's idea. She mulled it over for weeks, keeping it to herself until Will demanded to know what she was so preoccupied about. She told him her idea, then showed him the letter. It was from her brother James—in Mississippi.

Rebecca had kept only tenuous contact with her Kentucky family over the years. They had never been close, so the passage of time and the physical distance between Illinois and Kentucky had reinforced that isolation. Her parents were dead, her sisters married, her brother James a prosperous planter in Mississippi.

Will scanned the letter quickly. "Well, Ethan is certainly interested in the South. I think the trip would be a fine thing for him."

"I thought it might settle his ideas about the South. He has seemed so troubled by *Uncle Tom's Cabin*."

Will nodded. "It's a good idea. Good experience for him. And James sounds like he'd love to have him."

"For years he's been wanting us to send one of the children to meet their Southern cousins."

"Well, let's tell Ethan about it!"

Everything happened so quickly—packing, securing a steamboat ticket, saying goodbyes. Ethan would be gone at least six weeks. Grandmother Tufts came to the orchard house the morning of his departure to give him advice. "Don't drink any of those exotic-looking drinks with heathenish-sounding names. The southern people can be quite... Well... drinkers."

Ethan kept a straight face and nodded at all the appropriate times.

"And there will be gamblers on the boat, to be sure. You'll be tempted. They'll strip you to your... Just don't go near them and you'll be fine."

"Yes, ma'am."

"You don't have that book in your luggage, do you? Because it could get you tarred and feathered."

"No, ma'am."

"It's awfully humid down there. Sleep with your window cracked and a warm brick at your feet."

"And don't fall for any of those Southern girls," Will warned with mock seriousness, "with their haughty eyes." Rebecca nudged him in the side. Grandmother did not see this and continued, "That's true. Southern girls have such strange names."

"Like their beverages," Ethan supplied.

"Excuse me, but I'm a bit Southern!" Rebecca protested.

"Just a bit," Grandmother agreed. "But you're more Northern, and that's what counts."

"I'll be expecting a very expensive present from you when you get back," Libby said to him.

"I'll get you one, little sister, just send me the money!"

Will and Rebecca walked him to the gate. "Thank you both again for this trip," he said shaking his father's hand. Rebecca hugged him quickly, then he mounted his horse and with a broad smile and wave was gone down the lane.

On the river

It was a broad highway—a highway of water. It curved, ebbed and flowed in shallows and depths some twenty-three hundred miles, passing through ten states on its way south to the Gulf. In some places it was a smooth pane of glass, in others, turbulent and murky—uncertain, as unpredictable as a woman some steamboat captains were known to say. It teemed with bass, catfish, perch and bream. Its wide shores, bordered by forests of cottonwood, hickory, oak, willow and cypress, abounded with wildlife.

This watery turnpike was an artery of commerce for the nation. On any given night, music, song and laughter could be heard from a hundred or more steamboats, ferrying passengers and cargo north and south, their festive lanterns casting myriads of shimmering reflections on the river's dark waters. Lonely, hopeless melodies could be heard on this river also—the plaintive songs of negro slaves bound to a future as dark as the water.

This was the mighty Mississippi. Such a singular, powerful river, it commanded its own geographic standard. Schoolchildren learned geography in terms of "west of the Mississippi" and "east of the Mississippi." Indians called it *Meact Chass*, meaning "Ancient Father of Waters." When Ethan Alcott saw it, he thought it a fitting name. Perhaps it was not as awesome as the Pacific Ocean that Henri had seen, but to Ethan, it was no less impressive.

Ethan's boat, *Miss Delta*, was only one day out from his port of destination: Greenville, Mississippi. Day after tomorrow, this first leg of his trip would be over and he would begin a new one to his uncle's plantation.

It was his new friend, Hank the steward, who brought him the newspaper. Hank had befriended Ethan on voyage, answering all Ethan's eager questions about the boat and the river. There seemed no end to the young Illinoisan's interest. While there was daylight, Ethan remained on the topdeck, watching the huge engine, the workings of the crew, the river itself. With each turn and bend, the river seemed to change.

Hank handed him the paper as he lounged against the rail. "Heard 'bout it yet?"

Ethan shook his head. "No, what's happened?"

Hank nodded toward the paper. "Take a look."

Ethan unfolded it—and was stunned. "Dred Scott Decision Handed Down," the bold headline declared. Ethan was familiar with the case. It had preempted other news for weeks. Now, the United States Supreme Court had reached its decision. A Negro, whether free or slave, could not claim U.S. citizenship. Ethan swallowed hard. This was too incredible to accept.

"Already been a couple of fist fights in the bar," Hank interrupted. "Yes sir, this is a nasty piece of work if you ask me."

Fighting was not difficult for Ethan to imagine. Even Northerners, like his father, who weren't radical abolitionists, would be outraged.

"How can they do this?" Ethan murmured to himself.

"It's the highest court in the land. Reckon they can do anything they want."

Ethan refolded the paper and handed it back. He hadn't the stomach to read more. Suddenly, the clear, bright morning on the smooth Mississippi was spoiled.

"Seems like you're sailing into ... well, hostile territory, Ethan," Hank offered mildly.

Ethan looked at him sharply.

"Ain't you thought of that already? You're a Northern boy going South."

"It doesn't matter, Hank. I'm ... going to see family." But already Ethan felt the unfamiliar emotion of apprehension.

"Sure, sure. But where you're from, you can't ignore politics, Ethan. Not while you're down there."

Ethan shook his head and pointed at the paper. "The court decision may be politics ... but it's mostly insanity!"

Hank leaned forward, "Uh huh, and where you're going you better keep that little opinion to yourself."

Greenville, Mississippi

Perched on the seat of his fine carriage, Patrick Cash seemed to know instinctively which of the passengers disembarking the *Miss Delta* was his Northern cousin. It had to be the young man whose eager, boyish face scanned the crowd. He felt amused. Ethan looked like a boy searching the mob for a great adventure. Tossing his white linen coat aside, he went forward, smiling.

Any anxiety Ethan had been feeling evaporated at his cousin's warm and sincere welcome. After the initial greetings, Patrick steered Ethan through the crowd to the waiting carriage.

"Father couldn't come, since buyers were arrivin' this afternoon. Believe me, your comin' rescued me from the peril of a stuffy room of men hagglin' for hours over cotton prices! I'm eternally grateful to you, cuz."

Ethan had to listen carefully to understand his cousin through the thick Southern accent. It would not take long for Ethan to realize amusement and levity was the typical tone of Patrick Cash.

He brought Ethan to an open carriage where a black man stood waiting.

"Look here, Goodnight! I found him! No trouble at all."

Ethan had his first close-up look at a slave. He guessed the man to be in his early fifties. He swept up the baggage with a quickness that surprised Ethan. He was thin and wiry, his eyes big, friendly, brown-stained orbs.

"Welcome to Miss'ippi, Mistuh Alcott! Ain't no other state in all the Union half as pretty as she is! No better place to live, no suh!"

Ethan was momentarily stunned by this unpredictable greeting from a slave. Mississippi was a slave state after all ... He gave his cousin a quick glance and found him smiling that half-smile he would soon come to know so well. "Thank you," Ethan stammered.

Confused, he turned to the horses. "Beautiful horses," he said, running his hand over the smooth side of a chestnut gelding.

"My father's pets," intoned Patrick. "The near one is Shem,

the offside is Ham. Japheth is at home. Now let's part the waters, Goodnight, and take cousin Ethan home."

When Ethan finally stretched out for bed that first night in the Cash mansion, his mind was awake and rioting with a multitude of thoughts. He couldn't define what his expectations had been, but somehow, he felt they had been exceeded.

He and his cousin had taken to each other immediately. As their talk moved from tobacco and cotton to apple harvesting, they found common ground. Though slaves were in evidence everywhere, the subject was not broached by either.

Then they were winding up the curving drive, bordered by huge willows, to the red brick mansion that was Patrick's home. By Southern standards, it was modest, but to Ethan it was intimidating. His nervousness returned as Goodnight brought the carriage to a stop on the gravel drive. The door swung open and James Cash came down the steps with a wide smile. Ethan had a quick moment to assess him.

His uncle's face was mild, his hair already gone silver. He was lean, but not as tall as his sister Rebecca. Ethan could find nothing in the brief scrutiny to suggest this man was kin to his mother.

"Rebecca's boy! Welcome, Ethan, welcome!"

"Thank you, sir."

"A good journey?"

"Yes, sir. It was my first time on a paddlewheel. The Mississippi is pretty impressive."

They moved into the house where Ethan met his aunt and two nieces. Both girls were friendly and openly curious. Ethan vowed to himself he would take in as many details of the family, the house—everything. He would need to remember it all to deflect the barrage of questions that would surely come from his mother and sisters when he returned home.

James Cash interrupted Ethan's evaluations with an offer. "A drink, Ethan? Surely you're cotton-mouthed from that long drive."

"I know I am," Patrick said, helping himself.

His uncle extended him a slender glass of frothy green liquid. He noted Ethan's hesitation with amusement.

"It's a mint julep. Pretty tame."

"Thank you," Ethan returned, taking the glass, smiling as he remembered his grandmother's admonition.

James Cash appreciatively studied the face of Rebecca's son. He had wanted Ethan to come to his home for several reasons. Over the years, he had come to respect his oldest sister in a way that only time could bring. Their parents gone and his other sisters in Kentucky, he realized it was really Rebecca he had liked deep down all these years. Rebecca had spirit and conviction— when he hadn't. And he could not ignore what he considered her sacrifice: caring for Isaiah all these years.

So he wanted to establish some sort of communication with her, if only through her son or daughters. Then too, there was that desire to have a real Northerner in their midst, to dispel any archaic and false ideas about the South—even establish a little gooodwill between the two if possible. Perhaps Peppercreek apples, shipped down the Mississippi, might provide an interesting and profitable little business venture for him and his Illinois sister.

Over that first meal, he carefully questioned Ethan about the family business. He recognized Ethan's enthusiasm for the work by the way he talked. Any nervousness Ethan felt melted away. James Cash grew wistful. If only his son, the heir to all his efforts, would show greater interest. All he seemed to care for was painting. Painting...

Ethan had noticed the look of surprise his uncle had given him when they had met earlier. Now, James Cash was casting furtive glances in his direction. Finally the older man spoke with a chuckle.

"I'm sorry, Ethan, really."

"Sir?"

"Well, I keep lookin' you over. I can't help it. I just can't get over how much you look like your adopted father."

Ethan had been told this before.

Cash continued. "The build, the coloring, the jaw. It's so much like I remember Will O'Dell." He chuckled again. "Of course, I only saw him very briefly, just the time he came to Kentucky, and took our Rebecca away. You've heard the story of their... unconventional courtship, I assume?"

Ethan had of course—it was one of his favorite family stories. It was still on his mind as he climbed into the luxurious four poster bed later that night. His uncle had called the courtship unconventional, but Ethan thought the way his father chose a bride had been adventurous. Ethan was not interested in marriage—hadn't any prospects back home in that direction—but he could not help but hope that when his time came, he, too, would have an adventure.

The first two weeks of Ethan's visit sped by. Impressions came so quickly, crowding in on him, that every night was a struggle to fall asleep. Everything was new and different—from his kin's accents to their traditions: the slavery, the land itself, even the food.

He had not expected the food to be so distinctly different—in his naiveté he figured everyone pretty much ate the same foods, cooked the same way. But then he was introduced to she-crab soup, black-eyed peas and okra, sweetbreads, and lime pie. Without question, the spicy jambalaya was his favorite. Every morning was an experience as the Cash cooks loaded the huge mahogany sideboard. Never one to have to watch his weight, Ethan had to wonder if his middle might just thicken up a bit. He could imagine Libby's teasing without difficulty. Further, he wasn't working off the mammoth meals, as days were spent in the Southern tradition of relaxing and leisurely riding.

Ethan and Patrick spent most of their time together. Patrick showed him about the house and grounds. His face glowed with pride when he showed him a small studio.

"I paint here," Patrick explained hastily.

Ethan scanned the room. The west wall was glassed in and overlooked a lush garden. It was a typical artist's studio, with canvases propped up against the walls, a splattered easel, all awash in the strong smell of oil-paint and linseed-oil thinner.

"Father and Mother don't approve of course," he said with a shrug. "But, they've given up complainin'. That Cash stubborn streak, you know. It just seems to them a waste of my time, inappropriate for Southern gentry."

"I'm no artist Patrick, but you sure can paint!" Ethan enthused.

It was true. The Mississippi beauty that Ethan had seen so far had been faithfully captured in Patrick's brush. There were landscapes, portraits of his sisters, and, Ethan's favorite, a thoroughbred in full gallop across a field. So this was the passion of Patrick Cash—not the business of cotton planting.

At the end of the second week, Patrick came up to Ethan with a mischievous gleam in his eyes.

"Well, your fate is sealed, cuz."

"Oh?"

"Yessir! I've heard from reliable sources that the single ladies of the neighborhood are very eager to meet the, ah, eligible and handsome young man visitin' the Cashes!"

"Aw, Pat—"

"Oh I'm quite sincere! You're a real attraction, being a Northerner and all. Yes. I can see it now: You'll be writin' Aunt Rebecca sayin' you won't be comin' home. You've been snared by a Southern beauty!"

The following afternoon, Patrick was more careful over Ethan's attire than he was his own.

"Shall I just drop you off and let them swarm over you or would you like proper introductions?"

"You're making me nervous, Patrick! I'm not so sure that I even want to go, now!"

Patrick laughed heartily. "Nonsense, cuz. You must be a part of this important Southern tradition, the lawn party . . . We'll be at the Hunters' in a few minutes, so let me give you a few pointers. Is your tie straight? Ah, perfect." He then rattled off a list of young women who were either married or engaged. "That leaves you a field of roughly . . . a dozen or more."

"Patrick, come on!" Ethan said, unable to contain his laughter.

"Now, you will have a few competitors of course," Patrick continued, unperturbed. "I cannot guarantee Southern hospitality, times bein' what they are, but we'll hope for the best. You drift around in little laughin' groups, under the trees. Be sure to keep the lady's glass filled so she won't wilt in the heat. Tell them their skin is beautifully smooth, like a Georgia peach."

"I've never seen a Georgia peach!"

"Doesn't matter. And be sure and admire her hat. They spend a lot over those creations of vanity. Now, there will be drinks goin' around, but don't dip too freely, or you'll be in no shape to enjoy the barbeque."

"Barbeque?"

"Barbeque. Don't you know what that is?" Patrick was incredulous.

Ethan shook his head. "Never heard of it."

"Oh, my! And I was just thinkin' Illinois was civilized . . . Well, the main thing is you don't put any on the plate of the lady you're with."

"Why not? Don't they like it?"

"Love the stuff. Yet when you see it, you'll know why no decent Southern woman can eat it in public."

So, with much anxiousness, Ethan went to his first lawn party. The venue was the verdant lawn of a large estate and the place was alive with flirtations and laughter, with men in elegant white shirts and parasol-twirling women in flouncy dresses. Servants glided noiselessly between the groups. Ethan was widely introduced, receiving open curiosity, friendliness, and some cautious glances. He found the young men of his own peer group to be the most hesitant and reserved. To them, he was the young blood of the North, that source of scolding and rage over things that were not its business.

Patrick gradually drifted away from his side and Ethan found one attractive young woman particularly attentive. Her name was Madeline Hunter. She was a beauty with creamy-white skin, red hair and deep green eyes. She talked and laughed and made Ethan so comfortable that he felt no need to comment on her lovely skin or pretty hat.

It was only as evening approached that Ethan detected open hostility toward him. It came from a tall, handsome man of about his own age. Ethan had immediately noticed the man's stiff manner. He dropped anti-northern comments just low enough for Ethan to hear. Ethan looked at Madeline as she pulled him toward the long tables of food.

"He wasn't very friendly," Ethan said slowly.

She laughed, "No, I suppose he wasn't! He thought Madeline Hunter would be exclusively on his arm this afternoon. The arrogance of that Luke Bowers!"

"He's courting you?" Ethan asked with surprise.

"He thinks he is. But Ethan," she said smiling up at him, "never count on a Southern woman until the diamond is on her finger!"

When Patrick was busy or occupied with his painting, Ethan would wander or ride about the plantation, as his curiosity dictated. He most often sought out Goodnight, the slave. He would find him in the stables or puttering about in the garden. Goodnight was the family's most respected servant, it seemed to Ethan. He did not draw into himself when Ethan sat nearby to talk. He answered all the questions about cotton or horses that Ethan could put to him. After a few of these meetings, Ethan began to ask him more personal questions, about family and his past. In the garden one afternoon, Goodnight was digging a hole for a rose bush when he stopped a moment and Ethan could clearly see a look of pain cross his face.

"What's the matter, Goodnight?"

"Aw—nothin'," he said as he resumed digging.

"And roosters lay eggs!" Ethan returned.

Goodnight could not help but smile. The young Illinoisan had borrowed one of his own favorite expressions. "Nothin' at all, Mistuh Alcott. Just a little nag in my back. Have my Lil put hog grease on it this evenin'."

Ethan hopped up and snatched the shovel before Goodnight could protest. "Aw . . . no now, Mistuh Alcott, no suh. You can't do that."

"Of course I can, and I am. How many afternoons have I sat here and watched you work while I sat here like . . . a bump on a log?" Ethan said hotly. "Now please sit and let me work off some jambalaya."

"You'll get me in trouble if Mistuh Cash sees this. And you bein' a guest in the house—"

"I'll explain, so don't worry. I'll tell him I threatened you. I do work at home, Goodnight."

"I believes you," the slave said with a gentle smile.

But James Cash never knew about the little exchange. Ethan was surprised to receive an invitation two nights later for dinner in Goodnight's home "I been promisin' you a real southern meal

Mistuh Alcott. Yes suh, what you get up at the big house ain't
worth shakin' a stick at, compared to my Lil's cookin'...

Patrick took Ethan to Meridian one morning, on business for
his father. They were returning home, riding opposite the largest
cotton field of the Cash plantation, when Ethan was forced to
stop. He couldn't keep going.

It came like a wave—clear and strong. The slaves' backs were
bent, but their song was rising. Ethan had never heard anything
like it before—the perfect harmony of a hundred voices, young
and old, male and female. From somewhere in the middle of the
field, a single voice led the anthem.

> "Lift up your heads, O gates,
> And be lifted up, O ancient doors,
> That the king of Glory may come in!
> Who is the king of glory?
> The Lord strong and mighty,
> The Lord mighty in battle.
> Lift up your head, O gates,
> And be lifted up, O ancient doors
> That the king of glory may come in!
> Amen...and again!"

Ethan had never heard such a song of praise before. He felt he
had intruded upon some sacred time of deeply personal worship.
When he turned around, he found Patrick's eyes on him.

"I've never...heard anything like that!" Ethan stumbled.

Patrick appeared to study his horse's mane for a long time.
Ethan had never heard his cousin's voice so sad.

"I've heard it all my life."

They both looked back out over the field.

"Ready to go?" Patrick asked quietly.

◆◆ ◆◆ ◆◆

*7*he men were relaxing over their bourbons in the library, grateful they could drop all restraint since the women were cloistered in the parlor. An hour passed as the small group of men lounged in casual talk. Goodnight periodically appeared, silently and efficiently replenishing the drinks. The liquor loosened their tongues. Ethan tried to appear at ease, a part of things—and yet he wasn't. He smiled and laughed at the appropriate times, even when he didn't feel like it.

His uncle sat with his legs outstretched, his boots propped up on the low mahogany table, his eyes focused on the sculptured ceiling. The conversation flowed from politics to the economy to crops to weather to neighbors. When a planter launched a series of coarse jokes, Luke Bowers was quick to speak up. Ethan did not miss the sneer in his voice. "Careful, Father! There are tender ears in the room."

Ethan blushed in spite of himself, as all in the room turned his direction and chuckled.

"He's all right now," his uncle said lazily.

Ethan looked across at Patrick who sat with folded arms, gazing at the floor. He felt Ethan's eyes and looked up. He shrugged and gave Ethan a tired smile. Ethan knew his cousin was wishing he were somewhere else—as he did, himself. This conversation made him ashamed.

The men leaned forward, now animated with emotion. This subject, the growing tension between North and South, was close to all of them. That a Northerner was among them seemed completely forgotten in the heat of the debate. Scathing anti-slavery newspaper editorials had found their way south.

"To say we're not Christian men!" a planter snorted.

"They always drag religion in for a crutch," another agreed.

"We keep the North in tobacco and cotton and that's fact. Maybe if they had to do without, they wouldn't be so proud and fussy."

The oldest planter in the crowd spoke up, his voice haughty and angry. "I own 350 slaves and I treat 'em fine. They eat, wear decent clothes, have shelter, get attention for their sick. I'd like to see what they could make of themselves without my provision!"

James Cash knew that this discussion in front of his nephew was inevitable. Perhaps it was just as well that he see the way things truly were down south. He should see the sentiment of the men who owned the land, who voted. He could go back and tell his Northern friends the South was serious about its rights and wouldn't brook any interference. Surely he had judged his young nephew correctly—he would be fair.

Luke Bowers spoke up with heated passion. "The Northern men are a clan of hysterical, ignorant jackasses. They don't have any idea what they write about! All of us in this room treat our stock well."

James Cash sat up abruptly, his boots thudding to the floor. "Well, I think it's time we go enjoy the refreshin' company of the ladies."

Yet no one made a move—because a voice, calm and deliberate, stopped them.

"If . . . you all treat your . . . stock so well, I wonder which of you would trade places with them?" Ethan asked with a steeliness that made his throat tight.

He had remembered the words of a certain Illinois circuit lawyer years ago.

A silence as thick as the cigar smoke hung over the room. Then, Luke Bowers was on his feet.

"Like I was sayin', Northern men are fools!"

"Siddown Luke, siddown," his father said with amusement.

"Ethan, I don't think Luke meant anything personal in his reference to Northern men. But we do live in a time when men hold their convictions passionately . . . Still, I think you have insulted my guests," said James Cash, his voice moderate.

"Father, I think Ethan—" began Patrick as he stood. His father gave him an impatient wave and all eyes in the room focused on Ethan. Any reserved cordiality the men had shown James Cash's nephew from Illinois was replaced now by open hostility.

"I hold my convictions just as passionately," Ethan said

quietly. "But, if I've offended your hospitality, I apologize to you, sir." Ethan quickly left the room.

Ethan dressed slowly the next morning. He had spent a restless night, revolving the conversation in the library in his mind. Had he acted rudely to his uncle? They had been baiting him, and he had taken the bait. Would his parents be ashamed of his impulsiveness again? He was to leave at the end of the week anyway, but would he be sent home prematurely?

Ethan expected a summons from his uncle, but none came. Instead, James Cash stopped him in the hall with a friendly offer. "Ready for that ride to the river?" Patrick came up behind his father, waiting for Ethan's answer.

"Well, all right. If you're not too busy, Patrick."

The young man laughed at this. "Me ... busy?"

James Cash clapped both young men on the shoulder. "You boys get goin', then. Enjoy yourselves."

Soon they were on their horses, passing under the leafy, dreamy arches of the magnolias. They rode several miles without speaking.

Patrick finally broke the silence.

"Umm ... cuz, I detect a bit of uneasiness in you this fine mornin'. You don't seem your usual good-natured self."

Ethan glanced at him. There was that usual mocking light in his cousin's eyes. He wasn't sure what to say.

"You're worried about the feathers you ruffled last night aren't you?" Patrick asked.

"Well, yes."

Patrick slowed his horse and leisurely lit a cigar.

"Don't think you ruffled mine particularly," he said around the puffs.

"But ... your father," Ethan replied.

"Oh, well, father. He's fairly amenable. He didn't seem overly upset this morning, said nothing to me. He said what he did to you last night in deference to his cronies, not in anger at you. After all, Luke Bowers wasn't particularly courteous. Never is, in fact."

"Patrick, I don't understand you. Are you agreeing with what I said last night?"

"Let's see. What was your question? Would any of us trade places with our slaves?" He gazed out over the fields where the laborers were at their work. "Certainly none of the men in that room last night would. That would be an absolute absurdity. They would die first." His voice was mild. "And me? Well . . . I've lived a life of—what do your newspapers call it? 'Indolent laziness'. I'm heir to a thrivin' cotton plantation. The slaves do the labor, I'll handle the business end of things. It's that simple. Maybe . . . maybe I don't really like it . . . But do I have a choice, cousin? I'm a small and insignificant part of a system. What I'd prefer really doesn't matter."

The last thing that Ethan wanted was for this trip south to turn into a personal battle. He didn't want any strife between him and this family—or any of their friends—because of their differences on the slave question. Yet, here it was, turning up at every corner. How could he have been silent in the face of such hypocrisy the night before? Yet now he felt pangs of regret. He had developed a real affection for this passive cousin of his and did not want any enmity between them.

"So, you understand, Ethan?" Patrick asked.

"You're saying that slavery is a 'necessary evil'?" Ethan asked reluctantly.

"Most Southerners hold the view that slave labor is necessary, yes. Evil, no. Many feel they were destined to rule over inferior men, which is how they see the negro. But, Ethan, there are men here who have freed their slaves—men who hate slavery as much as any abolitionist back North. There aren't enough to change the system, though."

"Your father is a good man," Ethan replied. "I don't think he really likes—"

"Father is a transplanted Southerner," Patrick interrupted. "He came here, met and married my mother and inherited all the ways of the South. Good *and* bad. He did what he had to make this place profitable and successful."

"And it took slavery," Ethan said quietly.

"Success in the South means slavery," Patrick agreed. "He used it as a tool, but did not necessarily take the philosophy. Do you see?"

Their horses had come to a standstill.

Ethan pulled the hair above his ear. His face was troubled.

"No, I'm not entirely sure I understand. My father has always said slavery is a complicated issue."

"Bein' from a free state, this all seems unfamiliar, perhaps even repulsive to you. I suppose ... I've just gotten used to it."

There was a sad timbre in Patrick's voice that Ethan did not miss. His reply was gentle. "You know what I think, Patrick? I think you find it repulsive too. I think you hate the auction block and the whippings and the assaults on the women and the indignity of it all. I think you hate it, too."

Patrick turned a deep red and faced away from Ethan, a vein pulsing in his slender neck. "Then ... that makes me a low-bred coward, doesn't it?" he said quietly.

Ethan was instantly sorry for his words. His impulsive speeches were getting him nothing but trouble.

It was the night of the Rutheford ball. Ethan felt the thinly-veiled hostility toward him as he entered the grounds with his cousin. But Patrick smoothed things along, acting with nonchalance and indifference.

Then Madeline Hunter was at his side, smiling up at him, resplendent in silk and jewels.

"Good evening, Miss Hunter."

She linked her arm through his. "We are cordial people in the South, Ethan. As warm as the weather ... So, you'll call me 'Madeline'."

"All right," he answered shakily, tremendously enjoying her nearness. This night, he told himself, he would not bother to notice Luke Bowers' dark scowls—or slavery.

"I think Southern folks are very friendly, but I doubt I'm very welcome here tonight," he said as they strolled along. "I only came because Patrick pressed me to."

She laughed. "Ah, yes I did hear you were just a bit naughty the other night."

Ethan had to smile. He had not thought of his words as naughty.

"I like a man who speaks his mind, Ethan. Naughtiness is rather ... attractive sometimes. Shall we stroll outside?"

He could only give a dumb nod. As they passed out the door, he saw Patrick. His cousin winked at him.

"When will you be goin' back to Indiana, Ethan?"

"Ah, it's Illinois. I plan to leave the end of the week."

"So soon? Oh, that's a shame. If you stayed...longer, I'm sure you'd enjoy yourself." It was clearly an invitation and they both knew it. Ethan cleared his throat awkwardly.

"You work very hard at home, I would imagine." She was feeling the firmness of his arms. "Stay here and learn about cotton farmin'."

"I—" Ethan's voice squeaked, "I don't know anything about cotton."

"Cotton, apples...growin' plants is all the same, isn't it? All you need is a sharp mind and a good strong body...and you definitely have both."

Slaves, he thought as she leaned into him, you need slaves to grow cotton, that's what you mean. He stepped back from her, trying to regain his balance. Slavery wasn't supposed to come up tonight...

"Will you stay longer then? For me?" she purred.

"I...don't know. I had planned to leave. You know, fish and guests both smell after three days...I should be pretty offensive by now!"

She looked puzzled a moment, then smiled. "Is that a northern expression?"

"Well, actually it's a grandmother expression."

"Stay," she whispered.

"Ahem..." A voice had intruded into their privacy.

"Go away, Goodnight!" Madeline scolded. "No one sent for you."

"Ma'am, it's a telegram for Mistuh Alcott."

"Later," she insisted.

"A telegram for me?" Ethan asked as he stepped toward the slave.

"Yes suh. It came to the house after you left and I thought it might be important."

"Thank you, Goodnight."

Ethan quickly scanned the lines, his face suddenly turning into a frown.

"What is it, Ethan?" Madeline asked.

"My...mother. She's very ill." Ethan felt the blood draining from his face.

"Oh, I'm sorry. Hopefully she'll be better when you get home."

Ethan looked at her his eyes round with shock. "No, I have to leave immediately."

"Leave? But what about—"

"Madeline, it's my mother! She's very sick. It has to be serious or they wouldn't have sent a telegram."

"Go away then! You're just a little boy!" Madeline Hunter flounced out of Ethan's life.

Back at the Cash home, Ethan quickly packed his things. His cousin stood with folded arms, strangely silent. There was evidently something on his mind.

"Ethan," he began slowly. "I was wondering something, now that you're heading home."

"What is it, Patrick?"

"It's about our talk the other day—"

"Patrick, really—I'm sorry. I have this bad habit of saying things without thinking first."

"Ethan, you meant what you said, didn't you? Even if you wish you hadn't said it. I understand that."

Ethan sighed deeply.

"Ethan, when you get back home, among your friends and family, what will you tell them about your trip south?"

"I really hadn't thought about it, Patrick."

His cousin began to pace, his face flushed with feeling.

"Ethan, think! What will you say? Is slavery the only thing you've seen down here?"

"No, of course not."

"Will you go back and tell them it's like the papers say? Like *Uncle Tom's Cabin*? What will you tell them?"

Ethan pulled at his hair, distinctly uncomfortable now.

"Patrick, I know there is more to the South than slavery. I do know that. Your people are friendly and generous. There is great beauty here . . ."

"Ethan listen, this . . . is bigger than you or me. Don't you see that when I'm master of this place, I have to keep the slaves? I don't have a choice! It's not up to me . . . You know that I'll be good to them!"

Ethan returned to his packing, wishing this confrontation, which his cousin seemed so intent upon, could have been avoided.

"Say what's on your mind Ethan," Patrick said in a tight voice.

Ethan threw a shirt angrily into his suitcase.

"They're still slaves, no matter how you treat them," Ethan said evenly.

Patrick exploded. "I can't change that!" he shouted.

Ethan felt miserable that their last conversation would be an argument. "Patrick, please! Let's forget it."

Patrick Cash felt miserable too, but he could not forget it.

"The economy of the Southern states is all tied up in slavery," he said quietly.

"Yes," Ethan agreed tiredly.

"There's no end to it. Not by my hand. There are owners that have let their slaves go and still nothing has changed."

Ethan nodded, "Yes, it . . . would take something more."

"More? You know, Ethan, there's an old man in these parts named Hedikiah Bass. He's about ninety-five or so and quite the sage. I've talked to him a few times. Always thought he seemed to have a second sight about things or a deeper wisdom than most men have. You know what he says about all this trouble between the north and south over slavery?"

Ethan shook his head.

"War," Patrick said. "He says this country will have a war over it."

"No, Patrick. That couldn't happen."

"I don't know, Ethan. Men feel pretty strongly on both sides of the fence. Which side would give in?"

They looked at each other in silence.

"If it did come to war . . . we'd be on opposite sides, cousin."

Ethan ignored the statement and closed his baggage with finality.

"I'd like to ride with you, Ethan, but bankers are comin' in the mornin'. I'm sendin' Goodnight with you, though."

Ethan began to protest. "That's too much trouble! I can find my own way—"

"I insist," Patrick said. "You may not be Cash by blood, but you definitely have our stubborn streak." His voice was light once again.

He patted Ethan on the shoulder and extended his hand.

"I've enjoyed your time here tremendously, my northern cousin. Come back and fish the mighty Mississippi . . . and maybe I'll come North someday."

"Yes Patrick, that would be good. I'd like to have you in my home. Thank you for everything."

Their looks held a moment more—could they see into the future? Both taking up arms . . . Perhaps laying down their lives . . .

Peppercreek, Illinois
Summer, 1858

"Your pa seemed quiet tonight," Henri said.

Wyeth nodded, "I think he's thinking about Mother. Day after tomorrow would have been their twenty-ninth anniversary."

"It's hard to believe she's been gone a year . . . It seems so much longer," Ethan said softly.

The three of them were sitting on the front porch, Wyeth and Henri rocking in the swing, Ethan lounging on the steps. It was late afternoon—tranquil and quiet, the day was drawing to a close. Butterflies, bees, and other little winged creatures rose in hazy bunches around the flower beds. The sunset was brilliant scarlet to the west with fluffy golden-tinted clouds piled at the edge of the horizon. "The day is giving itself an evening bath in gold," Henri murmured. Ethan could understand that bit of poetry and agreed with it.

The reference to Rebecca sent his thoughts back . . . to a year ago.

The homecoming had not been what he had expected. No, not at all. He could still see himself riding up to the barn. A light rain was falling. He had started up to the back door when something drew his attention toward the hill. He could see between the white picketed fence of the small family plot—a fresh mound of dirt. He dropped his bags in the yard and ran. He leaned against the fence and stared, the rain coming down harder now. Before him was not one mound of fresh dirt—there were two. Two white crosses. He remembered as he stood there he felt as if someone had punched him very hard in the chest. He couldn't take in the shock of it. It couldn't be true. The telegram had said his mother was ill. Yet there it was right before him. Two crosses. One for Rebecca Cash O'Dell—and one for Libby.

His mother... This woman who had drawn him to her heart without hesitation from the first day he had come to Pepper-creek. His sister, fun-loving Libby. He closed his eyes and gripped the fence till his hands hurt. He could no longer feel the rain.

"Ethan," said a flat-sounding voice behind him.

He slowly turned around. Wyeth stood there, an umbrella in hand, her face as gray as the sky.

"I saw you ride in."

"Wyeth, the telegram... It said..."

Ethan's voice was hoarse and Wyeth winced at the pain she heard in it. "I know. We tried to get word to you again, but you had already started home. I know what a shock... It's been over a week and I still can't... grasp it."

"But she was just sick, Wyeth!"

"It was a fever. It came quickly and she just couldn't shake it. Doc Noble couldn't do anything for her."

"But... Libby..." His voice was breaking.

Wyeth began to cry. "Remember how she always said she and Mother got sick together? She just..." Wyeth couldn't finish. Ethan went to her and she took his hand. "Pa has been wanting to see you, Ethan."

A year ago.

"Ethan? You look miles away," Wyeth was saying.

He smiled slightly. He couldn't voice what he had been thinking.

Henri drew Wyeth closer to his side. "Since we're going to Quincy tomorrow, maybe that will help your father—give him something else to think about. The papers say the debates are pretty entertaining."

"Ethan, remember when Mr. Lincoln had dinner with us, years ago?"

Ethan nodded. "He rode the sorriest horse I ever saw!"

"Wonder if he's still just as skinny." Wyeth mused.

The debates. Yes, if anything could distract his father it would be the much-talked about debates, Ethan decided. Seven cities across Illinois were hosting these outdoor meetings, attended by hundreds. A holiday, party-like atmosphere prevailed at the gatherings, despite the fact that the topic debated was nothing close to party-like. Slavery. The debates were vocalizing the growing hostility about slavery.

Illinois was greatly enjoying the national attention two of her sons were receiving. Newspapers traded articles and editorials quite generously, so Abe Lincoln and Stephen Douglas were heard of as far south as Mobile, Alabama and Savannah, Georgia. For most Southerners, though, the lanky, long-legged Springfield lawyer was not very popular. His words were greeted with scorn.

"Where do you think this debate fever will end?" Ethan asked his father, once.

Will looked out across the fields and sighed. "The debates will end . . . but not what's behind it. Slavery is too much with us. And too much like that swarm of angry bees we worked with yesterday."

Then Will was silent, and Ethan instinctively knew his father was praying.

Life at Peppercreek was so different now. How quiet it was! The very house felt different. The course of their days was changed. Ethan's mother and sisters were all gone. With Wyeth and Louisa married and the deaths of his mother and Libby, it was just three lonely bachelors—himself, his father and Uncle Isaiah. His throat would ache when he thought of the times when he had come silently upon his father, his face buried in his hands, or just staring off into space. Yes, everything was different.

The difference was never more obvious than at mealtimes. Ethan smiled ruefully to himself. It was a wonder they weren't skeletons by now. Not a one of them could cook decently. He would never forget one night in those first painful months after his mother was gone. Will had made a stew for dinner. The three had obediently eaten in silence. Ethan would have sworn his father used dish water in the broth. Then Will had thrown down his spoon in disgust. Ethan could see he was fighting back tears. "You see, it's like . . . this stew! This mess called stew!"

"What, Pa?" Ethan asked gently.

"There's no seasoning . . . No spice in life without . . . my gal. Without Libby." He stood up abruptly and went to his room and Ethan wished he were a thousand miles away from this raw pain.

Then too, there was Uncle Isaiah. He had taken his sister's death as he had taken everything all his life—so calmly. He had held her hand at the end and prayed in his own unique way. Then he was gone, and they did not see him for three days. He came back even more aged and frail. When he tried to communicate, it was through a feather touch of his hand on Will's cheek and a trembling smile. Now, a year later, he too was thinner, slower to work, longer to rest. The fiddle he had once so enjoyed playing for Rebecca, now lay wrapped in a quilt—a part of his quiet past apparently over. It had been such a long, hard year—a year of hurt and, slowly, a year of healing.

Then he thought of his cousin Patrick. He had not thought a lot about him this past year. Patrick, who could paint southern sunsets and blooded thoroughbreds and waxy magnolias one moment, and add profit-and-loss figures in a cotton account the next. Ethan wondered what his cousin would think of the words of Douglas and Lincoln?

Two farmers had traded blows over slavery here in Illinois . . . Would it ever come to worse than that?

Autumn of 1858 was memorable at Peppercreek. A killing freeze, not due till after the apple harvest, came in early October. Old Baily, living almanac and historian, declared there had never been such an early freeze in fifty years. For once, Alice Tufts agreed with him. Only God's provision, hard work by the men, and Will's savings sustained them.

It was a memorable fall too, because Ethan became engaged— and unengaged—to a Peppercreek daughter. It was an ill-fated affair, Grandmother had said in her wisest tone, but Louisa still suffered the disappointment of a frustrated cupid.

Best of all that autumn, Henri and Wyeth had returned to Peppercreek to stay. Chicago was simply too harsh on Henri's still-fragile health. It came together perfectly, for Henri was offered the pastorate of Peppercreek's small but strong church.

"You must do what you and Henri want, of course," Will said, taking Wyeth's hand in his. Gazing into her green eyes, he could not help but think of his Rebecca. "This house is your home. You can change it, redecorate it, whatever gals like to do. Anything you like."

"You can certainly take over the cooking," Ethan said with a straight face. "We need you here for health reasons."

Wyeth smiled at these men she loved.

Will continued. "There's room for all of us. Why, you and Henri can have the whole upstairs! Make it into... What's the word?"

"A suite of rooms, Pa?"

"Yes that's it! A suite of rooms. Certainly big enough for a grandbaby someday!"

Wyeth blushed. "Henri?"

Henri was looking down over the orchard—still, silent and gray with the coming of winter. The beauty of this place—so unchanging, yet steady with the joys and sorrows of their life. God had led him to this valley, to this family, years ago. He turned back to them.

"Your father's right, Wyeth. This is where we belong."

Part III

MasterPiece

Chapter 1

Peppercreek, Illinois, 1860

◆◆ ◆◆ ◆◆

*W*ill O'Dell moved comfortably in his chair, readjusting his feet on the broad hearth to feel the fire's warmth. The only light in the room was the orange glow of the coals, becoming momentarily brighter as a log would crumble in sparks. The only sounds were the snapping fire, the mantle clock's steady tick, and aged Jumper, who lay beside him giving an occasional whine in his troubled canine sleep. Tonight was Christmas eve, 1860, and as Will sat alone he reflected on the changes that had come to his home. Had Rebecca been gone three years now? Oh, it seemed like so much longer to him. Yet, wasn't it yesterday he had made her laugh, seen the love for him in her eyes? The passage of time was a strange thing, he mused, sometimes terrifyingly swift, sometimes painfully slow.

Tonight he had looked around the brightly lit room, seeing the smiling faces of his family. Yes, he was happy too. The pain was not so sharp, though the ache of missing Rebecca would never leave. He had studied each face in the lamplight. Wyeth and Henri. He smiled to himself, his eldest was a happily married woman. Yet he also knew there was a shadow in her heart. He noted again the rich copper highlights in her hair, reminding him that the older Wyeth grew, the more she looked like his Rebecca. And Henri. His quick smile. Tall, slim Henri. His face still boyish though he was now thirty-four. He was the minister of the small flock of believers at Peppercreek, greatly enjoying the work to which he'd been called.

Louisa and her husband, Joe. Louisa, with her golden hair piled high on her head, her figure well-rounded with her second pregnancy. Little two-year-old Rebecca, his first grandchild, singing, climbing into laps, her chubby hands busy filling her mouth with sweets. Uncle Isaiah, with his fleeting smile, his eyes eagerly following little Rebecca, his head gently nodding to the music. He murmured perhaps half a dozen words all night,

185

thought Will, moving slowly between his own silent world and ours. Grandmother Tufts' place was empty this Christmas eve. She was caught at home with a fierce cold.

There was Ethan, his adopted son. Could a father ever love a boy more than he did Ethan? Had a father ever prayed so fervently for his son? He thought of him tonight—laughing, singing, tossing Rebecca high in the air, teasing his sisters unmercifully. And arm-wrestling. Will chuckled softly. Ethan could easily defeat the doctor, and—only lately—Will; but tonight, as usual, he could not beat his unmuscled brother-in-law. So tall and broad-shouldered this son of his, now turned twenty-four. It was no surprise Ethan was considered the catch of the county by its single women. He and Ethan worked alongside each other and it was no secret that Ethan's hard work and common sense had generated greater profit for Peppercreek Orchard.

Will stood and stretched. He crossed to the window and looked out. No snow had fallen this Christmas eve; only a piercing coldness wrapped the countryside in purple shadows, the stillness interrupted only by the solo flight of a night bird. In a way, the entire country lies in a type of shadow, thought Will. Abraham Lincoln of southern Illinois had become the sixteenth American president just last month. Now all the newspapers were describing the growing tension between the northern and southern states. South Carolina had seceded from the Union five days before Christmas. Where would all this secession business lead? It was as if the nation collectively held its breath. War was more than just a dark rumor. Will shook his head. Surely not war! Fighting a foreign country was hard enough, but a country at war with itself?

It was well after midnight, but Will was not tired. It seemed to him that as he grew older, he required less sleep. He spent long hours in the night praying. He drew a deep breath, the fragrance of pine boughs filling the room. Soon it would be a new year. He would pray now, for each of his family, then, his country. Then off to bed, alone. Sometimes, thought Will, bed was the loneliest place to be.

Christmas Day

Wyeth and Louisa were busy with Christmas dinner. Louisa

paused and pointed out the window. "Look out there," she said. "Ethan has Rebecca up on Bess again."

The sisters looked out in the yard. Little Rebecca, bundled up like a tiny fur mouse, sat atop the horse, clapping her hands as Ethan led the animal around. Wyeth watched Henri's face as he followed the little girl with his eyes. Wouldn't he love a little one like that, she thought. Louisa turned away, resuming her work. But Wyeth stood still, gripped for the thousandth time by a wave of longing for a child.

She and Henri were very happy, these two-and-a-half years together. Yet one thing lay between them. No children. It went beyond the raised eyebrows of friends or the careless comments of neighbors. That didn't hurt so much anymore. No, it was the simple longing of wanting a child to lie in her arms, to see a baby, pink and soft, with touches of her and Henri. A thousand little things caused her pain. Sometimes it made her feel she was a failure as a woman. But Henri understood. He had drawn her close to him so often, whispering words of love and comfort. "Wyeth, we have each other. Let's be patient with Him. Let's just trust Him. He knows our hearts."

Dinner was a feast. A small basket of straw was the table's centerpiece, an old custom from Will's family. It symbolized the Christ child who came in simplicity and humility. In tantalizing profusion around the basket sat a golden turkey and steaming bowls of vegetables and stuffing. Henri asked the blessing, then Will spoke, his eyes sparkling but his voice serious.

"I usually don't put conditions on the talk of my table, but this day . . . this day, only love and laughter. No talk of politics or troubles, please. Let's just celebrate His birth, His goodness toward us."

Later Wyeth drew Henri aside. "Henri, I've got Grandmother's food ready. Can we drive over with it?"

"Sure. I'll get the buggy."

It was late afternoon. The sun's passing made the day colder and gray. Wyeth looked toward the hill at the back of the house as she pulled on her coat. How well she could remember the pilgrimages her mother had made each Christmas day to that little white-fenced plot, to brush away the snow, to lay the flowers by the two little stones. Henri brought the buggy around to interrupt her thoughts.

"Ready, Mrs. Mullins?" Henri smiled as he helped her up. "Did I tell you how beautiful you are this Christmas day?" he asked.

"Only three or four times."

"Soon as we get around the corner, I intend to give you a very big Christmas kiss!"

"Oh Henri," she laughed.

"Just thought I'd warn you!" and Henri snapped the reins.

In January the nation's drama heightened with six more states leaving the Union. The country, still in its childhood, was about to be tested—in blood. In Illinois, January blended into February without ceremony, two long cold months. Evenings were spent in the living room before the fire. Often, as Wyeth sat with her handiwork or a book, she would watch Henri and Ethan, these two so close to her heart. As close as brothers she thought—and yet, so different. Henri: easygoing, even-tempered. Ethan: impulsive, quick-tempered, friendly. And then there were his unfortunate love affairs. Wyeth shook her head at the thought. She almost wished he would marry and end all these silly entanglements. Just last spring he'd been engaged to Elizabeth Cooper, a flaming redhead in the next county. Which of them had broken the engagement, only the two knew, but at the O'Dell house they were all relieved. Currently, a local girl had found his favor, and courting continued despite the frigid weather. Still, when Wyeth thought of each girl Ethan had courted, she was left just a little dissatisfied. She had that true sister's instinct, and felt that no girl was really suitable for her little brother.

Spring finally came in a rush of thawing creeks, warm soft winds and bouquets of verdant green. The orchard began to bud. Nature was not mindful of the nation's ills; it had more important business to conduct. With spring, life on the farm picked up its tempo. There was work to be done from sunrise to sunset. Winter storms had left repairs to be done on house, barn and outbuildings. Soil must be plowed for planting. There was work to be done on bee hives, cultivation and cleanup in the orchard. Foals on spindly legs were appearing in the pasture and cranky hens declared they were setting. Spring brought work, and a satisfying riot of new life and sounds and color.

Wyeth was at her garden with a passion. In a few days she and Henri had tilled and planted the kitchen garden, but with enjoyment she lingered in her flower and herb garden. Supper finished, they often sat awhile on the porch before turning in, watching the last rays of sun color the evening sky. Coming out of the house behind them, Will let out a sigh of satisfaction.

"I'm glad to get that north section done," he said. "Do you think we can do the south section in two days, son?" asked Will.

Ethan sat nearby, with his face intent upon the newspaper.

"Ah... I'll get the limbs up here and cord 'em tomorrow," Ethan said.

A look passed between Will, Wyeth and Henri that Ethan did not see. Ethan had never been an avid reader, yet they all knew what drew him to such intense study of late. They knew what sent him into town for the newspapers, what captured his interest in the evenings when the rest of them mused over the day and the night sky. The slide toward war—it was the theme of newspapers and most conversations. It was the steadily approaching storm cloud on the horizon.

Finally Henri spoke, "What's the news, Ethan?"

Ethan's alertness returned.

"President Lincoln has ordered a relief expedition from New York to Fort Sumter."

Fort Sumter, an obscure fort in the Charleston harbor, had become a point of focus for the nation. A federal fort surrounded by the newborn Confederacy, Lincoln was anxious that it should not fall into Southern hands. The troops stationed there were low on provisions.

"The Southerners won't let that expedition get through," said Henri, his voice sounding hollow. "It'll be the beginning."

In all the talks of the conflict in the O'Dell household, Ethan had said very little.

"What do you think, son?" asked Will quietly.

Ethan glanced up at his father uneasily. "Sir?"

"Henri's right. This will probably be the beginning of war. War," he said shaking his head. "One nation split in two. As the president said from God's Word, 'A house divided against itself cannot stand.' Everyone will take a side, sooner or later..."

All eyes turned on Ethan.

"I'm... not sure what I think exactly, sir," he hedged.

Events, like dominoes, fell predictably. Four days later, April 12, 1861, the Confederates fired on the fort. Henri, Ethan, and Will had been working in the lower pasture repairing a fence when a rider on horseback came galloping down the crossroads. He let out a whoop when he saw them and barely slowed his mount, "They done it! By durn, they did!"

They instinctively knew what his brief words had meant. Later Ethan rode into Peppercreek to wait for the news.

"I guess I never saw Baily's so crowded before," he reported later. "Seemed like everyone was there, in the middle of the day too. Then the mail coach came and dropped off the papers and folks were all over 'em like ants."

Ethan stopped and fingered the paper on his knee. The headline was bold for emphasis: "Fort Sumter surrenders, no casualties." Ethan waited a moment for someone to comment, but there was only the creak of the porch swing where Wyeth and Henri sat. Ethan shifted impatiently.

"More cake, Uncle Isaiah?" asked Wyeth and the old man smiled.

"Guess Baily was pleased with the crowd in the store," was Henri's laconic reply.

Ethan turned his face from them, feeling an unaccountable sense of frustration. Why were they so nonchalant?

Will stood up, leaning against the railing, his face turned toward the little white-fenced plot on the hill.

"This is what happens when a country refuses to humble itself before a sovereign God. Hasn't He blessed this country time and time again from the beginning? It's been a country of light . . . And now, darkness is swallowing up that light. Bloodshed of Americans will be the payment to that darkness. Back in 1761 we were on the eve of a war with the most powerful nation on earth. A struggle for freedom. Now, not one hundred years later, we're fighting within ourselves. A hundred years from now? That would be . . . 1961 . . . What will this country be like? Two separate nations?"

"Pa, maybe it won't come to war." Wyeth's young voice was full of hope.

But the next day Lincoln called for seventy-five thousand volunteers. In cities, towns and sleepy rural hamlets across the

North, upper class, middle class and country folk were coming together. It was the birth of two great armies.

Ethan and Henri worked and sweated together over a wagon wheel the next afternoon. Henri noticed Ethan was unusually quiet.

"Henri, I can finish this, you go on in. I know you have prayer meetin' to get ready for."

Henri laughed, " What's to get ready? You just—pray!"

Ethan did not smile at Henri's joke.

"Ethan, what's the matter?" Henri asked. "All afternoon you've seemed to have a bee in your bonnet, as Grandmother would say."

Ethan could not help but smile now. He threw down a tool.

"Yes, I guess I do, but..."

"What?"

"I guess I can't expect you and Pa to understand," he said simply.

"I'm not your father's age but we do feel alike," Henri replied. "Young men always thirst for the glories of battle. It—"

"It's not that!" Ethan's voice was sharp.

"What is it then, Ethan?" asked Henri calmly.

"Do you believe in slavery? Or does Pa? Of course not!"

"Well, it's not that simple. I dare say no one knows exactly the full reasons. It's—" but Henri stopped. Ethan's face was closed and his troubled eyes were on the ground. Henri knew this young man. He loved him as a brother, and he knew words were not right for now. They finished their work in silence, and Henri watched as Ethan strode to the barn.

"Yes, only prayer tonight..." he said to himself.

In May, Arkansas, Tennessee, North Carolina, and finally Virginia, joined the Confederate states of America. The new country now numbered eleven states. Now two hostile nations, so unprepared for war, devoted time, money and energy to little else. Military preparation became the fever across the land. From Bangor, Maine to Drip Hollow, Tennessee to Mobile, Alabama to Austin, Texas, men lay down plows to pick up muskets and rifles. Loyalty, patriotism and war fervor flooded Union and Confederate hearts alike, creating little problem in meeting troop quotas

Southern men weren't quite sure about the talk about states' rights and such, no Yankee government was gonna tell them they couldn't keep slaves. Yet Northerners were not all so deeply unprejudiced. In fact, many felt little genuine concern for black Americans. Still, they reasoned, citizens should do what the government decides and not be upstart smart alecks in thinking they could just pull out of the U.S.A. A good brawl should shape up those "Johnny Rebs," they thought. Headlong into a fight both sides bounded, no one imagining it could possibly last four long years or cost so much in human suffering. Two vast bodies of people, with uncertain motives and untested courage were about to collide.

Grandmother Tufts had come over for Sunday dinner, and now, in the living room with a summer rain dripping outside, they all sat, watching Grandmother's knitting needles flying almost as quickly as her tongue.

"It can't come to war! No real shots have been fired since Sumter. You can't believe those Northern newspapers!" she said hotly.

"The Southern papers are saying the same things, Grandmother, and the Southern delegation has left Washington. Everyone is spoiling for a fight," said Henri tiredly.

"Humph and hogwash... That I should live to see the day that Americans would fight Americans! Abraham must *do* something!"

They all smiled at Grandmother's familiar term for the President.

"I think he's doing all he can. Surely he wants war as little as anyone," Will replied.

"Yes, well... What about those Congressmen and Senators up there? Doing what, I ask? Raising taxes! Making foolish laws! Disgrace!" Grandmother was talking in exclamations this afternoon, her brown eyes snapping with her words.

"Your vinegar is up today, Grandmother," Henri said laughing.

She managed a clipped smile at the preacher.

"Indeed! Like naughty children, these seceded states. Need a good dose of 'what so.'"

Ethan, who had been uncharacteristically quiet and pensive, had to smile at the old lady. "What so" was her original term for discipline. It grew quiet a moment, and all were surprised at the milder, even sadder tone Grandmother's voice took.

"Indeed, my papa fought in 1776. Paid so dearly for freedom for this land. Now this..." Silence again.

Ethan had been thinking a lot these days. Everyone knew his trip South had made a strong impression on him, but they did not suspect the depth of that impression. He would never forget the frightened children separated from their parents or the resignation, despair, pain and exhaustion etched on so many black faces. The images had been burned into his young mind. This afternoon, the face of Goodnight, his uncle's servant, rose so clearly before him. Any discussion of slavery for him was not confined to numbers or abstract theories. Slaves had faces, were people. He finally excused himself, going down to the creek, heedless of the rain. He passed through the orchard and fields, this land he had grown to love. Perhaps out upon the land he would find some comfort.

His thoughts about the conflict were as tangled as a skein of Grandmother's yarn. Most of the local lads were mustering and heading over to Springfield, Galena, or Cairo. It was not uncommon now to see a solitary farm lad tramping down the sunlit road, eagerly offering himself as the pride of Illinois. Ethan had talked it over with other Peppercreek young men, but he had hung back, waiting, thinking.

A warm night in May found Ethan driving the carriage home, a full moon brightening the sky to a beautiful hue. He held the reins absently. He had taken Mary Chaney home after church, then they lingered at the gate as they always did. Yet, Ethan noticed, young Mary was not so gay tonight.

"Mary, is something the matter?" he finally asked.

She sighed. "No...."

Ethan smiled to himself, remembering Henri's words. "When you ask a woman if something is the matter and she says 'no,' you should be warned something is very much the matter."

"Mary, what is it?"

"Well, Ethan you know how much I—like you—"

Ethan smiled again. She must be trying to say something that was hard for her to say.

"Ethan, why haven't you enlisted?"

"What?" Ethan was startled by the question.

"It's just that some of Bob McDunn's crowd are saying— that...you're a coward."

"Is that what you think, Mary?"

"Of course not! I know you're brave, Ethan... Well, why haven't you enlisted? You'd look splendid in a uniform."

"I haven't joined up because I haven't exactly decided about ...all this."

Mary's eyes were intent. "Really?"

"I'm not going to go dashing off like I just can't wait to fight. There's more to it than that."

"Well, I'm glad you're staying around, because you're my best beau. Now you may kiss me."

The kiss was a peck on the cheek, for Ethan was suddenly not much in the mood for kissing. He turned down the lane at home. He hadn't told Mary everything. Nice and cute girl that she was, somehow she did not inspire his confidence. The fact was, he was already committed to joining the Union cause, but held back, sensing his father's feelings. He felt a deep desire to respect and honor Will O'Dell. There was no man living who held such a place in his heart as did his adopted father. They talked, laughed and prayed together. They had tramped through the woods hunting, and played fishing lines along Pepper Creek together. They worked side by side and decisions in the business now were made together. Ethan knew his father despised slavery, but this possibility of war was like a personal grief to him, shocking and horrible.

As he climbed down from the carriage, he heard voices. Wyeth and Henri were in the garden. They had not heard him drive in. But he could see them plainly in the moonlight. Then Wyeth was laughing and Henri pulled her into his arms. This was no perfunctory, in-front-of-the-family type kiss. Ethan turned away with a sigh. Their marriage reminded him of his parents'. So tender, so devoted, deepening so with the years. He thought again of Mary. Was she the wife for him? Maybe there's a girl somewhere for me, like Pa and Henri got... Maybe...

"...It was a tranquil summer morning with so much of the Virginia countryside in bloom, fields of corn ripening in the sunshine ... No less than fifty carriages of civilians parked at the crest of the hill to observe the battle. This reporter saw gentle-men in spotless summer suits and ladies in flowered hats, picnic baskets and bottles of wine—spectators to this first great en-gagement between the Union and Confederate forces. While clouds of dust and smoke obscured the actual fighting, the report of rifle and cannon was easily heard.

"In the capital the dull thunder of cannon played all day and citizens were confident of the Union victory ... But by late after-noon, the truth was apparent; the Union forces had been severely routed and were beating a hasty and chaotic retreat to the capital. The road back to the city was choked with the dust and terror of spectators and the fleeing army. Many fashionable car-riages were wrecked or commandeered to convey wounded ... Total and complete defeat for the Union ... Casualties are ex-pected to be nearly fifteen thousand."

Will finished reading aloud and slowly folded the paper. July 21, two days before, the first battle of the war had taken place at Bull Run, Virginia. The North was reeling in the humiliation of the rout. Ethan watched his father's face pale, his lips tighten.

"So ... Fifteen thousand lives lost in a single afternoon," he said.

Silence.

"This defeat—it's a blow to the pride of the North. More men than ever will enlist now," replied Henri.

"I think this won't be a quick, tidy little war. This is going to take awhile," returned Will.

"Freedom. Grandmother said her father fought for freedom." Ethan's voice was so unexpected, the others turned to him. He continued looking at his hands, not meeting their eyes. "I guess this war is about freedom, too. Freedom for six million or so negro men, women and children."

"Who's the enemy in this fight, Ethan?" asked Henri.

Ethan did not answer at first.

"We all agree slavery is a disease in the country. A bondage of Satan's own design. But—war, Ethan? Is that truly the only way?"

There was a sad timbre in Henri's voice, but Ethan met his eyes and his voice was now firm.

"How else, Henri? How else? Look, it's been a part of the South for over a hundred years! It's their way of life. Their economy is all tied up in it. They won't give up without a fight. How can they? You say it's a disease and you're right. But with a disease you have to cut it out. You can't hope it away. If there were another way besides war..."

He finished and met Will eye to eye. The father smiled slowly, loving this son of his so much. If Ethan approached him to ask permission to enlist, Will knew it was only a courtesy. He was a man now, old enough to leave home, old enough to make his own decisions. Will stood up and walked to the end of the porch and picked up Ethan's squirrel gun. Slowly he walked back toward them. He stopped in front of Ethan, who stood up. He stretched the rifle out to him.

"Ethan, you're a good shot. The best I know. You've killed turkey, deer, rabbits, squirrels, bear...bobcat, even."

He stopped and though his voice was deliberate, his eyes shone with pride. Ethan swallowed hard.

"Will you point a rifle such as this at a man and pull the trigger, as you will be expected to do?"

The silence was thick. Wyeth felt tears rising for her young brother, standing so tall and strong-looking. Ethan took the weapon from his father, but still said nothing.

"Son, you're your own man. You have every right to think and feel about this war as you like. Not to take my view or Henri's or anyone else's. Pray, and when the time comes to make a decision, you'll feel right. And... Whatever you do son, you'll have my never-changing love and prayers with you."

The first of July, 1861, Ethan left his home and rode off toward Galena, Illinois. He rode, not wanting to acknowledge the tightening in his throat. He did not look back. He would never have thought just riding off could be this hard. Wyeth had failed at hiding her tears and Louisa had clung to him. Grandmother trembled. Will's eyes were steady and his handshake firm. Henri had slapped him on the back and made some joke that he could not remember now. This was only a new bend in the road of his life, he decided. Perhaps, he could make a success of it and all their fears would be for nothing.

Chapter 2

Galena, Illinois, 1861

◆◆ ◆◆ ◆◆

*G*overnor Yates sat uncomfortably in his saddle. He was hungry, perspiring heavily in his black frock coat and suffering with a colossal headache—literally and figuratively. He had ridden up from Springfield to Galena to see for himself the condition of the huge army camp centered in the city. He quickly decided that the reports had not been exaggerated. Situated on the muddy bluffs overlooking the Tennessee River, Galena had become important in riverboat traffic. Like hundreds of other towns across the country, it had been totally unprepared for the huge tide of men and supplies that planted itself to grow into an army. Lacking leadership, supplies, uniforms and weapons, medical care, even basic sanitation—both sides were appallingly unprepared to begin such a big war.

A pall of smoke from hundreds of cooking fires hung in the hot air. The humidity was stifling. Already dysentery, measles and chicken pox were thinning the ranks. Previously clean, robust farm boys were suffering in the primitive conditions. Dysentery alone would claim forty-five thousand Union lives over the next four years.

Yates wiped his brow, wishing he were back at the capital. There were so many men ... so few officers, so few who had the slightest military knowledge. Over half the West Point graduates had gone South.

Yates hoped some of this chaos would be relieved after the appointment of that Galena storekeeper. He had been given command of all regiments of southern Illinois. Ulysses S. Grant, a veteran of the Mexican war, had impressed the governor and was quickly given command. Still the appointment had not solved all his problems. An aide came riding up.

"What is it, Jeff?"

"Another telegram, sir."

"Ah ... What else?" Yates studied the telegram a moment, then gave a brief smile.

197

"From an old friend. Well, I've seen enough, Jeff. Has Grant arrived?"

"Yes, sir, just now."

"All right, here." He scribbled something down and handed it to the aide.

"Go find what company this lad is in."

"Ethan Alcott is it, sir?"

"Yes, from a fine family. Always sent up apples to the mansion. Find him."

Dear family,

I've only a few minutes. I'm part of the 21st Illinois Regiment, off to Cairo. That's where General Grant is setting up his headquarters. I'm feeling fine and looking forward to the move. Galena has gotten kind of old. My commander seems pleased with my progress.

Ethan

Six weeks had elapsed since Ethan had left home to join himself to the Union army. With one signature, he had become a "Billy Yank," bearing arms against "Johnny Rebs." Those six weeks had been weeks of wide-eyed wonder for him. He was absorbed into camp life without formality and very little instruction. Diet, lack of organization, poor sanitation, and just so many talking, cursing, sweating men was somewhat of a shock to him. Army life changed however, when he went to Cairo. How he was sent there he would not know for some years.

At Cairo, a more orderly, more disciplined, better supplied camp was created under General Grant's direction. Grant ordered that they must learn the basics, thoroughly and quickly. They must know how to stand at attention, shoulder, clean and fire a weapon, get into marching form and then into fighting columns. They must do all of this no matter what the terrain or weather or nearness of the enemy. So drilling went on morning, noon and evening—every day. A routine set in, as predictable as the daily rations of hardtack, coffee, and beans.

Ethan began to distinguish himself. It seemed this environment brought out his natural leadership qualities. Of all the members of the company he was in, he knew the most about firearms and was the best shot. He quickly became well-liked and respected. The officers above him noticed. They were looking for leaders. Soon Ethan was given charge of a company of men. He took the promotion in stride and vowed to himself he would maintain the men's trust. Now life in the army became more of a challenge and he did not mind so much the monotony and homesickness.

Missouri, December, 1861

The wind had picked up and the temperature was dropping. A low bank of dark blue clouds, thick and twisting, moved in from the west. The sun would be down in another hour or so, yet the camp was busy with activity. It was not battle preparation or drills, but men hurrying into the adjacent woods scrounging wood to make their huts warmer. Winter camp had been established by Grants' troops in southern Missouri. Winter had halted the war for a season.

"May be snow for Christmas."

A voice behind Ethan broke into his thoughts. He turned and nodded at the soldier. Andy Mill from Indiana was one of Ethan's regiment and had become one of Ethan's friends over the months

"It'll be the first time most of us have been away from home for Christmas," Andy continued.

Ethan did not miss the touch of longing in the man's voice. Andy was a quiet man, often to be found reading his Bible. He was easy to talk to and had a teasing boyish humor. He shrugged off the taunts about his thinness and his faith.

"Hey, fellas! Christmas dinner!"

The two turned and found a soldier happily waving two rabbits and two squirrels. From the hut came a fourth voice, "Come on in, boys, soup's on!"

Ethan shared a hut with four other men with whom he had forged friendships. Curly Brown, a jolly man of forty, was the self-appointed cook. He had taken all the packages from home and promised culinary delights. Moses Cobb, a short and round little farmer from northern Illinois and Sam Bass, a ferret-faced, taciturn soldier from Michigan, completed the group. They looked to Andy, who gave the blessing over the food. The thin soup was good and more importantly, warm. Ethan looked into his cup and couldn't help but think of home. Home... He stretched out his feet toward the fire, smiling, grateful again for Grandmother's knitted wool socks.

"First Christmas of the war..." mused Moses.

"Hopefully the last," added Andy quietly.

"Aw, Andy, we haven't even seen any action," returned Curly.

"Let's sing some carols, fellas, and Curly, cut that poundcake! It's Christmas eve!" encouraged Ethan.

Dear family,

I'm sorry I haven't written sooner. A bad cold laid me up for a week or so, but I'm a lot better now. Many men have been very sick. Haven't had much snow, but it is very cold. Even out in the wind we drill repeatedly. It keeps us warm for awhile. Thanks for the Christmas box. You would like these fellas I share a hut with. They are honest and decent. Commander Pillow has been pleased with me and I'm a Captain now. We're heading down to Tennessee day after tomorrow. The men are eager to get going. It will be the closest we've gotten to the enemy.

Ethan

Tennessee, 1862

The March winds were soft as winter finally loosened its grip in northern Tennessee. Grant's troops were encamped for a few days, still in high spirits about the victories at Forts Henry and Donelson. Casualties had been low for the Union.

Hopefully, Sunday was to be a day of rest for the men. Drills in the morning for an hour or so, then free time the rest of the day. There would be races and wrestling matches, card playing, haircuts and letters home. Simple church services were held early in the afternoon for those interested. Even for those not so inclined, most enjoyed the hearty choruses and hymns that came from the chaplain's tent.

Ethan, who had spent most of the morning with division officers, now joined Curly, Andy, Moses and Sam, who lazed in front of their tents. Too relaxed to care, their dirty dinner plates were heaped in the center of the group.

"You know, 'bout now my ma and pa are gettin' home from meetin'," Moses sighed. "They been smellin' hell's smoke all mornin' and Pa's powerful hungry. Ma'll go in and put on her apron and before you can change your Sunday pants she'll have a big pot of—"

"Aw, hush up, Moses," interrupted Curly. "You do this every Sunday. You get to talking about food, and it's plumb cruel!"

"Aw, let him finish," said Sam. "Makes me hungry too, but I kind of like it."

"Now, let's all say what we'd eat now if we could have anything!" proposed Moses.

So, around the small circle they went, each giving a personal menu, receiving accolades of groans, competing to see who stimulated the appetites best.

"Just cornbread. Half a dozen skillets of it. Big mug of buttermilk and a big ol' onion," said Curly.

"Roast. Big, thick pot roast. Lots of gravy, potatoes, cabbage and Mama's hot rolls," was Moses's offering.

Sam grew thoughtful a moment, rubbing his grizzled chin, then broke into a rare smile. "I'll never eat another bean all my life!" he exclaimed. "What I'd take is a dozen eggs, pound of bacon and coffee—real coffee!"

This brought cheers. Army coffee was considered somewhere between boiled tree bark and dirt. Then everyone looked to Andy, who lay dreamy-eyed on his back, his Bible open on his chest.

"Well... Don't know how I'd have it, in a pie or just fried. But when I get home, no chicken in Cameron county is safe!"

They all laughed.

"Okay, Alcott. What suits your taste?" asked Curly.

Ethan sat thinking of what a good cook his mother had been and how good his sisters were.

"I wonder," he began slowly, "if we ever really thanked our ma's for all those good meals we've been describing?"

Moses and Sam frowned when they heard his serious tone. Then Ethan brightened, "Today I'd give just about anything for an apple from my pa's orchard. Sittin' in my palm like this, it'd weigh about eight ounces. Red, scarlet red. And so crisp that when you bit into one the . . . Rebs would come running! I could eat a dozen easy. Then I'd have a big pitcher of cider, so cold it would make the back of your throat ache. Pie. Hot, juicy pie. My sisters' pies can't be beat."

The boys were begging Ethan to be quiet. He had never been so eloquent!

"Well, gosh, fellas. Didn't know ya'll been hankerin' for a pie," piped Curly's thin voice.

They looked to him, surprised.

"Sure thing, got one right here. Wife made it before I left." He held up his boot . . .

Later, Andy and Ethan alone remained at the tents. The others had gone to watch a stone-throwing contest. Andy had been quiet a long time and Ethan was about to fall asleep.

"What do you suppose you'll do when the war's over, Ethan? Stay in the army?"

"I don't know, Andy. Haven't given it very much thought. Not very ambitious, I guess."

"Go home to grow the best apples in Illinois?" Andy laughed.

"No. The best apples in the whole Union!"

"And you say you're not ambitious!" said Andy, closing his Bible.

"What about you?" asked Ethan.

"Can't you guess, Ethan?" He smiled sadly, making Ethan feel a bit uncomfortable. Maybe Andy's mood was becoming too serious.

"I'm trained as a printer back home. But when this is over, I'll get me a good horse, take my Bible and ride across the land, telling folks about the goodness of Christ."

"You mean become an ordained preacher?"

"Like your brother-in-law? No . . . I don't have time for that. I'll just ride and work among them and tell them that Christ is real and really interested in them." He straightened up, his face and eyes animated, his voice eager. "You see Ethan, when this war is over there will be lots of hurting folks. Hurting in their bodies and their spirits too. What else will they have seen but pain and death? They'll be bitter. Bitterness between Yanks and Rebs even after the last shot has been fired. Some will want to forgive but they'll be too full of pride. What about the negroes, Ethan? If the Union wins, what will he be free for? Work? Education? Too many men count a man's color above everything else. From Maine to Mississippi there will be confused people. Mothers grieving over lost sons, children grieving over lost pa's. Who but Christ can help them in all that pain? Have you ever lay in bed at night and felt so small, so totally alone?"

Ethan did not want his mind to return to thoughts of years ago, when he was a small boy alone with his mother. Yes, he had felt that way before. He wished Andy would change the subject. He shook his head to clear his gloomy thoughts.

"There's Christ, Ethan. To take away the loneliness. I want to introduce folks to Him." He stood up, stretching.

"There's great work ahead for me. Just wish this foolish war was over so I could get started."

His work had started—and the foolish war, sadly, was far from over. Ethan smiled at his friend and Andy gave him a friendly pat on the back.

"Didn't count on gettin' preached at today, did you?"

"Guess I need to recommend you to the chaplain!"

The next day Ethan brought the news to his friends.

"We march tomorrow, fellas. Pittsburg Landing. General Grant takes control of all the Union forces there."

"Any Johnny Rebs around?" asked Curly eagerly.

"Scouts say there may be a few. Nothing to worry about. We're just to sit tight till Buell gets there, then on down into Mississippi, where a big division of Confederates is forming. Anyway—get your gear ready."

Ethan noticed Andy's face at the announcement—pale and tense. Ethan knew without asking that Andy was very reluctant to fight. Ethan never questioned why the young man had volunteered. Though they were friends and the same age, somehow Ethan felt a sense of protection toward Andy—like an older brother toward a younger.

Only ten days separated them from one of the bloodiest days of the entire war. The thirst for battle would be very well satisfied—and the few men who survived it would be changed forever.

Chapter 3

Shiloh, Tennessee

◆◆ ◆◆ ◆◆

*W*ith the Union capture of Fort Henry and Fort Donelson, the Confederacy lost Kentucky and half of Tennessee. With Grant following, the Southern troops pulled back to Corinth, Mississippi, an important regional railroad center. Moving down the Tennessee River, Grant finally encamped at a crude little riverboat port called Pittsburg Landing. He would wait there for General Buell and his thirty thousand men.

But Albert Sidney Johnston, commander of the Confederates, was not about to allow the Federals the advantage of reinforcements. He launched a surprise attack. It was April 6, a beautiful spring morning—near a little country church called Shiloh.

The land surrounding Shiloh was a quilt of pastures, meandering cow paths, orchards and woods. Farm houses were scattered in the thinly populated county. Corinth, thirty miles away, was the nearest town of any real size. The topography around Shiloh was perfect for picnics, grazing cattle—and fighting armies.

When the Confederates opened fire that morning, Grant had no idea how inaccurate his scouts had been in reporting the location of the Southern lines. If he had, he would not have encamped so close to the enemy before Buell's arrival. His army of forty-two thousand was about to engage in a brutal struggle with the Confederate army—numbering forty thousand.

By noon, Ethan felt his head was going to burst. The confusion and noise of battle was indescribable. He felt as if he'd been thrown into some gigantic caldron of screaming bullets, cannon fire and smoke. There were yells and curses and men falling in pain or death all around him. It was quickly apparent this was not going to be as easy as the battles at Fort Henry and Fort Donelson. His wildest nightmares could never come close to this. There was not a moment to rest, no time to think. No time to talk.

He knew his men were flanked near him, but in the smoke and sunshine it was difficult to discern anything clearly. He lost sight of Curly, Moses, Sam and Andy early in the morning. He only fired and kept firing. He was thirstier than he'd ever been in his entire life, but there was no time to drink.

Then a part of his regiment surged forward and he was caught up with them. Stumbling, they entered a densely wooded area. Even here, there was no relief from the hail of bullets. Ethan had lost his sense of direction.

Suddenly he felt a painful sensation above his right ear and a blow that knocked him backwards off his feet. His rifle flew out of his hand and he was lying on the hard ground, looking up through tree branches at the late afternoon sky. He lay still a moment, trying to catch his breath. Then he felt the warm trickle of blood down his neck as he slipped into unconsciousness.

The Confederates were winning. Aggressively they pushed the Union army back, north toward the river. Union officers were shocked to find hundreds of terrified, confused soldiers huddled at the river banks. The Confederate victory seemed certain by late afternoon. Then, General Johnston was killed. The officers who assumed command were hesitant and uncertain. The Union finally held a thin line of defense as darkness approached. Darkness was coming—and with it a night of agony.

Both sides had left many of their wounded and dead on the battlefields of that horrible day. In some stretches of land, bodies carpeted the ground. Groans and cries rent the night air.

Around dusk, Ethan woke up. Uncertain at first where he was, he finally managed to pull himself up into a sitting position. He was terribly dizzy. He scooted himself backwards till he came to rest against a tree. He worked his handkerchief free and tried to wipe the thick blood from his face. His eyes finally adjusted to the gloom—and in a way he wished they hadn't. Bodies lay scattered everywhere around him, one about four feet away. Arms and legs were at odd angles. There was eerie silence.

The dizziness came on in a rush and a searing pain on the side of his head doubled him over. He vomited helplessly. Never in all his twenty-six years had he ever felt so wretched, so alone, so fearful. Perhaps this was only a very horrible dream. He pushed himself back into a sitting position and kept his eyes closed— until something happened that frightened him even more.

A human voice, slow and labored, spoke in a monotone from the carnage around him.

"Those . . . who . . . live by the sword . . . shall perish by the sword."

Ethan trembled violently, not daring to open his eyes. Then he heard a racking cough.

"Lord, oh Lord, please forgive me . . ."

Ethan finally opened his eyes and found the voice. A man was propped up like himself, against a tree, about twelve feet away. His uniform was gray color. The man reached up and pulled off his cap, and Ethan could see he was young. One hand was thrust into the breast of his coat. His voice came again and this time it was firmer.

"They shall hunger no more, neither thirst anymore. Neither shall the sun beat down on them, and the Lamb shall guide them to the springs of living water . . . and God shall wipe away every tear!"

Ethan closed his eyes as a spasm of pain and coughing racked the dying Confederate.

"And the Spirit and the Bride say 'Come!' And let the one who hears come and take the water of life . . . without cost . . . I come, Lord!"

Silence resumed with the fading of last rays of light. Ethan sat waiting, unaware of his own pain. But no more words came from the other soldier. Ethan opened his eyes, barely able to see his stark white face, slightly tilted, eyes closed in death. Loss of blood continued to take its toll and Ethan lapsed into darkness.

Peppercreek, Illinois

It was a beautiful spring night in Peppercreek. A full moon hung like a brilliant orb in the sky and Henri and Wyeth stood on the front porch drinking in the beauty of it. They were silent, words unnecessary, for they shared a deep reverence for the natural works of God's hands: In the land that changed robes with each season, in the sky's tumbling clouds of pale blue or its canopy of a million stars, they saw profound beauty; never the same, never growing old.

A slight breeze stirred and Wyeth shivered. Instinctively, Henri drew her closer.

"Do you remember when I left to go to California, years ago?" he asked.

"I remember."

"That night, the first night back on the trail, was a night like this. The moon was so bright. I was staring into the fire thinking about your family, how much they had come to mean to me. Your face seemed to glow out of the flames at me. I felt a surge of love for you like I'd never felt before. I glanced up at the sky... and you seemed as unattainable to me as the stars." He sighed, drawing her closer still. "And now look! Another night, and you by my side, my unattainable star! How good God is to me!"

His arms encircled her and they stood that way a long time.

"Do you think Ethan... sees the moon tonight, Henri?"

He nuzzled her hair. "It's hard for you not to worry about that little brother of yours, isn't it?"

"Yes, I suppose my faith isn't very big right now. I read the reports in the papers this afternoon..."

Henri whispered, "The Word says, 'the prayer of a righteous man availeth much.' We believe—we *know* He has His hand of love on Ethan, even now!"

Shiloh, Tennessee

The light rain brought Ethan instantly back to consciousness. He was weak, but he could feel no real pain. He shifted carefully, rolling onto his knees, gasping for breath with the effort. He had never felt this way—so weak and exhausted, and now in the dark woods he knew he faced a fight for survival. None of his training had prepared him for this. The stark reality was that he was forgotten, weak and wounded, exposed to the weather, with no idea how far his comrades had pulled back—or in which direction. For all he knew, they could have left the field entirely and be gliding up the Tennessee River. He could not be sure that if he stayed where he was till morning, he would survive the night. But he wanted to be up and away from here—even if death was a hundred yards away—even if he was taken prisoner.

He would never forget this night. Never. Then suddenly, in his mind he saw Rebecca—and he was a boy again. She was reviewing memory verses with him and Libby. Their voices were in unison.

> *He who dwells in the shelter of the Most High shall abide in the shadow of the Almighty. I will say of the Lord, my rock and my refuge, my God in whom I trust...*

The words came easily back to his mind, though he had not read or heard them in years. He remembered waking up at night to find his new mother sitting by his bed, her lips moving in prayer. Prayer.

"Oh Lord, please help me," he moaned. It was a prayer born of desperation.

Finally he made it to his feet. A few hundred yards of stumbling and groping brought him to a clearing. Then he heard the distant thunder of cannons. Amazed, then sickened, he realized that fighting had not ended with the darkness. After depositing Buell's troops, Federal gunboats were lobbing shells at the Confederate encampments. No peace, even at night.

His thoughts now were as unsteady as his steps. He had become separated from his men and totally lost. He felt angry with himself. Above all other thought was the desperate desire to lay down and sleep, to be safe and warm for a time.

He stumbled over a root and slid down a slight ravine. Again he felt the trickling of warm blood down his neck. Now, he thought to himself, just let me die... I can't go another step. Ethan, who had always been so strong, so self-reliant, was at his very lowest ebb. He pulled himself a few feet more, crawling really, surprised by a sudden bit of moonlight. What was it he saw? Tents... Squatty, scattered tents. There were no camp fires.

Suddenly, as if rising out of the ground before him, appeared a man. After the initial shock, Ethan found his voice.

"Do you have any water?" he gasped.

The man stretched forward, handing Ethan a half-full canteen. He drank greedily, trying hard not to gulp the entire contents.

"Who is it, Dan?" A voice called from the darkness.

"Don't know," said the man in front of Ethan.

"I'm ... freezing," Ethan groaned.

"We've just got this tent up, lad. Crawl in with us. We've even got dry blankets," came the more distant voice.

"Blast it, Joe! Do you have to be so all-durn charitable? There's hardly room for us," grumbled the man who had given Ethan the water.

"Come on, lad," Joe admonished Dan. "It's been a tarnation of a day," he said patiently.

Muttering, the man called Dan pulled Ethan inside the tent.

"Just stretch out, lad," Joe said kindly.

They pulled coats and blankets over themselves. There was an audible sigh from the tent mates, then silence as each labored with his own personal pain.

Finally Dan spoke, "Well, seeing we're bunkmates, guess we should introduce ourselves."

"Ethan Alcott," Ethan simply stated, his body relaxing. Conversation was the last thing he wanted right now, just sleep.

"Got an injury? " asked Joe.

"Scrape on the head."

"How's your leg, Dan?"

"Hurts like blazes ... still, you won't catch me near the surgeon's tent! Where you from, Joe?"

"Mississippi. You?"

"Texas."

Suddenly Ethan laughed out loud. In his fog of exhaustion, he had not noticed their accents until now.

"What's so funny?" rasped Dan.

"I can't believe this run of luck! Lost from my regiment, hit in the head—a Billy Yank sleeping between two Johnny Rebs!"

There was silence at this. He waited. They could slit his throat. Instead—they both chuckled.

"I'll be all-durned," said Dan.

Ethan was drifting off to sleep, barely hearing Dan's last words.

"It's been the devil's own day."

Sunlight penetrated the tent with precious warmth the next morning. Disorientation took hold of Ethan for a short time when he woke up. There was a dull ache on the side of his head and he was hungry. Hearing cannon fire roused him to reality. He sat up, muscles screaming with soreness. He turned to his right and found the blank stare of the soldier named Joe. Death had crept into the tent during the night. He moaned aloud.

"He's dead."

Ethan almost jumped, for he'd forgotten about Dan. He reached over Ethan and tenderly closed the soldier's eyes.

"Well... We'd best pile out, Billy. Another day."

They both crawled out of the tent. Ethan hesitated, it seemed so harsh to leave the body there.

"You look pretty nasty, Billy Yank," said Dan.

"You do too, Johnny Reb."

Their eyes held a moment, and they smiled.

Morning fog had evaporated. It was another beautiful day— perhaps an apology for the night before.

"Thanks for helping me, Dan," said Ethan easily.

Dan shrugged, "Hope you find your men all right, Yank."

"You too."

Then there were hoofbeats and three cavalrymen swept into view. They were rounding up stragglers, deserters, prisoners. They were Union. They rode up to Ethan and Dan and stopped.

"Well look here!" Their eyes quickly took in the situation.

"A boy in blue and a Reb together!"

There was low laughter. One cavalryman jumped down and strode up to Dan and grabbed him roughly. The Confederate brushed the hand away with a curse.

"Leave him alone!" said Ethan sharply.

The Union soldier ignored him and made for Dan again. Ethan's arm shot out and sent the soldier sprawling on top of the tent.

"What's the matter with you?" a soldier screamed at Ethan, his hand reaching for his pistol.

Ethan drew up to his full height as he dusted off his clothes.

"This is one Reb you're letting go, soldier. I'm Captain Ethan Alcott and I outrank all three of you."

Pale, with a growth of beard, blood stained, his eyes like sharp steel points, his voice was hard enough to cause the two on horseback to hesitate.

"Now, where's the nearest Confederate line?"

The two shifted uneasily in their saddles. Finally one pointed west.

"Good luck, Dan." Ethan nodded to the gray-clad soldier.

Dan nodded back and was off. Ethan cast one more look at the tent. Then he jumped on the dismounted man's horse and spurred it north before any of the soldiers could do anything. Again, impulsiveness had ruled Ethan's actions.

The jolting of the horse hurt his head more, but it got him behind Northern lines quicker. Fighting had renewed now, with the Union having the advantage of fresh, eager troops. After thirty minutes or so of riding, Ethan located his unit. By late afternoon, it was obvious the Confederates were losing all the ground they'd gained the previous day. They were limping south toward Corinth, and General Grant wisely assessed his troops were too worn and wounded to pursue. The next few days were spent cleaning up the battlefields. Steamboats began chugging up river, their decks stacked with wounded. The fields of Shiloh lay silent again.

Ethan's injury was healing and his strength returning. Yet he was unusually quiet, staring gloomily into the fire. His friends did not know what to think of the change. Two days later he was summoned to his commander's headquarters. He had been expecting it.

Ethan arrived at the white tent of his commanding officer and found him behind his camp desk, an agitated and weary expression across his face. He was not alone. Another officer stood stiffly beside the desk, his arms crossed, eyes blazing.

"How's your head, Ethan?" Major Sullivan asked kindly.

"Fine, sir, thank you."

"Perhaps it was . . . the injury that caused this officer to act so—outrageously," growled the other officer, a Major Winston.

His tone was tight and acidic. This, then was the commander of the cavalrymen Ethan had encountered. Sullivan did not look up at the remark, but focused on a fly traversing his desk.

"Ethan, ah . . . it seems some of Major Winston's men have some complaints against you. Now we don't have much time to cover this. General Grant has issued orders we press on to Corinth day after tomorrow. We'll rendezvous with Halleck—"

Winston loudly cleared his throat.

"But," Major Sullivan winced, his eyes on the cavalry commander, "we do need to get to the facts of this episode. So, tell us what happened."

Ethan briefed them, keeping his eyes on Sullivan. Winston paced, muttering curses. Ethan could not help but be reminded of a bad-tempered stallion his father once had. He stopped pacing when Ethan finished and spat angrily.

"I'd rot on the ground before I'd tent with the enemy!" Winston hissed.

Ethan said nothing. Sullivan leaned tiredly back in his chair.

"You've told the truth, Alcott?" he asked finally.

"Yes, sir. I—"

"Of course it is!" snapped Winston. "Who would make up such blasted stuff?" He came up close to Ethan. His voice was seething. "To get yourself separated from your men by accident or design, to actually encamp with the enemy and then encourage his escape! Then, to strike a fellow officer and pilfer his horse! This is the worst case I've ever heard, Alcott!" He wagged his finger in Ethan's face.

"Now, Winston—" began Sullivan.

"Most unbecoming conduct for an officer!" Winston persisted. "Did you go temporarily insane, Alcott?"

Ethan was silent, studying the canvas above Sullivan's head.

"I want this blasted man out. Out!" Winston shouted.

"Winston, Alcott's record—"

"His record is manure!"

"Winston, we just don't have enough good officers to drum them out over any little thing. Alcott is well-liked by his men."

"He's unfit! He can't humiliate fellow officers and go unpunished. Move him!"

Ethan shifted uncomfortably, caught in a power struggle.

"An officer cannot allow the enemy to escape. Why have a blasted war at all?" asked Winston peevishly.

"Why, indeed?" mumbled Sullivan.

"I will not allow this man to go un—"

"Enough, Winston, enough." Sullivan's chair came back down with a thud. "You've quartered Alcott well enough. Now, let me alone . . . to dispose of the pieces, eh?"

Winston gave one final glare at Ethan, then stalked out. The tent was silent and Ethan felt totally alone. Sullivan seemed lost in thought.

"You'll have to excuse Winston, Ethan. He lost three quarters of his men at the peach orchard. He's not feeling very forgiving. Now, sit down. This is very serious business, Ethan. I won't ask you to explain why you did any of it; you probably don't even know. We all do things sometimes without any real reason. And these last few days ..." His voice trailed off.

Ethan suddenly thought of his father, something he had said years ago. "One of these days Ethan, I'm afraid your impulsiveness is going to get you into serious trouble. And it will be bigger than the Denham brothers." Apparently, Ethan thought grimly, that day had come.

"Sir, the man, the Confederate, he saved my life!" Ethan said fervently. "I couldn't do any less than let him go! He was one man, not a regiment. I ... don't know. Maybe I can't follow the rules of war so much anymore. I shouldn't have struck the officer or taken his horse. I acted without thinking."

Ethan's head had begun to pound again. Sullivan pressed his fingertips together, watching the young man.

"We throw out rules of kindness in war, Ethan. You say and do things ... you'd never dream of doing at another time. I went out with the cleanup detail yesterday. I couldn't believe ..." He spread his hands helplessly.

"But if I think about it too much ... Your Rebel may or may not have made it back to his line, thanks to you. Winston wants your hide, Ethan, and I'm powerless to help you. You're still a good officer to me. But—"

An aide pushed open the tent flap and handed Sullivan a note. The major read it quickly, chuckled and crumpled the paper.

"Our fearless leader is just that! Fearless—until it comes to newspaper people and Congressmen. Ha! Well, here now ..." He stopped to think, then continued.

"All right then. Secretary Stanton wants a personal dispatch about this engagement with the enemy. The press is giving him fits."

Outrage and grief was sweeping across north and south alike
as papers reported the unbelievably high casualties. How could
so many men be killed in roughly sixteen hours of fighting?

"I can't do much for you now, Ethan, but save your rank. I'll
write up Grant's reports, then you'll be the personal envoy to
deliver them."

"Washington, sir?"

Sullivan nodded. "There's a steamboat leaving in the morning."

"Then what, sir? I mean—after I deliver the report?"

"They'll find a place for you." Sullivan waved his hand non-
committally. He led Ethan outside.

"I'm sure this seems hard to you, son, but I'm sure you'll do
well in your new position. Don't think poorly of all us military
men, we— Ah, General!"

A man of military dress had ridden up, dismounted, and
come up to Sullivan. Ethan noticed his broad-brimmed hat,
luxurious mustache, flowing cape.

"Good morning, sir. Captain Alcott, this is General Wallace."

"Sir." Ethan saluted.

The officer gave Ethan a quick nod.

"Can't ride out with you, sir," Major Sullivan apologized.
"General Grant wants a report."

Wallace's gaze extended over the hazy fields, and Ethan and
Sullivan followed it.

"Pretty grim stuff, this battle at Shiloh," said Sullivan quietly.

"Shiloh," came Wallace's low voice. "Do you know what
Shiloh means, Captain?"

Ethan shook his head.

"Shiloh means 'place of peace.'"

Only Andy and Sam could accompany Ethan down to the
landing the next morning. He had said his goodbyes to Curly and
Moses the night before. The sun was slowly rising in a yellow mist
over the muddy river bank where the three stood waiting for
Ethan to board. An air of confusion hung over the scene: hundreds of wounded were being loaded onto the line of riverboats.
Officers' barked orders mingled with the groans of pain.

"Well, looks like your traveling companions won't be too sociable," said Sam dryly.

Ethan looked at the scene around him, feeling his throat tighten, still in shock over the sudden change in his circumstances.

"You're fortunate you're traveling healthy anyway," said Andy slowly, trying to cheer his friends up.

Ethan looked at him, knowing he should be at the surgeon's tent.

"This is sneakin' business anyway," growled Sam. "Sullivan is a skunk and Winston's a bigger one!"

Ethan had told them everything—except his time in the forest. He could not talk about that. He remembered the speech of the dying Confederate.

"Andy, where is this Scripture found?" he asked. "'Behold, I am coming quickly and my reward is with me, to render each man according to what he had done.'"

He had repeated it perfectly after hearing it only once. Andy could not conceal his surprise.

"That's from the book of Revelation."

Ethan studied his boots a moment. "How about this one? 'Those that live by the sword, shall perish by the sword.'"

Andy's already pale face blanched even more, for his gentle soul had recoiled at the bloody business he was involved in.

"That's in the gospel of Matthew. Why—"

But a call from the boat told Ethan it was time to say goodbye.

The three shook hands.

"I...wish you could go in my place, Andy. I mean, so you could get some decent food and rest."

Andy smiled. He would miss this friend very much.

"Don't worry about me, Ethan. Lord's watchin' over us."

"And I'll cover his backside," said Sam roughly.

The three laughed nervously. Goodbyes in times like these were often final. Ethan boarded the *Emerald Belle*, waving quickly to the two men on the bank.

He found a place in the stern. Some had curious stares for him, one of the few uninjured men on board. No one could fail to notice Ethan's air of dejection, as obvious as his soiled uniform.

He was frowning and sullen, daring anyone to speak to him. He sighed, knowing it would only be a matter of time before he was put to work among the wounded. He turned his face north as the *Emerald Belle* chugged up the Tennessee River.

Chapter 4

Washington, D.C., May, 1862

✦✦ ✦✦ ✦✦

*F*ort Stevens was only one of fifty forts that encircled the thirty-seven mile perimeter of the city. Ethan had been given a small, plain but private room. For ten days he waited for a word from the War Department after he had deposited Grant's dispatch. Staring out the window, he wondered when the fog would lift and give him a decent view of the city. He felt as if a fog had descended upon him too, leaving him frustrated and forgotten. The long idle hours made him pessimistic. A brilliant military career, or even a fairly significant one, had burned to ashes. He had not written his family yet—what could he tell them?

Suddenly the door to his room swung open, and a man walked in. The man's glance rested only briefly on Ethan, then traveled around the small room. Ethan looked him over quickly. The man, perhaps in his late fifties or early sixties, was dressed expensively, a jeweled hand resting on an elaborate cane. His brown eyes were keen.

Ethan grew impatient as the man continued his silent perusal.

"Guess I don't know you, sir."

"Are you certain of that?"

Ethan was in no mood for guessing games.

"I'm sure. You must have the wrong room."

"Captain Ethan Alcott, late of the 21st. Illinois Regiment under Major Woodrow Sullivan. Adopted son of William and Rebecca O'Dell, Peppercreek, Illinois."

The man lit a cigar, never taking his eyes off Ethan. Ethan said nothing, not particularly liking the advantage this man had over him.

"You a lawyer?" Ethan finally asked.

The man gave a short, hollow laugh. "No, I'm not a lawyer. I do have a few scruples left. The name's J.A. Packer, Captain Alcott." He extended his hand. "Why are you here, Captain?"

Ethan's voice was bitter. "You know enough about me, you should know why I'm here."

"I'd like to hear your side of it."

"Why?" snapped Ethan.

"I might be interested."

Ethan felt confused by this man's manner, but he apparently was not going to say anything else until Ethan answered him.

"There's not much to tell..." And Ethan, though not in the mood to talk, began to open up. He told the stranger everything, from the night in the forest near Shiloh, to sleeping with the Confederates, to the next morning and his mission east.

"Why did you allow that soldier to return to his line?"

The question was asked without accusation, yet it so surprised Ethan, he answered irritably. "Yes, he was just a Rebel, just a Johnny Reb. He shared his canteen and his tent. He probably saved my life. I hurt the same as he did. If I hadn't let him go, he'd have gone to prison. Somehow... I just couldn't do that. I've had a lot of time to think lately, Mr. Packer, and... I would do it again."

Ethan sat down wearily on his narrow bed.

"So, they shipped you off here, to figure out what to do with you," Packer said, walking to the window. "You still don't remember me?"

Ethan shook his head.

"New Salem Road, about twelve years ago."

"New Salem Road? You... and—a black fella!"

Packer nodded. "You intervened in a little disagreement I had with some local toughs."

"The Denham brothers."

"Yes."

"Well, talk about old trails crossin'!" Ethan said with a smile.

"I'm late for an appointment," Packer said. "I'll return tomorrow." And as quickly as he had appeared, he was gone.

Two days passed before he returned, striding into Ethan's room as abruptly as before.

"I've been looking into your story," Packer stated curtly, without preamble.

"You mean you didn't believe me?" Ethan exclaimed. "Would I make something like that up? Why are you so interested in my story, anyhow?"

Packer gave a curious half smile that Ethan would learn to know well. "I'm undersecretary to Mr. Stanton. In the War Department."

Ethan digested this. "Well, did he get the dispatch?"

"He did. Now, Captain, what are your plans?"

"Plans? You tell me, sir! You tell me."

"Your military record still stands well. This other matter... Does it suggest a disloyalty, I wonder?"

"Look, Mr. Undersecretary, I served eight months. I volunteered. I ... did my best. None of the men I knew particularly liked trying to kill a man. We followed orders. We chose sides. We don't know fully what this war is all about, but my turning that Confederate loose has nothing to do with my loyalty to the Union."

"And our President?"

"President Lincoln? I figure he's doing the best job he can."

Packer fingered his watch chain awhile. "You can still serve the Union... I'm prepared to offer you a position with the War Department."

"Doing what, sir?"

"Personal aide to President Lincoln."

Ethan said nothing, shocked at such an offer. Packer's shrewd eyes studied Ethan a moment before he continued.

"To work with the President's personal secretaries, Mr. Hay and Mr. Nicolay. To coordinate travel arrangements, advance details of public outings and such. To stop an assassin's attempt against the President's life... with your own life if necessary."

"What about this ... 'aiding the enemy' mess on my record?"

"All taken care of," stated Packer flatly. "If you're interested, and acceptable to Stanton, I'll send you to New York for a time. There's a West Point professor there who will tutor you. Give you a very quick, concentrated course on security matters. When he thinks you're ready, you'll come back to D.C. and serve the President. Are you interested, Captain?"

"Well, yes, sir. It's just that this is so sudden, it's hard to take in."

"I thought we were all insufferably slow-witted over at the War Department, Captain."

"Oh," Ethan flushed. "Listen, I'm sorry about my bad humor before. I guess this waiting just got to me."

"Get your gear together, Captain. You have an appointment with a man who does not like to be kept waiting."

To anyone who noticed on that cold yet sunny January day of 1863, the young officer who stepped off the 4:08 from Baltimore seemed confident and at ease. With the collar of his wool cape turned up, he looked like so many officers who passed through the city daily, always and forever, on business connected with the war. Editorials of the city's newspapers were often pointing out rather snippishly, with so many officers to be seen on Washington streets and in Washington bars, who was managing the war down south?

Still, Ethan didn't feel particularly at ease or confident. Arriving in Washington after three-and-a-half months in New York, he felt this was another beginning for him. He was nervous with energy and the deep desire to do this job well, to merit the confidence Mr. Packer and Secretary Stanton had shown in him. Securing a hack, he rode into the heart of the Union capital.

Washington D.C. was not a centuries-old capital of culture, sophistication and classical architecture, like European capitals. It was a new city, a city that hadn't changed much in the sixty years since its birth. A city with lofty dreams and ambitions—yet in 1863, it was little more than a sprawling, untidy collage of unfinished government offices, hastily built public buildings and private homes. It was the seat of government, set down in a wilderness.

Ethan leaned forward in his seat, not minding the cold, getting his first real view of the capital. The hack driver, realizing he had a newcomer to the city—and perhaps a heavy tipper—became loquacious through his woolen muffler.

With his whip he pointed out to Ethan all the points of interest in a definite Southern drawl.

"That's the Post Office. There's the Patent Office and the Treasury."

"The red towers there?"

"The Smithsonian Institute, gaudy if you ask me. They say there's all kinds of old stuff in glass cabinets there; I just don't know. And that, sir, is the humble home of our President."

The hack had stopped in front of the Executive Mansion. Foreign dignitaries were known to sneer, calling it rustic. It did remind Ethan of the mansions he had seen down South some years ago. An iron fence enclosed the grounds, but Ethan noticed the big open gates. He would soon realize this was one government that gave no pretension to its leader's home. The public came and went at will.

The driver pointed out Lafayette Park directly in front of the White House.

"That statue there is of Andy Jackson...and I'll leave you to your own opinion."

Ethan smiled. "That's the War Department through the trees, isn't it?"

The driver nodded, "Where they manage...or mismanage the war, yes, sir."

Then came the drive by the Capitol. Even in its state of incompletion, Ethan was impressed. It stirred him inexplicably— its tall marble columns and marble extensions. The original dome was gone and the new cast-iron dome was surrounded by scaffolding.

"The dome ain't finished yet, as you can see. The President has taken considerable fuss over spending the money to finish it. Know what he said 'bout it?"

"No, what did he say?" Ethan leaned forward to catch the words of his soon-to-be boss.

"Says he, 'If folks see the work go forward on the Capitol, it will help them remember the Union goes on too.' That's what he said, yep."

The driver then turned north, and gave Ethan a quick tour of a section of fine homes and churches.

He revolved his wad of tobacco saying, "Now I'll take you down the Avenue, and you'll have 'bout seen it all."

Pennsylvania Avenue had also been conceived under vaulted hopes, a broadly majestic thoroughfare connecting Capitol and Executive Mansion. While it indeed had become the city's main artery, it was hardly imposing. The thin cobbles had given up in despair under constant traffic and poor drainage, and had become a road of bone-jarring ruts and bumps. After days of rain the avenue was slick with mud. In summer, that mud would turn to a fine, dry dust that rose to choke riders and pedestrians.

There was every kind of conveyance on the avenue that afternoon—riders on horseback, enclosed carriages, hacks, farm wagons and ox carts. Ethan watched in fascination as an elaborate carriage had to stop to allow a dozen hogs to pass by on their way to the government butcher. Boot blacks and newspaper boys hailed from every corner.

"I need a place to stay, a hotel," Ethan said finally.

The driver was pleased to be asked. After all, let Mr. Lincoln run the government. He, a hack driver, really knew Washington.

"There's the National and that one with the marble columns is Brown's." Here he reached a corner. "This is Willard's and I guess I know it's the place."

Ethan thought a moment. "Drop me there, please."

Willard's Hotel, located at the intersection of Pennsylvania Avenue and Fourteenth Street, was considered more the seat of government than the Capitol. Willard's was the place to be. With its long bar and extravagant dining room fare, politicians, military leaders and foreign dignitaries all found a place.

Ethan stepped through the door and was immediately amazed. Every tongue and tribe was represented here and the din from the public rooms was almost deafening. A cloud of blue smoke floated from the bar, testament to at least a hundred puffing Union cigars. To Ethan's right came the clang and clatter of the enormous dining room. From the parlor directly in front of him, he could see men in groups, gesturing, arguing, debating. Ethan began to have his doubts about this place. Could a man actually get any sleep here?

Fifteen minutes later Ethan closed the door to room #410. It was amazing, but he could hear nothing of the crowd of life below him. The room was not Willard's finest, but was certainly suitable and luxurious to Ethan. Soft Oriental carpet, double beds, a small table, two chairs, a washstand and wardrobe comprised Ethan's new home. He crossed quickly to the windows. He was glad to have two. He would be able to see up and down the avenue.

He looked around the room again. So, this would be home. He must write his family as soon as he had something to eat. They would be eager to hear from him and there was so much to try to describe. He stood before the window, hands thrust deeply into his pockets—lost in thought. The turns his life had taken this past year ... Home to army camp, to Shiloh, to New York ... now here. Through the bare tree branches he could see the silver thread that was the Potomac River and, to the north, the roof of the White House. A new beginning ...

"To protect the President, Alcott, you've got to know who his enemies are—those who make themselves known, and those who don't. It's very wise you chose Willard's. When you're not on duty, you'll feel the pulse of the public there. Absorb the talk, the sentiment of the people. Absorb ... much else, and you'll be useless to me."

Ethan smiled but Packer did not return it.

"It would probably surprise you to know the vehemence some folks feel against a man who hasn't been around D.C. that long."

The two rode toward the War Department in Packer's personal carriage.

"Don't think because folks liked him in Springfield, Illinois, they like him here. Fact is, Washington is a southern city. Just happens to be planted on the wrong side of the Potomac. Three daily papers and only one pro-Union. There's enough Rebel blood in this town to compose several impressive regiments." Packer's voice was clipped, factual, unemotional. "The President has enemies in the Senate, the Treasury, the War Department, the newspapers, even the clergy. Folks don't like him because he doesn't go to their church, or they don't like him for his beard, or his top hat or his jokes. They don't like him because of his wife, or his sons, or because he didn't give them a job that they thought they had a claim to. Abolitionists don't think he's tough enough and the 'Sesh' think he's out to get them personally. See my point?"

"Yes, sir."

"Any one of them could put a bullet through his head, given half a chance. You're not to give them half a chance. You may be strong in limb, Alcott, but your ears and eyes will be the most important in this job. This isn't loafers' work. You may wish quite a few times you were back at the front."

The carriage came to a stop at the War Department and they started up the steps.

"Mr. Packer, sir . . . I want you to know how much I appreciate this opportunity you've given me. I'll do my very best, sir. You won't be disappointed."

Ethan's voice had that eager, boyishly innocent, want-to-please quality that was not lost on the older man. He turned away from Ethan, a bitter smile crossing his lips. Young, innocent, eager . . . Yes, J.A. Packer had been that—once. An awkward silence followed, and Ethan realized this man would not be one given to easy confidences.

"I have every expectation you will do your best, Captain."

The lives of these two men, twined years earlier, grew more so—with a future neither could imagine.

Dear family,

I am well and hope you are also. I am in Washington now and have been one week. I've seen so much I don't know where to begin. I live in a room in a fancy hotel called Willard's. I'm on the fourth floor so that I can see down the "Avenue." Pennsylvania Avenue is the main street of the city and you've never seen so much going on in your life. I'm still getting used to the noise of it at night. Ambulances and army supply wagons go up and down it at all hours of the night. Can you imagine a place that doesn't serve breakfast till eleven in the morning? And then it's oysters and blanc mange *and other fancy stuff. Don't worry, I go to a quiet place nearby to eat. I won't ruin my digestion, as Grandmother says . . .*

Today I went to the White House for the first time. Mr. Packer wanted me to ramble around it while the Lincolns were away. The doorkeeper, Mr. McManus has been at the White House forty years and says he can tell me plenty! Well, this letter can't tell you all what it's really like inside. Sorry girls, I know you want details. There is thick carpet, chandeliers, gold-frame mirrors and wallpaper that has fabric on it! The state dining table will sit sixty people. Mr. Hay was telling me they have a real problem with folks coming in and

cutting pieces off the drapes or wallpaper for souve-
nirs, can you beat that? As Grandmother would say, "I
just wonder where they're from." Anyway that will be
part of my job, to watch over and organize all the
people who come to see the President. I haven't met
Lincoln yet and I guess I do feel nervous about it . . .

Ethan

The White House, January 1, 1863

The President carefully pulled off his glasses. His voice, Ethan noticed, was tired—yet firm.

"An aide, Mr. Stanton, as you well know, is just a fancy name for a bodyguard. Switching titles doesn't make a horse chestnut a chestnut horse."

"We've been over this before, Mr. President—" Stanton's voice was testy.

"Indeed we have, Mr. Stanton. You know my feelings. It is unbecoming for the Chief Executive of a democratic nation to have an armed bodyguard."

Stanton was clearly exasperated. "It is for your own protection! You know there have been threats."

Lincoln stood up and strolled to the window. "I remind all of you, if anyone wants to kill me he will do it. Carrying a cane as Mrs. Lincoln insists, or a bodyguard as you suggest will not change that."

A tense silence filled the President's office.

Packer spoke up. "What we propose, Mr. President, is for Captain Alcott to serve as an aide for you here in the White House, run errands for you, and so forth. A capacity not unlike your personal secretaries. Mr. Hay and Mr. Nicolay do very well, but cannot possibly do everything—screen people for appointments, for example. Outside the White House, Captain Alcott would be merely an escort. If you insist, we can compromise. Captain Alcott will not be armed."

Ethan saw Stanton move to protest, but Lincoln cut him off.

"Very strategic, Mr. Packer," Lincoln smiled. "Perhaps you should be one of my generals. Well, why don't you two go hunt up some tea or something until Seward gets here. Let me get acquainted with my new . . . aide from Illinois."

Ethan sighed inwardly, relieved that Lincoln had agreed, but still stiff with nervousness. Lincoln indicated a leather chair for Ethan while he himself took the one just opposite. Ethan had the opportunity to study the leader now, to see how much, if at all, the years had changed him. Lincoln slouched in the chair rather than sat, his long legs sprawled far out in front of him, his long arms draped over the sides. His eyes were the same as Ethan remembered: deep set and dark, under eaves of shaggy brows. He looked as if he had combed his hair with his fingers. His face was much more lined. His ears, mouth and nose were as generous as the papers described. But it was the eyes that drew Ethan—a mixture of sadness, fatigue and tenderness. Ethan would have months to learn the mobility of that face, the theater of emotions that played across it. It was a challenging face, a face beyond definition.

Lincoln finally broke from his personal reverie to focus on the young man in blue before him. Ethan could not know Lincoln's thoughts of course, but Lincoln was pleased at the healthy, strong picture of manhood across from him. Lincoln had not wanted to give in to Stanton—but, these days there was so much . . . It was too tiring to battle over everything. He spoke.

"It's been a rule of my life that if people won't turn for me, I'll turn for them. You avoid collisions that way." Lincoln smiled slowly. "'Course that's not always easy."

"Yes, sir."

The President drew out his watch. "Tell me where you're from exactly, Captain."

"Peppercreek, Sangamon County, sir."

Lincoln's face lit up instantly and he slapped his knee.

"Well, that Packer is a shrewd one!"

"You came to our home once, sir, when you rode the circuit."

"Oh? Then I know your family?"

"My father is William O'Dell. Your horse had thrown a shoe and my father helped you. You stayed to dinner."

"You see! I *was* a politician back then! Yes, I remember now—the best apple pie I'd ever had."

Ethan smiled. "Yes, sir."

They both laughed. The weariness seemed to drop off the leader. His voice and gestures became animated as he talked of home. Thirty minutes passed effortlessly as they swapped fishing tales and talk of families they both knew, and weather and crops. Ethan could not help but relax.

"Mother'll be happy to know that we have someone from home here with us," Lincoln said. "Sometimes . . . she feels the capital isn't an altogether friendly place."

Then Lincoln's eyes swung to focus on the wall where a large map hung. Ethan had glanced at it when he had entered the office. He knew what the red and blue pins indicated. Lincoln ran a bony finger down the bridge of his nose. His words were slower and deeper.

"Mr. Packer said you were at Shiloh."

"Yes, sir." Ethan felt a tightening inside.

"Do you know I've never met General Grant? What's your opinion of him?"

Ethan didn't have much opinion, since he had no direct contact with Grant. So he could say little as Lincoln turned from pleasant home memories to the present. The President wanted to know about life in the army for the enlisted man, and Ethan could tell him about that.

Then young John Hay stuck his head in the doorway.

"Mr. Seward's here, sir."

"Fetch Packer and Stanton, will you, John?" said Lincoln, rising.

"Thank you, Mr. President," Ethan said. "I enjoyed our talk, sir."

Ethan felt the full strength of Lincoln's penetrating eyes. Some said the man had a way of looking so closely at you, you felt he could see clear to your back button.

"Since Mr. Stanton and Mr. Packer must have their way, Ethan, and we'll be together a good bit, call me Mr. Lincoln and I shall have a resting spell from 'Mr. President'." His voice was friendly.

Ethan hesitated and Lincoln extended his hand. They shook as Seward, Stanton, Packer and the two secretaries reentered. Seeing Lincoln's cheerier face, Stanton gave Packer and Ethan a quick nod.

The deal was settled. The chief executive had a bodyguard.

Secretary of State Seward placed the broad sheet before Lincoln at his desk while the others grouped around him. No one said a word as Lincoln dipped his pen in the inkstand. This was too large a moment in human history for worthless chatter—and every man there felt it.

The signature would be a paradox—an ending and a beginning, a birth and a death.

Lincoln's pen hesitated. "I have been receiving calls in the East room all morning, shaking hands, till now my arm is stiff and numb. Now this signature will be examined closely, and if they find my hands trembled they'll suspicion I had some reservations."

Everyone chuckled. He carefully wrote, then passed the pen to Seward. January first, 1863. The Emancipation Proclamation was now the law of the United States of America.

"I've never in my life felt more certain than I am about signing this paper. It's done."

It was a momentous day for the lawyer-turned-president; a momentous day for all Americans; and an unforgettable first day of work for the young "aide" from Illinois.

In a few short weeks, Ethan became familiar with the geography of the capital city. He had met Mary Lincoln, sons Tad and Robert, the White House staff and several Cabinet members. Congressmen and senators who came and went, he knew by sight. John Hay had helped him in this education and Ethan was very grateful. When the President was in the White House, Ethan helped with the great number of people who came seeking an audience. Ethan was amazed at all whom Lincoln would see in just one day. "He's determined to be available to all the people," Hay had said aside to Ethan, "even if it kills him."

Often he rode to the Capitol for the President, carrying legislation. When Lincoln rode to the Navy Yard, Ethan rode beside him. Every day they crossed the White House lawn to the War Department. Lincoln wanted all the news firsthand.

Lincoln, generous and obliging, accepted Ethan quickly, liking the company of the personable captain. They never talked of war, always home. When the reports of a battle were forth-coming, the tired face grew even grayer. "I can feel bad news in the wind," he would sigh.

One noon Ethan and Packer sat in the dining room of Brown's, finishing their meal, discussing the callers who had come to the White House that morning.

"So, the congressman just kept on and on at Lincoln. The door was open and John and I couldn't help but overhear. We kept waiting for the President to get irritated with the fellow, and when the man finally takes a breath the President looks over his bald head and says, 'My, how close you shave!'"

Ethan went off into another gale of laughter and Packer himself allowed a slight smile.

The congressman went off in a great huff and Mr. Welles says to the President, 'Do you manage all Congress that way?' The President replied, 'You don't suppose strategy is all with the army do you?'"

Ethan noted Packer's quick change of mood as a man approached their table. Packer's smile faded.

"Well J.A., good afternoon. This must be the new aide I haven't met."

Ethan stood up and extended his hand. Packer didn't rise.

"Ethan, this is Senator Sims. Sims, Captain Alcott."

They shook hands and the senator drew a chair up to the table.

Trenton Sims was a lean man of strict economy. He gave out smiles infrequently. He never wasted words or publicly vented anger. He was the perfect picture of a man in control, quite satisfied with himself. He was one of the wealthiest men in government. He was a man of purpose and goals—and he had failed in precious few so far.

"So, how is Mr. President this afternoon?" Sims asked.

"Fine," clipped Packer.

"Glad to hear of Burnside's resignation. Not much of a general."

The resignation of Union General Burnside was not yet public knowledge.

"The President had faith in him," countered Packer.

"Our President is loyal to his generals, that's true. Despite the fact we're turning out a record lot quite unsuited for our loyalty. However," he turned his gaze back on Ethan, "I'm sure he knows best. Hooker will be better."

No one said a word and Ethan felt distinctly uncomfortable.

"Well, Captain Alcott," Sims continued, "how do you find your new job?"

"I like it, sir. It's very interesting."

"I can imagine."

"Daddy, there you are!"

A feminine voice interrupted them and all three men stood. A young woman had come up to the table in a flounce and flurry of silk.

"Amanda, this is Captain Alcott, President Lincoln's new aide. Captain, this is my beautiful daughter, Amanda."

Whatever Ethan managed to bumble out he forgot as he looked at the lovely young woman. There was nothing lean or economical about Amanda Sims. Ethan would later learn she was Washington's most eligible and sought-after young woman. Many considered her Washington's real hostess, far above the dowdy Mary Lincoln.

Yet Amanda Sims was no brainless beauty. She made no secret that her ambition matched her brilliant father's. She would have him as president, while she reigned as first lady.

Her smile was friendly as she held out her hand to Ethan.

"An aide to the President? How exciting! Captain, you must come see me sometime and tell me about your work."

Ethan was speechless.

"Yes, Captain, come by sometime. Well, Amanda."

"Nice to meet you Senator, Miss Sims," Ethan finally managed.

The two moved off and Ethan stood a moment, absorbed in thought.

"Think we can go back to work, or are you too addled?" Packer asked coldly.

"She's so beautiful!" gushed Ethan as they headed out the door.

"Yes, there is a certain beauty to spiders, I suppose," Packer murmured to himself.

Chapter 5

Peppercreek, Illinois, July, 1863

◆◆ ◆◆ ◆◆

*W*yeth sat in the shade of the oak by the creek wishing there was at least a breeze. She stretched her bare feet into the cool water. She could feel herself growing sleepy. Hasn't the Lord been so good to me, she thought drowsily...

She slept for only a few minutes, until suddenly a shadow passed over her face and awakened her. She sat up, fearful someone had been close without her knowing. Yet no one was in sight. What an odd sensation... Suddenly she felt she must close her eyes—not in fear, but in expectation and reverence. Never had she felt such a powerful urge to pray. Then, one thought rang clear in her mind.

"Have you thanked Me for your childlessness?"

So clear and penetrating, Wyeth never doubted it was from the Lord. Perhaps there was a split second of hesitation before she lay down that one petition...so painful, so close to her heart. Tears came, but Wyeth felt a deep sense of trust for Him with whom she had trusted her life. "Everything, Lord," she whispered fervently, "even my desire for a child...even Henri, and my family...everything to You."

One evening some weeks later, Henri and Wyeth were in their room preparing for bed. Wyeth stood before the mirror brushing out her hair while Henri sat tugging off his boots. His voice was excited. Today fourteen-year-old Toby Johnson had come to Henri with questions about the Lord. It was a beginning they had both prayed for, especially since Toby was nagging to join the army. Wyeth crossed over to Henri and sat in his lap, leaning her head on his shoulder. He became silent as his arms went around her. Henri relished the fragrance of her hair, her nearness.

Her voice came, almost childlike, "Henri, I'm so thankful God brought us together. I love you so much and I need you so much. I don't know if I'll ever...be able to give you a child. It's what I've wanted, but I don't think it's His plan. But...I have peace about it now."

Wyeth was surprised that Henri said nothing for several minutes. She could only feel his steady breathing.

"Wyeth, I love you more than I can possibly tell you." Finally Henri stood, carrying his wife across the room.

"Henri put me down! You'll hurt your back!"

"As if you were heavy!" laughed Henri. "I'll not put you down. I enjoying carrying my wife. Besides, I have a question."

"What?"

"I'm glad you've come to a peace about children. But—"

"But what?"

He nestled his face in her neck. "We ... can still try, can't we?"

Washington, D.C., July, 1863

Ethan stood before the mirror in his room, carefully combing his hair. He smiled at the reflection. He'd begun to take more care with his appearance of late—and he knew why. Last month Amanda Sims had suggested he grow a mustache. She had held his arm and looked up into his eyes, smiling. "It would make you older looking, more distinguished, and even more handsome."

So he had endured the scratchy business and taken all the comments from those he worked with. When it had become fully apparent what he was doing, the President had looked over his spectacles a fraction longer than usual, but said nothing.

Personally, Ethan didn't like the growth of hair on his upper lip. It felt so strange. He had the vague feeling he was trying to be someone other than himself. Then Amanda had studied him critically as he escorted her to a Washington party.

"No, Ethan, I was wrong. Shave in the morning. You look like a Rebel prisoner!"

So he had shaved at the fair lady's request, relieved, and glad his family back home hadn't seen him that way.

Now he was preparing to go with Amanda to a lawn party over in Arlington. It was a sultry afternoon, and Ethan knew he'd be mixing with the cream of Washington society. Since February, when he'd met the Senator's daughter, he had been with her four times, always at her invitation. She was always so interested in his work, and could talk politics as forcefully and knowledgeably as any cigar-chomping Unionist swilling drinks at Willard's bar. She would smile up into his eyes and Ethan would believe he was her favorite beau.

Satisfied with his appearance, Ethan hurried downstairs. He threw a quick glance into the parlors where the predictable blue smoke hung. Willard's was at peak capacity despite the oppressive summer heat. Gossip was thick in the city these last few days. Reports were sketchy, often contradictory. However, one theme prevailed in all the rumors: General Robert E. Lee was moving north with a massive portion of his army.

Amanda greeted him gaily as they climbed into her carriage. "Oh Ethan, you look so much better!" Her hand rested lightly on his clean-shaven cheek and he liked the softness of it. Her ivory face, so young and lovely, was close to him, and he wanted to lean down and kiss her.

Turning away, Ethan clucked to the horses. "It's a hot one today."

Amanda had seen the desire in his eyes and it pleased her. She raised her parasol. Her lips formed a pout. "Daddy's leg is much better. We're leaving for the coast next week. It'll be so much cooler up there."

"Is it safe for you to travel?"

"Why not?"

"Well, Lee, the rumors..."

She tossed her hair, "Oh Ethan, Bobby Lee is a very small concern for me. I'll have my vacation. It's just a rumor, like every summer. Hooker will put some fear in that Rebel."

Ethan knew from War Department reports this was not true. Hooker was not ready to fight. Lincoln had haunted the War Department telegraph office all week with Ethan at his side. A cot had been set up for him to rest while waiting for news.

"Will you be able to come to the Independence Day dance, Ethan?" Amanda was asking him. But he didn't hear her question. They were just driving past the War Department and Ethan saw a crowd gathering on the steps. It could only mean one thing: they were waiting for news. One of the rumors had become a reality. Ethan recognized a clerk he knew and called to him.

"What is it, Hal?"

"Lee's attacked," the clerk said grimly.

"Attacked? Where?"

"Pennsylvania. Little place called Gettysburg."

"Pennsylvania. That's General Meade. He won't be ready," Ethan murmured. "I'm sorry, Amanda," he said, turning to her. "You'll have to leave me here. The President—"

"This is your day off! What about the picnic?"

Ethan looked at her, surprised. A picnic on a day like this? He climbed down.

"Well, what about the Fourth, then?" she continued, the annoyance obvious in her voice.

"The Fourth? I . . . don't know."

"Goodbye, Ethan," came Amanda's tart reply as she snapped the reins and rode away in a cloud of dust.

For once, the rumors were terrifyingly accurate. Lee had intended to invade the north, but then he had encountered the vast Federal army at the sleepy country hamlet of Gettysburg.

Ethan stood across from the desk in the tiny telegraph cubicle. Only the President sat, his shoulders hunched, his gray face fixed on the floor. Stanton stood in the doorway smoking moodily, while Packer stood in the shadows, his arms crossed, his eyes bright. Gideon Welles stood near, trying to comfort the President. The battle of Gettysburg was over and the death toll, still trickling in, was already staggering. Over seventeen thousand Union soldiers had fallen in the three days of fighting.

Lincoln had moaned when he heard the news. His voice choking, "Here I am! A man who could never even cut off a chicken's head, with blood flowing all around me!"

Yet now his despair became even greater. It seemed General Meade was cut from the same cloth the previous Union generals had been. Lee was slipping away through Maryland and Meade was too cautious, too reluctant to pursue him. Throughout the North, the opinion prevailed, an opportunity to end the conflict had slipped by—all because of a hesitant general.

Lincoln sprang to his feet, ashamed of his emotion, yet overwrought with anxiety and frustration.

"Good Lord! We had them within our grasp and nothing I could say or do could make them move! This will be put on my account."

He threw a crumpled telegram in the wastebasket. A strained silence fell over the small room. The President's passion was rarely so ignited. Packer stepped forward, his voice calm, deliberate.

"Mr. President, shall we step into my office? I have some excellent tea going."

Ethan could almost discern a trace of gentleness in Packer's usually brusque manner. Lincoln seemed unfocused a moment then nodded to Packer and followed him from the room. Stanton heaved a deep sigh of relief.

"How long can our army go on like this?" he grumbled.

"How long can my good friend go on like this?" said Welles sadly.

September, 1863

It was a beautiful autumn day in Washington—if you had time to notice it. Days were warm and nights crisp. The trees along the Potomac were slowly exchanging their capes of green for yellows and burnt reds. The air had the perfume of fall in it, which made this the best time of year in the capital city. But the administration could not afford to appreciate this natural splendor.

Abraham Lincoln had never been more unpopular than he was this fall of 1863. "They put all the blame on whomever is most visible," Packer had said succinctly. And Lincoln was certainly the most visible. Daily he was lampooned in newspapers across the nation. It seemed to the public that the war was entirely his fault—especially Gettysburg, just two months previous. They could not and would not forgive him. Ethan knew the President was putting in sixteen-hour days followed by sleepless nights. He stalked the War Department for good news, but there wasn't any. His face, already lined and shadowed, became more so.

Radical abolitionists screamed of Lincoln's incompetence and boasted they would remove him next year. His own Republican party lashed out at him and hinted he would not be their

candidate in the next election. There was ambitious scheming in
the Cabinet. Even closer to Lincoln, known only to the White
House staff, the First Lady was on another of her refurbishing
binges—a costly thing that would bring embarrassment and
anxiety to her husband.

On this fine September day, Lincoln summoned Ethan to his
office. Another inventor was just leaving the President.

"A good war always creates more scoundrels than it kills . . .
Now, Ethan, let's saddle up. I need to get out for awhile. I want to
go see our brave boys."

Ethan knew their destination and soon they were riding
south from the White House. Amory Square Hospital, situated
across from the imposing Smithsonian, was only one of the many
hospitals quickly built in the capital city to accommodate the
vast tide of Union wounded. Because of its central location,
Washington was a natural medical and supply base. When wounded
soldiers survived the primitive field hospitals, the painful, crude
ambulance, train or boat rides, they usually found themselves in
Washington. Even then, conditions were often not much better
than the field hospitals. There were simply too many men and
too few supplies and staff.

Ethan slipped from the hospital ward out into the hallway to
draw a deep breath. The smells out here were only slightly better,
yet he'd heard Amory Square Hospital was one of the cleaner,
more efficient army hospitals of Washington. He would wait here
the remainder of Lincoln's visit with the men. Though he would
not admit it, coming here always made him a bit uncomfortable.
There was something unsettling about the wounded men who
looked up at him from their beds. Ethan saw the fright and pain in
their eyes. Here he stood, so tall and strong, spotless in his blue
uniform, while they lay so twisted and broken. Did they look at
him with accusation, he wondered? They had risked their lives,
he only followed the President around. Was his work really a
coward's job? He had asked himself this many times—without an
answer. After all, in the nine months of service to Lincoln, there
had not been any danger to him.

Ethan's musing was interrupted by a loud, cackling laugh. It
came from around the corner and he recognized it immediately.
Moses Cobb was leaning against a wall as a nurse stalked off.

"I don't think she's much impressed with you, ol' fella!" Ethan smiled.

Moses swung around and his face lit up. "Ethan Alcott!"

"Hello, Moses!"

The two shook hands warmly.

"Well I'll be jiggered! Never thought I'd see you again!"

"I knew it was you when I heard a donkey brayin'."

Moses thumped him on the back.

"What are you doing in Washington, Moses?"

"I ask the same of you. None of us heard from ya after you left."

Moses did not miss the quick frown that passed over Ethan's face.

Shiloh was still difficult to think about.

"I work for the War Department now, Moses."

"You? A paper pusher?" Moses was incredulous.

Ethan's smile returned. "No, I'm on the President's staff. I'm an aide."

"Old Abe? Are ya pullin' my drawers, man?"

"No, I'm serious, Moses. He's in that ward there, right now."

"The President is in there?"

"But Moses, what are you doing in Washington? Besides chasing nurses."

"She was a might frisky wasn't she?" Moses chuckled. "I'm headin' back to the front, but I can't get a pass. This town is a devil of a place—"

"But Moses, Amory Hospital is no place to get a pass."

Moses' face became serious. "Andy is here, somewhere."

"Andy Mill is here?"

"Just found out yesterday. He's either at Carver or here. Haven't finished checking here yet."

"We'll look here when I get off work," Ethan said excitedly.

He sent Moses on to Willard's to sleep in his room. When Ethan returned to his room later that evening, he found Moses stretched across the bed, snoring loudly. Ethan decided to let his friend rest and returned to Amory alone.

It was twilight as Ethan entered the main halls. He searched on his own for an hour without success. He turned down the last dimly lit hall and found a nurse unloading boxes. He hurried up to her.

"Excuse me, I wonder if you could help me?"

"Yes?"

"I have a friend who is supposed to be here. But I'm having trouble finding him. His name is Andy Mill."

"Yes, I'll help you."

It was toward the end of the ward that Ethan stopped. He gripped the bed rail.

"Have we found him?" whispered the nurse.

Ethan could only nod. Andy Mill lay before him, his chalk-white face covered with a matted beard, deep purple circles under his eyes. Andy had always been thin, but now he looked almost skeletal. Ethan could clearly hear his labored breathing. He stepped up to the bed and leaned over. Andy's eyes opened.

"I thought... it was you, Mother... Could I have a drink please?"

The nurse hurried forward and helped him. Ethan spoke up, his voice breaking, "Andy, it's me, Ethan Alcott."

Andy's eyes finally focused. "Ethan... you?"

"It sure is."

"Praise God... I get to see my friend again."

Ethan grasped his hand, unable to speak. Finally Andy managed a weak smile.

"Where am I, Ethan?"

"You're in Washington D.C., Andy."

"You too."

"Yes, now go back to sleep, fella. I'll come back tomorrow."

"Tomorrow..."

Andy seemed reluctant to let go of Ethan's hand. Ethan and the nurse moved back into the dim hallway. Ethan turned toward the wall, overcome with emotion. *Andy looks so bad, and here I am, so healthy*... His fists clenched in a choking anger. He was almost annoyed to see the nurse still waiting quietly beside him. He could not see there were tears in her eyes, too.

"Please," his voice was husky, "what's wrong with Andy?"

"He has pneumonia."

"Pneumonia. Will he be all right, Miss?"

She hesitated. "Well, he is very weak and malnourished. He has a high fever as well. Your friend is very sick, but hopefully the medicine has taken hold fast enough."

Ethan stood silently considering this.

How many once-strapping farm boys of the Union and Confederacy had been reduced to illness by malnutrition? Boys like Andy who had never really been off their farms.

Ethan sighed deeply and they began walking toward the entrance.

"Thank you for helping me find him."

"You're very welcome... You know, I notice you have an accent," she said.

"Me—an accent?" Ethan's laugh was shaky. "I've never been accused of that before."

He was grateful for the release of tension. "Where do I sound like I'm from?"

"Well, let's see. I'm not sure exactly. Somewhere west?"

"Yes."

"Ohio? No—farther. Perhaps Illinois?"

"Right again."

"Yes, I thought so. Say President Abraham Lincoln for me."

"President Abraham Lincoln for me." They both laughed.

"Yes, definitely Illinois. Southern Illinois?"

"Gosh, you're right!"

"You say your 'a's' flat, like someone from... Sangamon County."

Ethan stopped. "I can't believe it! You're absolutely right."

They had stopped under a gas light and Ethan could see the nurse in full light, not shadow.

"Hello, Captain Alcott." She extended a small hand to him and smiled.

Ethan's mind raced trying to recognize the young nurse.

"Don't you know me, Ethan?" her voice was full of laughter.

"Roy's sister! Sara James!"

He impulsively hugged her and they laughed again.

Sara smiled. He had not immediately recognized her, but she had known him the moment he had walked up. Certainly, some years had passed, but how could she not recognize the boy she had a crush on all her growing-up years? He had changed though, from a handsome boy to a good-looking young man. Broad-shouldered now, but the same green eyes, dark curling hair, quick smile. He reminded her of a magazine cover in his immaculate blue uniform.

"Sara, how long has it been?"

"Oh, let's see... about ten years, I think."

Actually, she knew quite well how long it had been, the last time she had seen him vivid in her mind. He had been a tall and lively lad of seventeen when she had moved away. Sara's family had returned to Peppercreek from Chicago shortly after Ethan had joined the army.

"You've grown up!" he enthused. He was surprised at the changes the years had brought to his old friend's little sister. Of course, there was no reason why she wouldn't change—yet it was difficult for him to reconcile the image he remembered of a skinny, long-braided tag-along with the young woman who stood before him.

Her dress was dark and drab, the uniform of all nurses. She wore a linen cap that pulled her hair back. He could see it was blonder than he remembered, the color of honey. He had to wonder at the pinkish glow of her cheeks, not dimmed by hard work. But it was her blue eyes that caused him to recognize her— big, cornflower-blue eyes.

"You make me think of Libby, seeing you again."

He frowned just an instant, then continued. "How long have you been in Washington?"

"I came last summer, a little over a year ago."

"Tell me about Roy." It had been years since he had seen him as well.

"He's with Sherman. I haven't heard from him in three months. He managed to get home last Christmas."

"How do your folks feel about Roy being in the army and you so far off, here in D.C.?"

"It's just Mama now, Ethan. Papa died four years ago. . . . Oh, she was reluctant to let us go, but we were both pretty determined."

"I haven't been home since I enlisted. I . . . Well, it's almost like I don't want to go home until this war is over."

Sara nodded. "Are you on furlough or stationed here in Washington, Ethan?"

"I was with Grant at Shiloh. Then, I ended up here. I'm an aide to the President."

"Oh Ethan, that's wonderful!"

Ethan laughed, "Well that's a nice reaction for a change. Just last week I had whiskey splashed on my coat by a gent who didn't like our President one whit!"

"I've seen Mr. Lincoln just a few times from a distance, here in the wards. He has such a kind face. He stoops down to speak to the men, and you can tell he cares. They just love it when he comes."

Their walk had brought them to the main lobby. Ethan sighed and they lingered there, both reluctant to break this easy conversation between childhood friends.

"Of course I wish Andy were doing better, but this has been a great day for me, Sara. First I find an old army pal, then Andy. Now I find you!"

There was enthusiasm in his words and Sara could not understand why she was blushing. She gave him her hand again.

"Yes, it has been nice to see you again, Ethan. Well . . . I've got to go now."

He didn't release her hand immediately. "Are you still on duty, Sara?"

"Just another hour."

"Why, it's almost ten! Sounds like long hours of hard work. Where do you stay?"

"Those barracks across the path there."

Ethan thought of his comfortable room at Willard's.

"Doesn't look too—" he didn't know how to finish and Sara laughed.

"Well, first we were in tents, so this is an improvement."

"I'll be coming over to see Andy every day. I know he'll get better." He thought of Andy's ambition. He closed his eyes a moment. If only there was some way he could help his friend . . .

Sara reached out and touched his arm. He could almost feel the gentleness in her voice. "He's a good friend, isn't he?"

Ethan nodded, then cleared his throat awkwardly.

"Listen, I'd like to hear about how you ended up in Washington and talk over old times. Do you suppose we could go to dinner some evening?"

"I don't have a lot of free time . . . but yes, I'd like that."

"Well, then . . ."

"Goodnight, Ethan."

"Goodnight, Sara."

Sara James, despite her bone-deep weariness, had trouble falling asleep that night. A face from her past crowded out all the sights and sounds of the long day. It was a relief. There was a feeling of security in drifting back over memories. She smiled in the darkness at his comment "long hours of hard work." Yes, it had been that and so much more. Even though she was still a young woman, she sometimes felt she'd lived a lifetime.

She had been happy at home, moving in the accepted circles of home life and church work. Yet, there had been a vague restlessness in her as the war accelerated. The stories were horrible enough, but the rumors of meager and primitive medical provisions for the wounded seemed even more chilling to her. It came to a climax when she listened to a wounded man from Peppercreek who had been sent home. He lingered ten days—then died. The story he told haunted Sara. He'd taken a mini-ball, then later a saber cut while fighting. He told of lying wounded for three days without any medical attention—some men twice that long. He told of field dressings that went unchanged for a week because of lack of supplies. He had survived two serious injuries only to die of typhoid from lack of proper medical attention. Most men were giving up their lives, not from battle wounds, but from maladies like typhoid, dysentery and pneumonia. With deficient diets, men had low resistance to the diseases that stalked the camps like silent, secret armies.

One spring afternoon not long after, the recent copy of *Godey's Lady's Book* lay idle in Sara's lap as she sat thinking. She suddenly remembered Libby O'Dell. Libby had loved to play nursemaid and Sara knew that if she had lived she would have been at a battlefront or army hospital. Certainly doing more than knitting socks for Peppercreek lads. So, her resolve was set: She would find an active way to help, for her old friend's sake—and her own. She picked up the *Springfield Register*. Three quarters of it were devoted to war news. She found the story she had read earlier and reread it. It detailed how the Union capital had become a city of hastily built hospitals. Wooden buildings and white tents dotted the hillsides. Churches, schools, public buildings, hotels, and private homes were being requisitioned by the Army of the Potomac for the wounded.

Sara hesitated a moment at the thought of leaving all she knew. Besides the few years in Chicago, Peppercreek was all she had known. She put the paper down—she would go to Washington.

So, in the spring of 1862, she had left home. The long railroad had chugged her away from her family's home, traveled across the Midwest, then deposited her without ceremony into a smelly, crowded city that was her nation's capital. That particular spring day the humidity had soared, leaving Miss Sara James grimier, hotter and wearier than she'd ever been in her whole life. It was a terrible beginning. For two weeks, she trudged from offices to hospitals and back again with no encouragement. Her meager savings were dwindling fast in this city of three-dollar-a-day hotel rooms.

Generals and their armies were mobilized and fighting, but the medical machinations of the Union were stagnating. Women as nurses were still viewed by most doctors as a "necessary evil." Hence, some rigid regulations were established for weeding out the fainthearts and females seeking romance and glory.

"Plain looks, no less than thirty years of age, married. My dear Miss James, you fail all three criteria. The regulations are in place for obvious reasons." ＿

Sara had heard this before, and her frustrations finally boiled over.

"Your regulations are ridiculous! They mention no medical training. I didn't come hundreds of miles to be turned down, because...I'm not an old married hag! My age or looks have nothing to do with my coming here to help. I—"

The man smoothed his walrus mustache and held up his hand to stem her tirade.

"Do you have any medical training?"

"No. I—"

"Have you ever tended sick, delirious men? Been in contact with rough men? Changed filthy bandages *ad infinitum*?"

Sara felt deflated. "No."

The man pressed his fingertips together and studied the young woman in front of him.

"All I have," she said wearily, "is the desire to serve. I can do that. The very fact that you can list so many needs, proves you need help. I can work hard."

He stood up and came around from his desk. He scratched something on a card and gave it to her.

"Here, this will make a place for you at Amory Square Hospital." He opened his office door, "You'll find out soon enough just how hard you can work, Miss James."

She had left the Sanitary Commission office feeling both elated and fearful. Doubts rose like never before. Perhaps she couldn't do the work after all. Perhaps contact with so many men would be terribly frightening. After all, compared to this she had led a pretty sheltered life.

Most of the doctors at Amory Square Hospital were older men, thoroughly entrenched in their way of doing things, thoroughly entrenched in their bias against women in the wards. Therefore, Sara was greeted with cold indifference by most of the medical staff. This she expected. What she did not expect was the tense reception of the other female staff. Sara was the youngest admitted and they resented it. She only found one woman who befriended her.

For two months she was given the most menial drudgery possible. Cleaning and cooking only; no contact with the men. Long days of hard physical work followed nights of exhaustion when a quick prayer was all she could manage before falling onto her hard bed. So many nights she cried herself to sleep, thinking of all the pain she had seen, and feeling she had made a monumental mistake by coming to this mean city of mean work.

Finally, acceptance came with the bloody battle of Antietam. Hundreds of injured men poured into the hospital. Patients filled the corridors. Now everyone had to be both cook and nurse. Everyone had to help with round-the-clock surgery. In ten days of hellish work, Sara quickly learned the most basic nursing skills. Her efforts did not go unnoticed.

A doctor had said it succinctly: "Anyone can stir a pot of soup! I need the lass in here with me. She's steady."

The dour-faced matron handed her only one condition as she was moved into a limited nursing position.

"Keep your hair covered."

Sara rolled over in her narrow bed. Her life had become the life of the hospital. She had one friend and very little time away from her work. It was a very limited existence for a healthy country girl, but proving to be the best experience of her young life.

Her thoughts returned to today. It was funny how she had instantly recognized Ethan after ten years. But then, his striding down the hospital hallway had not been unlike the first day he'd walked into Peppercreek school years ago: head erect, smiling, confident. Of course, everyone had heard about the boy who had come to the O'Dells' that summer of 1844. It was a strange story about a runaway boy. She remembered how she and all the other scholars of Peppercreek had craned their heads around to stare at him. Libby had told Sara everything, so Sara felt in a way she already knew him before she saw him. She snuggled deeper under the covers, remembering...

School days came back—Ethan running races or stumbling over verb tenses and conjunctions. There was always some adoring girl to help him with his sums—or anything he asked. There was the face of Jip Denham, the one boy Ethan never got along with. There were the times when Roy allowed her to tag along fishing with them. Ethan would always put the worm on for her and never pulled her braids like other boys did. Then, she thought of the last time she had seen him. Had it really only been ten years ago?

He had looked so tall and manly to her as he stood shaking hands with Roy. The Jameses were leaving Peppercreek for Chicago, and Sara was losing her best friend and her heart's secret crush. She and Libby hugged and cried, then Ethan hoisted her up in the wagon. He had given her that big smile and she couldn't meet his eyes.

"What will you do, Sara, without Libby to lead you into trouble?"

Then the wagon rolled down the road toward Springfield and through her tears she saw them waving. She would never see her dear friend again—years later, the letter would come saying that she and her mother had died.

It had been difficult for her to keep a secret from her friend. It made her feel like a traitor. They shared everything—but this. She had no idea how Libby would have reacted if she knew Sara had such a crush on her big brother. Would she have scoffed, thought her terribly silly? How she would have hooted if she knew Sara kept a cigar box full of Ethan's discarded school papers under her bedstead.

Ten years ago . . . Or was that just a month ago? thought Sara. It seems so vivid to me, even now. So much has happened in ten years. Here I am, a grownup girl living and working in Washington. A friend from her girlhood days had entered her world of the present and it made her feel strange to realize that the friend flustered her as much now as he had ten years ago.

♦♦ ♦♦ ♦♦

*C*oming to the hospital now became a part of Ethan's daily routine. The first week Andy had lain in the grip of fever and was not coherent. It gave Ethan a frustrated feeling that he could help in no tangible or effective way. He didn't see Sara and he wondered if he'd imagined her. Then, he began to pass her in the hallways as she hurried by on her rounds. Their words were brief and mostly about Andy's condition. It was the second week before Andy could sit up. Ethan found Sara with him as he came up to the bed.

"Well! The prophet is revived!" he grinned at Andy.

Andy laughed and they shook hands.

"I thought you were just a hallucination, Ethan."

"I've been called worse before."

"But Miss James has told me otherwise. It's good to see you, Ethan."

"I'll let you two get reacquainted for awhile," said Sara. "But not too long, Ethan," she admonished as she left.

Ethan found that he did not mind the atmosphere of the hospital nearly as much now. He looked forward to the visits with his friend and the feeling was mutual. Andy told him very little about the battles he had been in or how he had come to Washington. It became quickly apparent that Andy was not like other men who liked to swap battle stories. He did not want to talk of the war at all. He preferred to hear about Ethan's life, about Lincoln. Ethan told him all he could and they talked of boyhood days.

By October, Ethan grew busier as the fall session of Congress opened. The Washington population seemed to swell overnight. Congressmen, officers and would-be inventors were multiplied in the White House corridors. He was still able to come to the hospital each day, even if it was only for a short time in the evenings.

Amanda Sims was yet another claimant on his attention. One night they had gone to the theater. He could never remember the name of the play they saw. All he recalled was the nearness of her as they sat in the darkened theater. She had leaned on his arm and all he could smell was the delicate scent of flowers. Another

247

night there was dinner and Amanda did not see Ethan's eyebrows rise when he received the bill. Then there was an evening of playing whist in her parlor with another young couple. He was infatuated with her . . . and it was a costly infatuation.

Early one evening, Ethan met Sara in the hallway of the hospital. She was carrying a basket of soiled linen, her dress-front blood-stained. She was very pale.

"Sara, are you all right?" His concern was genuine.

"Oh, hello Ethan. Yes, I'm fine. Have you been to see Andy yet?"

"No, I was on my way now."

"I promised him yesterday I would write a letter for him. I have to be back in surgery so I won't be able." Ethan blanched inwardly at the thought.

"I could write for him," he volunteered.

"I'm sure he would like that."

Arriving at the bed of his stricken comrade, Ethan pulled the stool close to Andy's side.

"Sara talked me into being your secretary, Andy. Now, if you don't hurry and get better she'll probably ask me to give you a bath, and I'll have to draw the line there."

Andy chuckled as he pulled himself up in his bed.

"I suspect that you'd do just about anything Miss James asked you to do," Andy said with a wink.

"Oh, now Andy! She's like . . . a little sister to me."

"Oh?"

"Come on, now. This is the only time—"

"The prophet has your full attention?"

"Right."

So Andy began his letter, as if he were talking to his mother in person and Ethan was not there. It was the closing paragraph Ethan penned that he remembered years later.

> . . . *Ma, I've had a lot of time to think while I've been lying here. I think about being a boy again, like when I'd go fishin' with Boon. And just yesterday I remembered the time old lady Tupper gave me a switchin' for*

saying Revelation was in the Old Testament. She called me a heathen and said I always would be one, remember? I've thought how I've hated this war, hated the bloodshed, wondering if I shouldn't have come when they asked me to... I fired my rifle, Ma, when I had to. I never aimed at a particular man, I couldn't. When I was shooting, I half-wished I would get shot so I wouldn't have to do this anymore. Yet it seemed the Lord's good pleasure was to preserve my life out there, though I wondered why, sometimes.

I am one man, one soldier, and I did no good toward ending this fighting. It makes me think about what makes a person's life really important. Does land, or cattle, or cash in the bank? My friend Ethan told me President Lincoln said this in front of him: "In my young days I always wanted my life to count, to do something to make another human remember I had lived." Ma, all I know of the importance of my life is this: While I served the desperate call of my country, I helped four men come to know Jesus Christ. I hope I've been a servant He would be pleased with. Your son loves you. I'll see you at home.

Andy then carefully scratched his signature on the letter. Ethan felt an awkward silence. Andy had opened up his most personal self in front of Ethan. The letter had stirred him and he didn't know what to say. Finally he coughed. "Maybe you can be home with your Ma for Christmas."

Andy smiled tenderly at his friend's misunderstanding. "Yes— maybe I'll be home..."

It was fashionable to drive out in carriages to Georgetown or Arlington on Sunday afternoons. Picnickers found pleasant spots around Mount Vernon, Columbia College, and Meridian Hill. The Virginia creeper looked beautiful on the fine old brick homes of Georgetown. As Ethan and Amanda swung the carriage back toward Washington, Ethan could not help thinking of how Georgetown was such a quiet, peaceful place compared to the capital. It had a quaint, gentle sophistication that Washington could not boast. Amanda sighed as she slipped her gloved hand over Ethan's arm, and cuddled closer.

Ethan smiled down at her. She did make a pretty picture in her lilac-colored silk and cream bonnet. He had never seen her lovelier. She did most of the talking—about romances of her friends, of operas scheduled, of parties, and a shopping trip to New York in December. Ethan suddenly realized how far out of his price range the proper courtship of Amanda Sims could be. It was only a matter of time before his salary would stretch no farther. Because he didn't own a carriage, Amanda always generously offered her own. Ethan could not help but wonder if in some way her respect for him was lowered. If it was, it didn't reflect in her attitude toward him.

"One of these mornings soon, we'll wake up and find frost. The weather for drives like this will be over till spring," Ethan remarked.

"I won't mind too much, though today has been nice. I prefer the winter. The theater always has better shows!" She gave a little bell-like laugh.

Thinking suddenly of Moses, Ethan said, "Let's hope this is the last winter of the war." He felt her stiffen at his side. Apparently he had said the wrong thing.

"Do you suppose dear Mr. Lincoln feels the way you do?"

Ethan could not miss the hardness in her voice and was surprised at it.

"What?" Ethan turned to look at her, but her return gaze was steely-eyed.

"Daddy thinks it's outrageous the way the Union keeps blundering through its generals. George Meade is a friend and doing well, we think. But dear Mr. Lincoln is unhappy with him."

Ethan said nothing, but kept his eyes riveted on the horses in front of him.

"Well, Ethan, is Lincoln going to replace him?" she persisted.

"I haven't any idea about that, Amanda. I can tell you President Lincoln wants this war over as much as anybody. You must know that."

"You know that?"

"Of course."

"Yet you don't know about General Meade." There was a flash of sarcasm in her words.

"No, I'm not privy to that kind of information. I'm not in on the Cabinet meetings."

"Yet you're with him all day."

Ethan felt distinctly irritated now.

They came to the outskirts of the capital city as dusk fell. The gas street lamps twinkled like small handfuls of tiny stars. He drove directly to the Sims mansion and helped Amanda down. Her hands lingered on his broad shoulders and then she leaned forward and kissed him on the cheek. Whatever had stirred up her stormy spirit had passed just as quickly.

Peppercreek, Illinois

Henri slipped up behind Wyeth and slid his arms around her waist, kissing her on the neck.

"Henri! You startled me."

"Sorry... What are you doing in here?"

Wyeth was in her father's room, standing before a small oak chest.

"Pa brought this down from the attic and asked me to go through it. He thought there might be some baby things of ours Ma kept that Louisa could use. This was just about the only thing Ma brought to Illinois as a bride."

Henri placed a gentle kiss on Wyeth's forehead. "Shall I open it for you?"

Wyeth nodded and Henri opened the lid. The aroma of cedar filled the room. Soon Wyeth was absorbed, fingering linens and laces and carefully preserved baby smocks. Henri leaned on the table, only taking in half what Wyeth was saying as his mind wandered over a sermon he was working on.

"Oh, here's Ethan's bundle, I think."

She lifted out a small packet of faded, frayed blue homespun. She untied it and held up a worn pair of trousers, holes at each knee. Then came a flannel shirt.

"Hard to believe Ethan was ever that small," Wyeth laughed. "These were the clothes he came here in."

Something dropped from the pocket and fell under the table.
Henri stooped to find it.

"Seems like the orphanage didn't keep him very well dressed,"
Henri was saying.

"What do you mean? Have you found it?"

"Well," Henri was searching in the dimness, "the clothes
look pretty worn out. Did he look like that when he came?"

"Henri! Are you joking?"

Henri's hand finally closed around the object.

"What is it? Henri?"

Henri's face had an odd, inscrutable expression on it as he
slowly moved to the bedroom window. He opened his hand and
looked at the object. Wyeth came up to him.

"Henri, are you all right?"

Henri said nothing for a few moments.

"What were you saying about Ethan? About an orphanage?"
His voice sounded strange, almost tense, to Wyeth.

"Did you actually think Ethan came to us from an orphanage?"

"Yes, I suppose I did."

"How amazing! You've been in the family all these years and
you didn't know. You knew his last name was Alcott, not O'Dell,
didn't you?"

Henri nodded slowly.

"We found Ethan when he was about eight, near the woods
by the crossroads. He was delirious with fever. Henri, what is it?"

"This."

Then Wyeth looked at the object that had slipped from
Ethan's shirt pocket. In Henri's palm was a smooth wooden heart,
actually half a heart. A jagged line cut through the center. Wyeth
carefully turned it over. Inscribed and still visible were the letters
"to R Alc fro wi lo 1815." Wyeth scarcely noticed Henri leave the
room and then return. His hand trembled as he opened a worn
paper packet. First he drew out a letter, then he tipped the packet
and half a wooden heart slipped into his hand. Wyeth gasped.

The two halves fit perfectly.

Leaning toward the light, they read, "To Rachel Alcott from
Pa with love 1815."

"Henri, what can this mean?"

Henri sat on the bed.

"You know I've told you I was raised by my aunt."

"Yes."

"I always thought, of course, she...was my mother, until after she died. She left me this letter and this wooden heart from my real mother."

He had thoughts, years back, of going East, of trying to find his mother, but really there weren't many clues. If Caleb Mullins had found a cold trail how much more so would he, some twenty-five years later?

"Rachel Alcott was my real mother's name...Alcott is Ethan's name. We don't know his background, but, these two hearts..."

"It's..." Wyeth was stunned.

He took her hand in his, tears in his eyes.

"Your adopted brother is my real brother."

Wyeth sat mending one of her father's shirts, but her thoughts were hardly on the work in her lap. The house was so quiet, she could feel the quiet—and it stirred the tears forming in her eyes. Henri was gone.

It had happened so fast. Only four days ago their world had been fine. Now... She knew he was bothered about something. He was unusually quiet and rarely touched her. They could always talk things over, yet he had closed himself off to her. She found their bed empty at night, Henri strolling out in the orchard. Finally he told her, taking her hands, loving her with his eyes.

"Wyeth, love, I'm going to tell you something, and don't say anything yet. I'm going to join the army as a chaplain. I don't really want to go, to leave you. I'm a coward, but it's what I think the Lord wants me to do."

"Henri...you're not strong enough. You know what Dr. Noble has said. Life in an army camp...Henri..."

"Love." he was smiling now. "You know I'm stronger than when he said that. If I'm not fit to carry the Gospel to hurting men then I'm not fit for anything!"

"But Henri, I can't let you go!"

He pulled her to him. "There are men dying every day, Wyeth. We've read all about it. How can I not go?" He fingered her hair. "I'll be back, Wyeth. I'll come back to you. I'll come back just like I did when I rode the circuit. I'll come back to hold you in my arms, to feel your skin against mine. To laugh with you and to pray with you. I'll be back!"

Two days later he left. He must go quickly he had told her, to keep his resolve.

Henri had been gone twelve weeks when Wyeth visited Dr. Noble. She left his office radiant—a part of Henri was growing inside her.

Chapter 7

Washington, D.C.
◆◆ ◆◆ ◆◆

*L*ate one afternoon, Ethan entered the hospital as Sara was leaving.

"Sara!"

She liked the happiness she heard in his voice at seeing her.

"Ethan! Hello."

"You're going out?"

"You're going in?" she teased.

He smiled at her words, that broad smile she knew so well.

"I'm off duty for the rest of the day," she said.

"So am I. How's Andy today?"

"About the same."

"Good. Say, since they're turning you loose for awhile and I'm off too, how about dinner? We really haven't had a chance to talk much. Could you get ready while I visit with Andy?"

"All right."

"Thirty minutes?"

"I'll be ready."

"Andy looked better today I thought," Ethan commented.

He and Sara were walking toward Pennsylvania Avenue, for Sara had declared this day was "made to be out on." Ethan looked at her from the corner of his eye. It was the first time he had seen her out of her dark nursing frock. She wore a simple navy calico dress and carried a scarlet-colored shawl. Her clean white collar was edged in eyelet and fastened with a plain gold pin. Her outfit reminded him of something Wyeth or Louisa would wear. Her hair was caught up in a loose bun. She had transformed in thirty short minutes and the lightness of her mood infected him.

"It's a beautiful day, Ethan, did you know?" she asked him as they began walking. Her face was tilted up to him with a smile, and for one quick moment Ethan thought she looked like she was waiting to be kissed. He shook his head to clear the silly thought.

Until she had pointed it out, he really hadn't noticed what it was like outside. Except for his trips to Amory Square, his world was really a triangle—Willard's, the War Department and the White House. Watching clouds scuttle across the sky in advance of rain or sunlight reflecting off the Potomac or trees turning in autumn afternoons hadn't been a priority with him.

"Miss James, I do believe you feel like a schoolgirl let out for term end!"

"Or maybe a schoolgirl playing hooky!"

"That's not a reference to my past is it?" he asked, and they both laughed.

Ethan had led Sara to a small establishment just off Pennsylvania Avenue. He came here often, for it was quiet. It would be easier to talk here. After the meal, they still sat talking and laughing over days past—of friends, teachers, adventures. Ethan stopped speaking a moment and looked down at the table.

"You're thinking about Jip Denham," Sara said.

He was surprised, "Well, yes! How did you know that?"

"Lucky guess." She knew the way he thought.

"I don't like to have enemies. Jip and I couldn't get along for some reason, from the very first."

"Tell me about your work, Ethan."

So he did. He found himself saying more than he realized was in him. He looked at her, startled. "I've done all the yakkin'. Now you. How did you get into nursing and end up in Washington?"

"Nursing is . . . a pretty generous term for what I do. I found out quickly that what was needed was just a willingness to work."

She told him about coming to Washington and what it had been like for her. "It was so different at first, to be away from home. And hard sometimes. What I mostly do is cook and clean and change bandages and try . . . to bring some measure of comfort to the men. My efforts aren't very much, though. They're usually so broken when they get to us."

"I think you do very well, Sara—more than you know."

His voice was so low and earnest, she couldn't look at him. She suddenly felt lightheaded.

"I know you've helped Andy a great deal," he continued.

It was so quiet in the small café that Sara suddenly had the feeling of being completely alone with Ethan. She became very aware of his nearness, his presence, his manliness. She was close enough to see the flecks of gold in his eyes, the shadow of beard on his cheek, the curve of his mouth. She thought about that mouth a moment... then looked down at her plate to dismiss such thoughts. There was a firm strength about him that threatened to overwhelm her. His voice broke the spell.

"Will Andy be all right? Maybe go home for Christmas?" She hesitated. "I'm praying so."

They drank their tea in silence. Ethan marveled that he had talked more in the past two hours than he had in the last six months. Sara marveled that she suddenly felt so nervous with him.

"Well, I suppose we'd better go," Ethan finally said with reluctance. "We both have long days tomorrow."

Ethan hailed a hack, for now twilight had fallen and with it an early chill. Soon they were at the steps of the nurses' dormitory.

"Thank you for supper, Ethan. I enjoyed it very much."

"I did too, Sara. You would let me know if Andy's condition... changed, wouldn't you? You could send me word at the hotel."

"Yes, of course."

She wanted to turn, to hurry in, but found herself looking into his eyes. Finally, she looked up, and there was the friendly face of the moon, a gauzy halo of clouds drifting around it.

"It'll rain tomorrow," she stated. Ethan followed her gaze.

"You're still a country girl, Sara," he said smiling.

She gave Ethan her hand and said goodnight. The doors quickly closed behind her. Ethan stood a moment, surprised that the touch of her small soft hand had stirred him so.

A subtle change came over Sara James in the next few weeks. A change that she was aware of only in her innermost being. It seemed she moved in a slightly preoccupied frame of mind. Her closest ally, Claire, noticed it, but didn't mention it because it seemed so indefinable. A year-and-a-half of hard work had created a more resilient person in Sara James. Yet there were many mornings it took a great deal of inner motivation to get up again to face the physical hardships, the misery, to witness death do its work. These days, however, Sara got up humming to herself, and

Claire looked on in wonder. The work load hadn't lessened, the biting sarcasm of the head matrons hadn't changed, the food hadn't gotten better or the living conditions any more comfortable. So, what was it?

When Sara lay in her darkened room, night after night, one solitary face came into her mind. It didn't matter if she had seen him that day or not, she had memorized his tone of voice, the way he walked, the way he mechanically ran his fingers through his hair just above his left ear when he was deep in thought. She could see that quick smile that seemed to intensify in his eyes. When she was with a patient her mind was on the patient, but when she rolled bandages, washed dishes or hurried down the halls her mind was exclusively on Ethan. It was double-edged though. She liked thinking about him, wondering about his day at the White House, or what stories he might bring to Andy. Still, it frustrated her. She told herself that it was nothing more than a deep affection from childhood. A perfectly harmless thing...

Sara sat talking with Andy when Ethan came into the ward. He carried a large basket.

"What have you got there, Captain?" Andy asked, his voice cheerful.

"Only the best apples in the U.S.A.!" Ethan announced as he removed the cover with a flourish.

"Oh, Ethan, they're beautiful!" enthused Sara.

"Of course they are! Enough for the prophet and the whole ward!" Cheers went up from the men in the surrounding beds as the rich aroma of apples filled the ward.

"Apples for everybody!" Ethan began tossing apples to those beds where men stretched out eager hands. There was laughter until the double doors banged open and Matron Hix marched in. She surveyed the scene, which had become deathly quiet, and came up to Andy's bed, her eyes blazing.

"Miss James, what is your friend doing?"

"He—"

"Apples! Young man, you can't possibly be serious! These men are on strict, low diets. They are very sick. They can't digest rough apples!"

"Well, Ma'am—" began Ethan humbly.

"Take them up immediately!" she snapped.

Ethan sheepishly began to retrieve the apples.

"Miss James, what can you possibly be thinking of, to permit this?" Her voice dripped acid.

"I was about to tell him that the men couldn't have them. But . . . It just seemed to cheer everyone up, and I didn't think it would hurt anything for a moment."

" 'Didn't think' is too true! I think your young man has addled your judgment."

Sara tried very hard not to blush. She was grateful Ethan did not hear the woman's remark. Matron Hix moved to take Andy's apple when her arm was stopped in a strong grip.

"Don't you think the men could keep just one apple on our table? Promise not to eat them?" Andy's voice was gentle but firm.

"What's the point of keeping them, young man, if you can't eat them?"

"Well, it would be like an encouragement to the men, a hope that they'll be getting better. We've been told these are the best in the country. Besides, they smell good—like home, not a hospital."

She hesitated, then casting Ethan and Sara a final furious glance she hurriedly left the ward. Ethan passed the apples out again to the happy patients, then said goodbye to Andy. Andy called him back a moment.

"Ethan . . . thanks."

There was something about his voice that caused Ethan to pause, smile, then hurry out after Sara.

"Sara, wait! Please." He caught up to her. "Sara, I'm sorry if I got you in trouble or got you on the matron's wrong side."

She smiled, "It's all right, Ethan. I'm usually on that side of her, anyway. Thank you for the apples. It cheered the men and . . . that's as important as any medicine."

She reached for one of the scarlet fruits and inhaled deeply. Ethan watched her as she closed her eyes.

"It does smell like home, doesn't it, Ethan?"

He had thought the same thing earlier. He nodded. She seemed to touch his emotions in a way he couldn't explain.

"You work so hard, Sara. Wouldn't you like to go home?"

She sighed. "I'll be glad when...this is over."

He was surprised again at her conviction, her passion for her work. Amanda Sims' face flashed into his mind. He shook his head. Just yesterday, over lunch, she had vented her concern...

"Ethan, being in that hospital every day is unhealthy for you."

He had thought of Sara when she said that. Sara certainly looked healthy...

He'd smiled. "Packer says the same thing. Says I'm going to catch something and give it to him."

"He's right for once."

Ethan stopped eating. "You don't like Packer, do you?"

Her eyes sparkled as she leaned forward. "I don't trust Mr. Packer."

That was her explanation and she resumed eating.

Ethan studied his plate a moment. Packer didn't like the Sims' and the Sims' didn't like Packer. Why? Sometimes being with Amanda left him with a nameless confusion inside. Yet, it was a heady feeling too. He had the arm of one of Washington's brightest belles. Their relationship, in the brief months that they had known each other, had included a few drives in the country, a few dinners, escorting her to two parties. He hadn't kissed her, but he had wanted to. He hadn't given any serious thought to why this young woman, who could snap up any eligible officer or businessman or Congressman, would be interested in a lowly presidential aide. He really wasn't, after all, so very different from the man he worked for—a backwoodsman come to the big city.

"So, you'll stop going there so much?"

"I can't, Amanda, I told you. Andy is a good friend and I know he depends on my coming..."

Sara's voice penetrated his reverie. "Hello?"

"Oh," he smiled awkwardly. "He's getting better, isn't he, Sara?"

She nodded. "He hasn't had a fever in a few days, and that's good."

"His color is better, and did you notice his coughing spells aren't near so bad anymore?"

"The doctor saw him this morning and was 'cautiously optimistic'. But Ethan, conditions can change."

"He looks better, sounds better—I'm just plain optimistic!"

They stood in the shadows of the hallway, Ethan leaning against the wall.

"I told him I won't be around for two days. We're going up to Gettysburg. The President has been asked to speak at the cemetery dedication there. Andy's already eager to hear about it."

"You're good . . . for Andy."

Her voice was so soft that Ethan looked at her closely. She sighed.

"Sara, are you all right?"

She just nodded, suddenly very tired and emotionally drained. Their eyes met. It was a moment of total quietness in the corridor. It could have been an intimate moment. It could have been . . . Sara had the overwhelming desire to put her arms around Ethan, to lean against him, have him hold her. It would be so nice to lean on someone for a change, even for just a short time. If only he would fall in love with her . . . What if I just kissed him, right here, right now, she wondered. What would he do? What would he think?

"Well . . ." Ethan felt awkward again. What was this strange feeling replacing the easy friendship he'd been having with Sara? His voice was hurried, "I've already given the President the apples that my father sent for him, so just keep these for the staff." He passed her the basket.

Then he was gone, and Sara hesitated, smiling to herself, daydreaming about what might have happened if she *had* kissed him.

Gettysburg, Pennsylvania, November 19, 1863

The train chugged out of Gettysburg at 6:30 in the evening, bound for Washington. The presidential entourage ate, talked and laughed. The President was quiet, finally stretching out across some seats with a wet towel over his eyes. As the train pulled out, Ethan had overheard his frustrated remarks to Secretary Seward.

"That speech was a flat failure! Folks will be disappointed, just as I was."

He was partly right. Papers across the country and across the ocean carried his words and were mixed in their reviews. The *Harrisburg Patriot* called the speech "silly and not to be thought of again." The *Chicago Times* called the remarks "ignorant rudeness, dishwashy" and the *London Times* "ludicrous and dull."

Yet the *Chicago Tribune* described the Union leader's address as "remarks that would live forever," the *Cincinnati Gazette* "right words at the right time" and the *Providence Journal* "inspiring and beautiful."

The monotone of the train along the track was soothing to Ethan. He felt agitated. He and Packer sat apart from the others. Packer did not bother to light the gas lamp by his seat and sat slowly revolving an unlit cigar. Ethan leaned forward, wanting to talk.

"What did you think about Mr. Lincoln's speech, Packer?"

As usual, Packer was cagey. "He's grumbling about it himself. You were out in the crowd; what were they saying?"

"Some said it was too short, some said it was fine. I saw quite a few folks moved to tears." Ethan thought a moment, "Didn't see anyone teary over Mr. Everett's speech."

"Can't cry when you're sound asleep," grunted Packer. "But it's obviously on your mind. What did you think of it?"

Packer did not want to answer Ethan's question. He felt too deeply stirred by Lincoln's words to verbalize his feelings. The emotion Ethan felt, sparked by the speech, was nothing compared to the turmoil inside J.A. Packer. Ethan sensed something about his boss that was making him more taciturn than usual. But Ethan needed to talk. Tonight he wished he were on his father's front porch, telling him all about the day.

"I can't really explain it," he began, "but I thought . . . it was powerful." Ethan shrugged and sighed. He couldn't articulate his feelings. Packer leaned back in satisfaction. He need not worry, he realized; this boy had heart.

Ethan looked out into the darkness. He would tell Andy tomorrow. Tomorrow would be easier, and Andy would understand.

Washington, D.C.

Sara was reading from the Psalms while Andy slept. The shaded lamp by his bed cast a soft, tranquil glow on the otherwise dark ward. Labored breathing and coughs were the only other sounds of the night. Sara had the painful experience of being with dying soldiers these last few months of her life. It had been an experience that left her feeling raw and wounded herself, each time she experienced it. Tonight she kept vigil not just for Ethan's sake, but for her own as well. She had come to love Andy as a brother in the brief weeks she had served him. More than that, they shared the bond of faith.

Andy had been asleep since dinner. He had managed only a few spoonfulls of broth before falling asleep. At least he can sleep, Sara thought, though his life hangs like a vapor. She knew instinctively he couldn't continue like this much longer, but she was determined to stay the night with him.

Ethan would be in Gettysburg tonight, she remembered, perhaps back here tomorrow. Would Andy linger that long? But then, would it be good for Ethan to see his friend dying? How would he handle it? Andy stirred.

"Sara, are you still here?"

"Yes Andy, can I get you anything?"

"No . . . No thanks. I'm fine. Sara, you can't sit here all night."

"I'm the nurse and you're the patient. Now, what can I read you?"

"Please read me the fortieth chapter of Isaiah, Sara."

So she read and when she finished she found his eyes fastened on her. His skin seemed transparent, a fever burning within him that no medication could quench. Purple shadows hung about his eyes. It seemed to Sara, just hours after Ethan left yesterday, Andy had suddenly grown worse. Involuntarily, tears filled her eyes and threatened to spill over. She took his hand and bowed her head.

"Andy...I'm...so sorry," she choked.

"Sara, Sara...don't cry. I'll...be all right soon."

"Andy, are you afraid?"

"No, I'm not afraid, Sara. How can I be? He's right on the other side of the door, just like He promised. Sara...He's so good, isn't He?"

"Yes, Andy, He is."

He patted her hand. "Tell Ethan I wasn't afraid. Tell him..."

Now tears came to Andy's eyes. "Ethan was like the brother I never had. Do you know why I liked him right off, Sara?"

She shook her head.

"He didn't try to tear down my faith, or ridicule me. I knew he didn't feel exactly as I did, but it didn't matter. He gave me the name 'prophet,' and I didn't mind. He respected me."

Andy was spent from the effort of talking and now drifted back to sleep.

Sara made herself comfortable as much as possible. Ethan had been a good friend to Andy and that made her so proud of him.

It was just at sunrise, just before the ward began to stir, that Sara was awakened by a strong, clear voice. She blinked, straightened up, despite the sore muscles in her neck and shoulders. She hadn't meant to sleep that long. She found Andy watching her, smiling.

"You love him, don't you?" he was asking her.

She forgot how sick he was, confused at first by his direct question, but then certain of his meaning.

"I..." She had to smile. "Yes, I do love him, Andy."

"He will be a good man for you, Sara."

"Andy, you must be feeling better! You're playing prophet this morning!"

He continued smiling at her.

"Oh, Andy, we're just friends," she said, flustered by the certainty in his eyes.

"But you love him." It was a statement, not a question.

"Yes. Now, you're feeling better. Let me feel your pulse."

"Sara, don't worry. Ethan will come to know God."

His pulse seemed stronger, the fever not so hot. Now to get him some food.

"Sara, go get some rest."

"I'll be back at dinner."

Sara left with a lifted heart. She had misjudged; he was getting better. And if Andy could see her feelings so clearly, perhaps Ethan would. He would be back soon.

When she came back at dinnertime, she was tired from the night's vigil she had kept, but happy. She found Claire outside the ward—her face became tense when she saw Sara. By her expression, Sara knew immediately what Claire would say. She closed her eyes a moment.

"He's gone, Sara," Claire said quietly. "I'm sorry. I know he was your friend."

"Not gone, Claire... He just went through the door," she whispered.

Ethan walked with swinging strides and a beaming face down the hospital hallway. It had been difficult for him to wait until he was off duty before he could come to Amory Square. But he was here, whistling until a nurse shushed him. He gave her a cheery wave and turned into Andy's ward. He could not wait to tell Andy about his trip to Gettysburg, about Mr. Lincoln's speech. He could read it to him in the paper, but could he convey the way the President had delivered it? Could he describe the rapt attention he had seen on so many faces when Lincoln spoke? He would tell Andy everything. Then, he would find Sara and tell her.

He approached Andy's bed and suddenly realized no one had called out the usual friendly greeting. He swung around and looked at Henry Jacks, in the next bed to Andy's. Jacks turned his face away from Ethan. Then, he looked down at Andy's bed. A pale, haggard face looked back at him. It was not Andy. He threw a quick glance around to make certain he had stopped at the right bed. He had.

"Where have they moved Andy?" he asked the stranger. The man could only continue to give him a vacant stare. Ethan was back down the ward in a flash, hurrying down the hallway to the nurses' cubicle. His mind was in a near-frantic turmoil and he wouldn't listen to its whisperings.

Ethan pushed his way through a covey of nurses, till he reached the head matron. Her head was bent over a clipboard.

"Where's Andy Mill?" he asked abruptly, his voice suddenly hoarse.

The matron waved an absent hand at him.

"Where have you moved Andy Mill? Answer me!"

She looked at him, her eyes glinty and hard.

"Young man—"

"Where have you moved him?"

All the nurses grew quiet.

"He was in his bed two days ago," Ethan rasped, "recovering just fine. Now, where is he?"

"He has either been released or died," the matron said in a flat, professional voice.

"That's a lie!" Ethan slapped his hand down on the desk. "Tell me where you've moved him!"

"Young man, lower your voice immediately. This is a hospital!"

The matron's own voice had risen considerably.

A doctor was beside them. "What's the problem here?"

"You!" Ethan almost jumped on the startled doctor. "You said he was getting better. You—"

"Who? Now calm down, soldier."

"I'll calm down when you tell me where you've moved Andy Mill!"

Sara had been farther down the hall when a raised voice told her Ethan had returned. She walked up to him and took his arm, pulling him away from the doctor who was now growing angry under Ethan's tirade. Ethan tried to shake her off till he saw who plucked at his sleeve.

"Oh, Sara, I'm glad you're here! I can't make them tell me where they've moved Andy!"

She hurried him wordlessly down the hallway, until they reached a small corridor that led to the rear of the hospital. She turned and faced him, her hands gripped behind her back. She had never seen him look this way before. How could she tell him? It would hurt him so deeply. She knew he had grown to love Andy.

"Ethan..." She felt helpless.

"I went to ... Gettysburg, you know," his voice sounded like that of a frightened child. Sara felt her throat tighten.

"Ethan, Andy died yesterday."

He continued to look at her, a cold hard stare. She felt trapped by his look.

"I wasn't on duty," she continued nervously, "Claire said he was very calm. I stayed up with him last night and he ... he wasn't afraid, Ethan. He wanted you to know that." She waited, tense.

"He was getting better," Ethan said flatly, suddenly unable to meet her eyes.

"He's out of pain now Ethan, and—"

"Why didn't you do something?" Ethan fairly yelled. "What are the doctors for, anyway? Frauds—all of them! Why ..." He slammed his hat down against a nearby table.

"Oh, Ethan ..."

Then he saw that the door behind Sara led outside, so he pushed past her. In the rear of the hospital grounds were stables and sheds. He hurried past these, then across the meadows that sloped down to the river. Sara followed him, having to almost lift her skirts and run to keep him in sight. Finally he stopped. He let out the most wrenching cry Sara had ever heard—as if all the pain and anguish of years had been pent up in him. It seemed to him he suddenly felt the grief of years wash over him. Rebecca. Libby. Now Andy.

Sara walked up to him and touched his shoulder. He swung around and she was shocked by the whiteness of his face. It seemed to her that he looked through her. Suddenly he grabbed her by the arms and pulled her close. His look was almost wild. Sara longed for his embrace—but not like this!

"Ethan, you're hurting me!" she cried, wrenching herself free.

They stared at each other. Ethan lowered his head, and when he finally looked up again, he was crying. Sara stepped up close to him.

"Sara ... Why?"

She drew him into her arms like a penitent schoolboy.

How long they stood there holding each other and crying, Sara was not certain. Yet she felt as if her love for him had been nothing compared to the feelings now swelling within her heart.

"I'll come back tomorrow," he said, wiping his eyes, "and apologize to ..." He gestured toward the hospital.

Sara said nothing, unable to speak.

The sunset had dropped its misty curtain, and Ethan had to be going. He felt terribly tired.

"I . . . wish I were home tonight," he said quietly. "Goodnight, Sara."

She would wait for another time to tell him the last words of his friend. She turned toward the cold, lonely room she must face. Her heart ached to comfort him—to bring him to Andy's God . . . and hers.

◆◆ ◆◆ ◆◆

*S*ara heard that Ethan had come the next day to apologize to the head matron, but she was busy and didn't see him. Three days later, he came again. He was so pale and worn-looking, Sara thought he might be ill.

"Look, Sara," he began directly, "I can't stay, but I'm sorry about the . . . other day. I don't know what came over me. I hope I didn't hurt our friendship."

Sara swallowed the lump in her throat, then smiled bravely. "No, it was my arms you hurt, silly."

He missed the joke and just stood, twisting his hat in his hands.

"Ethan, would you like to write Andy's mother? I could—"

"No." His voice was strangely sharp. She looked into his eyes.

"Ethan, are you all right? Would you like to go somewhere and talk?"

"No, I'm fine."

He was cross and tired of everyone asking him if he was all right.

"I can't write or anything right now. And I won't be able to come by much anymore. I'm very busy at work. Goodbye, Sara."

He turned and left, a sinking feeling in his spirit. It seemed the grief turned like a knife inside him. He hadn't meant to be so abrupt and harsh. And, he had lied to her.

He had less to do at work lately, for the President had fallen ill after his return from Gettysburg. He had been diagnosed with a mild case of chicken pox and would be quarantined in the White House.

Sara went back to her work. She now accepted what she had held at bay in her thoughts—with Andy gone, Ethan hadn't any real reason to come to Amory Square.

Peppercreek, Illinois
December, 1863

Wyeth was reading Ethan's Christmas letter to her father and Isaiah one rainy afternoon.

269

... I think Mr. Lincoln's favorite present so far this year was a pair of knitted stockings from an older lady in Ohio. They are red, white, and blue, with a Union flag at the top of the sock, and a Confederate flag at the heel! He sure got a good laugh from that one. Doesn't that remind you of something Grandmother would do? Thanks for your package. I'll be a good boy and not open it till Christmas day. I can smell Grandmother's fruitcake... It will be another lonely Christmas away from home. I miss you.

Ethan

The room was quiet; the rain had stopped. Wyeth tried not to cry, but Ethan's letter, like Henri's the day before, brought all her emotions back to the surface. This was the first Christmas she and Henri had been separated in their marriage. And with a baby on the way.

"It'll be a quiet Christmas this year," Will's voice was low.

"But, we'll get along!" said Wyeth with forced cheerfulness.

"Of course we will! Now, I'll go put the tea on. You slice that cake, and let's begin Mr. Dickens' new book."

Eastern Kentucky

"All right fellas, whoever is going to listen, come on."

The crude bark hut of the preacher was cramped but warm. Outside the winter wind howled across the frozen Kentucky countryside. Had the twelve men come for the diluted hot cocoa Henri offered, or the words? He didn't know, and in a way it didn't matter, for he genuinely liked these men. All of them were homesick and war-sick. He looked into their chapped, grizzled faces.

"You've got a grand wife to send you all these goodies, preacher."

"The best, Danny!"

"Now, hold on there, preacher. My Agnes is a prize winner, sure."

They all laughed.

"I reckon we'd all like to be home tonight," Henri said. He looked down into his tin cup. "I know I would. My wife is going to have a baby, and I... This hot cocoa and a story is all the Christmas cheer I can give you fellas... If your ma had sent you a big box, with it wrapped up in beautiful paper, filled with all your favorite things, and you took one look and said 'Aw, just keep your old box,' what would you be?"

"Crazy!" piped up one soldier.

"'Pears to me you'd be ungrateful, like," suggested a timid young man.

"You're exactly right, Seth. Now think about that as you hear this story I'm going to tell you. You've probably heard it before, but really listen to it this time. Listen with your heart...

"There was a man whose wife was going to have a baby, soon. When her time came, the only place for them to stay was in a stable, with the animals."

"Bet it was cold," someone interrupted.

"Sshh!" admonished another.

"Yes it was," Henri continued, "a cold night like this night. A clear night. Out on a hill, like we are, away from their families, was a group of shepherds, with cold hands and cold feet. Just like you fellas. It was about to become a night they'd never forget... And suddenly an angel appeared with a multitude of the heavenly host, praising God, saying 'Glory to God in the highest, and on Earth peace'... And Mary gave birth to a son, and laid him in a manger...

"Fellas, that's the gift, plain and simple. A little baby named Jesus, sent from God to become a man, to live a sinless life, to die on a cross for your sins and mine. It's the biggest and best gift anyone will ever give you. It's up to you if you accept it or not..."

Henri lay looking up at his ceiling some hours later, tears streaming down his cheeks. Tonight had been precious to him as he prayed with some of his soldier friends. He lay now in his quiet hut, praising God. He thought of all the men separated from their wives. He thought of his Wyeth, in her bed alone in Illinois, so far away.

"But though I miss her," he whispered in the darkness, "You, Jehovah, are with her. Tell her I love her tonight..."

Washington, D.C.

The social season of Washington was spinning at its height.

The war had gone into hibernation. The third Christmas of the war found Southern cities faced with despair—there was no hope in sight for an end to the conflict and the long hoped-for aid and intervention from Europe had never come. Economic hardships were becoming increasingly painful to Southern citizens. Yet, hardships were unheard of in Northern cities, and certainly in the fun-loving capital. Bread lines might be seen in Richmond and Atlanta, but in Washington there were theater, parties, fairs, and no short supply of food and drink.

Amory Square Hospital was receiving a good dose of benevolent Christmas cheer from ladies' societies and church groups of the city—those who remembered the ailing multitudes of the army on their very doorstep. With their baskets of greenery, they decorated the hospital, looping pine boughs over the Union flags that hung in the wards. The scent of ginger, cinnamon, tea, and pine mixed with the antiseptic hospital odors. They brought newspapers, Bibles, magazines and novels to read tirelessly to the patients.

Because of this added help, Sara was able to take a much-needed break from her work. She and Claire were traveling to Claire's small hometown in northern Maryland for a few days.

"We'll drag out Father's sleigh and go for long rides. We'll sleep late and drink Mother's special nog and just—get away!"

So Sara had agreed. It was too far to go home to Peppercreek, but at least she could be away from the hospital for a time.

A blast of winter wind slammed against the window, causing Sara to look up and frown. If the weather continued this way it would make traveling more difficult tomorrow. Already the sky was a flat white, with all the promise of snow in it. Sara drew her shawl closer around her. The thin boards of the barracks were flimsy against the penetrating cold.

She thought of Thomas, a Tennessee farm boy turned soldier. Gentlemen to the marrow, he was always telling Sara about his girl back home. There was no threat to Sara to draw close to him. She thought of his words to her as she had bid him goodbye.

"Are you sure you ain't runnin' off to your sweetheart, Miss James?"

"Now Thomas, I told you I'm going home with Nurse Hatch."

"Well, you just have to have a beau somewhere."

"Why do I?"

"Are you fishin'?" he asked, teasing.

Her laugh bubbled over. "Of course not! Why must I have a beau?"

He cocked his head. "Cause you're plum pretty—though o'course not so much as my Sall—and sweet as a peach."

"Thank you so much. Now lie down, and try to behave for whomever cares for you while I'm gone. I know it will be difficult for you."

"Aw, Miss James, why don't you have a sweetheart?"

"You're part Tennessee bloodhound, Thomas! I don't . . . have time for romance."

Thomas's face grew very serious. "No time? Why that's no good, Miss James. Things of the heart are powerful important!"

She looked out at the white slate of sky. She didn't want anything to spoil their trip tomorrow. Christmastime was so special.

"Mr. Lincoln's back." Claire's voice interrupted her thoughts.

"Mr. Lincoln?"

"Yes, he's out in the wards."

The President was fully recovered and returning to wish the men his best Christmas greetings.

"I'm almost finished packing," continued Claire. "Just think, Sara! This time tomorrow we'll be home and enjoying the fatted calf!"

"Was he alone?" Sara asked casually.

"Who?" Claire returned with equal innocence.

"Mr. Lincoln."

"No, the First Lady is with him this time. She's a short, plump little gal, isn't she? The papers have been right about that much."

Sara smoothed a well-starched hanky and did not meet Claire's eyes to ask, "Just—Mr. and Mrs. Lincoln then?"

She did not see Claire's quick smile.

"No, there was an escort with him, I think. Very handsome fellow. Seemed on the lookout for someone."

Sara had said nothing to her friend about her feelings for Ethan. In fact, she had never even mentioned his name. She was saved a response by another nurse appearing at the door summoning Claire away.

"They're probably still in ward C," Claire called over her shoulder.

But Sara did not move toward the door. She would stay just where she was, she told herself. Sara had not seen Ethan since that last abrupt time six weeks ago. She hungered to see him, but it was too painful. Why go now?

"I'll get over him, I will!" she whispered fiercely to the glass.

She could hear the wind outside. It seemed to moan Thomas's words at her: "Things of the heart are powerful important..."

Ethan poured himself another cup of tea, squeezing a liberal amount of lemon into it. Perhaps this would help, but before he could drink it he threw out another racking sneeze. He leaned back in his chair, groaning. He ached from head to toe.

"What a wretched, miserable way to spend Christmas," he said to his empty room. "Watch it, old boy. It's getting dangerous when you start talking to yourself!" he laughed.

He looked around the room and his eyes rested on the box from home. Why eat the fruitcake, he thought bitterly, if I can't even taste it?

"Blast colds anyway," he mumbled again.

He sighed. He couldn't go home, and was stuck in his room, sick.

On his table lay two theater tickets. They were for Sara, but she hadn't been there when he had gone to see her a few days ago. A small Christmas gift he thought she'd enjoy, a chance to be away from the hospital. Sara. He hadn't seen her in over a month, though he started to go to her half a dozen times. He felt guilt about that, but he was just now feeling a lessening of grief over Andy. He wouldn't admit it to himself, but in his mind Sara and the pain of Andy's death were linked.

Tonight was Christmas Eve. He decided the best he could do was to remember, remember Christmases in the past. That first one at Peppercreek. Muted laughter from the hallway vaguely penetrated Ethan's room. But in the darkness, he celebrated Christmas, 1863. By remembering....

Chapter 9

1864

♦ ♦ ♦ ♦ ♦ ♦

*T*he flurry of parties was over, and the grim business of war was taken up again with the arrival of spring. Frozen roads now thawed into rivers of mud, giving passage to troops and supply wagons. Northern sentiment held that this must certainly be the final spring of the war, fighting General Grant must bring it about. In addition, rumors came daily of desertion in the Southern ranks. The Rebs were losing the heart for fighting and there seemed no hope left in Jeff Davis's troubled government.

This was an election year, and things looked gloomy for the President. Optimism for the war's end didn't seem to matter to the public. There were ills in the government and surely Mr. Lincoln was responsible.

When Ethan turned into the hallway leading to the President's office after dinner one afternoon, he smelled something familiar. Lilacs. He was surprised. Miss Amanda Sims stood at the end of the corridor, gazing out a window. She stood in silhouette. Her parasol twirled daintily by her side. In that moment of undetected gazing, Ethan had time to again confirm that she was indeed a beauty. Now dressed in a red striped gown, she reminded Ethan of a peppermint stick. The hallway was quiet and deserted. He cast a quick glance to see that the small waiting room was already full of folks eager to press claims on their easily accessible leader. Ethan's step made no noise on the carpet, but Amanda turned. There was a grim line about her mouth and a cold look in her eyes. It seemed to Ethan she looked like marble. She recognized Ethan, and the pleasant mask went up again.

"Ethan! Hello. I thought I might run into you here. What a delight."

"Hello, Amanda," he said coming up, taking her extended hand. "You're the nicest thing I've seen in these hallways in a long time."

Her smile broadened at this.

"It's been awhile," he continued.

She dipped her chin slightly. "Very true. Been busy, or..." She let her words dangle with a smile.

"Yes. You know, with the campaigns and election, it's been pretty busy around here," he said.

"Election. Well, things don't look too favorable for Mr. Lincoln just now, or so the papers say," she said, arching an eyebrow.

Ethan was grateful the President's door was closed. Somehow, this seemed to him an inappropriate conversation to be having in the White House hallway.

"Well, not many newspaper editors like President Lincoln. Still, a lot of the voting public do."

"Newspapers are rather, oh, influential, don't you think?" she purred.

"Are you waiting to see him?" asked Ethan.

She answered with a bell-like laugh, "No, of course not! Daddy's in there with him. He's concerned about this absolute flood of wounded into the city. It's shocking!"

"Can I get you a chair?"

"No, I'm fine, thank you. I just couldn't sit in there."

She pointed to the waiting room where a farmer in overalls was entering. "Too many people. Besides—the smell! Why do I smell turpentine in the White House, Ethan? Is Mary having something redone again?" There was a trace of sarcasm that Ethan missed.

"No, it's from the dining room. An artist from New York has moved in to make a portrait of Lincoln and his Cabinet."

One of Amanda's eyebrows arched again. "A portrait?"

"Yes, he's recreating the signing of the Emancipation Proclamation on canvas. It's pretty impressive."

"But why?"

The President's door suddenly swung open with several senators emerging, Sims included. He crossed over to his daughter.

"Sorry to keep you waiting so long, my dear."

"Oh, don't worry Daddy. Look who kept me company."

"Hello, Senator."

"Captain Alcott, how are you?"

"Fine, sir, and you?"

"Considerably rattled, I'm afraid. This rush of wounded is quite fearful. Disease could run rampant through the city if precautions aren't taken immediately. Well, Amanda, where can I drop you off? I'm going to take another look, make a fresher report."

"I'll go with you."

"Certainly not."

They had begun down the hall, Amanda easily linking her arm in Ethan's.

"It's no place for a gentlewoman," the senator continued.

Amanda laughed. "Oh Daddy, don't be silly. I'm certainly strong enough to take the sight of a little blood. Besides, I've done extensive charity work for the Sanitary Commission, haven't I?"

"Of course. And I'm very proud of you. But this is hardly the same thing, my dear."

Ethan wished he could escape, but Amanda was tightly possessive of his arm. He thought they had forgotten him, but of course she hadn't.

"Now Daddy, I'm going with you. Here, let's take Ethan with us for protection!" She finished with a laugh. "If any delirious soldiers rush our carriage, Ethan will be there!"

Ethan felt terribly embarrassed. Amanda's light banter irritated him, but he didn't know what to do.

"Well, Alcott, what do you say to my daughter's proposal?" The senator's gray eyes were piercing. "Could Mr. Lincoln manage awhile without you? It might be useful to have someone on his staff see firsthand the condition of things. Perhaps he respects his bodyguard's opinion better than those of the senators around him." His voice was bitter.

"Sir, I . . . hardly have the President's ear. I mean—"

"Can you go with us?" asked Amanda.

"I'll go speak with Mr. Hay."

They drove toward the wharf district, and when the Senator was satisfied with a place to stop, he directed his driver to pull the carriage over. "I'll be back directly, Amanda. Wait here."

There were nurses, doctors, citizens and wounded everywhere—a mass of unorganized people, an odd mosaic of life and
death.

"Look at all those stretchers!" exclaimed Amanda. "It's
frightful—so many poor men. Look at all the women here!"

Ethan said nothing. This scene was not new to him.

"I can't believe it! There's Lydia Bragg!"

Amanda could not conceal her surprise at seeing a friend
from the cream of society in such chaos.

"Amanda, what does your father want the President to do
about the wounded?"

She looked at him, almost having forgotten he was there.

"Establish more field hospitals. This is ridiculous, flooding
the city with dying men. There simply isn't room for all the men
and supplies."

"And there is at the fronts?" Ethan returned incredulously.

"Father thinks so. And I agree. Why, Washington is becoming
a virtual hospital city! Think of the possibility for the spread of
contagion to the civilian population."

Ethan swallowed hard, thoroughly indignant now.

"Not to mention the sight it gives foreign dignitaries. They
come to the capital of a great nation and see this! They must
think we can't manage things very well."

Ethan looked down at his hands, his mind reeling with things
he could say.

"I must go speak with Lydia." Amanda was out of the carriage
before Ethan could protest.

Ethan followed her, becoming instantly sorry he had. It was
too absurd, this contrast they made in the crowd. He, tall,
healthy, spotlessly dressed, escorting a woman in flounce and
furbelows, her wide hat bobbing in the crowd. They looked like
the sugar figurines on a wedding cake. They drew immediate
attention, and Ethan was never so embarrassed in all his life.

"Amanda! Your father wanted you to stay in the carriage. We
should go back."

"Nonsense! I will see Lydia."

Then, he saw her. Sara was bent over a man on a pallet,
readjusting a bloody bandage across his forehead. Even at a
distance, he could see she did it with great tenderness, speaking
something to the man that he could not hear.

"Sara." He spoke her name gently, happier to see her than he had been that first time in the hospital months ago. His eyes were beaming. She whirled around, startled, nearly dropping the bucket she carried. She was too tired and too surprised to see the gladness in his face.

"Hello, Ethan."

They had but a moment to study each other. They had not seen each other in nearly four months. Ethan quickly assessed that he had never seen her looking worse.

"How are you?" she asked, forcing normalcy into her voice.

"Fine. And you?"

She gave him only a tired smile for an answer. She wanted to move on.

"Ethan! There you are." Amanda swept up beside him, linking her arm in his. "You left me."

"Amanda, this is a friend of mine, Miss Sara James. Sara, this is Amanda Sims."

"Hello, Miss Sims."

Sara was not surprised by the name. One day she and Claire had been reading the newspaper's society page for laughs, when they came across Ethan and Amanda's name linked together. Sara had not been surprised then either. Of course he would be courting a young woman.

So, here she was. Yes, Sara admitted, she was as pretty as the papers loved to describe.

"You're a nurse," Amanda enthused. "How brave!"

Sara said nothing, shifting the bucket of smelly linen to another hand.

"We're friends from back home in Illinois. We grew up together," Ethan volunteered.

Amanda turned her full attention upon Sara and Sara did not flinch under the gaze. Nor did she fail to notice an almost imperceptible tightening of Amanda's grip upon Ethan's arm.

"How charming," murmured Amanda.

"Well, I better go," Sara said in a moment. "Nice to meet you, Miss Sims. Goodbye, Ethan."

She quickly melted into the crowd with Ethan gazing after her. For a moment, he had forgotten Amanda.

Amanda shook her curls. "It's warm. Let's go back to the carriage Daddy may be there "

Back at the carriage, she fanned herself in silence. Finally she spoke. "How does Lydia do this?" There was an edge of wonder in her voice.

Ethan sat in silence.

Her color was slowly returning. "Miss James is rather young to be here, don't you think? But so brave..."

Before Ethan could reply, Senator Sims was climbing in the carriage. Ethan sighed deeply. It would be good to get back to work.

Ethan woke up feeling restless that Sunday morning in May. It wasn't just restlessness—he was homesick. It seemed overnight he'd become sick of Washington, sick of everything about the war, sick of this room that had become his home. It was not unhappiness with his work with the President however. That was still a privilege.

He stood looking out the window of his room, frowning. Outside, the day was perfect: calm, warm, the sky a smooth sheet of cerulean. Still, he couldn't enjoy it.

Spring was planting time. He could see it in his mind. Wyeth would be in her garden. His father would be plowing up the fields, hiring someone to help because Ethan wasn't there to do it. The trees would be in blossom. He wanted to go home.

Then Sara's face came to mind. He hadn't seen her since the time at the wharf two weeks earlier. When he was with her, he felt like he was home. Sara...home. He grabbed his hat and hurried from the room.

He found her sitting with Claire on a veranda the staff used. He surprised her with his forthrightness.

"Hello, Sara."

"Ethan! Hello."

"It's one of those days to be out on, don't you think? Let's go rowing."

He hadn't asked, he just stated it. Claire looked down at her needlework, wondering how her friend would respond. Sara felt his eyes upon her, awaiting an answer. She was tempted to say no, but for no real reason—especially since she so wanted to go.

A handful of rowers could be seen on the Potomac, and occasionally a steamboat. Ethan rented a small skiff and soon they were drifting lazily along the shoreline. Ethan had said perhaps a dozen words, then fallen into an absorbed silence. Sara sat thinking about him, wondering what serious thoughts made him so unusually quiet.

Why hadn't he taken Amanda Sims rowing? she mused. Was he still seeing her? Sara had no way of knowing. She was a generous girl though. He had asked her out rowing and that was all that mattered.

She was content to study his profile, the way his dark hair framed his head, his jawline, his eyelashes. She knew every line of his face, and smiled to herself, knowing he probably didn't even know the color of her eyes. Finally she broke the silence.

"What are you thinking of, Ethan?"

He shook his head, embarrassed that he'd grown so silent.

"Home," he said simply.

She looked out across the water.

"And I guess I'm thinking about Andy," he added slowly. "Ah, Sara, I'm sorry about when Andy died—how I acted, I mean. Like I blamed you or something. I don't, of course."

"It's all right, Ethan. I know you were hurt."

"I'm not very fit company today. I don't know what's the matter with me."

"Look around, Ethan! Look at the hills!" she encouraged.

And he did. He inhaled deeply, for the fragrance of spring-time was strong in the air. A kaleidoscope of color was all around him. Springtime in Washington could be every bit as beautiful as springtime at home.

"Miss James, I think you're trying to tell me there's more to life than this war and Washington and..."

"And your work. Yes, much more. We see so much of the work of men's hands around us every day that we forget to look at all the work of God's hands."

He studied the oars a moment, digesting her words.

"Sara, you see the wounded, the dying every day. Ten hours a day. I only read about them. You work ten times harder than I do! How do you keep going when you see that constant misery?"

She had to think carefully before answering him. "Some days I don't do very well. I decide that I'll tell the matron I'm finished and I'm going home. Then, I remember that my life right now is larger than this, is more than just where I am and what I'm doing

today. This is but a season, like springtime. The war will end and
I'll go home. It will be another season of my life and I'll take up
whatever new work He has for me."

His eyes were intent upon her. She had never looked lovelier
than now with the sunshine radiating all around her. Ethan could
see that out in the fresh air, the deep pink had returned to her
cheeks.

"And I know He'll give me strength because He called me to
Amory Square. He wouldn't call me to something without giving
me the strength to do it."

She had never shared her faith with him and she didn't know
what he was thinking. She knew his family, his upbringing as well
as her own. Yet she did not know his heart.

The personal way she referred to the Lord made him think of
Wyeth.

"Usually you remind me of Libby, but now you're reminding
me of Wyeth," he said.

She smiled. He was referring to her faith, the same faith his
sister had. So, that's how he thought of her—as she had already
guessed—a little sister.

"I'll take that as a compliment, then."

He pulled the hair above his ear. She could almost imagine
tears in his eyes. She felt a wave of tenderness for him. There
would never be anything more than this, she had decided. Yet the
good friendship between them would always be special.

"There's no one I respect more than Wyeth," he said. "She . . .
is like my mother was."

He could not talk anymore, so he rowed in silence.

As they came around a point of land Sara exclaimed, "Oh,
Ethan!"

A lush hill of jade green sloped down to the water, and farther
up was a well-cultivated orchard. It was obviously part of a
wealthy estate. The orchard was a showy panorama of white and
pink blossoms.

"They should have a good crop of fruit this year, I'm betting,"
commented Ethan.

Sara turned back to look at him.

"You're missing the famous Peppercreek orchard, I'm guessing!"

"You seem to have the knack of hitting the spot, Sara."

Their laughter floated over the water.

"As nice as it is here today," he admitted, "I was still wanting to be home, with my father, working in the orchard."

"Tell me, then," she urged. "Tell me exactly what you'd be doing if you were home. Tell me everything, Ethan." He did not hear the longing in her voice.

So for over an hour he did that. The oars lay idle in his hands. He became relaxed and cheerful talking about home. The earlier gloom fell away. He told her of plans, of things he'd like to do for the orchard and his father. Plans that had lain dormant in his mind for nearly three years. Plans he had never voiced to anyone. He finished by telling her of his desire to bring Andy Mill home to Illinois for a visit, yet he did not grow sad.

"I've used my strength talking," he laughed. "You may have to row us back, Sara!"

It was her turn to be lost in thought. He had grown warm with the rowing and rolled up his shirtsleeves. She could see the firm muscles swell as he pulled. She wondered how those arms would feel around her, closed in a gentle embrace...

Ethan lay in his darkened room that night, tired and fighting the creeping feeling of loneliness. He had shrugged it off for those hours he was with Sara, but now it returned. It made him feel strange inside—almost frightened. Frightened because he'd never been like this before. He'd always been confident, optimistic, and content. He had talked so much today. Why? Why did he always do that with Sara? He rolled over, resolving to work even harder, if it would drive away these strange feelings.

Sara sat brushing out her hair that night when Claire entered the room they shared. Claire could read nothing in Sara's passive face.

"So, how was rowing on the Potomac with the Captain? 'Let's go rowing, Sara'." She imitated Ethan in her sternest voice. Sara burst out laughing. Then her smile faded as she slowly replied, "It was a wonderful day, Claire. And a terrible day."

On a bright Sunday afternoon, a large crowd gathered on the White House lawn to hear the Marine Band play. It was the first time since little Willie Lincoln's death that the First Lady had allowed the Sunday concert tradition to continue. Now ladies strolled on the arms of gentlemen, their parasols twirling by their sides, gay chatter and laughter mixing with the music. It was a beautiful spring day, oblivious to man's designs. A day when all the fresh, vibrant spirit of spring seemed to come up from the ground and infect people. Folks were smiling, the sunshine was mellow, the sky was an intense blue, as if the ocean had rushed up into it. The thunder of cannon and clash of steel southward seemed a continent away.

Ethan was on his way back into the city and a late dinner when he heard the strains of music from the lawn. He turned his mount toward the lawn, ignoring his growling stomach. It would be nice to listen to the band awhile, instead of the clatter and clang at Willard's or the silence of his own room.

Tying his horse in the White House stables, he sauntered over through the crowd. He selected a tree to lean against and listen. The band was a skilled group, entertaining the crowd with waltzes, popular songs, and marches. The laughter of a couple across the way drew Ethan's attention away from the band. Amanda was sitting, leaning toward a handsome officer. Their heads were close together. Ethan shifted, surprised that he felt no jealousy.

A little cart with a striped canvas top had rolled up, dispensing lemonade for a nickel. Ethan sauntered toward it.

"Hello, Captain."

A feminine voice stopped him. Well, for once I surprised him, Sara thought to herself.

"Well, Sara! Hello!"

She looked so fresh and young and . . .

"Enjoying the concert?" she was asking.

"Yes, it's—"

"A wonderful day to be out on," she finished for him.

They both smiled. It was a private moment—just them, sharing a smile, with everyone and the music in the background. She clasped her hands behind her, that nervous, tumbly feeling growing inside her. She was too much in love with him now to deny it.

They talked a few minutes and she noticed him glance toward the crowd, as if he was looking for someone. Now that she had this chance encounter, she fidgeted with her dress as she worked around to what was uppermost in her mind.

"Ethan, there's to be a dance next Saturday night. The Christian Commission is putting it on with the Patent Fair. To raise money, you know."

"Oh? I hadn't heard." He kept looking above her head.

"An orchestra from New York, and everything. It's supposed to be quite—"

"The Christian Commission putting it on? Hmm... That should be interesting."

Sara colored slightly, but Ethan didn't notice.

"I was wondering if you'd like to go."

Somehow, normally easygoing, uncomplicated Sara James could not squeeze "with me" on the end of the invitation. It seemed to stick in her throat.

Ethan pulled at his hair absently. He could see Amanda in the distance. There was just enough desire and ego in him to not want to be easily put off by her. He wanted to walk up to her, easy and friendly, to show her he didn't mind this officer. He had only listened to Sara with half attention.

"Well, maybe, Sara. I don't know what I'll be doing then— what's going on, you know."

Sara turned slightly and saw the object of Ethan's attention. Amanda Sims.

For as long as Sara could remember, she had never really been angry with this boy/man she'd known so many years. But now, she was angry. She felt the hot flush of anger and hurt feelings. She straightened up, losing any hesitancy she'd been feeling.

"You're right, Ethan, it probably will be a country bumpkin affair to you. Never mind."

Ethan's face registered surprise. He'd never heard Sara's voice so bitingly calm. "Sara, I only meant—" But she was stepping back over to her friends, her back ramrod-straight.

She knew Ethan was standing behind her, but she would not turn around. The little drama had taken less than five minutes, but Sara's sensitive soul felt as if it had been stabbed. She gritted her teeth against the tears that threatened to come.

Ethan stood there a moment, shrugged, then headed toward the stable. Perhaps he should have chosen food over music today . . .

Within a few days, Ethan realized how very wrong he had been about the Christian Commission dance. It might not rank as the social gathering of the season, but it was certainly no backwoods barn raising. He heard talk of it from the tables at Willard's and in the society pages of the newspaper.

Saturday afternoon found him moping in his room, but at six that evening he decided to go alone. Sara might be there, and he could apologize.

When Ethan arrived, the auditorium was already surrounded with carriages. Even unused ambulances had been pressed into escort service. Light and music pulsed from the windows. There were officers in blue and gold braid everywhere, their mustaches well waxed. There was laughter and gaiety, no sobering war talk. Society was enjoying itself for the night. Silks and crinoline rustled along the dance floor with the clicks of shiny boots.

Ethan grabbed a glass of punch from a passing tray and idled from one group to another, staying on the fringe and taking no active part. He began to wish he hadn't come. After an hour or so, he found an alcove and stood absently watching the couples glide across the floor. In front of him was a group of officers who kept up a steady commentary on the feminine allurements on display. Ethan listened for lack of anything else to do.

"That's the beauty of the dance, there," declared one tall young officer loudly. "Wish I could get near her." There was murmured agreement. Another officer joined the group and was asked his opinion.

"There, that one. The blonde. I'll get a dance with her before the night's over," he said confidentially.

"And Jeffy always gets what he wants!" someone laughed.

Ethan's curiosity was thoroughly awakened now to see what woman was provoking such admiration. More than likely it was someone from Amanda's set of friends, someone he had been introduced to.

He followed the officer's gaze until he found the dancer they all watched. She wore a silk dress of watered strawberry, but with so many dancers he could not see her clearly. He could see her dress was not low cut in the back like so many others. She was also easy to spot because of the way she wore her hair. She was the only woman in the room who did not have her hair piled up. Instead hers was loose, flowing past her shoulders in waves of honeyed blonde. Such a hairstyle was causing quite a scandal among the womenfolk and admiration from the men. He could see her head tilt forward like she was frequently laughing. Ethan stepped to the edge of the dance floor to get a closer look.

Dancers came between them and he could only follow her from the splash of color from her dress. Now, she was coming closer, and he could see she had changed partners again. She was swinging into his view, her face toward him. It was Sara!

He stood transfixed as she whirled by, her cheeks glowing pink. Sara! He could hardly believe it! From the drab brown uniform he had usually seen her in, her hair severely pulled back, to this! A glittering, shimmering, radiant young woman. "She's beautiful!" he gasped.

"You're right there, Captain." It was the officer who had assessed Sara earlier. He flashed Ethan a cocky smile. "I'll have her next."

Ethan studied the arrogant lieutenant a moment, but said nothing. Two older women had stepped up to the edge of the dance floor also. They stood with their tiny beaded purses, flashing pearl handled fans. Their comments were as easy to hear as the officers'.

"They say he's second only to General Grant..."

"He's dancing again, and not with his wife!"

"That young woman, look at her hair. It's positively heathenish! Why, someone should speak to her about it!"

At that instant the music ended and Ethan found Sara only a few feet from him. Her partner was bowing over her hand as the officer beside Ethan moved forward to his conquest. Ethan stepped up to her also. She looked up and found Ethan and another officer in front of her.

Sara James had never been known as a beauty, either in Washington or at home. Too often her face reflected exhaustion or sadness. Only the soldiers she cared for thought her really lovely. It was some quality of sweetness they saw coming from the inside that radiated beauty on the outside. Tonight she was enjoying herself, and it showed.

It had taken a few days to shake off the hurt from Ethan's rudeness. Then she had decided she would go, forget work for one night, forget Ethan and have fun. She had been amused when Claire took over her preparations with such seriousness. She tossed aside the plain gown that Sara had and presented her with one of her own elegant dresses. Sara had chosen to wear her hair down.

"I always wear it pinned up! I'm wearing it down like I do at home. I'm going to go and have a good time, after all!"

At first she had been terribly embarrassed by the attention. Then, she ceased to really care. After all it was only one night; reality would come with the dawn. Now Ethan stood before her, looking as handsome to her as ever. With all her strength she forced herself to stay calm. Please don't blush, she ordered herself.

"Miss—" began the officer at Ethan's side.

"Good evening, Sara," interrupted Ethan, taking her hand.

"Hello, Ethan."

There was nothing else to say so Ethan led her back into the surge of dancers. He relished the look of shock on the face of the lieutenant.

They danced in silence, Sara finding she did not really want to look at him. Surely he could hear her heart beating, she thought.

Finally Ethan spoke. "Sara, you . . . I almost didn't recognize you! You're radiant tonight!" he enthused.

"I didn't think you were coming," she said calmly.

The hurt had fallen away at his voice and touch.

"Well, I didn't either, until the last minute."

Ethan didn't feel like talking and neither did Sara. They danced until the music ended, then he steered her to the table where punch was served. Sara watched the dancers, Ethan watched her.

"I'd imagine you'd be pretty thirsty with all the dancing you've done. You're the belle of the ball tonight, Sara!" His voice was teasing.

"Oh, Ethan . . ."

"No, really! Everyone is talking about the lovely young woman with the scandalous hair."

They both laughed and Sara grew calmer, toying with the edge of her cup.

"This isn't the first time we've danced, you know."

"It's not? I'm afraid I forgot."

"Sally Ann Hudson was your date that night."

"Oh, now I remember. I don't remember us dancing, though."

"You humored me. Besides," Sara added, laughing, "you were addled over Sally Ann, according to your little sister."

She watched him over the rim of her glass, as he remembered that long-ago night.

But now his mind was completely on the present. He knew if they stood there much longer another admirer would try to claim Sara. And strangely, he didn't want to dance any more after this first dance of the night. He wanted to be somewhere alone with her. Would she be willing to step out of the spotlight for him?

He touched her arm. "Sara?"

There was nothing else, just a simple appeal. He glanced around and spotted an archway that led outside. It was quieter and deserted on this outdoor pavilion. Sara offered no resistance to going outside and Ethan was relieved.

It was shadowy and cool here, a breeze gently tossing the branches in a music Ethan and Sara recognized better than the tunes that the orchestra played inside. Sara stood smoothing her dress, a part of her wishing she had not allowed him to lead her here. Why had he, anyway? Ethan leaned against a railing, his arms crossed. Perhaps he had learned to court Amanda Sims, but somehow, this was different. He couldn't be glib or superficial with Sara and he knew it. Why had he wanted her alone? After all, this was Roy's little sister. Yet...

"I said you looked radiant tonight. I meant that. You're absolutely lovely tonight, Sara."

There was that schoolboyish quality in his voice that she had not heard in a long while. It caused her to smile inside.

Ethan was confused, nervous. Why do I feel this way? he asked himself. He meant to apologize, but it seemed all words stuck in his throat. Sara wasn't saying anything, wasn't even looking at him. Perhaps he should take her back. Perhaps that's where she really wanted to be.

He stepped up to her and took her hand. The moonlight, pale and friendly, glowed in a springtime canopy of stars. Somewhere in the distance a horse neighed and someone was laughing, but to Ethan and Sara, the two of them were the only ones on earth.

Who moved forward first could be a matter of debate. Perhaps only the moon and stars knew. Ethan leaned forward and Sara met him in a simple, gentle kiss. Then he pulled back. This was a beautiful woman—the skinny schoolgirl was a thing of the past. He stared into the clear blue depths of her eyes and she did not care now if he did see all the love she felt for him mirrored there. There was a slight smile playing about her lips.

"Yes, you are very lovely, Sara," he whispered hoarsely. He was surprised as her arms slid up around his neck. She pulled him closer as his arms encircled her. Now, their kisses were not so quick, not so gentle. He smelled and fingered her hair, she caressed his neck and touched his curls. They stood this way for a time, conscious only of each other.

Finally Sara pulled away, breathless, lightheaded, and thoroughly shocked with herself.

"Do you want to go back in and dance, or are you ready to leave?" Ethan asked quietly, reluctant to release her hand.

"I'm ready to leave," she agreed softly.

Ethan fetched their wraps and hailed a waiting carriage. Finally they were in the carriage and while the driver made ready, Ethan turned to look at Sara, half afraid he would find her angry with him. But she wasn't angry, and returned his smile. Impulsively, he kissed her. Then, with a jump, the carriage started.

It seemed natural enough to them both, that here in the relative quiet and darkness of the carriage, they should kiss each time the driver stopped at a corner. So, they did. Too soon, they arrived at Sara's dormitory. Ethan helped Sara down and told the driver to wait. The squatty little building lay in darkness, but lights from the hospital cast shadows on the ground.

They faced each other on the steps. Ethan felt that his head was in a whirl and couldn't think what to say. Sara looked at him in expectation for a moment, but then after an awkward silence, quickly said goodnight and hurried into the building. Ethan stared after her. The carriage horse gave an impatient stamp and Ethan climbed back in. As he rode along toward Willard's, he thought of how, only moments ago, Sara had been so close to him, her slender arms around his neck. He still felt the sweet passion in her kisses. He sighed deeply. Tonight had been so different than he had expected...

Chapter 10

Peppercreek, Illinois

✦✦ ✦✦ ✦✦

*I*t's strange to be celebrating another Independence Day, and the country still at war."

There was a sad tone in Wyeth's voice that caused Grandmother Tufts to look up from her knitting. War indeed, Grandmother sighed to herself, and here was Wyeth with her time so near—and Henri hundreds of miles away. Grandmother shook her head. This war was dragging on so that even her sturdy optimism was being severely tested.

"Have you heard from Sara lately, Helen?" Grandmother asked.

"I had a letter a week ago. The hospital is a bit less crowded lately, so her hours aren't as long," said Mrs. James.

"Such a brave girl," praised Grandmother.

"Such a wicked city!" Agnes West interrupted. "I'd imagine she sees no end of sights! Why, lands, I don't suppose I'd sleep a wink at night for knowing one of my young'uns was in that big city."

Grandmother, knowing the West children as she did, gave a wry smile. "Sara's a good girl. Have you heard from Roy, too?"

Mrs. James face paled a bit. "Not in several months. He's not much of a hand to write."

"Neither is Ethan," put in Louisa.

"But Roy James is a soldier on the front lines, not in Washington D.C.," added Mrs. West pointedly. She always felt the O'Dell clan—and Alice Tufts particularly—put on airs that Ethan was an aide to the President. And an adopted son at that...

Wyeth withdrew from the conversation and gazed out across the meadow. It was a small gathering this Fourth. Many folks had stayed at home. The sky was a beautiful blue with fleecy clouds scattered like coconut shavings across it, a perfect day for a picnic. Wyeth shifted, trying to find a comfortable position with such a protruding belly. Her hand went to her stomach, smoothing it protectively. No doubt if Henri were here he would make tender, teasing jokes about her figure. If Ethan had been home, the combination would have been unmerciful.

She smiled. Henri, her Henri. A soon-to-be baby after so many years of longing. It was almost a reality. But what if . . . What if something went wrong during the birth? Or what if something happened like the choking spell with the Baxter baby—and Henri not here?

"What's to be the name of your little tyke, Wyeth?" Mrs. West asked sweetly.

Wyeth was lost in thought and did not hear.

"Wyeth?" Louisa touched her sister's arm.

Mrs. West repeated her question. Grandmother rolled her eyes. Really, was there no end to this West woman! Plain to see she was a newcomer to Peppercreek . . . It's common courtesy not to ask the name of a baby-to-be. Wyeth was not troubled, though.

"Well, Mrs. West, we haven't chosen a name yet. Names are too important. I'll have to see our little son or daughter first to make sure the name fits just right. You couldn't put Mary on an Amy baby, you see. So for now, it's just 'blessed baby'."

Mrs. West looked down at her lap a moment. Oh the strange fancies of Wyeth Mullins! And hadn't she heard Wyeth's mother had been just like that?

"I reckon Rufus and I always allowed that naming our young' uns from the Good Book was the best way. All our girls are real biblical."

Wyeth dared not meet eyes with Louisa or Grandmother.

"You look absolutely blooming, Wyeth. I'd imagine your time isn't far off," spoke up Helen James.

"Thank you, Helen. Joe says two weeks or so."

"And the doctor is always right, you know!" laughed Louisa.

Grandmother smiled. She did like to hear Louisa laugh, such a fearless laugh. Then, her smile faded and she pointed an accusing knitting needle at Wyeth, "Louisa says you're still in that upstairs bedroom, Wyeth."

Wyeth smiled, knowing well Grandmother would eventually bring up this point. "I'm fine, really. I don't climb the stairs but once a day, I promise."

Grandmother was not without her stock of superstitions. "Climbing stairs has been known to mark a baby, as I've well told you."

Mrs. West nodded vigorously and added, "Hanging laundry can do the same." She smiled importantly, grateful to be on Alice Tufts' side at last.

It was just before sunrise the next morning when Wyeth eased herself down the stairs to her father's room. She knocked softly, calling, "Papa?"

"Wyeth? What is it gal? Are you all right?"

Wyeth could not help but smile at his anxiety.

"Papa, I think...you need to send Uncle Isaiah...for Joe."

"Joe?...The baby! Well, not for two weeks, didn't he say?"

"Papa, you know little ones come when they're ready."

"Yes, but are you sure?" Stepping into the hallway, he could see her face clearly. It was his own Rebecca's, years ago.

"Yes, gal, now you sit down. I'll fetch Joe. Now stay there. Isaiah!"

Wyeth managed a weak chuckle. No, she didn't feel much like going anywhere.

Washington, D.C.

July Fourth dawned on a hot and listless capital. There was little interest in celebrating. Besides the Union's sinking of a Confederate steamer off the coast of France, there had been little encouraging war news. Congress had adjourned and the city slipped into its predictable summer lethargy. On normally busy street corners, cabs and hacks idled with sleepy horses while even sleepier drivers nodded on their benches.

Ethan waited with other War Department staffers as news trickled in over the telegraph wires. Confederate forces were moving down the valley toward the capital. Yet no one was taking the reports too seriously. It was probably just roughriders or scouts, maybe a small cavalry unit. Even when the news leaked to the public, they were not unduly alarmed. After all, hadn't every summer of the war held rumors of Lee's attempts to capture the Union seat of power?

As the next few days passed, the reports increased, with boatmen arriving from nearby Georgetown declaring that the

Rebels were crossing the Potomac. No clear estimate of the size of the troops could be agreed upon. Washingtonians accepted the news with a yawn. Besides, the War Department still looked somnolent and passive. If there was any truth to the reports, the place would be lit up and bristling with officers, congressmen and clerks.

Then the reports described torn up railroad tracks, burned bridges and severed telegraph wires. This was beginning to sound like reality, not rumor. That same day refugees from upper Maryland arrived in the city. Frightened, they clogged the streets with their household belongings piled crazily on farm carts.

Stanton jabbed his cigar in Ethan's direction. "Get up there and bring him back."

Lincoln and his family were at the Soldier's Home again. The President's summer residence was too close to Georgetown. He must return to the relative safety of the White House.

While D.C. was surrounded by forts, they were very weakly manned. Nearly all able-bodied men had been sent to reinforce the Army of the Potomac. What the public did not know was that the city was virtually without defense. And it would be days before reinforcements could arrive. As Ethan saddled up, he thought over Packer's earlier comment.

"The city's defenses? Ha! A bunch of biddies with broomsticks! Mr. Lee or any other Confederate commander could waltz up Pennsylvania Avenue and ask the President for a cup of tea."

Returning to Washington, they hurried directly to the War Department telegraph room. A report was coming in from Baltimore. Union General Lew Wallace had gone out to confront the invading Southern troops, only to be severely routed with considerable losses. Faces grew tense. Yes, this Confederate threat was very real indeed.

Over his midday meal, Ethan's mind traveled back to Shiloh, where he had met the dramatic Lew Wallace. Now that seemed so long ago.

"Worried we're about to be attacked?" Packer asked, noting Ethan's serious face.

"Ah . . . no. Actually I was thinking about Shiloh. I met General Wallace there."

Packer drew a long drink of his dinner wine. "Not a particularly pleasant subject for digestion, I would think."

Ethan smiled. "True."

They ate in silence a few minutes more.

"You haven't been around to Amory Square Hospital much anymore," Packer stated blandly.

Ethan looked surprised, and colored a bit. "No, I haven't."

Packer knew that a close friend of Ethan's had died there the year before, but was there some other reason for him to visit the place? So far he had not been able to ferret out that answer. It was of little importance he supposed, yet, he liked knowing all he could about this young man. "And the illustrious Amanda Sims?"

Ethan was still mulling over Packer's comment about the hospital.

Cagey. Yes, that's what my father would think of you, J.A. Packer. Shrewd as a fox. "You don't like Miss Sims, do you, Packer?"

Packer leaned back in his chair, his eyes concentrated on the ceiling. "I don't care for her father," he stated bluntly.

"I wasn't courting her father," Ethan said with a touch of irritation.

"It's been my experience, Alcott, that men beget children who are mirrors of themselves."

Ethan stopped eating and leaned forward, "You don't like the Senator. Why?"

"Do you?"

"I've no reason not to. He's been nothing but cordial to me."

"Cordial..." Packer drew the word out with obvious contempt. "He despises Lincoln. You know that."

"No, I don't know that."

Packer resumed eating, despite Ethan's angry glare.

"You're not telling me anything," Ethan hissed.

Packer leaned back, tossing his linen napkin aside, gazing over the other diners, his face as bland as if they'd been talking about the weather. Finally he focused on Ethan, his eyes narrowed and steely. "You remember that secret little social that came up last year, about the First Lady? A sophisticated lynch mob." Packer's tone was biting.

Ethan nodded. He remembered it well, for he had seen the President's sad, weary face afterwards. Mary Lincoln, an unpopular First Lady from the beginning, was suspected of treason against the Union. Yes, treason in the White House, all because, being from Kentucky, Mary Lincoln had Southern kinfolk. Surely she had passed Union secrets to them, the rumors ran. It was absurd, yet senators who did not like the President at all, hastily met in secret to consider the charges. The first morning of the meeting, the gathering had been shocked when the gaunt-faced President had walked in. Embarrassed, they could say nothing. But Lincoln did not give them a chance. Without preamble he stated that he positively knew there were no treasonable communications from his family in the White House with the enemy. He slipped out as quietly and as quickly as he had entered. With great discomfort, the senators disassembled.

"I saw the report on that, and Senator Sims' name was nowhere on that," Ethan defended.

"Of course not!" Packer snapped. "He wouldn't be so stupid to be there in person. Still, he put the whole tidy tea party together."

"That meeting, it was supposed to be in secret. How did the President find out about it?" Ethan asked, though he already suspected the answer.

"I told him," Packer said without emotion.

"Mr. Lincoln has lots of enemies," Ethan said slowly.

"Yes indeed, and one's marching toward Washington right now. We'd better get back."

As they mounted the War Department steps a bit later, Ethan stopped.

"You know a lot about me."

"I know . . . a good bit about a lot of things."

Suspense hung heavily over the capital city. The boom and shudder of cannon and artillery could be heard in the suburbs. For two days the Confederate and Union troops sparred north of the city, smoke drifting from the battlefield like an ominous veil. Then confusion struck the Confederates, and they slipped back across the Potomac. The South had squandered its best chance. It would not penetrate so far north again.

Shenandoah Valley, Virginia, August

It had been a quiet, sultry day, oppressive with humidity.

Mid-morning found Henri sitting alone in front of his tent, trying
to get rid of a nagging headache. The rattle of a wagon drew his
attention. It was the mail wagon, unseen for ten days. Excitement
pumped into the camp as the men hurried forward to claim the
possible messages from home. Henri hung back, yet his heart was
racing. Perhaps there would be a letter from Wyeth.

The grizzled man on the mail wagon let a torrent of brown
juice spew out before he called, "Hi-ho, preacher!"

An envelope came sailing toward Henri, who caught it carefully, almost hugging it to his chest.

"Thank you, Mr. Cheevers, thank you!"

It was difficult to find a place of privacy in an army camp and
Henri couldn't face the stifling tent. He wandered over to the
eastern picket line until a sentry stopped him.

"Could I just slip over there to those trees for a little while?
You see, I have a letter from my wife."

"Now, preacher, what would happen to me if some Reb sniper
picked you off? The General would have me for dinner!"

"You know Johnston isn't that close. There's no danger.
Please, Alfred. It's from my wife," Henri pleaded.

The sentry shrugged.

"Please."

"Aw right, just stay where I can keep a bead on ya."

Henri sauntered over to the grove of trees, selected a shady
spot and sat down.

> *Dearest Henri,*
>
> *. . . Separated by hundreds of miles, yet tonight I feel
> so close to you because, my love, I have a part of you
> right here beside me. God has given us a healthy son.*

Henri stopped and drew a long breath, his head bowed, tears
spilling down his face.

> *I lie here beside him, clean and feed and kiss him,
> and yet I can't quite believe he's real! He is three days
> old tonight and I've looked him over hundreds of times
> and my heart overflows with gratitude at what God's
> created . . .*

*Henri, how I longed for you when the time came,
and cried out for you when I thought I couldn't go
another minute, but He gave me strength, and finally,
Joe said, 'Wyeth, you have a son!' Uncle Isaiah is
transfixed by him, and honestly, Papa hasn't stopped
smiling. Your new son's name? Caleb William Mullins... Grandmother says it 'suits him just fine.'*
    I love you so much, Henri...

Wyeth

He finished the letter and folded it, slowly putting it in his
shirt pocket. A war might be in progress, but new life was still
going on...

Alfred, the sentry, shook his head sadly. The preacher must
have gotten bad news from home—he was on his knees and he
looked to be crying. In a few minutes Henri returned to camp,
though, and while his face was tear-stained, it was radiant, too.
He came up to Alfred and gave him a hearty slap on the back.
"Congratulate me, Alfred! I'm a father!"

Washington, D.C.

Sara sat folding bandages, her mind hardly on the work in
front of her. It had been over a month since the dance and she had
not seen Ethan since that night. The dance where he had told her
she was radiant and lovely. He had held her and kissed her...

As the days stretched into weeks, Sara knew that, though it
had not been a dream, that one night had been just that—one
night. Apparently Ethan had yawned about the entire episode
and dismissed it. At night when she lay awake in the darkness,
she returned to it and played each detail over in her mind. It hurt
deeply that she had misunderstood him. She knew what she had
felt when she kissed him. But what had he felt? The look she
thought she had seen in his eyes...

Ethan felt a vague sense of urgency to see Sara as he rode
along the crowded streets toward Amory Square Hospital. He

had suddenly realized how much he missed their talks. Then there was the night of the dance. He had pushed that memory to the back of his mind and avoided going to see her. Well, he would just greet her in the old familiar way and drop by the hospital more often. Everything would be all right and if there were more to his feelings—or hers, they would have time to discover it.

The matron did not seem pleased to see Ethan. She remembered his temper. Ethan had found the wards strangely quiet.

"Could you tell me where I'd find Miss James, please?"

Two nurses exchanged glances.

"Somewhere between here and Virginia, I'd imagine."

"Excuse me?"

"Miss James is part of the staff that has gone to Cold Harbor, Captain."

"She's not here? Why, Cold Harbor is the front!"

The nurses ignored him now.

"When did she leave?"

"Five this morning. Good day, Captain."

The women left, leaving Ethan standing in the hallway, feeling shocked. Sara not here? It was hard to fathom. He really was alone in Washington. Now he couldn't try to make things right or explore new feelings. He leaned against the wall, feeling helpless and frustrated. He didn't notice the man who was quietly sweeping the floor, eyeing him with amusement.

"It's still here."

Ethan was surprised at the voice. His face betrayed his confusion at the man's words.

"The train to Cold Harbor is still here. 'Least it was an hour ago, when I took a load there."

"But it's two in the afternoon! The matron said it left the depot at five this morning."

"You're with the War Department, right?"

"Well, yes, but—"

"Then you know about the call for civilian help at the front."

"Yes."

"Well, there you are. Every do-gooder and sensation seeker has turned out. Half of them drunk. What you have at the Washington depot is a royal mess and—"

But Ethan was already out the door. He had never ridden so fast through the city. Undoubtedly, some he passed thought the young officer on horseback carried urgent military messages.

It was like Packer had warned Stanton—only worse. Men and mules, ambulances, supply wagons, and luxury carriages congested the station in such incredible chaos that the train had been unable to leave. After thirty minutes, he finally spotted her. He touched her arm. "Sara."

She heard his voice above all the noise around her. She sighed. Here he was again, surprising her. It had been a long, tiring day of being ready to leave and yet unable to. She couldn't miss the relief in his voice.

"I . . . I found you," he said momentarily out of breath. He swept off his hat and smiled. He really was glad to see her and he would tell her.

"Sara," his voice jolted her. She looked around quickly to keep her mind off the night of the dance. His voice brought back the pain of rejection she had tried so hard to forget.

He laughed nervously. "I can't believe I found you! They told me you left at five and then—" he stopped, his face growing serious.

"Are you really going to Cold Harbor?" he asked.

"Yes. They expect the casualties to keep growing and—"

"I've seen the report. Sara, this is the front!"

"They're very short of supplies and staff. It's desperate."

"But it's the front, Sara! There's fighting!"

Sara managed a tired smile. "There is no danger for us. The medical tents are well behind the lines."

"Still, Sara, are they making you go?"

"Of course not!" Sara answered tartly. "I volunteered. I wanted to go."

"Sara! They say we're leaving," Claire called.

"Are you sure?"

The shrill call of the train whistle confirmed Claire's words.

"Well, I have to go now," Sara said quietly.

Their looks held a moment, but she dropped her eyes to the ground. He was looking too much like that night . . . She felt a wave of anger at her feelings for him, tempting her to tears.

"Sara . . ."

"Goodbye, Ethan "

She picked up her box and turned to go. So, that was it. She was angry and hurt and there wasn't time for him to try to make it right. He touched her shoulder in spite of the fact he knew he shouldn't.

"When will you come back to Washington, Sara?"

"I don't have any plans. Just work."

"Sara, why didn't you get me word that you were leaving?"

He regretted the question as soon as he had asked it. Finally she lifted her eyes to his.

"I would have left you word, but...I wasn't sure..." Her voice was a whisper. Someone jolted her.

"I have to go. Goodbye."

She slipped through the crowd. He didn't see her tears.

♦♦ ♦♦ ♦♦

Chapter 11

*E*than was summoned to a city hospital during the night. Lieutenant Meadows from the War Department was waiting for him.

"What happened?" Ethan asked without greeting.

"We don't know, except that Packer was stabbed in his study, sometime early this evening."

"Stabbed?"

Meadows nodded. "The room was torn up. The housekeeper found him unconscious."

"How bad is he?"

Meadows shook his head. "He's not as young as you or I, Ethan. The doctor says he's lost quite a lot of blood. He's been asking for you."

Ethan went inside and leaned over the bed. Packer's face was a dull white against the pillow. "Packer?" Ethan whispered.

The older man's eyes fluttered open. "Ethan..." He smiled and Ethan did not fail to notice the use of his given name, rather than the usual "Alcott" that Packer called him. "You...came."

"Sure. What happened, Packer? Who did this?"

Packer waved his hand weakly, and Ethan knew this was his way of dismissing the question.

"I've been lying here...thinking. Thinking a lot, lately, about ...God. Was married, Ethan, years ago, to a fine Christian woman. I've been reading her Bible lately. Mr. Lincoln reads the Bible, you know."

Ethan nodded, beginning to think that his boss was incoherent.

"I'm in my right mind, Ethan. I know almost everything about you... You were raised in a God-fearing family, brother-in-law's a minister. Do you believe in God, Ethan?"

"Yes, of course."

"Why 'of course'?" Packer was still able to snap in his weakened condition. "What will you do when the war is over, Ethan? Stay in Washington?"

"I don't know, Packer." Ethan felt frustrated that he could not question the man about his attacker.

"Don't stay in this city. Go home. Go home, Ethan, and marry that little nurse..." He broke off in a fit of coughing and Ethan helped him to a drink.

"Packer, tell me who attacked you."

Packer's eyes were still sharp. He studied Ethan a moment. His voice softened. "Forgive me, Ethan."

"What? What are you talking about?"

"I betrayed you. I put you there to... Then I... You're like a son to me..."

"Packer, listen to me. Hush all this talking. Lie still."

Packer slipped down in his bed, his voice deeper, slower, tired.

"I didn't like Lincoln at first, then... I couldn't help it. He just made me like him. He's a good man."

"Packer..." The man was dying and Ethan knew it. He gripped the man's hand, afraid for him. "Hang on, Packer. It's going to be all right."

"No... No more hanging on. I've made my peace with God... They'll come for you, Ethan..."

"Who? Who'll come, Packer?"

Packer squeezed Ethan's hand and gave him one of his rare smiles. He closed his eyes and sighed deeply. Ethan kept holding his hand, minutes after, till it could no longer hold his own.

"Did he have any family?" Stanton asked.

"Don't think so, never spoke of any. Packer was a very private man."

"Meadows, you make the funeral arrangements. Bad business. Mr. Lincoln's pretty well shook up. He liked J.A. Did you look over the room carefully, Alcott? Alcott?" Stanton's voice was testy.

Ethan ran his hand wearily through his hair. "Yes, sir. All three of us did, then the city police. Nothing stolen that the housekeeper could tell. Just a struggle."

Stanton gave Ethan an owlish look. The young aide was visibly tired and upset. They all were.

"Well then, if it wasn't a common robbery, why Packer?"

"He was a private man," repeated Meadows.

"There are always conspiracies afoot. Perhaps they want to slowly eliminate those closest to the President. We'll add extra protection for the next few days. See that the President doesn't go out much."

Meadows laid Packer's broken cane across Stanton's desk.

"Well, I have a feeling Packer knew his murderer. Put up a struggle. Here's the personal belongings that were on him at the time." Meadows spread some personal articles on the desk.

Ethan picked up a frayed train ticket. It was a ticket to Baltimore. Ethan flipped it over. There was a barely legible address written across it. He carried it to the window.

"Ethan, I want you to talk with the D.C. police. They must have their report and I'm in no mood," said Stanton.

"Yes, sir." He headed toward the door. "I'll look into this case myself, sir. After hours."

Stanton's eyes were beady as he nodded. "Yes, quietly . . . and carefully. Captain, Packer's enemies could be yours, too."

It was nearly a month before Ethan could do anything about looking into Packer's death. Humid August faded into September. The summer-dulled capital came to life with the return of Congress. It may have been an uneventful summer for most Washingtonians, but Ethan was slow in getting over the loss of Sara and the death of Packer. There were changes going on inside him—changes that he couldn't define.

While he worked at the White House, his mind returned to Packer's last words: "They'll come for you. I betrayed you. I put you there. Forgive me . . ." What could all those disjointed words mean? They stirred so many questions. Did any of them reveal the identity of the killer? He had to smile to himself. There were those words of a different theme: "Marry that nurse." Somehow Packer had known about his friendship with Sara. But why? Then too, there were his brief words about his faith. It was a nagging mystery in Ethan's mind—and he did not much care for mysteries.

Finally, one Saturday morning, Ethan boarded the train for the ride to Baltimore. He was tense with expectation. He had no idea what he would find—perhaps, Packer's killer.

"You're Amos Jones?" Ethan asked.

The two-hour search had finally led to this man. The black man indicated a chair for Ethan.

"My name is Ethan Alcott."

"Yes, I know."

"You know me?"

Jones gave Ethan a slight smile. "The years haven't changed you so much, Captain. Just growed you up some."

Amos... Ethan studied the face before him.

"You were with Packer on the New Salem Road!"

Jones nodded. "Around 1850, I think." He extended his hand. "I didn't get to thank you proper-like, that day, for what you did."

Finally, Ethan spoke again, slowly. "Do you know about Mr. Packer's death?"

The brown eyes softened. "Yes, I read it in the papers."

Ethan looked around the room and its book-lined walls. He came back to focus on this man named Jones. The neatly dressed, quiet, calm man before him hardly looked like a killer, yet...

"The paper said an investigation was underway surrounding J.A. Packer's death," Jones continued.

"The investigation is finished. The Washington police didn't find anything."

"The War Department is looking into this, then?" Jones asked.

Ethan was in civilian clothes. How did Jones know of his official capacity? Ethan could not conceal his surprise. "No... I'm trying to find the killer on my own."

Jones said nothing. An awkward silence followed.

"How did you know I'm with the War Department?"

Jones drew a long breath. "James Packer was my friend, Captain. We've been friends for over twenty years. His death..." Finally the brown eyes dropped to the desk in front of him as a look of sadness that could not be counterfeited passed over his face. Ethan instinctively knew this was not the killer.

"Mr. Jones, can you tell me about Packer? I want to find out who killed him and why. I didn't know that much about him, though we worked together. I felt we were friends."

"Yes, Captain, Packer had grown quite fond of you—in his own fashion."

"Then he told you about me?"

"Some. You know as well as I that Packer was no great talker. Something about James you need to understand. He always paid his debts. Felt almost a passion about it. What you did that day with those boys on that road—well, you saved our skins and that put Packer in your debt."

"But I didn't do that much."

"That's not the the way he felt. Did you receive a set of books on your eighteenth birthday?"

Ethan was astonished. "Yes, I did! We never knew where they came from. He sent them?"

Jones nodded, "I knew James and knew what he had in mind. He wanted to keep his eye on you, no matter how distant."

Ethan tugged at the hair above his ear. This was all so strange.

"When you went to Galena, he sent a telegram to Governor Yates. They'd been cronies in college. Packer suggested to Yates that you would make a good officer. Funny thing was, Yates already had his eye on you. Wrote Packer you were a fine Illinois lad. I reckon this all seems pretty astonishing to you."

"Yes . . . it is."

"Seems he'd lost track of you when you went down to Tennessee with Grant. Then, you were on his doorstep with a dispatch to Stanton."

"He got me a job with the President." Ethan spoke slowly.

Jones stood up and walked to the window.

"Why would anyone want to kill him, Amos?"

"I've asked myself that since I read of his death. When we were in Cincinnati, he worked a lot, but was very close about exactly what he did. He seemed to grow hard those years, and more to himself. Bitter. Sometimes he worked for a senator."

Cincinnati . . . Ohio!

"Sims? Senator Sims?"

"Yes, Captain. Sims. Packer never talked about his work . . ."

Ethan didn't notice the Maryland countryside as he traveled back to Washington. The visit with Jones had left him tired, confused and feeling as if he was peering into a dim hallway.

Ethan stood sipping champagne, grimacing inwardly since he didn't much like the stuff. This was a party Amanda Sims was giving for the celebration of the fall social season. He watched the dancers absently and nodded at appropriate times to the officer who had cornered him. The fellow had definite opinions on how the military campaigns should be conducted and felt required to share them with any available listener. But Ethan wasn't really listening.

Ethan had been very surprised when he'd received the gilt-edged invitation. He had not seen Amanda for several months. He had stared at the invitation, stirred by a dozen impulses. He had all the information from Amos Jones to digest in the long hours, though he had come up with very few conclusions. Sims. Sims and Packer. So, from curiosity more than anything else, he had come.

Ethan had no illusion about where he stood with Amanda Sims. There was no relationship between them—and he was no longer bothered by that. When he lay awake at night, it was not Amanda's face that filled his mind. It was not the tilt of her chin or the waves of her hair he thought about. It was not her words he could remember, or the rich timbre of her laugh. And, it was not Amanda's kiss that seemed to burn on his lips.

Toward eleven that night, Amanda came up to him. "Daddy wants to see you, Captain Alcott."

Ethan smiled at her formality. "It's Captain Alcott, eh?"

She smiled. "Well, I haven't seen you in awhile, sir."

Then she took his arm. "Come on. Daddy's waiting."

As she led him down the hall, he asked, "What does your father want, Amanda?"

She only smiled and knocked on the paneled door. She gave his arm a quick squeeze and disappeared down the hallway.

"Come in," said a voice, and Ethan stepped into Senator Sims' personal study. The room was illuminated by the light from a small shaded desk lamp. When his eyes finally adjusted, Ethan found the senator seated behind a massive oak desk. As he crossed the room, he saw two men from the corner of his eye—one slumped on a couch to his left, the other standing in the shadows to his right. Though he couldn't see their faces clearly, he could feel their penetrating stares on him.

"Sit down, Captain, sit down." The senator's voice was pleasant as he indicated a chair directly in front of his desk. It gave Ethan a distinctly uneasy feeling to have the two men at his back.

"Smoke?" The senator's words pierced his thoughts and Ethan finally focused on him. The man had removed his evening jacket and now sat in shirt sleeves.

"No, thank you, sir. I don't smoke."

"A drink then?"

"Thank you, but no."

Sims said nothing, seemingly absorbed in the rising thread of smoke from his cigar. The room was very still and Ethan tried to organize his thoughts. Why did this man want to see him?

"My daughter throws a rather fine party, wouldn't you say?"

"Yes, sir."

"Having a good time?"

"Yes, sir."

"You haven't been around in awhile to see my daughter."

"I've been pretty busy lately."

The senator leaned back leisurely and it was then Ethan noticed that Sims toyed with an object on his desk, sometimes spinning it or revolving it in his hand. In the dim light, Ethan could not see what the object was.

"You're quite the chaste young man. Illinois must know how to grow 'em. Our beloved President, the illustrious General Grant . . . you. It suddenly occurs to me that you just might be too tame for my daughter. Besides, a captain's salary would keep Amanda in stockings about one month." He gave a short laugh at his own humor.

Ethan shifted in his chair, wishing Sims would change the subject—which he did.

"You were with Grant in '62?"

"Yes, sir."

"Fought at Shiloh."

Everything was a statement, not a question.

"That was quite a blunder for General Grant, as I recall. I imagine it was rather nasty business for you, also. Very fortunate for you that Mr. Packer came along with such a safe job."

"It's been a very good job for me."

"This war needs to be over. We're all pretty tired of it. Bad for the economy, bad internationally. Think our President is tired of it, Alcott?"

"I imagine he's most tired of it, sir. In fact, I heard him say just a few days ago he thought he was the tiredest man on earth."

"Said that?"

Ethan suddenly realized he had spoken out of turn. He wanted very much to get up and leave. The senator drew out a crystal canister and poured himself a drink.

"Well, Captain, I did have a reason for asking you in here... What are your ambitions, Captain?"

"To serve the President as well as I can."

"When he's out of office, very soon, you'll be out of a job. Back to the farm?"

"I'm confident Mr. Lincoln will be reelected, Senator."

"Ah well, your confidence is sadly misplaced, I'm afraid. He won't be reelected. He's more interested in country jokes and writing out pardons for squeamish cowards. He's no leader... He's a buffoon. You may like him as a man, but he's not good for this country. Not good at all. Listen to the good people of this land and you'll realize they're sick of this blasted war. Let Mr. Lincoln go back to Springfield and swap stories and spit with other farmers."

His voice had risen considerably. This was a side to the controlled Trenton Sims that Ethan had never seen before.

"You despise him, don't you?" Ethan asked, suddenly very angry.

Sims ignored Ethan. "This administration will be swept away next month. Where will you be, Captain? I have the influence to assure you a position that would put Amanda in more than just stockings."

Ethan was silent and Sims fidgeted.

"You seem like an intelligent young man. You have all the facts."

Ethan leaned forward. "Do I Senator? What can you tell me about J.A. Packer's death?"

Someone stirred behind Ethan but he ignored it. Sims grew very still.

"To use a phrase you would understand, you're barking up the wrong tree," Sims said tightly. Ethan could tell the man behind the desk was trying to keep his voice calm.

Ethan drew out his words slowly, "I don't think so, sir."

The senator gave a short, hollow laugh. "Perhaps I gave you too much credit, Captain. I am not a man who tolerates threats."

"It wasn't a threat, sir. It was a question," Ethan said calmly.

Again, there was a movement behind Ethan.

"Packer made threats!" Sims exploded. "He was a fool!"

"Harsh name for a man that worked for you for years."

Color drained from the senator's face. It was a gauntlet Ethan had dropped, one he had only guessed at. Yet with Sims' reaction, there was no mistake. The mighty senator was tied to Packer's death and they both knew it.

"Perhaps it was threats ... that killed my boss," Ethan said softly.

"I was prepared to help you, Alcott. To give you opportunities like you'll never get again. You're a bigger fool than Packer." His voice was reduced to a menacing snarl. "Now you fancy you know things and the fact is that you know and can prove—nothing."

Ethan stood up. "Goodnight, sir." He turned to go.

"Alcott!" The senator's sharp tone stopped him midway across the room. "I'd keep a look out for my backside from now on, if I were you."

Ethan's hand was on the doorknob.

"And this time, Captain, you won't have J.A. Packer to cover it for you."

Once in his room, Ethan got ready for bed, mentally noting the President's plans for the next day. He turned out the light and lifted the window sash. He gazed out on the avenue. It will be a river of mud in the morning if this rain keeps up, he thought. Washington D.C.—so far removed from Peppercreek, Illinois. What would they have been doing at home tonight? he mused. What would his father have thought about his meeting with Sims? Had he been too impulsive?

He sat on his bed. He had to think. He had to make some sense of what he'd learned from Amos Jones—and tonight, from Sims.

Packer and Sims had some sort of working arrangement. Then, apparently, Packer had come to despise Sims. Perhaps he had wanted to sever any connection with the Senator. Had it cost him his life? Sims had revealed his contempt for Lincoln—just as Packer had said—and asserted Lincoln could not, would not be reelected. Could Packer's killer stalk Abraham Lincoln? For all his cold hatred of the President and his personal ambitions, Ethan could not envision the dignified legislator as a murderer. Still, what about those two men who sat in the shadows?

Had Packer intended for him to work for Sims? Ethan wondered. Then, had he changed his mind? "You're like a son." Ethan groaned out loud. Forgiveness... Packer could not sacrifice Ethan to Sims' designs. Ethan would never know how correct his speculations were.

Then his mouth went dry. He remembered. The object that Sims had toyed with on his desk was the head to Packer's ornate cane.

Election Day, 1864

The café was quiet, with only a few diners like himself, and Ethan was glad. It had been a long, noisy day. So many had come to the White House to congratulate Lincoln. But the reelected President had taken the news of the victory with typical humility. A slow smile had lit up his tired, deeply lined face. He had pulled at one of his big ears, drawling, "Well, after all, folks know it's best not to swap horses in the middle of a creek."

Ethan leaned back. A glad feeling enfolded him, pushing away the grief, gloom and anger of the last few weeks. Lincoln would lead the country four more years. Ethan knew unquestionably that Lincoln was the best man for the monumental task. The tide of war was favoring the Union now. It was just a matter of time before the Confederacy would be too weak and ravaged to continue. Wish they'd all just lay down their weapons tonight and go home, he mused. That would be a grand election gift to Mr. Lincoln.

"More tea, Mr. Ethan?" a waiter asked, coming up to his table.
"Yes, Jim, thank you." He raised his cup. "To Mr. Lincoln!"
"Yes, sir! God bless Mr. Lincoln!"

Ethan sat at the table he and Sara had shared only last summer. That seemed to Ethan so long ago. Perhaps... perhaps he had come here to stir up that memory. Tonight he wished... Her face came into his mind. He realized he thought of her more often now than he had when she had been just blocks away from him at Amory Square. Where was she tonight? he wondered. With the admiration she felt for the President, he knew she would be feeling the same gladness he was for Lincoln's victory. It would be nice if she were here with him tonight.

Then he thought of the last time he had seen her, nearly four months ago. She was looking as if she wanted to say something else, and there was that sadness in her eyes. What could she have been thinking of, but not saying?

He stood up and hurriedly paid his bill. He would go to his room and write her a letter.

A group of congressmen and senators had come to congratulate Lincoln. They were men who, having little or no liking for the President, nevertheless were prudent enough to act as if they did. Courting favor was part and parcel of politics.

Ethan stood with John Hay in the secretary's office, the door open so they could observe who came and went. Hay stopped talking as he followed Ethan's gaze. Senator Trenton Sims and others had emerged from the President's office.

"Ethan, you all right?"

"Excuse me a minute, John."

Ethan walked up to Sims. "I need a word with you, Senator."

The senator looked into Ethan's face. For the first time in a long time, he felt a slight tremor of fear. Ethan's eyes were hard and riveted on Sims. His youth and his manliness dwarfed the man before him. Sims coughed nervously.

"What do you want?" he asked tersely.

Ethan waited a moment before speaking. "Killing innocent creatures seems to me below your... dignity, Senator. Or rather, having it done, I should say."

Ethan's horse had its throat slit two days earlier.

"You're a damned idiot," Sims said through clenched teeth.

"I can't prove anything, like you said, but—"

"Get out of my way."

The hallway was deserted and no one could hear them. Ethan glanced around. Of course, the shadow men were not in visible attendance of the senator.

"Just one thing, sir. While President Lincoln is in the White House, don't ever put your hypocritical foot in this place. If you have something to say to the President, send it by courier."

Sims snorted. "Who do you fancy you are, Captain?"

"I'm just one lowly presidential aide who has some speculations that the papers might find more interesting than war news, just now. Don't cross the threshold of the White House again."

They locked eyes and Ethan had no reason to expect an attack by some of Sim's lackeys. Perhaps his impulsiveness would cost him his life. Sims stalked off and Ethan was left shaking.

Northern Virginia

The six Confederate scouts had been trailing the lone wagon for over an hour. Impatience and hunger finally prompted them to act. The merchant grew quite frightened by the rough-looking soldiers. With casual indifference, they stole his wagon. He had shouted at them that he was a certified mail carrier of the Federal government. They laughed good-naturedly at this, and soon the cold little merchant was left standing on the frozen road.

"Merry Christmas!" called a Confederate over his back as the merchant's horses and wagon were driven off into the frigid Virginia woods.

A mile later the scouts stopped and made quick work of the wagon. All foodstuffs were grabbed up in a frenzy of pathetic hunger. The wagon itself was a prize—valuable fire wood for thinly-clad and very cold soldiers. It was hacked up in record time with the mail sacks providing the final torch. There was a great shout of laughter as the soldiers enjoyed the plunder and bonfire at the Yankees' expense.

The letter from a lonely presidential aide to a lonely Union nurse went up in spiraling smoke.

Chapter 12

Cold Harbor, Virginia, December, 1864

◆◆ ◆◆ ◆◆

*F*rank, I can't accept this."

"Why, Sara? Don't you like it?"

"Yes, of course, it's beautiful." She turned the gold locket over in her hand.

"It's just... You shouldn't have done this."

"Sara, Sara." The doctor took her hands in his.

She could not help but think of the matron back in Washington, how scornful she would be if she saw this little drama between a doctor and a nurse.

"Please, Sara. You know I haven't really said anything. I've tried to be patient. Yet, you know how I've felt, haven't you?"

"Yes." Her voice was barely audible. "Yes, I've known how you felt."

"They've asked me to go to City Point and head up the staff there. I told them I would go."

Sara would not meet his eyes.

"I leave day after tomorrow and I wanted you to have this little Christmas gift. I hoped we could have some kind of understanding about... us. I don't know how long I'll be down there."

Still Sara said nothing. Yes, she had known for some time how the dedicated doctor felt about her. She had tried ignoring him, avoiding him—and she had tried falling in love with him.

Finally, she looked into his face—such a nice, kind face.

"Sara, when you first came here, well, there was hurt in your eyes. It finally left, but now as I speak to you I see it again. Is there someone else you care for?"

She couldn't speak at first, she'd tried so to get over those feelings.

"No, there isn't anyone else, anymore. But, it still..."

"Hurts?"

She nodded. His head came close to hers. "I won't risk losing you by rushing you. We'll talk more when I come back."

315

She watched him resume his duties. It was not difficult for her to imagine that he would make a passionate lover. He really was a good man and a compassionate doctor. She had worked beside him for long hours and witnessed firsthand his gentleness with the wounded. When they'd both been exhausted, he had made her laugh. She should fall in love with him. She should...

Washington, D.C., December 25, 1864

Ethan was sick of Washington. This past fall had put a stress on his emotions like he'd never experienced before. He had planned to go home to Illinois for Christmas. Then a winter blizzard dropped down with fury out of Canada, leaving train travel frozen and impossible.

Somehow, word reached Lincoln that Ethan was not able to go home. He had taken his young aide aside. "Mother and I were talking the other night. Since the election is behind us, and it seems the tide of war is with us, we're going to take a vacation back to Illinois. Take Tad fishing. You'll go with us, and be our body—I mean, personal escort." There was a twinkle in his kind eyes.

That was not the only disappointment. He had written Sara over a month ago, but there had been no reply. He knew mail delivery was slow and uncertain. Still, he felt she had chosen not to reply. Apparently she was still angry with him. Eighteen sixty-five was just around the corner, and Ethan never felt lonelier.

Peppercreek, Illinois, December 25, 1864

"The first Noel, the angels did say, was to certain poor shepherds in fields where they lay, Noel, Noel..." Wyeth was singing to Caleb. It was a frosty, clear Christmas morning as she stirred the pot of oats and turned pancakes and sausages. Singing would keep her spirit lifted. Another Christmas, and Henri and Ethan were not home.

She turned as she heard the tramp of boots. Her father and Uncle Isaiah came in.

"It's mighty cold out there this morning!" Will said. "Sharp as ice. Fine Christmas day the Lord's given."

Wyeth smiled at the two men, one so silent, one so animated. Isaiah bent over Caleb's basket, extending one finger to touch the baby's downy head. Will and Wyeth exchanged a smile. Isaiah seemed fascinated with the baby. He straightened up and surprised them both with one of his rare, awkward speeches.

"'Ismas Day baby . . ." He pointed at Caleb. "Ah good a baby on 'Ismas Day. Like baby along ago, Jesa!"

Wyeth hugged him as Will said, "Yes, Isaiah. A baby in the house on Christmas day is a blessing indeed. To remind us again of Him who came on Christmas day for us!"

Will's voice had tears in it and Wyeth knew there was joy and sadness in his words. She knew he remembered a baby son who was born and died on Christmas day, so many years ago.

"Well, let's eat!"

The meal was nearly over when Will pointed toward Old Jumper, who lay curled in sleep before the stove.

"Has he been out this morning?"

"He put his foot out the back door and honestly, he looked like he frowned!" They all laughed. "But I shooed him out anyway. He was back in a few moments, whining like a pup and giving me a very reproachful look."

Old Jumper, who had only recently received the prefix to his name, opened his rheumy eyes, raised his head and began to slowly, very slowly, thump his tail. They all stopped to watch him.

"Must have heard us talking about him," laughed Will.

The dog stiffly raised himself up. His nose pointed toward the door. He was motionless, almost expectant. Then his tail thumped more vigorously.

"He acts like someone's coming, but who would it be, this early and on Christmas morning?" Will asked.

"He would have barked," said Wyeth, simply.

Why is my heart suddenly pounding? she asked herself. Then she recognized that feeling she'd felt only once before in her life. It had happened a few years ago . . . Jumper pushed the hallway door open.

Wordlessly, Wyeth passed Caleb to her father and followed the dog. She didn't bother to grab her shawl from the peg, or take off her apron, or look out the window.

She flung open the front door—Henri was standing at the end of the snowy lane.

Married women usually give up running, but Wyeth took it up effortlessly. Never mind the blast of cold or the snow filling her slippers. No, never mind any of that.

The wagon had dropped Henri off at the beginning of the lane because he wanted to enjoy the full pleasure of coming home. He wanted a long look at the place so close to his heart. Now he had seen the house and the trees fringed with snow, the smoke curling up in lazy tendrils from the fireplaces, the wreath of red and green on the broad front door. Then the door opened, and Henri began to run too.

He held her, and hugged and kissed her. They laughed and cried all at the same time. Neither could say a word, nor feel the cold. He buried his face in her hair and didn't want to let her go. Finally he released her just so he could look at her.

"No sight will ever be more beautiful than you are to me right now. You're real . . . You're not a dream anymore. Wyeth!"

She held tightly to his neck. He had come home—he had come home on Christmas day! Then, she turned back to the house. Henri looked past her. Will was standing in the open doorway with something blanketed in his arms.

Wyeth took his hand. "Henri, come and meet your son."

Louisa's little house was festive, decorated with fresh evergreens and bright red bows. It looked and smelled of Christmas with the rich scent of turkey, nutmeg and cinnamon mingled with pine. After the meal, they moved to the parlor where a crackling fire danced in the grate. Everyone was especially happy with the surprise of Henri's homecoming. Wyeth had been tempted to cancel coming so that she could keep Henri all to herself. They had had no time alone. But they came and talked and laughed and enjoyed the afternoon.

A small fear clutched at Wyeth. Henri was so thin, thinner than she had ever seen him. His healthy coloring was gone and everyone noticed the deep cough that would often shake him. Wyeth had not missed the glance Louisa had given Dr. Joe. Yet no one said anything about it.

"Henri, how long will you be home for Christmas? I haven't heard you say," asked Louisa.

Wyeth raised her eyes from Caleb. She had not allowed herself to ask Henri that question.

"Well, I'm not sure. The chaplain commander wants me to stay home till I get over this cough."

"With Wyeth's cooking and rest you'll get better in no time!" Louisa enthused.

"Yes, with Wyeth, I'll get better." He was not embarrassed with the intense look he gave her across the room. Then he smiled tiredly. "I wanted to come home... and stay home of course." He looked down at his chapped hands. "But the men seem to need me more during the long winter months. They're all cooped up in their tents or huts. I have a captive audience! They talk and listen, tell me their fears, their hopes. When they get a package from home, they're happy for awhile. Then they slide into depression because they're away from their loved ones."

"Why don't the generals send them home for the winter?" Louisa asked innocently.

"They must have them for the spring campaigns. If they send them home... they fear they won't get them back."

Silence filled the room. Wyeth wanted to hurry Henri home, he looked so tired. Earlier, when the gaiety of the carols and gift giving had gone on, she could feel his eyes on her at every move she made. He had talked, laughed, held his son, but he had watched her. Wyeth knew tonight when they were alone, his touch would be full of tender passion. And she did not feel ashamed that she would be equal to it.

Will cleared his throat. "We pray this will be the last Christmas we'll be separated from our loved ones."

Goodbyes were said and the buggy was brought around for the short trip home. Stepping out the door, Henri caught Wyeth's hand in his. "Wyeth look, it's beginning to snow!"

The house was quiet and though a fierce winter wind rattled the windows, the rooms were warm. The fireplace cast a warm yellow glow in Henri and Wyeth's bedroom. Henri sat on the small sofa, his feet extended toward the fire, watching Wyeth as she made Caleb ready for bed.

"I'm so thankful that you got home today before this storm hit," Wyeth said. "Are your feet cold?"

"I doubt they'll be thawed out till spring! I'm sorry if you think you've climbed in bed with a chunk of ice."

Wyeth smiled, "I doubt I could think that."

Their eyes met. This was the first time they had been alone since Henri had come home. She could see love for her in the depths of his eyes.

She sat on the edge of the bed. Little Caleb began to fuss. She patted and cooed to him. Henri watched.

"Is he wet? I have so much to learn about our son!"

"No, he's not wet," she said slowly. "He likes to eat before he goes to sleep."

"Smart boy!" smiled Henri.

Yet Wyeth made no move. She suddenly felt shy in front of Henri. Nursing was so personal, and he hadn't been there from the first.

"Love, aren't you going to feed him?"

Wyeth didn't look at him until he came to sit beside her.

"What is it, Wyeth? Are you nervous about me seeing you since it's been awhile?" he asked softly.

She nodded. "I know it's silly."

"No, I understand."

Slowly Wyeth unbuttoned her bodice and Caleb, giving up his protest, settled into delighted contentment. His eyes were open and gazing up at Wyeth, his chubby little hand resting on her skin. Wyeth could only hear the slight noise he made as he ate, the sweep of the wind outside, the crackle of the fire. Henri did not speak and when Wyeth finally turned to him she found him crying.

"Henri..." Her hand rested on his cheek and he turned it over to kiss her palm.

"Wyeth I didn't know... I mean, you and our son. Why has the Lord been so good to me? I'm home with my family. I'm whole and well, and yet, so many men..." He coughed, and unsettled Caleb momentarily.

"Henri, that cough! Are you all right?"

He reached out and slipped the pins out of her hair. He gently shook out its length. His kiss lingered a moment at the hollow of her neck...

"I'll be fine, now that I'm with you," he said huskily.

Soon Caleb was finished and Henri carefully placed him in his cradle. He leaned over it and Wyeth knew he was praying. She undressed and slid under the quilts. Henri added some more logs to the fire then came to Wyeth.

He whispered, "Tonight... Tonight I just need to hold you."

Washington, D.C.,
1865

Ethan had been up since four in the morning and by ten his body felt tired from tension. Yet there was no time to relax or let down—this would be one of the most important and demanding days on the job for him. It was Saturday, March 4, 1865—Inauguration Day.

He thought of Packer as he hurried to the War Department just before five, the sun not yet up, the smell of rain in the air. Mr. Lincoln would not have fair skies under which to take his oath of office. It seemed to Ethan so much had happened in the nearly six months since Packer had been killed—Sims, the reelection, the swinging tide of war.

Ethan gathered with Meadows and a few other staffers around Secretary Stanton's desk to review again the security details of the day. The additional stress made Stanton's voice more gruff than usual.

"Details aren't any good at all if we don't expect the unexpected! All of us know very well that he will do his utmost to lumber around out of our plans. The man's positively infantile when it comes to security."

All in the room knew his caustic remarks covered his very real respect for the chief executive. In fact, there was no one in the Cabinet who respected Lincoln as much.

"The city is absolutely packed with every form of human life." Ethan smothered a smile. "And, in particular, Rebel deserters! I've seen them taking the oath to the Union over at Lafayette

Square. Like little rats fleeing a sinking ship, if you ask me." He held up a stubby finger. "The facts are any one of them could decide, in a positive fit of passion for ol' Dixie, to take a crack at the Chief."

He shuffled papers and plopped wearily into his chair, already exhausted though the day was still young and no important ceremony had yet taken place.

He shifted his beady eyes to Ethan. "You'll be closest to him most of the day, Captain Alcott. Try, try, to keep him reasonably within our plans."

So, Ethan had been sent to work, to stay as close to Lincoln as possible without being obtrusive. Stanton had insisted he be in uniform. All day he would feel the hard pressure of the revolver under his coat, as Stanton had also insisted. He hoped he could remember everything for a long letter home.

By mid-morning Ethan knew Stanton's prediction was true. He and Lincoln rode alone to the Capitol, where Lincoln spent the morning signing bills. The President shrugged off the military escorts planned for his carriage. Ethan knew by his determined look it was useless to protest. He could only hope the rear guard would sensibly ride just out of Lincoln's view.

Lincoln was unusually quiet, Ethan noticed, on this important day. The only comment he made the entire ride was directed toward the pair of size eight gloves that lay on his knee.

"Gloves are cruelty to animals!"

Now the leader seemed lost in thought, and Ethan sensed they were melancholy thoughts. Rain began to fall from the lead-colored sky and a strong wind chopped at the carriage as it headed down the avenue. Yet the weather did not much dampen the arrangements for the day. Military patrols in dark capes sat on their horses at each intersection and police lined the sidewalks. Only one long bony finger tapped the leather seat and Ethan knew his boss was disgusted with all the security attentions.

Around noon, Ethan was in the Senate chamber with the droning of Vice President Andrew Johnson's speech in the background. He scanned the immediate crowd closest to Lincoln. The place was packed with dignitaries, foreign ambassadors, senators and congressmen. Mary Lincoln sat stiffly in the diplomatic section also, a tight smile on her face. He spotted a face near

Stanton's that he did not immediately recognize. He was curious. It was apparently someone important. It was a proud, haggard face, the face of a man not well. He nudged Meadows who stood beside him. "Old Hickory," Meadows whispered. So, here was the veteran, Andy Jackson, no particular friend of the reelected president. Ethan scanned the crowd further, pleased that the capital police were well in evidence.

He returned his attention to Johnson's speech. There was something not quite right here. His voice would rise to a feverish pitch then plunge to a near whisper. Ethan could make very little sense of his words. He noticed Stanton looked terribly agitated and many Republicans in near agony. Meadows gave a whispered interpretation again. "Andy's drunk."

Then it was over, and Ethan followed the senatorial procession that lead Lincoln to the East Portico for his short address to the crowds outside. Just as Lincoln passed, a man from the line rushed forward. The police were on him like a magnet. Ethan and Meadows had unceremoniously tumbled into another fellow trying to assist. The intruder was hustled to another chamber. Ethan got up, anxious to get back to Lincoln. The man he had bumped was rearranging his cape with great care. Ethan spoke to him amiably. "Sorry about the bump, fella."

The man smoothed his mustache, an obvious smirk on his face.

"That fella was too close to the President," Ethan further explained.

"I could care less," came the cultured, sneering voice. He breezed out the exit, giving his gloves a final flick.

Ethan pushed his hat back in surprise and Meadows, who had overheard, came up to Ethan chuckling.

"Kind of a sour one!"

"Don't you know who that was, Ethan?"

"Should I?"

"Only if you go to the theater much. Ladies are said to go in a swoon over him!"

"I don't go to the theater at all."

"That was Mr. John W. Booth. Actor and lady-killer."

"Well, he sure seemed out of sorts."

Ethan hurried out to rejoin the inauguration process. A wave of cheers was still thundering as Lincoln stepped out before the crowd. With the cheers the cloudy veil split, and the sun came out in dazzling radiance. Lincoln gave a quick glance skyward, then down at the small iron table where his tattered paper lay. He waited for silence, cleared his throat, and began to speak.

Ethan felt that same surge of emotion he had felt at Gettysburg. The president's voice was calm, clear, slow and gentle. "... Malice toward none ... charity for all ..."

Applause thundered again as Lincoln finished. The Chief Justice moved forward with his open Bible and officially made Lincoln a second-term president.

Ethan did not ride back to the White House in the carriage with Lincoln. He rode guard behind. It was a personal time for the President, and Ethan did not want to intrude upon it. Young Tad sat at his father's side, wildly waving a small Union flag from the carriage window, enjoying the show in his father's honor.

It was nearly eleven when Ethan finally stretched out on his bed. He was bone-tired, yet pulsing with impressions of the grand day. There were faces crowded in his mind: the sober-faced military guards along the Avenue, the groups of cheering negroes waving happily at the corners, the proud, indignant face of Andrew Jackson, the flushed face of Andrew Johnson, the plump, pleased face of Mary Lincoln, the impish, delighted face of Tad Lincoln. He thought of Lincoln as he spoke, so sad and weary, yet alive with hope.

He rolled over, drifting to sleep, grateful tomorrow was a day off. Perhaps he could use the day to write a long letter home—write of today's events while they were fresh in his mind. Grandmother Tufts, he knew, would expect complete details. His final thought was of Sara. Sara ... somewhere on the front. He wished he could write her, also.

Chapter 13

City Point, Virginia

◆ ◆ ◆ ◆ ◆ ◆

*S*tanton was irritated—and because of it, Ethan received a choice assignment. Choice, because it would mean being out of Washington for a few days. A Union general down at the huge army camp at City Point was sending the Secretary daily complaints. Complaints about Grant, troops, supplies—anything and everything. Disgusted, Stanton ordered Meadows to send someone to personally assess the situation. Meadows selected Ethan.

Before Ethan could leave, however, Meadows handed him a small revolver. Ethan started to protest, but Meadows was insistent. "Ethan, you're riding through Virginia. Confederate snipers are known to roam the woods. These are men who know the war is almost over and only want to satisfy their bloodlust."

"But a revolver won't do me any good if they're waiting to pick me off from the trees."

"True, but a revolver could come in handy if you need to defend yourself."

Ethan was reluctant. Shiloh had changed forever his feelings about raising a gun on another man.

"I—" he began, but Meadows stopped him.

"Take the gun, Ethan, if you want the assignment."

As he rode, he thought about the trip he had made with the President just a month before. They had taken a steamer down the James River to City Point. One night, the President had sat on the steamer deck telling stories. He was supremely relaxed. He had surprised everyone in the group with a display of strength. Holding an axe in either hand and extending them full arm's length, he raised them to shoulder height. No one on board could match the feat. Ethan realized then that for all his lanky, loose jointed, slouching ways, Abe Lincoln had latent strength—physical as well as emotional.

The following day Lincoln reviewed the Negro troops with Grant at his side. The soldiers crowded around Lincoln's horse, cheering and crying. They touched him with gentle hands and blessed him. They called him their liberator. The President was so moved he could not speak. His chin rested on his chest and before Ethan himself looked away, he saw the slow descent of tears. Grant looked away and tugged at his beard. Ethan would never forget the sight.

Ethan reached City Point at dusk of the second day. He dined privately with the commander to whom he had been sent. Gratified to have an ear from Washington, the general talked to Ethan for two hours, ignoring Ethan's yawns. Finally Ethan excused himself, deciding the man was mostly hot air.

A few officers lounged near the mess tent drinking coffee. Though he was tired, he ambled over to them. It would only be fair to get their side of the story. They were talkative and friendly. It was only when the group broke up for the night that Ethan noticed one who had sat apart, not joining in the conversation. He had faced sideways to Ethan, so he could not be seen clearly. From the corner of his eye, Ethan had seen the man add frequently to his coffee cup from a small silver flask. There seemed something vaguely familiar about him.

He was ready to leave for Washington the next afternoon. The general wore a petulant face and Ethan carefully told him it would be best to avoid contacting Washington quite so often.

It was just before dusk when Ethan's past caught up with him. He had made good time leaving City Point but would soon have to camp out for the night. That pleased him—another night before he returned to his room at Willard's. Out-of-doors, he didn't feel his loneliness so deeply.

The calm was broken when, some twenty feet in front of him, a rider broke out of the trees and onto the middle of the road. Ethan's horse shied with the surprise. The rider drew his horse to the middle of the road and stopped, facing Ethan. Quickly Ethan could see the rider wore the Federal blue uniform. But his stomach tightened when he recognized his old schoolyard enemy, Jip Denham.

The war years had not been unkind to Denham. He had never been seriously wounded, though the left side of his face bore a jagged saber scar. He had risen in rank by virtue of his ability to bully and play politics. His men served him out of dogged fear. Still, it was inside that Jip had not fared so well. He had lost both his older brothers—one at Antietam, the other at Champion's

Hill. Lost them in a blasted war that he had never believed in. He often mused that he should have been fighting for the South if at all. His belligerence and military skill were well known, along with his excessive drinking. His bitterness had found fresh vent when he recognized the Washington courier the night before.

Ethan drew up, their horses almost touching. Ethan hadn't seen Jip in eight or ten years and was not surprised that Jip's look was less than friendly. Their eyes held and neither spoke for a full minute.

"Hello, Jip. You were in the mess tent last night, weren't you?"

Jip had been the sullen officer who had taken no part in welcoming the presidential aide. Ethan extended his hand, but Jip held his reins fast.

"How are you?" Ethan asked, suddenly feeling a tentative nervousness.

Jip looked past Ethan, toward the trees, as if he was measuring something. Then he spat in the dirt beside his horse.

"And how are you, Mr. Aide-to-our-beloved-President?" Jip's sneering voice was hard. Ethan said nothing.

"You work for that—" and Jip turned loose a string of foul epithets for Lincoln.

"I'm sorry you feel like that, Jip. Mr. Lincoln really is a great man."

"What a mushmouth you've become, Alcott! 'I'm sorry you feel like that, Jip,'" he mimicked, then laughed.

"Look Jip, I know we had trouble when we were boys, but gosh, that's a long time ago. Let's forget—"

"You're afraid of me, ain't ya?"

"Afraid? No, why should I be afraid?" Ethan asked sincerely.

"What a —— you are! Can't you see that I've followed you?" Denham growled.

Ethan shifted in his saddle. There was raw hatred in this man's eyes.

"Yes, I guess you did follow me. Why?"

Jip carefully drew out a bottle and took a long drink. He wiped his mouth and gave Ethan a steady look. Jip had always been in the bullying shadow of his brothers, and now Ethan could see he had matured into a bully greater than his brothers had been.

"I'd offer even you a drink, but I know your precious family of Christians don't drink." He cursed Ethan again.

"I'm on my way back to Washington, Jip. I'll be going now."

Jip nudged his horse across Ethan's path, and Ethan's horse flattened her ears in nervous alarm. Ethan spoke soothingly to her.

"Don't you see why I followed ya?" Jip asked, leering.

"No! And I don't care, Jip," flashed Ethan irritably.

"This war has given me...an appetite you might say. An appetite for killin'."

Ethan swallowed hard. "Do you hate me that much, Jip? Why? From the first day of school you were set against me, when we could have been friends."

"Spoken like a true coward, Alcott. You've grown soft, I'm thinking. You were such a fearless leader in school. Winnin' the races, perfect hunter, and handy with the girls too. Now, you just sound yella'."

Ethan looked at his hands, his mind racing. He was talking to a madman. And this madman wanted a fight.

"Jip, for my part I'm sorry. If that sounds like a coward to you, fine. I'm sorry I made you hate me enough to want to kill me."

"*Going* to kill ya," Jip corrected, his voice like steel.

Ethan felt a small knot of fear. Jip tossed his empty flask in the road.

"You were awfully brave that day on the new Salem Road with that fat man and nigger boy," Jip gnashed. "Jumped out, rifle in hand, tellin' us to be off like we were a pack a' hounds! So brave then, Alcott...not lookin' so brave now."

"Is that what this is all about?" Ethan asked.

"I should have smashed your ol' granny, coming and tellin' us Denhams we best leave you alone or lose our right a' way."

"I'm going now, Jip."

Ethan urged his horse forward, pushing past Jip and his mount. Ten feet away, Jip's voice rang out clearly. "Alcott!"

Ethan turned to see Jip aiming his pistol at him. He was close enough to see Jip's hand was less than steady.

"Go ahead and reach for your gun, Alcott! Go ahead!" Jip shouted.

"No, Jip. I'll not fight you again. Not anymore."

Jip hated the calm that was in Ethan's voice. But he shrugged and cocked his gun.

Ethan swung back around, coldly certain the shot would come in seconds.

"Pretty speeches," Jip slurred as he steadied his aim. The shot rang out in the dusky sunset, and Ethan felt only a momentary flash of pain. He thought of his father as he slid into darkness.

Cold Harbor, Virginia

Sara strolled alone through the meadow near the encampment. Her fingers absently brushed the long grasses, dozens of butter-yellow butterflies darted at her touch. She barely noticed them, however. Finally she stopped walking, gazing across the meadow toward the camp. The surge of wounded had abated somewhat and now the staff and patients alike talked about the future again. A future with no war. A future which promised homecoming.

She focused on the line of horses picketed in the distance, the officers' horses. She could tell from their manner they wanted to be romping and galloping in the pasture instead of tethered in camp. Tomorrow a roan mare would arrive in the camp and be tied to the post near the medical tent. Her suitor, the doctor, was returning from City Point.

He would want an answer tomorrow, and there was no real reason to delay giving him one. What would she say? Did she love him? Love him as she had loved Ethan? *Had loved* Ethan? No, try as she might, she could not dismiss her love for him so easily. Hadn't it been a slowly growing love whose roots went back to her girlhood? How could such a bond that stretched over the years be broken? No, but it had to be. It had to.

Tears filled her eyes. "I've always felt I belonged to him... And he belonged to me," she whispered. "Now, see the pain all your foolishness has caused you."

Virginia

The impact of the bullet propelled Ethan out of his saddle. He fell face-down on the road. Jip sat watching a moment, dismounted and casually walked over to Ethan's body. In the twilight he could already see a pool of blood collecting under his victim. He waited another second for some movement or sound from Ethan—there was none. With his boot, he rolled him to the edge of the road, then savagely kicked him down the incline into the woods.

He remounted and lit a small cigar. He seemed lost in thought, in no hurry to move on, relishing the thought he had at last bested an old rival. Still, there was the regret that neither his father or brothers had lived to know that he had put arrogant Ethan Alcott in his place. In his mind he had avenged the New Salem Road incident very nicely.

He eyed Ethan's horse speculatively. "She'll bring a bit," he chuckled to himself.

Claiming her reins, he began to ride. Not back to City Point, or even north as Ethan had been. Desertion did not matter to him now. He headed south. Perhaps he would settle down in war-ravaged Savannah or Charleston. There would be many opportunities for a man like Jip Denham. He smiled a drunken smile as he goaded his horse forward.

When Ethan fell down the ravine he was fortunate, for the brush and fallen leaves padded the way. He quit tumbling and came to rest under a sumac bush and rotting log. He lay unconscious for nearly two days. Blood was soaking through his shirt as his very life ebbed out. It was Shiloh again—only worse.

On the third day, Ethan woke up, completely disoriented. The slightest movement caused terrible pain. When his mind could pull away from the pain, all he could feel was extreme thirst. He did not hear the noise near him.

"Samson! Come on, boy! Let's go!"

There was a rustling of leaves near Ethan's boot.

"Samson! You dog, you! Come here! Thee will be getting me in trouble."

The blue tick hound gave a low throaty growl as he sniffed Ethan's leg. He made no move to go to his young master.

"Dog! What have thee got there, boy?"

A boy of nine or ten emerged from the brush. His overalls and homespun shirt testified that he was a native of this countryside. One hand gripped a rifle, the other, three dead squirrels. He approached cautiously. Samson was known to track and tree most anything. He seemed to have a particular passion against snakes.

"Oh!" The young boy's eyes grew wide when he finally saw Ethan's leg across the log. He was nervous as he pushed aside the bush. Ethan was not a pretty sight, especially to a young lad so early in the morning. His shirt was plastered in blood, his face chalk-white, with purple bruises and scratches. One eye was swollen shut. The boy dropped his squirrels.

"A dead soldier!"

Ethan tried to feebly raise his hand, but the boy turned and ran. Samson lay down at Ethan's feet.

Martha Chester glanced out the small window for the third time.

"Where is the boy?" she muttered. She turned back to the fire where she cooked their breakfast. Apparently he had wandered farther afield in his hunting.

"Ma!" Daniel burst into the small cabin.

"Son! Does thee want to frighten thy mother to an early death?"

"But Ma! There... there's a man! In the woods, he—" the boy leaned against the table to catch his breath. Martha could see he was very upset.

"A man? Who?"

"A dead man!"

"Oh son! Is thee certain?"

"Yes, Ma. He is lying in a bush near the road. He's all covered with blood. Samson stayed with him."

"Well, perhaps there is still life in him. Go fetch Marcus and I'll hitch the wagon."

Back at the cabin, they stretched Ethan on the common-room floor of the cabin. Martha was a strong woman and certainly no novice to nursing, but Ethan lay so still, and had obviously lost a great deal of blood. There was a terrible wound high on his shoulder. She could not ignore the odor that came from it.

"Ride to the village, Daniel and fetch the doctor. Quickly!"

She closed her eyes in the stillness. There was nothing to do but pray for this poor young man. She did not hear the doctor's step inside the cabin sometime later. "Are you praying, Mistress?"

Her eyes opened, smiling briefly at the big Quaker man. He began his examination. Despite the booming voice and manner, the doctor was actually a very gentle man. "Indeed, Martha, you did well to pray. Hmm..."

Finally he stood up with a sigh.

"How is he?" she asked slowly.

"Healthy and young. That is to his credit. But..."

"The poor boy has lost so much blood," offered Martha.

"Yes, he's given up a great deal. Thee sees his shoulder?"

Martha could not look as easily as the doctor, but nodded.

"It is a bullet wound, and I would say whoever shot the man was very close. The ball has completely shattered the muscles, nerves and bone of his upper arm."

"Can it be mended?"

He shook his head, and Martha knew he was struggling with something. "Martha, thee can smell. When he was first shot I would have had a better chance, but now..."

She recoiled at the thought of amputation.

The doctor continued. "Look at his hand, his forearm. From his elbow down it is fine and healthy. From the elbow up the gangrene has ruined it."

The doctor walked to the window, stalling his decision, hating the thought of cutting off a partially sound limb. He turned around brusquely. "I will go to the village for help to move him."

"Move him? Why?"

"I will wait on his arm. I have stopped the bleeding and will give him eight hours to see which way he may turn. I can watch him, and make my decision. Either way he will require great care."

"He is too sick to move. I can take care of him just fine," the mild Martha replied tartly.

The doctor pulled at his lower lip to disguise his smile. He nodded to her. "All right, let's clean him up and move him to a bed."

Cleaning Ethan up, they came across his wallet. Now he had an identity. The doctor would send someone from the village to City Point to see that the War Department in Washington was notified. Daniel had searched the woods for the soldier's horse, but without success.

The doctor returned at twilight. His examination was painfully brief. He turned to Martha, and she could see the regret in his eyes.

"It's no use. I'm going to the village for Duncan to help me." He held up his hand as she began to protest. "You've done enough for one day. It must be done tonight. Boil water for me, please," he said, hurrying out.

The surgery lasted a little over an hour. After seeing the extent of the wound, the doctor knew he had made the right decision. The gangrene was checked but Ethan was in no less critical condition.

Martha entered Ethan's room at the doctor's summons. The room was spotless and bore no trace of the ghastly operation. She bent over Ethan, tenderly smoothing back the hair on his brow. He was so desperately white and still.

"His breath is so faint," she said.

He nodded, "As fragile as his life is right now."

Five days the fever was at its highest, the delirium at its worst. The doctor came into the room as Martha was sponging Ethan's face. He checked the pulse and the wound and laid his hand on Ethan's forehead. He straightened up, frowning. "The fever rages worse this day, yes, Martha?"

"He has been this way all day. I—" She broke off, not trusting her voice. She had grown to care deeply for this young man who had come into her keeping. The doctor patted her shoulder awkwardly. "Martha! Thee has done all thee could do. A man could have no finer nurse. And thee has carried him in prayer to the great Healer, as well."

"His shoulder?"

"It is an ugly wound but I see no sign of worsening. Tonight, I think the fever will either burn itself out, or he shall die by morning. He cannot hover between life and death much longer."

"And there's been no word from his family?"

"No, I think it will be a few more days before we have word. Washington is very busy just now. The officer at City Point told Duncan that our Captain here is an aide to President Lincoln!"

"The President!"

The doctor nodded. "A celebrity with us, hmm?"

It was early morning when Ethan's eyes cracked open. If only I could focus on that voice, he thought. He found himself looking into the ruddy face of a boy. The lad's eyes were tightly closed and his hands were clutched together in a desperate appeal.

"Jesus, please heal the Captain. He works for the President! Please don't let him die!"

The boy's eyes opened at the end of his prayer, startled to find the wounded man's eyes fastened on him. Ethan managed a very weak smile.

"Doctor!" the boy gasped.

The big man started in the chair where he had finally dozed at sunrise. He stood up quickly, sending the chair over backwards.

"Look, Doctor! His eyes be open."

"Yes, Daniel, they are indeed."

He felt Ethan's forehead and pulse. "His fever has broken. He will get well now. Go call thy Mother, Daniel."

"I'm here," said Martha behind them.

Ethan was surprised to see a little woman in Quaker garb, coming up to his bedside. Her smile trembled, her eyes overflowed with tears.

Martha leaned forward, "Good morning, young man."

"Good morning," Ethan whispered.

The three nearly jumped for joy and hugged each other. Ethan was amazed. Was this Peppercreek twenty-one years ago? Hadn't he waked in a strange bed then, too?

For two more days Ethan did little more than sleep and eat the broth the Quaker woman fed him. His extreme weakness left him no ability to protest over his dependence on her. His shoulder throbbed so painfully at the slightest movement that he remained very still. In his weakness he knew there was something different about his left arm—a strange tingling sensation, but he did not bother to raise or inspect it.

The third morning he woke to the steady drumming of a

spring rain. His eyes adjusted to the morning dimness and for the first time in days he didn't feel like falling back to sleep. He had to figure out where he was and how he had come here.

The door opened and the man he only knew as "Doctor" strode purposefully into the room. He carried a tray that Ethan knew contained his breakfast. Ethan had a moment to appraise him. A man in his mid-forties perhaps, Quaker in dress, tall and powerfully built. Nothing at all like the frail Dr. Noble back home. He set the tray down and pulled up the chair. Resting his hands on his knees, he scanned Ethan with eager eyes.

"Thee is feeling better this morning, hmm?"

"Yes, thank you."

"Yes, thy color is better. Thee look less like Mistress Chester's fresh cream. Still a bit cheesy, though. Ready for a drink?"

The man helped Ethan to a long drink of tea.

"Thank you. Can you tell me what day it is, please?"

"Certainly. It is the third day of April, 1865."

"The third of April?" Ethan repeated, feeling confused.

"Correct. Now I can see questions in thy eyes. Let me try to help thee sort things out. Thee has lain ill for ten days. This is the home of Mistress Martha Chester and her son, Daniel. She has been thy nurse. Her skills and the mighty hand of God have given thee back thy life. Her son Daniel found thee in the woods near this cabin."

"Where is this place, this cabin?"

"Brainerd County, Virginia. The nearest village is Lancaster, two miles west. And I am Dr. Jeremiah."

"My name is Ethan Alcott."

"Indeed, your personal effects told us so. Now, to your breakfast."

"Can I...I think I can do it myself. Thank you, sir."

The doctor raised an eyebrow, but said nothing. Ethan ate slowly, trembling with his right hand.

As he finished the doctor spoke again, "Is thee up to more conversation?"

"Yes, sir."

"Tell me how thee feels."

"Well, my shoulder hurts. Actually my entire left side, arm and neck. They throb when I try to turn my head or lift my arm.

And, I feel so weak, I don't think I could stand up if my life depended on it."

"Nor should thee attempt to. Thee have lost a lot of blood. Thee must be patient to let thy body regain its strength. Thy shoulder... Does thee remember how thee received thy wound?"

Ethan leaned back, searching the ceiling. "No..." he said slowly. "I came from Washington to City Point. I thought I got there, but..." His voice trailed off as he tried to clear his foggy mind. "Yes, I did get there and talk to the men. Then, I left..."

Silence filled the room as Ethan stumbled along in his thoughts.

"Thee was shot high in the left arm, a tearing wound that went up into thy shoulder. I'm no expert, but I would suspect thy assailant shot from very close range."

A shot in the shoulder... at very close range. Ethan closed his eyes as a wave of nausea swept over him. He could see Jip's drunken face in his mind, a face contorted with hatred. Yes, that was it. He had been on his way back to Washington when Jip shot him. The doctor wiped off his perspiring face and gave him another drink.

"Is thee all right? Shall we talk later?"

"No... No I'm all right. Yes, he was very close. Not much farther than from here to the door. I didn't expect to live. He wanted to kill me."

"But he missed."

"He was drunk, and he never was much of a shot. Still—"

"Thee knew the man?" the doctor broke in, astonished.

Ethan nodded.

"The man aimed to kill thee but the Lord did not desire it."

Ethan said nothing. Had another miracle intervened to save his life?

"We have talked enough I think. I will return this evening," the doctor said, rising.

Out in the common room, the doctor found Martha cleaning up the breakfast dishes. She looked at him anxiously. "How did he take the news about his arm?"

Dr. Jeremiah sat down wearily. "I did not tell him. He has nothing but pain, so he doesn't know the arm is gone. He is a strong man and I sense he will not take this loss too easily. I will tell him tonight."

"And I will keep on praying," said Martha quietly.

Martha sat with Ethan that evening after he had eaten. They were talking when the doctor stepped into the room. Ethan felt there was a tenseness about the man. He pulled up the stool and regarded Ethan soberly. He rubbed his forehead and finally spoke, "Thee received a severe injury in thy upper left arm, Ethan. I could not fully repair it. The bullet sliced through vital muscles and tissues. Thy arm was nearly severed. But He designed our mortal frames quite well. Thee lost an abundance of blood and after twenty-four hours of that loss, gangrene quickly attacked those damaged tissues."

"Gangrene?" Ethan felt his mouth go dry. Gangrene was what...

"I could not save thy entire arm, Ethan."

Martha moved closer to the bed, tenderness radiating from her eyes. Ethan turned away from them, the pain shooting down his neck. He slowly lifted his right arm to touch his left. There were bandages on his shoulder extending about six inches down his left arm—then, nothing. Nothing. There were no fingers to flex.

He leaned back and closed his eyes. He felt a wave of darkness and dizziness swell up in him. His arm had been amputated.

"I had to take thy arm to save thy life," said the doctor sorrowfully.

"My arm is gone," Ethan whispered dully.

He felt Martha's hand lay lightly on his forehead.

"Thee have thy life, Ethan. Thee will recover," she said softly.

During the night, Ethan woke from a sound sleep. He groped for the vacant space on his left side. Yes, he sighed to himself, it was real and not a very bad dream. With one shot, he had become like veterans he had seen daily on the sidewalks of Washington— grim-faced men with an empty sleeve dangling at their sides. He struggled with deep anger that long dark night that he lay awake. How could this horrible thing have happened to him? And this badge of conflict, this empty sleeve had not even been earned honorably on some battlefield. It had come from the chance meeting with a bitter, drunken enemy from school days. Ethan groaned out loud at the absurdity of it. Fleetingly he thought of the doctor's words about the Lord preserving his life when Jip had fired at such close range. Had this thing that had happened to him not been a mere chance at all? Had the Lord allowed this crippling? He did not sleep all night. The dark, quiet room gave up no answers and Ethan could not wrestle with it any longer. At sunrise, he grew calmer, feeling dull and resolved to this ugly thing that had happened to him.

It was midday of the following day before Dr. Jeremiah put in his appearance.

"I'm sorry I couldn't come till now, Ethan," he apologized. "Babies take their own time about coming. Martha, thee will be pleased to know Lancaster has two fine new lads this day. Jacob and Esau." He stroked his chin, his eyes twinkling. "Let's hope they get along better than their namesakes, hmm? Now, Captain."

He began to unwind the bandages and Ethan watched the big man's face. He had been glad to see the doctor this morning.

"When I rode up I could tell the mistress had put her good herbs to work, and they seem to be doing very nicely indeed."

"Sir, I want to thank you for what you've done for me. Please don't feel . . . badly about my arm."

The doctor continued looking at the arm before he could speak.

"Taking your arm when only a part was severely damaged was a very difficult thing for me to do. But it was the right thing. I hope soon there will be medical advances to prevent such things . . . or better, that men will forever grow weary of war."

He straightened up and looked kindly at Ethan. He had taken a liking to this young man. "Thee has lost thy arm and I know that it is a difficult thing. Thee will have to adjust to how thee does things. Difficult yes, but certainly not impossible. I suspect thee is a man of strength and determination. And thee will do quite well in time."

Ethan was silent as he considered the man's words.

"I must go now." He turned at the doorway. "I am no Bible

scholar, Ethan. Yet in the book He said, 'Let not your heart be troubled, neither let it be afraid.' Good afternoon, Captain."

Finally Ethan was allowed up, slowly, tentatively. It was so odd the first few days when he sat or walked, to feel that absence on his left side. Often his right hand would automatically reach for his left arm. It still gave him a queer shock not to find it. It made his whole feeling of balance different. He became angry one morning as he struggled to pull on his boots. Just the day before he had mastered putting on his shirt after much work. Now the boots. He had wanted to throw the boots across the room and would have if the house had been empty. "Make adjustments, yes, adjustments!" he had muttered viciously under his breath. He grew tired with the exertion and when Martha looked in and found him scowling she knew to quietly withdraw.

He came to the table later, silent and pale, eating his food without looking at the woman or her son. He did not see Daniel's worried glance nor Martha's sorrowful ones. Herb draws she could make, fevered brow she could sponge, but this was one battle Ethan had to face alone.

"Good news, Ethan!" Dr. Jeremiah called as he rode into the yard the next day.

Ethan stood up quickly, expectation dissolving his gloom.

"Richmond has fallen!" said the doctor.

"Richmond has fallen. Yes, sir, that is good news."

"Then the end must be soon?" Martha asked from the doorway.

Ethan nodded. "I think the war will surely be over soon."

"President Lincoln would be a very happy man tonight, wouldn't he, Ethan?" ventured Daniel.

"Yes, Daniel, very happy."

Martha and the doctor did not miss the tremor in Ethan's voice. Ethan was not there, at the President's side, to share the glad news.

Later, when just Ethan and Dr. Jeremiah remained outside, the physician sighed deeply and turned his attention back upon his new friend. "Another week or so and your strength will be better. Your arm is healing well, your color is improving." He paused as he traced something with his pipe stem on his leg. "What are your plans, Ethan? Does thy ... impairment prevent thee from still working for the President?"

His voice was deep and kind and it made Ethan think of his father.

Ethan drew a long breath and looked up into the night sky.

"I ... I don't know what my plans are. I've given it a lot of thought though ... Just this afternoon, I couldn't clean the fish we caught and yesterday I couldn't raise an axe very well. Cutting firewood ... It's just made me see all sorts of ordinary things that I can't do anymore."

"Adjustments, Ethan, adjustments," encouraged the doctor.

"Like ... shooting a rifle ..." Ethan returned with some exasperation.

"Does thee shoot rifles a great deal, on duty for the President?"

Ethan could not help but laugh. "No, Mr. Lincoln doesn't even allow a pistol."

"What else then?"

"Lifting things, getting on a horse." He broke off helplessly. The doctor was trying to be helpful, but ...

"Harder yes, Ethan, I grant you that. But not impossible. Thee will learn new ways of doing ordinary things." He leaned forward, placing his hand on Ethan's shoulder. "It will bring out the best in thee, I know! Aren't thee a man who has risen to challenges with courage all thy life?"

Ethan looked down at his feet. "They will have replaced me. A one-armed bodyguard would be pretty ridiculous. I wouldn't be in much position to defend him."

The doctor did not reply and they both turned their gaze back to the night sky. They watched as a single falling star blazed across the darkness. An owl hooted and a chorus of crickets began their night melodies.

"Did thee see that, Ethan? Everything goes on. Richmond is captured by Union troops, thee are without a job, but a star still falls in the night sky. The stars are hung out each night. There is a plan behind it all. Thy problems are not so very large when thee look at the sky. Perhaps thy injury is part of a plan."

"I ... can't see any reason for it," Ethan replied calmly.

"Perhaps thee have not looked behind it, at the One who allowed it."

Ethan stood up impatiently and the doctor followed him, placing an arm around his shoulders.

"Ethan, I am thy doctor and thy friend. I am a very imperfect man who believes in a very perfect God. I believe for thee, until thee can believe for thyself, that He has allowed thee to lose thy arm, thy job, for a part of a plan. It must be so."

Despite his fatigue, Ethan could not drop off to sleep easily that night. He turned to watch the moon slip into the square of his window. The same moon was shining in Peppercreek . . . Sara's face filled his thoughts. Where was she tonight? Mistress Chester had told him he had cried out for her in his delirium. He felt so confused, so lonely. If only Sara . . . He thought of the way he had seen her care for and comfort the men in the hospital.

"Sara, I wish you were here to put your arms around me tonight," he whispered to his room.

◆◆ ◆◆ ◆◆

$\mathcal{S}$aturday afternoon, Ethan walked to the village with Martha and Daniel for supplies. He could feel the curious stares he drew. Everyone knew of the presidential aide who was recuperating at the Chester place. He carried a letter back from Will and Wyeth that he looked forward to reading. As he came into the yard he stopped short. Sitting on a horse, looking very different in riding clothes, was John Hay. He laughed at Ethan's surprised expression.

"There you are! I was about to give you up. I had rather primitive directions out here. Hello, Ma'am." He tipped his hat at Martha Chester.

Ethan finally found his voice. "Mistress Chester, this is John Hay, secretary to the President."

She curtsied quickly, a bit in awe—as if the President himself had come to her humble home.

"I'll get thee something to drink for thee and thy guest, Ethan. Come, Daniel."

Hay extended his hand and the two shook warmly. Ethan indicated a bench.

"This is a real surprise, John."

He laughed easily. "I can tell from your face it is!"

"Have you ridden from the capital?"

"No, took the train till Martinsburg then hired that nag to load my bones the rest of the way."

He pulled off his hat and looked around appreciatively.

"Pretty country, these parts. Thought I'd better come check on you." He lowered his voice, "Thought maybe a pretty Quaker lass was keeping you down here so long."

Ethan laughed. "No, just a very good family."

John Hay looked squarely at Ethan a moment, his eyes resting briefly on the empty sleeve.

"So, Ethan, how are you?"

"Better John, really. My shoulder is just sore and I'm getting my strength back. I'm slowly getting used to one arm, I guess."

"Tell me what happened, Ethan."

Ethan did, keeping his voice as light as possible.

342

"That's all rather curious, Ethan. Do you suppose the fellow got away? Will you look for him again at City Point?"

"No, I'd rather just leave it alone."

"Oh, before I forget." Hay stood up. "I bring you personal greetings from the President. 'Get well soon and get back up here. We have a trip to plan.'"

Ethan's voice was husky. "How is he, John?"

"You've heard about Richmond."

"Yes, we got the news a couple of days ago."

"Tomorrow Lee will surrender to Grant over at Appomattox."

Finally, it had happened! A moment of silence passed as Ethan treasured the news.

"You can imagine how the old man is feeling now. He looks better and yesterday he came in singing some ol' Kentucky tune. Dreadfully off-key, of course!"

"That's great! No one will appreciate the war's end like he will."

Hay nodded. "Yet, he says, there's a long road of healing ahead. He's been laying out plans; reconstruction without harshness. No revenge against the seceded states."

"I'd imagine the city itself is in an uproar."

"Very nearly. Great cannons going off, flags and banners everywhere. The place may explode when they hear Lee has surrendered. The place is ready to celebrate in high style."

"And Stanton?"

The secretary chuckled. "Fit to be tied! Biting through cigars right and left! Jawing at the old man about being careful. But ..." Hay grew still a moment.

"What?"

"Oh, Stanton has rubbed off on me, I guess. He's concerned about the President."

"Why now, more than usual?"

"Well, he says Washington is in a ferment. Lincoln-haters and Union-haters bitter about how things are ending up are going to come out of the woodwork. He doesn't want the President out in public for awhile."

"And you agree with him?"

"Well, yes, I guess I do this time. There's also the old man himself, his ... dream." Hay's face grew troubled, a look not often found on the easygoing young man.

"A dream?"

"I know it's absurd to even think about. I . . ." He took time to collect his thoughts. "How much fact or fiction is in dreams? How much stock should we put in them? You see, a few days ago, at a cabinet meeting, Lincoln told about a dream he'd had the night before. I'm a little surprised he mentioned it, but then, I suppose he was still troubled by it. He said he dreamed he was walking through the White House late one night and he went into the East room and found a soldier guarding a flag-draped casket. Naturally he was shocked and asked the guard, 'Who has died in the White House?' The guard answered, 'The President has been killed.' I'm sure it must have been very realistic to him. Anyway, Stanton doesn't want the President out celebrating."

"The President has a mind of his own. He'll go out or not, in spite of Stanton," Ethan returned.

"Yes that's true, but he does have more than just his own mind." Hay gave a short laugh. "I know better than you, Madam President will have her way about socializing. Dropped me a note yesterday to say they plan to go to Ford's Friday night. Even asked Grant and his wife. Stanton hasn't heard about it yet, but he'll pitch a royal fit."

"A theater party should be harmless enough, with proper escort." Ethan looked toward the forest a moment, "Who's the aide to the President now?"

John fidgeted a bit, "Lieutenant John Humner."

Ethan nodded slowly.

"The President has missed you, I can tell you that. Has asked Stanton about you."

Ethan's smile was sad. "That's awfully nice of him. He does know about my arm, doesn't he?"

"I think Stanton told him. Listen, Ethan—I'm sure that they'll find—"

"It's all right, John. I know that shot took my job as well as my arm. They'll pension me off, especially now that the war is ending."

"I'm sorry, Ethan." His voice was sincere.

"It's all right, really. I know I had a great privilege for a time, working with Mr. Lincoln."

Finally John stood up, "Well I better stir up that equine beauty there and see if she can get me back to Martinsburg to catch the train."

Ethan stood up, saying, "Thanks, John, for taking the trouble to come down."

"No trouble. I enjoyed the escape from wicked Washington. Has your doctor said when you'll be fit?"

"Another week or so."

"Well, take your time about getting good and well. No need—"

He stopped, his face reddened, and their eyes met in understanding. There was nothing for Ethan to hurry back to.

"Goodbye, John."

"Goodbye, Ethan. Come to the White House as soon as you come up."

"Thanks. And John," Ethan felt that tightness rising in his throat. "Tell Mr. Lincoln . . . tell him, 'thank you.' Just thank him for . . . everything."

The same tightness was in Hay's throat as he nodded and urged his horse forward.

The valley was deepening with late afternoon shadows and a light breeze ruffled up the trees. The dust settled as if John Hay had never been there. Ethan leaned against the tree, thoughtful.

He would be leaving this place soon. As peaceful as the place was, and enjoyable as the friendship of the Chesters and Dr. Jeremiah was, he could not stay indefinitely. He must return to Washington and some semblance of his old life. Things would settle down, and Lincoln would get on with a post-war administration. Ethan wondered what it would be like to work for the great man when his mind was not so abstracted by the crush and clamor of war. He shook his head. What would his place be now?

April 16, 1865

Ethan was returning from the creek where he had peacefully spent the morning. As he entered the cabin yard, Daniel came tearing in on horseback. Ethan was surprised for he had never seen the boy ride the old mare so hard. Martha came to the doorway and they both saw the chalk whiteness of the lad's face. The face was twisted in fear or anger—Ethan couldn't tell.

He jumped off the horse and flew into Martha's arms, burying his face in her skirts and sobbing. Ethan hurried up to them.

"Oh Ma, oh Ma!" was all the boy could manage to cry out.

"Son, son, what has happened to thee?"

Daniel couldn't speak, and Martha sensibly gave up asking and just held him. Ethan looked on anxiously, hurt that his young friend was so upset. Finally Daniel grew a bit calmer and Martha stooped down, wiping his tear-streaked face with her apron.

"Now, thee is all right. Tell me, son."

The boy's face blanched in pain. "Oh Ma...they...they killed him!"

Then Daniel saw Ethan and he drew a deep breath, his eyes wide.

"They killed him, Captain," he said again, without the sobs, but with all the sorrow.

"Killed who, Daniel?" asked Ethan, his voice not betraying the sudden, inexplicable panic he felt.

"The President! Mr. Lincoln's been killed."

A dreadful silence followed, though Ethan felt a dull roaring in his ears. Ethan stepped back from Daniel, his face now as pale as the boy's.

"Son, who has told thee this?" Martha asked.

"James Penn. He rode over from Martinsburg... with this newspaper and everyone crowded around...and it said that ...that Mr. Lincoln had been shot last night."

Ethan stood silent, and Martha felt afraid of the look in his eyes.

"Dr. Jeremiah came up to the crowd and he had a different paper and it said the same thing...Ma, why would anyone want to kill dear Mr. Lincoln?"

Ethan turned from them and walked slowly back toward the creek. Daniel looked at his mother for explanation, but she could only shake her head.

Cold Harbor, Virginia

The doctor watched the nurse from the corner of his eye, aching that he could not comfort her. Her face was so white, so tense, so sad. He glanced around. Staff and patients alike—they all looked like that: sad, sober and pale. Just yesterday there had been laughter and talk of victory and going home. Now . . .

Of course, going home, even before today's shocking news, had left a bitter taste with the doctor. Sara would not be going home with him as his wife. She had told him she did not love him as she should to become his wife. "But you could grow to!" he had protested forcefully. He remembered the softness of her hand on his cheek, the tears in her blue eyes. No, it was no use. He was too good a man, she had said and her heart was . . . That had been weeks ago, and he wondered when he'd ever stop hurting over it. Didn't he dispense aid and medicine to the wounded? Yet he had nothing for himself.

It was late evening when Sara started toward her tent. If only she could sink into sleep and forget. It was too horrible! A good man like Mr. Lincoln . . . And just when the peace had come. A step sounded behind her and she turned to find the doctor had followed her. They had exchanged only a few words during the long day. He walked up to her, nearly touching her, as miserable and lonely as she was.

"Hold me," she whispered hoarsely, "please . . . just hold me."

She did not care who saw them. The doctor held her there, in the moonlight, as she cried, grieving over herself, grieving for the slain president.

She cried, knowing that miles away in Washington, Ethan would be in agony over the loss of a very special friend. Ethan . . . He seemed to her so far away, it had been so long since she had seen him. She clung to the doctor, hating herself that she could not return his love. If only . . .

Virginia

The doctor was waiting for Ethan when he came back. Twilight had fallen and they exchanged no words as they entered the cabin for the meal. Ethan only glanced at Daniel, not wanting to see the boy's pleading look. He wanted to say something comforting to him, but he could think of nothing. The two men remained at the table after Mistress Chester had cleared it and led the exhausted Daniel off to bed. The doctor drew out the newspaper.

Ethan sat studying the smooth oak table before him. The paper with its bold black banner reading "LINCOLN KILLED" lay between them. Ethan felt too sick at heart to even touch it.

"It's early yet, but witnesses at the theater say—" the doctor began.

"Ford's," Ethan said dully.

"Ah, let's see... Yes, Ford's Theater."

Ethan groaned. All Stanton's worries...

"Witnesses say it was an actor who shot our president. An actor!"

Ethan felt chilled. "Booth?"

The doctor was surprised. "Why yes! How did thee know?"

"The War Department had a report from a fellow who had come in saying there was a plot against the President headed up by this Booth fellow. We didn't do anything much about it. There were always threats made toward the President, but nothing you could exactly follow up. I..."

The doctor was at a loss how he could help his young friend in his hurt. Ethan stood up and went to the fireplace, staring into the embers. The peace of this place had been shattered. He needed to leave now. He swung around and faced the doctor who could easily see the determination in Ethan's face.

"Could you get me a horse in the village? By early morning?"

"Yes," the doctor admitted slowly. "I think so. Perhaps not as fine as you're used to."

"It doesn't matter. Any horse will do."

"Ethan, you're not strong enough. It's too soon to undertake such a trip." Martha had come noiselessly into the room.

"Mistress Chester, I am stronger. Besides, I have to go back, sooner or later, you see."

"But—your shoulder—"

"It's healing. It hurts less each day."

"Dr. Jeremiah, could bumping along on a horse possibly be any good for Ethan's shoulder?"

"Well, no, Martha. I'd prefer Ethan wait out the week. But—"

"I appreciate your concern, both of you, more than I can tell you. But I must go back."

"Ethan, my friend, does thee think thee can do something for the great man now? What's done is done. We all feel the terrible weight of this tragedy. But thee can't let grief work too much in thee."

Ethan said nothing, swallowing hard around the lump that was in his throat. He felt an intense pain, born of failure and bitterness, that he dared not speak about. It had been a shock to lose his arm, then to lose his job. Now, another shock. Another person he cared for was gone... He felt a black cloud of bitterness descending on him. He had to get away.

The doctor stood up wearily. "I'll bring the horse around by first light, Ethan. Let's all try to get some sleep. It's been a long, long day."

The doctor left and Ethan came to Martha. "It will be early in the morning, so I'll say goodbye now. Please tell Daniel how very much I enjoyed our talks and fishing together. That's a fine lad you have there. I can't tell you how grateful I am for all you've done. I will miss all of you."

It was still dark the next morning when Dr. Jeremiah road into the yard with Ethan's mount. Ethan sat at the table, slowly drawing on his boots in the light of a single candle. The doctor watched and Ethan managed a faint smile. "You see, it takes me a bit to pull these things on, but I'm adjusting, as you said."

"I have never doubted that thee... would adjust very well." Ethan looked at the big man and saw he was sorrowful.

"How much for the horse?"

The doctor named the price and Ethan paid him.

"Thee paid me too much."

"For your services. They do pay doctors in this county, don't they?" There was a smile in Ethan's voice.

The doctor tugged at his chin. "Oh, sometimes. Mostly in currant preserves or a basket of potatoes or a dozen eggs."

"I haven't any of that, so accept this."

"It's too much."

"You people of Lancaster are hard to thank. I'm sure you could use it toward medical supplies. Maybe, maybe, you'll need bandages to patch up the squabbling Jacob and Esau one of these days, eh?"

The doctor had to smile.

"Thank you, sir, for saving my life. And I've enjoyed our talks together very much."

He extended his hand and the doctor shook it warmly. Then he gave him final instructions about caring for his arm.

"God bless thee . . . son."

Ethan felt tears coming so he quickly prepared to ride. Suddenly Martha was there, silently, quickly pressing a kiss to his cheek. Awkwardly, he mounted the horse and headed for the road. He could not look back.

Fingers of pink dawn moved across the sky as Ethan began his ride. So much had happened since the last time he had ridden. Lincoln . . . There would be no fishing trip to Springfield.

Chapter 15

Washington, D.C., April, 1865

◆◆ ◆◆ ◆◆

*E*than was shocked at the crowds of people who thronged the streets of Washington. Soldiers and civilians were everywhere, many with black crepe paper pinned to their sleeves. Black bunting hung from nearly every doorway and Lincoln's portrait was placed in public shop windows. All business and government offices were closed. Ethan frowned to himself. The city was a bit tardy in its respect for the great man, he thought bitterly. A definite sense of shock and tension prevailed over the city. The capital of the victorious Union was reeling in humiliation.

Ethan was unsure of his plans. He knew his room at Willard's had been released, even as he drew up to its front. Valances of black silk swathed the big double doors. He secured his horse and went into the lobby. He was surprised at what he found. Despite the throng outside, Willard's was quiet inside. A gold braided rope stretched across the barroom entrance. The hub of Washington would respect the fallen president with temperance.

Ethan found Ben, his favorite employee of the hotel. Ben brought Ethan's few belongings to him. "Sure am sorry about your room, sir."

"It's all right, Ben. I'll try to find a place somewhere."

Over breakfast Ethan tried to form his plans. A newspaper had been left on his table, and while a part of him hated to read the cold sobering facts, he decided perhaps he should learn the details before he went to the War Department. The funeral was set for Wednesday at noon, but the public could view the President lying in state, in the East Room of the White House, beginning the following morning.

Ethan was given a small yet comfortable room at the Soldier's Home. Accommodations were precious since the city was overflowing with people coming to the funeral. He stretched out fully dressed on his bed, tired from the long ride, but full of a thousand thoughts. He thought of the time, nearly three years earlier, when he had come to Washington under a cloud, his future plans uncertain. Then he had brooded in an inhospitable room at a city fort.

"Well, old fella, you're hardly on top of the heap anymore, as Grandmother would say," he said bitterly to himself.

He thought of his family and he felt he would be returning home a failure. As his room grew dimmer with the coming of evening, his thoughts turned to Sara. Was she back in Washington? He wanted to see her with all his heart, yet he knew he would make no move to. He reached over and felt the still tender stump of his arm. Sara had treated men like him. When she saw him next, would there be only pity in her eyes? He dropped off into an exhausted, troubled sleep.

It was midmorning the following day before he reentered Washington. Reluctantly he rode toward the path between the White House and War Department. He had walked that path daily with the President. He would never forget Lincoln's long strides and swinging arms as he walked. A local paper had described the President's gait as "the swagger of a long-legged, long-armed monkey." Lincoln had laughed and said that for once the paper had printed the truth about him.

There was no one on the path today—it was quiet. He could reminisce alone for awhile. He thought of the last day he had seen Lincoln before he had left for City Point. It was the dinner hour and Lincoln had walked down the hall with him, talking. He could not recall now what the President had been saying. Someone was vigorously pulling the front doorbell and McManus, the doorkeeper, seemed tardy in answering it. It was not unusual for the President to answer the door to the Executive Mansion himself. Lincoln opened the door to a middle-aged woman in country garb. She held the hand of a boy in knickers and carefully slicked hair.

"What can I do for you?" asked Ethan.

"We want to see Abraham the Second!" piped up the little lad eagerly.

Ethan could see Lincoln tugging at his beard in concealed amusement.

"And who is Abraham the First?" asked the President.

"Why bless you!" laughed the boy. "Abraham the First is in the Bible and Abraham the Second is our President!"

"Oh I see . . . Well, young man, the President isn't in his office just now I'm afraid."

"He isn't? Well, where is he, then?" the boy asked fiercely. "We've come a long way!"

"He's here!" boomed Lincoln.

Ethan left for dinner with the deep chuckle and the boyish laugh ringing in his ears. The memory stirred Ethan so deeply that he knew he could not face Stanton and the others at the War Department yet. Slowly he turned his horse around. He would return to the quiet of his room at the Soldier's Home.

Ethan rode into the city the next day, tethered his horse and started walking. He crossed Lafayette Square, fully intending to go to the War Department. It was time to be putting in his appearance there, no matter how apprehensive and reluctant he was. But the crowds filing into the White House pulled him along.

He was amazed. The lines were filled with civilians and military personnel alike, there was no social distinction; a man in overalls stood in front of a diplomat in silk; a Union private helped along a crippled black woman. All faces were etched in grief. Ethan had no intention of viewing the President, and was finally able to pull aside out of the line. He didn't move away immediately, however. He was now caught up in watching this progression of pain and sorrow. He felt uncomfortable with such open emotion; yet, there was something communal, almost comforting in seeing others grieving for the slain leader.

Just as he turned to leave, he noticed a small group of negroes, huddled under the eaves of the mansion. Apparently they had just viewed the President. Now, they seemed reluctant to leave. Lincoln had come to represent their freedom, their future—and now the future looked so uncertain.

One young man stepped away from the others, his eyes fixed on the East Room window. Ethan could see he clutched his hat tightly, his large brown eyes swimming in tears. He opened his mouth and Ethan was transfixed as a deep baritone voice filled the air.

"Mine eyes have seen the glory of the coming of the Lord ..." The young man was singing a popular anthem. Written by social reformer Julia Ward Howe, it stirred the hearts of many Northerners, for it reflected the spiritual passion of the long war.

There were hundreds going up and down the steps, most silent, absorbed, some talking in low voices. Yet all talking and movement abruptly stopped as the rich, plaintive voice rang out.

"Glory, glory hallelujah ... His truth is marching on!"

Ethan, who had not yet cried, wept openly now, as did many others. He could not have stopped the tears if he had wanted to.

It was afternoon before Ethan finally made his way to Stanton's office. He took a deep breath, knocked, and entered.

"Alcott!" Meadows sprang forward, greeting him warmly. "How are you?"

"Hello, Meadows."

"How's the shoulder?" asked Stanton gruffly and without preface.

"Healing fine, sir, thank you."

"Ethan, I'm sorry your assignment to City Point turned out as it did for you," Meadows said kindly.

Ethan shifted uncomfortably. "Losing my arm is small in comparison ..." There was an awkward silence.

Ethan leveled his gaze at the third occupant of the room—Humner, the aide who had replaced him.

"I'm sure you know tomorrow is the funeral, Alcott. Wear your uniform. The War Department staff will sit together in the East Room," said Stanton.

"I'd rather not, sir. I mean, I didn't plan on going to the funeral, sir."

"What's this?" Stanton snapped testily.

Meadows came over to Ethan, his manner gentle. "Ethan, are you feeling responsible for what happened, because you weren't here?"

"Manure!" Stanton bellowed. "Look here, we all feel badly. It was no one's fault."

Humner left the room.

"Ethan, do you feel hard at Humner? He wasn't even at the theater," Meadows explained.

"Yes. I'm sorry, but I'm feeling hard at everybody just now, I guess."

"I tell you, he was warned!" Stanton was in a royally bad mood. "I told him not to go, especially to the theater!" Stanton sat back, deflated, closing his eyes in frustration. "Are you sure about the funeral?" he asked quietly.

"Yes, sir."

"All right, then, go talk with Meadows about your pension and such," he said, waving his hand absently toward Ethan as he pulled a sheaf of papers before him. Ethan knew the important man was dismissing him. He had more pressing business than the plans of a one-armed, ex-presidential aide.

Outside the office, Meadows sighed loudly. "Sorry, Ethan. He's been pretty frosty since..."

"Just since?" said Ethan, attempting to make a joke for his friend.

Meadows laughed, glad to see the captain had not really lost his sense of humor, even if his eyes now looked so sober.

"Yes, frostier than usual. Will you head home to Illinois now, Ethan?"

Ethan looked down at his feet a moment. "Yes...soon."

"Your family will be glad to have you back. You'll be farming in no time. I can see it. You were made for the land, Ethan, not the city, I think."

"I hope so. I haven't done too well in the city."

His words were said simply and without pity. Meadows placed his hand on Ethan's arm. "The President liked you very well, Ethan, you must know that. No other fellow could have made him as comfortable with having an aide. Be proud of your work. Now go home and raise those—apples, is it?"

Ethan nodded.

"Raise those apples and a bushel of little Alcotts and you'll be just fine."

Ethan was awakened the day of the funeral like every other Washingtonian. Great booms of Federal cannon began the slow solemn tribute. All businesses were closed and by midmorning hundreds were pouring into the streets to view the funeral procession. Ethan could see people on rooftops and in the trees. Trains arrived every hour depositing new arrivals. Bands added sobering music as they joined the processional. The sky was spotless, as April would give no more concessions to winter.

Ethan wandered among the crowds with no fixed purpose. When he heard the church bells begin their toll, guns fire, and bands playing, he knew the prairie lawyer was making his final trip up the avenue. He stopped as the black-draped hearse pulled into sight. When many around him saw the casket, they began to sob, and Ethan found his own heart racing. Then Lincoln's horse followed, with its master's boots backwards in the stirrups. Ethan turned and headed back for his room at the Soldier's Home.

The next day he headed for the depot. "When's your next train going west, to Springfield?"

The grizzled man at the window squinted over the schedule. "Wal, let's see . . . 'bout midafternoon tomorrow. Schedule all cat-a-wampas with the funeral train, you see."

Ethan fumbled in his pockets, not wanting to wait until the next day to leave the city. He wanted to leave today—now.

"Wal, young man?"

"When's the next train?"

"Where?"

"East."

"Baltimore in twenty-seven minutes."

"A ticket, please. I want to go to New York."

The decision made, Ethan felt relieved. Of course he knew he had no reason for going to New York, but that didn't matter. He felt so stirred up inside, he reasoned he couldn't go home yet. Purchasing some paper, he wrote a quick message home. Ethan deposited the letter and boarded the train.

Peppercreek, Illinois

Caleb had been fussy all morning and Wyeth was grateful Henri had taken him along on a visit to a church member. She needed an hour or so of quiet. The baby's crying had jangled

severely on her nerves—and she knew why. She was preoccupied. Her mind was on the letter they had received yesterday.
Now, sitting on the broad front porch, she turned to it again,
hoping she could understand it better with a second reading.

> *Dear family,*
>
> *You know it has never been easy for me to write
> letters; this one is not easy either. I know you are
> expecting me home soon, but I am writing to tell you I
> can't come just yet. I'm waiting for a train that will take
> me east, probably all the way to New York. I don't
> know why I'm going, I just can't come home yet and I
> can't stay in Washington any longer. I have been pen
> sioned out of the army and the War Department staff. I
> don't know what my plans are. My shoulder is healing
> and I'm getting used to one arm. I know this letter
> makes no real sense and I'm sorry. I will write again
> when I have some plans.*
>
> > *Ethan*

They had all read the letter the evening before when Henri
had brought it from town. A silence lay over the room as they all
considered his words. He had not been home in over three years
and their disappointment was very real. It was obvious he was
hurting in more than his shoulder. Will had risen slowly and gone
to his room. Henri and Wyeth had sat close together, not talking.
When they rose to go to bed Henri had said simply, "Losing his
arm, his job, Mr. Lincoln—I know he's deeply hurt. He's confused
and I trust the Lord is drawing him. We shouldn't despair. He'll
come home soon."

Her thoughts were broken as a horse and rider came down
the lane. Sara James rode up to the front porch. She's so fresh and
pretty, thought Wyeth.

"Good morning, Sara!"

"Hello, Wyeth. I rode over to tell you Mother said the music
would be fine for Sunday."

"Oh Sara, you needn't have ridden all the way over for that."

"I wanted to! It's such a beautiful morning, I just had to get
Flame out. I can't get enough of riding and being outdoors since I

got home. Mother says Flame and I have been over the county and back in the month I've been home!" she said, laughing.

"Come sit with me awhile before you're off on another trek."

"Where is everyone?"

"Isaiah and Papa went to New Salem to deliver a colt and Henri has taken Caleb—"

"The most beautiful baby in Sangamon county!" interrupted Sara.

Wyeth smiled, "Well, he was the most fussy baby this morning, so Henri took him for a ride."

They talked of other things a few minutes. Their age difference had precluded them from friendship growing up, but they had known each other all their lives and now that they were women, they had a friendship that years would not change.

"Louisa tells me that you and Tom Springer..."

Sara blushed, "Your sister is a hopeless romantic, Wyeth!"

"Now you see why my folks were so relieved when Joe came along. Somebody had to slow her down!"

"Tom has been coming over since I got home," Sara admitted slowly. She fiddled with her dress. "But, we don't have much in common, really."

They both grew silent as the morning sun heightened in the May sky. Sara detected something was troubling Wyeth.

"Wyeth, is anything wrong?"

"Hmm? Oh, I'm sorry." She smoothed her hand over Ethan's letter in her lap. "Sara, you've seen Ethan more recently than any of us. When you were in Washington... Well, how was he, really?"

"It's been over a year since I saw him. Do you mean besides physically, how was he?"

Wyeth nodded.

This was a subject painfully close to Sara's heart. Talking about it was not easy. It wasn't his fault, she had reasoned, he simply hadn't returned her love. In all her thoughts, she was trying to get over him. Falling out of love, she was learning, was a much more difficult proposition than falling in love.

"I think he was struggling, in a way. Losing his friend Andy hurt him deeply. He told me he felt something change inside him at Gettysburg, something he couldn't explain. I think... I think he is never quite content with himself, like there's an empty spot inside. I know I'm not making sense."

"Oh, no, you are! I *do* understand you. I think Ethan has always been that way. Henri says he is satisfied with himself physically and mentally, but emotionally and spiritually there is an emptiness, like you said."

Sara gazed out at the orchard a moment. "I can imagine how hurt he is over the death of Mr. Lincoln. He respected him very much," she said quietly.

"Yes and losing his arm..."

Sara had learned about Ethan's injury when Henri had spoken to his congregation about it. Henri, of course, didn't know how his words had affected a certain young woman in the fellowship that morning. She heard absolutely nothing of the sermon, and afterwards went home to her room and cried. Losing an arm didn't make him less a man to her, but she could feel what it must surely be doing to him. His hurt became hers because she loved him. She lay awake long at night, absorbed in thinking about each detail of him—his face, voice, walk...

"We received a letter from Ethan yesterday," said Wyeth.

"Is he coming home soon?" asked Sara too eagerly, leaning forward in the swing. Her face had brightened and Wyeth did not fail to notice it. She had picked up a few things from sister Louisa...

"It was written over two weeks ago," said Wyeth, extending the letter toward Sara.

"Oh Wyeth, you don't, I mean... Don't feel like you should offer to let me read it." Sara felt suddenly flustered and their eyes locked.

Wyeth kept the letter out and Sara slowly took it.

It was the same quick, careless scrawl she remembered so well from school days when she had secretly saved all his discarded papers. She read it quickly then handed it back to Wyeth. Wordlessly she walked to the end of the porch. The O'Dell farm was so beautiful, she thought, with the honeysuckle vine growing over the low stone wall, the white fence that bordered the lane, the barns, the redolent orchard beyond.

"Oh Lord, please help me," she whispered. Tears were streaming down her cheeks when Wyeth came up to her.

"Sara?"

Sara turned and Wyeth took her hands.

"Sara... Are you in love with my little brother?" There was calm happiness in Wyeth's voice.

"I'm trying hard not to be! But I'm not doing very well."

"Oh Sara..." The two hugged.

"Does he know how you feel?"

"No, he was courting Miss Amanda Sims when I left Washington. I don't think he loved her, really... I'm like a little sister to him."

"Is that why you left Washington?"

"Partly. They needed nurses at Cold Harbor, so I volunteered. I'm selfish, Wyeth. It became too hard to... love him and not have it returned."

Wyeth led Sara back to the swing.

"Henri says he thinks Ethan will come home soon and I think so too. God is trying hard to reach Ethan. Listen, Sara, my mother was a woman of prayer."

Sara smiled, "I remember."

"She prayed for all of us, of course, but I think Ethan even more. She didn't know what his spiritual heritage was. Even though she went to heaven not seeing the fulfillment of her prayers in her lifetime, she kept on praying! She believed Sara, and so shall we. We'll keep praying for Ethan, praying that he'll come home soon."

Sara nodded.

"Home to... all of us," added Wyeth with a smile.

Chapter 16

Washington, D.C.

♦♦ ♦♦ ♦♦

*T*he train porter, a man named Dilling, did not know what to do about the young man slumped in his red-cushioned seat. He must be drunk, reasoned Dilling, though he couldn't smell any alcohol about him. Dilling had a well-practiced nose when it came to that. The passenger certainly didn't look very good. His plain clothes were rumpled, his face was covered in a scratchy looking beard and a purple bruise was coming up on one of his cheeks. He'd been crumpled in his seat the entire trip.

"Say there, young fella! Time to wake up!"

The man in the seat merely groaned.

"Washington be only five minutes off."

Dilling began to shake him gently. "There, there, that's fine. You awake."

"Goodnight?" Ethan's voice was croaky.

"Good night?" Dilling's laughter bubbled out. "No, suh, it's good mornin', more like."

"Your name isn't Goodnight?"

Ethan's foggy brain was remembering his uncle's slave.

"Laws, laws! What kinda name be Goodnight? No, suh, my name is Frederick Ambrose Rufus Dilling."

Ethan pulled himself up to get a better look at the man. "That's a pretty long name."

Dilling chuckled, "Well, I was an only child, you see. Folks'll be callin' me Dilling, though."

"That's reasonable," Ethan said, pushing back his hat. "Where am I, Dilling?"

"'Bout to be in Washington. You did know you were on a train, suh?"

"I . . . do now."

Dilling moved off with a shake of his head, satisfied that the passenger was awake, at least, and sober.

The 8:05 from Baltimore arrived in Washington, shrouded in thick folds of gray smoke. Ethan wandered along the platform until he came to a glass window that had just been washed. He saw his reflection for the first time in days. He was shocked—he looked worse than he had imagined.

He began to walk toward the hub of the city—totally aimless. He came out of his reverie to realize someone was walking beside him.

"Now, it's a peach of a mornin', wouldn't you say, suh?"

"It's Dilling, right?"

"That's right, suh."

"Not Goodnight or Goodbye."

The man laughed and Ethan joined him—it was good to laugh suddenly like that. He hadn't laughed much, lately.

"My name's Ethan Alcott, Dilling."

Ethan extended his hand and Dilling hesitated, then shook it.

"First time in Washin'ton, suh?"

"Ah, no. Listen Dilling, I've never had someone call me 'sir' before and I don't really want to start now, all right? It's just 'Ethan'."

"All right."

They kept on walking.

"So, you been to the city before. Family?"

"I don't have family here. I used to work here. Do you have family, Dilling?"

"Ah yes," he said clapping his hands. "I am a married man . . . chained by love to a good, good woman." They both laughed again. "And we have four boys. My sons, bright as new pennies and pride of they dear daddy's heart, yes, suh!"

Ethan smiled. Then he began to notice how crowded the roads into the city were. "A lot of folks in town this morning," he said.

"'Spect so," Dilling agreed.

"I would have thought they would be gone after the . . . funeral."

"Oh, these ain't the same folks, Ethan. Didn't ya see when we came into town this mornin', on the hills around the city? All the tents?"

"Who are they, Dilling?"

"All the troops are in town, even from the West. Been comin' in for days upon days. Camped thick around the city, like so many fleas."

"Why?" Ethan's voice trailed off in confusion.

"Today's the grand review of the Union armies, Ethan! That's why I got to hurry home. My boys'll be givin' my woman fits to get out to see the parade."

"Parade," said Ethan flatly.

"Yep, they'll march down the avenue and pass in front of the White House and General Grant and President Johnson. Take most of two days, they say."

Ethan stopped walking, feeling weak. "It'll be hard to get a room, then." His voice was dull.

"Don't you have a place to stay, Ethan?"

"No, I haven't any plans. I . . ."

Ethan felt a wave of shame that he was without a plan, without a place to stay, and almost penniless.

"You'll come home with me, of course," Dilling said cheerily.

"Oh no, I couldn't, Dilling, thanks." Then he realized how the black man might interpret his refusal. "I couldn't impose on your family," he added.

Dilling carefully measured Ethan a moment. His normally smiling face was sober. "You hungry, ain't ya?"

"Well, yes . . ."

"'Course you are. You'll come home with me."

Soon they entered a very small cabin in the black quarter of Washington. "Woman of mine!" boomed Dilling through the door. "The man of your heart is home!"

Suddenly, four little brown bodies were climbing and clinging all over Dilling. Ethan stood in the doorway as Dilling's family welcomed him home.

"Now, now, all right, don't choke your daddy off! Get back, you scamps. Where's your Mama?"

A woman stood by the table as the children greeted their father, suddenly made shy by the stranger with her husband. A white man had never been on their street before, much less in their house.

"Now, Rose, no need to shy off, like. This is my new friend, Ethan Alcott. We got acquainted on the train, you see."

"Hello, Mrs. Dilling."

Rose Dilling nodded slightly and smiled. Then Dilling turned to the four little boys who stood beside their mother, openly regarding the stranger with awe. They could not pull their eyes from the empty sleeve.

"Now scamps, you all come here." The boys edged over to their father. "This here is my oldest son, Frederick."

Ethan shook their hands in turn.

"This bright-eyed lad is my second son, Ambrose. This big lad is my third son, Rufus, and this hound dog puppy is Abraham."

"Very handsome boys you have, Dilling," Ethan declared.

"Daddy, when we gonna go to the parade?"

"Soon as my belly's full, so patient up, now."

Seated around the plain table, Ethan began to relax and enjoy himself. The boys too, became less concerned about Ethan's presence. Soon, the meal was finished, and Ethan felt much better for the good food. Dilling tipped his chair back, his hands behind his head, his eyes closed. Rose busied herself wiping faces and tucking in shirts.

"They'll be bands!" piped one boy.

"And think of the pretty horses!"

"And the uniforms and shiny swords!"

"Daddy, you should see all the flags up, everywhere!"

Ethan watched the preparations with amusement. Yet Ambrose did not take part. He stood silently at the window, his hands clasped behind his back.

His voice was wistful. "Just wish Mr. Lincoln could see the parade."

Everyone grew still and Dilling straightened up in his chair. Ethan's hands clutched under the table, and he was surprised to hear his own voice. "Maybe . . . Maybe he will, Ambrose. Maybe the Lord will draw back a curtain in heaven, and let Mr. Lincoln watch."

Ambrose gave a little nod.

The boys lost all their hesitancy about Ethan then, and beamed with friendliness. Soon they left and the little cabin was quiet. Ethan stepped out into the bright May sunshine, and began walking toward Pennsylvania Avenue.

The city had taken off its veil of black to replace it with patriotic finery. As one of Dilling's sons had said, red, white and blue banners and bunting were everywhere. Many people waved tiny Union flags. There was an unmistakable holiday spirit in the air. The long bloody conflict was over, the formidable task of healing the nation lay ahead—but for today, Washington was determined to celebrate.

Ethan squeezed into a place with thousands of others as row upon row of soldiers marched by. He hoped Sam Bass, Moses and Curly Brown were among these passing ranks. Bands were playing and sunlight flashed off swords and sabers. The steady cadence of boots marching filled the air and hundreds of horses pranced by with braided manes. Yes, if only Mr. Lincoln were here... He walked all day till sheer exhaustion led him back to Dilling's.

If any of the adults had hoped to sleep a bit late the next morning, that hope was quickly dispelled. The four boys bounced from their beds, eager and animated to describe yesterday's grand sights. At breakfast they could hardly eat for all they must tell Ethan.

"Did you see the Zouaves? Didn't they have funny-lookin' hats?"

"Did you see the colored regiment, Ethan? Did you see how straight they marched?"

"Did you see the horses with the purple plumes?..."

"Did anyone see the Twenty-First Illinois?" Ethan asked, finally.

They shook their heads. "Were you ever in a regiment, Ethan?" Dilling asked casually.

"Yes, I was in the Twenty-First till...Shiloh."

"You were in the army?" gasped Frederick. "The Union army?"

"Well you don't think it was the Rebel army do you, boy?" snorted Dilling.

"Did you get shot somewhere?" asked Rufus eagerly.

"Look at his arm, dummy," snapped Frederick.

Rose gave her eldest son a sharp pinch.

"Actually, Frederick, I didn't lose my arm in battle."

"Shiloh is in Tennessee," said Frederick. "What did you do till now?"

"Frederick, you sound like a two-bit trial lawyer, askin' Ethan all these questions. Mind your own business, boy," warned Dilling.

"It's all right, Dilling. I don't mind. I came to Washington after Shiloh."

The boys were looking at him with expectation and even Dilling leaned forward in his chair.

"I worked in the War Department."

"You were a secretary?" asked Frederick, the family authority on the war. He was plainly disappointed.

"No, I worked in the White House."

Everyone's eyes were round and their breathing seemed suspended.

"I worked for Mr. Lincoln. I was an aide to him."

Ambrose jumped up from his chair and came around to Ethan's.

His voice was barely above a whisper. "Oh Mr. Ethan, you ain't tellin' lies, are you?"

"No, Ambrose, I'm not lying to you. I wouldn't do that. I was an aide to Mr. Lincoln. I ran errands for him and rode with him when he went out, in case someone tried to hurt him."

No one said a word. It was almost beyond belief. This ragged, crippled man had not only seen Mr. Lincoln, but talked and worked alongside him.

"Here." Ethan went over to his valise and took out his uniform. He brought the coat back to the table and pointed out the lapel.

"See that pin, Ambrose?" he said pointing to a small bronze pin.

"That was given to everyone from the War Department who worked in the White House. It was like an identifying badge."

Everyone gathered around to look, then began talking at once.

"Did you eat with him?"

"Once or twice."

"Were his feet really so big?"

"Nearly as big as your daddy's and mine put together," Ethan said, laughing.

"Did you ever meet Tad? He's my age," asked Frederick.

"Yes, I knew Tad. Sometimes I had to get him out of the office when important men were coming to see his daddy. They had a special knock between them that Tad used to come into the office."

"Really?"

"Yes. Mr. Lincoln liked boys very much."

"Did he ever laugh?" asked the young Rufus.

"Oh, yes, Rufus, Mr. Lincoln loved to laugh. He was always telling jokes and stories. Sometimes when the war news was really bad, he'd tell a funny story to the men that worked with him, so they wouldn't forget to laugh at themselves."

Then Ambrose pushed his brothers aside and stood right before Ethan. He looked at him a moment then climbed into his lap, his arms clinging tightly to Ethan's neck. Ethan could feel the boy shaking with sobs. Dilling cleared his throat and Ethan could hear the tears in his voice.

"Ambrose did love Mr. Lincoln," Dilling explained. "He was always findin' a newspaper to read about him. Once he saw him pass in a carriage. Talked on it for days and days."

Ethan held him close, trying to think of something to say. "Ambrose . . . You see, it was my job to protect Mr. Lincoln. He had a lot of enemies. Maybe you read about that in the newspaper. A lot of people didn't understand him. Mr. Booth was like that."

"Did you carry a gun?" Frederick interrupted.

"No. Mr. Lincoln didn't like that."

"Were you at the theater, Ethan?" asked Frederick.

"No, Frederick, I wasn't." Ethan looked down at the floor trying to steady his emotions. Dilling reached out and patted Ethan on the shoulder. "I was in Virginia, and I got shot. Then . . . Mr. Lincoln was killed."

Frederick patted his knee. "I think you did a good job, anyway."

Ethan took a deep, hard breath. "I'm sorry, Ambrose, that I wasn't here to protect our friend. I'm not sure what I could have done, anyway. Men like Mr. Booth are pretty determined."

Ambrose withdrew his face from Ethan's shoulder. "Will you tell me all about him? "

"Yes, Ambrose, as long as you like."

They all moved out of doors, onto the front stoop. Bands could be heard in the distance as the second day of the grand review of the troops got underway.

"Now, there isn't all sadness about Mr. Lincoln you know. He wouldn't like that. He really did like to laugh, and especially at himself. He told stories, but he said he never told an original story . . ."

So Ethan began talking and the morning faded into a mild afternoon. The more he talked, the more he remembered. And the more he remembered, the more he enjoyed it.

The Dilling family now knew, to some detail, what the White House looked like inside, what things Lincoln laughed about, how he walked. Ethan told them of the trip to City Point where Lincoln had demonstrated his strength with the two axes. Frederick's eyes grew round at that. Ambrose cried when Ethan told them about Gettysburg.

Rose brought food, but they scarcely touched it. Ethan was giving them something priceless in their humble lives and they didn't want to lose a word. Rufus listened while drawing pictures of plumed horses on scraps of paper. Ethan could see the boy had an amazing artistic talent for one so young.

Ethan talked till dusk, finally growing hoarse. The boys were yawning now as the stars and night breezes came out. Ambrose came to Ethan. His face had lost that solemn look.

"Today was better than yesterday," he said.

"I'm glad, Ambrose. I enjoyed it too. Goodnight."

Each boy, except baby Abraham, came up to Ethan and shook his hand. It was the only way they knew to thank him. Ethan found himself feeling very touched by this family. He stood up as Rose took the boys off to bed.

"I think I'll go for a little walk, Dilling. I'm kinda stiff."

"Sure," said Dilling stretching. "Like my son said, today was real special, and we thank ya more than we can tell ya."

"I may be late, so don't wait up or anything."

"All right, but be careful," he said, nodding toward the heart of the city. "The streets can be kinda rough."

Ethan chuckled. "That's true. Goodnight, Dilling."

Ethan had no particular destination in mind as he began walking. He had to think. His money was gone and he could not impose on the Dillings much longer. There was no money to buy a train ticket and he cringed at the thought of wiring home for some. No, he couldn't do that.

As Ethan drew closer to the city's main streets, he could see the saloons were doing booming business, since most of the troops had not yet left for home. There were fist fights on nearly every corner as regiments jealously guarded their reputations. Groups of swaying, singing soldiers filled the streets.

Ethan went all the way up to the Capitol, closed of course, but still glowing with celebration lights. At the War Department he studied the darkened window of the office that Packer had used. What would he think of me now, mused Ethan. With a sigh, he turned back east toward the residential part of town. He stood in the shadows, looking at the Sims mansion. It was dark and silent. He suddenly remembered the night Amanda had told him he was the most handsome man she knew. He laughed out loud at the thought. I wouldn't be fit to be her gardener now, he said to himself. He gritted his teeth at the thought of courting her when there was a girl like Sara...

His trampings brought him down Pennsylvania Avenue and across from Willard's. Light, music, and laughter poured from the open doors. He grew tired and started back for Dilling's. Several black employees were leaving from a side door, their shift over. They walked behind Ethan, since they were going into the black quarter, as he was.

Ben Jones, a waiter from Willard's, could not fully join in the conversation of his companions, for he was watching the man in front of him. He prided himself on studying the men who came under his scrutiny in the hotel. Who was this man just ahead? There was something familiar about him. Block after block passed and Ben grew agitated, certain that he knew the man in front of him. Young, an empty sleeve... Ethan turned a corner in the colored district and was lost to Ben's view. An empty sleeve ... of course! It was the young captain that had lived at Willard's and had worked for Lincoln! He hurried forward, calling Ethan's name. He had something to tell him, something that might be important.

He stopped in frustration, he had lost sight of him. What was he doing in the black quarter anyway?

"Doggone," he muttered, "maybe I'll catch sight of him again."

Peppercreek, Illinois

Sara stood at her bedroom window, her arms crossed, a frown on her face. She was angry with herself. Angry that she wasn't enjoying anything to the fullest since she got home. And that bothered her—bothered her very much.

Young Tom Springer had been coming over in the evenings, trading war stories with Roy. Of course, it was not really Roy that he came to see.

Everything in her life seemed whole and well. She should be very happy. Tom Springer was nice. There had been the doctor at Cold Harbor. She knew he had really loved her. Still, she had turned him down. Now there was Tom and she knew that he would be a persistent suitor. Why is life so complicated? she sighed. When all I want... She was angry with herself because her heart was tied to someone who did not love her. "I can't love anyone, Lord, till I get over him. Why is this so hard? Wherever he is, Lord, please be with him... Please keep drawing him to you, and bring him home..."

Washington, D.C.

Frederick Dilling lay in bed, one arm behind his head, the other arm pinned under one of his brothers, thinking of yesterday and the day before. Thinking on all he had seen at the big parade and then all he had heard from the man his daddy had brought home. He couldn't stay in bed a moment longer. Surely all his young friends had seen the parade, but did any of them know someone that had actually worked with Abraham Lincoln? No, it was too much to contain. He must go tell someone.

He quietly pulled on his overalls and carefully stepped over Ethan, who still lay sleeping on the floor. He was out the door soundlessly.

Later, Dilling was passing Ethan some syrup for his corncakes when he announced, "Ethan, I have to be at work just after noon today. You're welcome here and you know that plain."

"I appreciate that, Dilling. But I need to get out and get a job and earn some money to get home, or, something. But—"

Ethan was interrupted as Frederick burst in breathlessly through the door.

"Whoa there, boy! Where you been? Don't need to be missin' your Ma's cookin'."

"Where ya been?" asked Rufus.

"Went to Toby's house. Had to tell him about Ethan knowin' Mr. Lincoln!"

"All right now, sit down and eat," insisted Dilling.

"But Toby's daddy heard me talkin' and he's comin' right behind me!"

Dilling stood up as Toby Jones' father entered the cabin.

"Mornin', Ben!"

"Howdy, Dilling!"

Ben looked past Dilling. "It *is* you!" he said as his eyes came to rest on Ethan. "Thought it had to be, with all Fred was saying. Well, this is somethin'! Imagine you at the Dillings' all along!"

"Hello, Ben."

"You know Ethan?" Dilling asked incredulously.

"Sure do. Seen he had sense not to eat them rich vittles that Willard's passes off."

"I lived at Willard's," Ethan explained to Dilling.

"I'm glad I found ya, Captain. Saw ya last night, then lost ya. I wanted to tell ya, thought it might be important."

"What's that, Ben?"

"That a letter came for ya, 'bout three weeks or a month ago. Came to the hotel."

"I'll go get it now," said Ethan.

"No need. Sent my boy for it, should—"

All turned to the doorway as they heard the sound of someone running. A teenaged boy came into the cabin and handed the letter to Ethan.

"Thank you." Ethan took the letter. It was from home. He looked around the room. Everyone was silent and looking at him with expectation.

"Thank you, Ben. Thank you very much. I think I'll go for a walk to . . . read this. I'll be back before you leave for work, Dilling."

"Hope it's good news for the young man," said Dilling to his family after Ethan had left.

Ethan walked with renewed energy until he came to a grassy bluff near the Potomac. It was still early morning, not yet hot, the rising sun shimmering silver and gold on the glassy surface of the river. His heart was racing as he opened the letter.

Dear son,

   *You come by your difficulty in letter writing hon-
estly I suppose... The girls said we should all pitch in
and write and as usual they're right. I sold Maggie's
colt for you like you asked me to, years ago. Enclosed
is what she brought. I've been praying for you, son, like
you must know. You also know we want you home. I
am proud of my son.*

                                    Pa

Ethan fingered the paper, treasuring what his father had
written. He felt the emotion surging up in him as he unfolded the
next letter.

Ethan,

   *You are such a silly boy! I can only write you a quick
note, I'm the busy mother of two now, so very responsible! Goodness! Why aren't you coming home? Do
you have grand ideas that you are irreplaceable?!
Well, you are! Come home, little brother...*

                              Love, Louisa

Dearest Ethan,

   *I'm a busy mother too, and if you don't come home
soon little Caleb won't have a thing to do with you. He
has six teeth and is taking wobbly steps... The war is
over and we're so thankful. We know you're hurting,
but did you know that it doesn't change our love for
you? The Lord flashed that lightning years ago and I
saw you. You became a forever part of us. Nothing can
change that. Please come home.*

                                   Wyeth

Ethan drew a long breath and unfolded the final page.

   *Ethan, I'll save most of what I want to tell you till you
come home. But this you must know. I wanted to wait,
to tell you in person because it seemed too important*

for a letter. Yet now seems right. This will be very
surprising to you but remember we belong to a God
that does not shy away from surprises. You and I are
brothers, blood brothers. My mother's real name, I
learned long ago, was Rachel Alcott, the same as your
mother's. I have everything to confirm it. Come home,
Ethan, your brother longs to greet you.

Henri

He closed his eyes as tears slid down his cheeks. He had a
brother! It was almost too incredible to believe. His family from
miles away had reached out across the distance to touch him
when he needed it most.

Midmorning was drawing on, clouds floated passively in the
sky, fishing boats bobbed along the shoreline. He hopped up,
feeling more alive and hopeful than he had in months. He started
at a brisk pace toward the depot. A train with connections to
Springfield was leaving at one o'clock that afternoon. He quickly
purchased a ticket.

It was just before noon when Ethan came down Dilling's
street. Frederick had been hanging around the corner most of the
morning, telling stories with great relish and license to the dozen
or so small boys who were his eager audience. Frederick Dilling,
like Ambrose, could not help but secretly hope that the letter
Ethan had received would not take him away from them. His eyes
were wide as he saw Ethan's cleaned-up appearance and the
bundles he carried under his arm. A boy hurried behind him with
a small wagon of more bundles.

"That's a whole lot of stuff there!" Frederick enthused, coming up to Ethan.

"Bought out the store, Frederick!" Ethan laughed.

Dilling was on his doorstep, his face lighting up when he saw
Ethan. "Have you had good news, Ethan?"

"Yes, I have, Dilling. I'm going home!"

"He says he bought the whole store, Daddy!" explained Frederick.

In the cabin, Ethan unloaded the wagon and placed all the
packages on the table. He paid the boy that had helped him then
turned to the Dillings.

"Now . . ." his voice was full of anticipation. Most of the larger bundles were foodstuffs: potatoes, meal, flour, sugar and a box of oranges. There was a box of assorted hard candies and chocolates that left them speechless. Then Ethan sat down.

"You've all been . . . so good to me. I really didn't have any place to go and you took me in. I couldn't even pay you and you knew that. I really thank you for that."

"You let us meet Mr. Lincoln," said Ambrose.

"I was glad to, Ambrose. Here, now." He handed Rufus a box. "This is yours."

Slowly the boy opened the package. It revealed a flat metal box of colored pencils and two thick pads of creamy white paper.

Ethan smiled. "I fully expect to get some fine drawings in the mail one of these days."

The boy could not speak as he touched the art supplies with near reverence. Rose could not speak either, but her eyes were shining.

"Boy won't have to use scraps of that ol' brown stuff anymore," murmured Dilling.

"Now, this is for you, Frederick."

The boy did not take the deliberate care that his younger brother had, but tore into the brown paper with vigor. Inside a smooth wooden box lay a pearl-handled pocketknife.

"Every boy needs a good pocketknife."

Frederick nodded soberly and shook Ethan's hand.

"That big box there. That's for everyone." He opened it up and they all peered inside. There were two neat stacks of crimson bound books.

"Books," whispered Rose Dilling, her hands clasped together.

"Yes, they're classics, I guess. Should be some adventure stories in there you'd especially like, Frederick. I hope everyone enjoys them."

A little box was opened next. It contained a shiny wooden top and bronze train for Abraham. The baby boy clapped his hands in glee. Then a small footstool was unwrapped for Rose and bolts of fabric. Finally Ethan handed a small box to Dilling. The black man was reluctant to take it.

"You shouldn't have done all this," he said, emotion strong in his voice.

"Go on now, open it," Ethan urged.

Slowly he opened the velvet covered box. On the silk lay a gold pocket watch. The ticking could be heard in the expectant stillness. Dilling carefully clicked the cover open. It was 12:02. He looked up, tears spilling out of his gentle brown eyes.

"Don't know near what to say," he whispered.

"None of us have said 'thank you'," spoke up Rose.

"Seems like thank you ain't powerful enough," returned Dilling.

"Well, I figured all good train porters need to know the comings and goings of the train business, right?"

Dilling nodded. "It's just too fine."

"It's about too late, Dilling! Look at your watch. You've got to go!" Ethan said, laughing.

Ethan bent down on one knee and called Ambrose to him.

"Hoping ya didn't forget 'Brose," stated Frederick, matter-of-factly.

"No, I didn't forget. It's just . . . well, I couldn't find anything that I thought would fit you, Ambrose."

"'S all right, Ethan," the boy said soberly.

Ethan pulled a very small velvet-covered box out of his shirt pocket. Ambrose took it with trembling fingers. He lifted the cover. Inside lay Ethan's White House staff pin.

"I thought . . . this would mean more to you, Ambrose, than anything I could buy. I have . . . memories to remember Mr. Lincoln by."

Ambrose stepped closer to Ethan, staring at the pin. Then he put his arms around Ethan and he could feel the boy's tears on his neck.

"I love you, Ethan."

Ethan tightened his arms around the small boy.

Goodbyes were said as Ethan hurried after Dilling. At the corner they heard running feet behind them. It was Frederick.

"This . . . This is from Rufus," he panted. He thrust a folded paper into Ethan's hand.

"Goodbye, Ethan," Dilling said warmly when they reached the depot.

"Goodbye, Dilling." Their looks held as they shook hands.

"That's right, Ethan, it's 'Goodbye' not 'Goodnight'!" he said as he boarded the train with a wave.

From his seat Ethan watched the suburbs and heights of the capital city slide by. He watched from the last curve, catching the final sight of the Capitol dome, brilliant in the afternoon sun. He was leaving the city he had called home for almost four years.

Only when the train had chugged into the Maryland country-side did Ethan realize he still clutched the paper Frederick had pressed into his hand. He carefully unfolded it. Drawn on crude brown paper, but with obvious skill, was a drawing of Mr. Lincoln delivering his address at Gettysburg. Rufus had apparently listened closer than Ethan realized, for he had captured the President perfectly. Even the intent faces of the audience were depicted by the boy. Ethan lay it carefully in his valise. He knew he would always treasure it.

He looked forward out the window. He was heading west again.

Chapter 17

Peppercreek, Illinois

◆◆ ◆◆ ◆◆

*I*t was a warm morning in June when the telegraph suddenly sparked to life in Baily's little office. There had been no clicking across its wires for nearly a week. Baily was asleep and his nephew Martin had to call twice to rouse him. "Uncle Baily? Sir?"

"Huh?"

"The telegraph, sir, it's—"

"What? Oh, yes..."

Baily straightened up immediately, waving Martin off with an irritated face. *Young whippersnapper, trying to move in on my territory... I heard this infernal machine for myself.* He adjusted his spectacles and found his pad and pencil. The message was from the capital. *Well, now that was interesting... Click, click. To Will O'Dell.* Baily scribbled the message then clicked his acknowledgement.

Well, Well! Ethan Alcott was on his way home. The old man was pleased. Ethan had always been one of his favorites among the Peppercreek youth. He had also been rather indignant when the celebrations had gone off without waiting for the boy's return. After all, he had served the President! He straightened his stiff old body, tucked the telegram in his shirt pocket and fetched his hat.

Will and Henri had been hard at work repairing broken shingles on the roof, but now in early afternoon they took a break in the cool shade of the broad front porch. Henri eyed the coral-colored liquid in his glass and thought of Wyeth. She had made the punch for a quilting bee that she had attended with Louisa.

Then Henri and Will both peered down the lane at a cloud of dust rising in the afternoon air. Jumper got up reluctantly, wagging his stumpy tail.

"Too early for Wyeth to be coming home, isn't it?" Will asked.

Henri nodded and moments later Old Baily's medieval buggy jogged to a stop. Baily carefully stepped down, giving his mare an appreciative pat.

"Afternoon, O'Dell! Mullins!"

"Welcome, Baily!" Will returned, indicating a chair for the older man to take. Henri handed him a glass of punch.

"This is a surprise, Baily," said Will.

Baily nodded, but his attention was on the glass. "What's this you're servin' me, Mullins?" Baily asked suspiciously.

"Just fruit punch. Wyeth made it for a quilting bee she's gone to."

"What brings you out our way, Baily? Has my seed come in?" asked Will.

Baily gave him a patient smile. "Oh, don't reckon seed is so all-important to hitch Matilda up for. She's gettin' a bit lame— like me, I guess... And, I don't reckon I came out just to drink Wyeth's fine punch."

Henri and Will did not immediately catch Baily's attempt at subtlety.

"I can't trust Martin with... all the deliveries, can I?" The storekeeper was relishing the drama he was creating.

"A telegram!" Will finally guessed. He moved forward eagerly in his chair.

Baily withdrew the paper from his vest with an exaggerated flourish, extending it to Will with a beamingly proud face. Will opened it, scanned the short message, then handed it to Henri.

"Fine June day," Baily said expansively, plucking at his suspenders.

"You're the bearer of good news today, Baily," Will said with emotion. Baily swelled a bit more.

"Thank you for coming all the way out. I appreciate it."

"The boy don't say when he'll be here, though," said Baily.

"He's on his way, that's what matters," said Henri.

Will shook Baily's hand again and Henri jumped up.

"I'm going to ride over and tell Wyeth!"

Will nodded and smiled at his son-in-law. The tiredness that both felt seemed to evaporate.

"Don't mind if I have another glass of punch, do you, Will? To celebrate," said Baily with a sly grin.

On the Central Pacific Railroad, somewhere in the Midwest

· After Ethan had looked about at the passengers around him, he watched the countryside, mile after mile. And as he watched, he remembered . . .

Spring had flooded the little Ohio valley, that spring of 1844. As Ethan tramped home from some afternoon fishing, his shoulders drooped with dejection. The small boy of eight had caught his usual stringer full of fish, but he had fished half-heartedly this day.

The chill of winter had fled, but Rachel Alcott could not seem to find much warmth. Spring had come, but she had barely noticed it. She was so weak, so tired; keeping food and fuel in their little home had worn her down. The decision years ago to live without the protection and provision of a man had been a difficult decision, and their life had always been a struggle. She had taken back her maiden name, Alcott, to put her troubled marriage behind.

Rachel had been as faithful to her son as she possibly could. She had taught him to read from her well-worn Bible. She had told him her people were originally from the far-off country of Scotland. His grandfather and great-grandfather had been ministers, she had said. During the war with Great Britain, his ancestors had been patriots from the very beginning. One of her brothers, Henri Taylor Alcott, had worked for Sam Adams. He had fought and fallen at Camden. Ethan had listened wide-eyed to his mother's stories.

Ethan lay the fish down on the stump where he always cleaned them. The little stool his mother had been sitting on was still there in the square of sunshine. His throat swelled as he remembered his mother pulling him on to her lap. He had been embarrassed at first; he was too big, and she was so frail. Still, she had been firm in her weakness. Holding him against her, she had placed a worn hand on his head, growing still and quiet. She was praying a blessing on him. Praying that he would become a godly man. Praying that the pain of his childhood would not forever scar him. When she prayed that, she cried. She had prayed that same prayer years ago for her firstborn.

Ethan put down his knife, the fish untouched. His mother had been waving goodbye . . . He walked slowly toward the cabin. He stepped through the doorway, his eyes drawn to his mother's bed. He came close, certain in his eight-year-old heart of what he would find. It seemed to Ethan another woman lay in the bed. Rachel had let her hair down, and though the waves were streaked with gray, they were still glossy. Ethan was transfixed with her face. The lines were gone and a slight smile was on her lips.

There had been happy times, times before she became so weak. He remembered one night vividly. They were sitting beside the fireplace and she was telling him stories. She had made a plate of hot buttery scones, and showed him how to cut fancy shapes and snowflakes from paper.

Then the rough oak door banged open, and a swirl of snow unwrapped John Edwards. This was his father, and he stood staring at them for a moment like they were aliens. Ethan could still see the great buffalo coat he wore and the little slivers of ice that clung to his beard. His eyes were bloodshot and he brought the smell of alcohol with him.

Ethan had crept to his mother's side, while the man stood before the fireplace rubbing chapped hands. Not a word was spoken. Minutes passed with him looking into the glowing ashes. Rachel smoothed Ethan's little hand in hers. Ethan had never seen this man very often, yet everytime he did, he thought how strong he looked. Ethan had felt his mother tense beside him. His father's voice was steely as he leaned across the table toward his wife. "Where is he . . . Where is Henri?"

Now, years later, on a train chugging across the country, Ethan remembered that question his father had asked. He felt the fear that had knotted his stomach. He could still hear his mother's reply.

"He died, John, he died . . ." she whispered.

The table flew over in a flash and John Edwards slapped Rachel. Tears formed in Ethan's eyes as he thought of that memory. In his mind he could see his eight-year-old hand clenching in anger at his father. Would he have tried to strike the man, given the chance? But John Edwards had again vanished into the night and the boy had felt instinctively he would never see his father again.

Why was he thinking of all this pain now, he wondered? Now, when he was going home. A tangled fabric of his early years was unfolding, memories that had been confused, vague and buried for years. Apparently Rachel had given his brother Henri up years before he was born because of the brutality of his father. He sighed to himself. As painful as this was, it gave him a measure of comfort to know he had Henri to help him sort through it.

He closed his eyes. This long journey home gave him a lot of time to think... There was nothing, no one left for him after his mother died. He had heard about the west from talk in the general store, talk of a good life for anyone who had the tenacity to go. That's what he would do.

He took only a small portion of food, his knife, his mother's Bible and the odd little wooden necklace that his mother always seemed to treasure. He tied these few belongings up in a square of sturdy blue cloth.

Ethan began to remember with startling vividness those first few days and nights of his trip. Sleeping under the stars' blanket, listening to night sounds, eating only fish, squirrels, roots and berries, and always pointing himself westward. He was careful to stay off main roads and avoid towns.

Walking and finding food became Ethan's entire life. The hunger and harshness, the loneliness, did little to deter his will. He grew lean and browned from the sun, his bare feet were calloused. He walked days without seeing another human. In Indiana, he lived with an aged woman and her blind husband for a week, doing chores for meals and sleeping in the warm barn. He rode in wagon beds when he trusted the looks of the driver.

Crossing Indiana had been quick, since he rode with a family in their wagon. He had been traveling now for over two months. He had grown rail-thin. One night, a sudden rainstorm caught him in the open and drenched him. The night was cool and he became chilled. Curled up and trembling, his little boy heart longed for his mother and their home.

That was all Ethan could recall. He did not remember staggering with fever, malnutrition, and exhaustion for two more days. Unknowingly he had altered his course more north than west. One night, near collapse, he slept under a tree, deciding he must find a farm or village the next day. He could not go any farther like this. Putting his bundle in the crook of a tree the next morning, he staggered toward a road, then fainted. When he woke up, he lay in a warm, soft bed—his life altered forever.

Ethan smiled to himself as the train clicked on. He had faced his past and there was nothing to be afraid of anymore. His mother of years ago was a woman he could be proud of and proud to share with Henri.

He glanced up just in time to see a Union flag fluttering lazily from a fence post. He had entered Illinois. Then he remembered a different train. One that, some months back, had carried the midwestern lawyer slowly home to Springfield. The flag had been a farmer's simple way of paying a final tribute. Lincoln had gone home. And I'm going home too, he thought. Home...

Springfield did not look a great deal different to Ethan after four years, when he stepped off the train one mid-morning. The war was over, Lincoln buried, and now life was resuming its predictable, even tempo, just as in thousands of other villages across the battle-scarred nation.

Ethan hurried to the stagecoach office.

"Peppercreek, eh?" The dispatcher scratched his sideburns. "Well, I'm going far as Blackhollow Road today. Can drop you there, or you could wait till tomorrow."

At four that afternoon, Ethan stood at the crossroads after the coach had dropped him off. Peppercreek lay ten miles south. He could make the town sometime after dark. He looked up into the summer sky. He'd been on the train for days, then the coach. He felt like walking. He would camp out that night, then be home for breakfast.

It was dark by the time Ethan found a camp spot he was satisfied with. The place was on the edge of a small clearing with the woods behind him. He knew exactly where he was. He had tramped these woods often as a boy with a fishing pole or squirrel gun over his shoulder. It took little time for him to gather wood and kindle a crackling fire.

He settled in to listen to the night sounds: owl and cricket; the wind that had come up with the twilight and stirred the trees. He closed his eyes to smell, to feel the forest around him, to drink it like a thirsty man. The sky was a dark canopy with a million stars, and he felt his smallness when he gazed up at its vastness.

He felt too excited to sleep. The walk from Springfield had, if anything, invigorated him. His eyes fell upon his satchel, and without a second thought he opened it and dug out his mother's Bible. He smoothed the cover, seeing her face as she had read it years ago. He had leafed through its pages half a dozen times in the intervening years. Yet, he had never failed to esteem it worthy of a place of honor among his few things. He had carried it from Ohio to Peppercreek, from Peppercreek to Shiloh; to Washington, now home. With no particular reason or objective, he opened it and leaned toward the firelight. He began at the gospel of John. Sometime later, he finished, closed it and stared into the dancing flames.

This Jesus of John's gospel was the same Jesus of his real mother, of Rebecca and Will, of Wyeth and Louisa. The Jesus that Henri preached, the Jesus of Dr. Jeremiah and Martha Chester, the Jesus that Andy Mill had loved with all his young heart. Sara James seemed to know this Jesus, too.

He opened the book again. John, chapter one. He would know Him now. With the determination of his nature, and the prayers of loved ones encircling him, he began to reread. The moon was climbing to its highest when he finally closed the book and crawled into his bedroll. He fell asleep almost instantly. Four hours later, he woke up, feeling rested and unable to sleep. He rolled over on his back.

He knew if he got up now and began walking, he would be home for breakfast. He could help with the morning chores. It was a tempting thought. Instead he lay looking into the heavens, thinking—just thinking. Thinking of the pages he had read earlier. Thinking of how he had relived so much of his past in the last few days. He pulled himself upright to lean against the base of a tree, all possibility of sleep gone. He built up the fire again. He would read some more, he decided. Then he remembered the letter from his family, the part from Henri. There was a scripture listed in it that he had not looked up. He would do so now. After hunting a bit for it, he finally found the passage in the forty-third chapter of Isaiah.

> Do not fear, for I have redeemed you. I have called
> you by my name, you are Mine!

He could read no farther. "You are called by my name..."
Ethan could not stop his sudden tears. He saw now, as never before, the Lord's hand upon his life. He had preserved the Book for him, He had preserved his very life. The tears came from a man broken-hearted, his still-strong body shaking with sobs.

It was a beautiful day. Will lay dozing in the front porch hammock, all pretense of reading gone. Isaiah sat on the steps, carefully, slowly, carving little wooden animals for Louisa's girls and Caleb.

Henri and Wyeth sat on a quilt under the big oak, laughing as Caleb took unsteady steps between them. They had never been happier.

Wyeth sighed. "I better get up and go start dinner."

Henri took her hand in his. "Why not wait awhile longer? It's so nice out and—" his words stopped and Wyeth glanced up. She followed his look to the brow of the hill. Henri stood up, his heart racing—his brother had come home.

♦♦ ♦♦ ♦♦

Chapter 18

*W*ill and his son tramped over every square foot of the land in the early morning mists. Ethan ran his hand over the orchard trees, greeting them like old friends. Will talked of making things to ease Ethan's handicap. His voice was full of enthusiasm and Ethan's heart swelled. They talked of plans for the orchard and the horses heavy with foal in the pastures.

The sun came up. The orchard wore a gown of gold and crimson. They stood, silently watching.

"I love this place," Ethan said quietly.

"I know you do, son. I saw it in your eyes from the very first. You love it even as I have."

Will gazed out at the trees planted by his grandfather of long ago. His eyes welled with tears as he picked out the younger trees that he and Rebecca had planted. It had been a special time in their marriage, that planting of trees together. He looked with pride at his son.

"It's yours, Ethan. Always was meant to be. I can't tell you how proud Rebecca and I were to pass it on to you. We talked of it often."

"Pa..." Ethan couldn't speak.

Will's arm went around his son. "You love the land, but I know where your first love is...and that's far above land. No father could be prouder or happier than I am. I...I like to think Rebecca and Rachel and Anne know all about this. I expect they're celebrating, too."

Old Baily rode out from town to shake hands with Ethan, to thump him on the back and welcome him home. He insisted Will throw a potluck picnic so neighbors and town folk could welcome him home also. Will agreed to the plan. Baily also felt obligated to acquaint Ethan with any town tales that Alice Tufts or the family had neglected. Ethan believed that between Grandmother and Baily, nothing had happened in Peppercreek in his nearly four-year absence that he didn't know about. Of course, everyone liked to hear Ethan talk about Abraham Lincoln.

385

"There were folks coming to the President every day, about all sorts of things that had nothing to do with the war or the government. Trying to sell him things—junk mostly. Sometimes they pestered him for an appointment to this office or that. Apparently, campaign managers had made many promises to get Lincoln elected, promises he didn't know about and certainly couldn't keep."

"Poor Abraham," interrupted Grandmother.

"Well, one day he just got fed up with them all and sent them packing. He looked at me, shook his head and said, real serious like, 'Just too many pigs for the teats, Ethan.'"

Everyone burst out laughing.

"There was certainly no false sophistication about Mr. Lincoln," said Will.

Baily, who was not to be outdone, spoke up. "He always paid his bills in cash—never credit. Many's the time he would ride up, dustier than a back-porch rug and say he could only stay a minute. He'd perch up on the cracker barrel and start tellin' tales for an hour or more. Was always good for business. Sure am sorry to see he ain't leadin' the march no more."

Ethan was happy to be with his sisters again. They made him laugh. He was helping in the kitchen one noon, when he suddenly wished he had stayed out in the barn with his father.

"I guess losing an arm does have a few advantages. You won't be putting me to peeling potatoes like you used to do."

Louisa gave him a knowing look. "One of these days, little brother, you'll have a wife and she'll have you doing all sorts of things, and you'll like it!"

"I'm home four days and you're already marrying me off! You're hopeless, Louisa!"

She laughed. "I'll not be completely happy until you're properly domesticated!"

"Oh no!" groaned Ethan.

Wyeth did not look up from the pot she was stirring. She had been patiently waiting for the proper time.

"Speaking of domestication, Sara tells me Roy is courting a girl over near Alton. Served with her brother in the war. Had you heard that, Louisa?" Wyeth did not allow herself to look at Ethan at the mention of Sara's name.

Louisa handed Ethan another plate to dry. "I hadn't heard that. But, what about Sara herself? Things look pretty serious with her and Tom."

"Tom? Tom who?" asked Ethan, with forced casualness.

Louisa turned to Ethan. She did not know what Wyeth knew, but Wyeth could trust her to keep the conversation on track.

"Tom Springer. Didn't you see Sara in Washington, Ethan?"

Ethan looked down at the plate. He was trying hard to visualize the stocky Tom Springer with Sara. He had known this moment was bound to happen.

"Yes... I did."

"Nursing certainly seems to agree with her. She's such a pretty girl," continued Louisa.

"I think she's the prettiest girl in Peppercreek," said Wyeth slyly.

"Well, I certainly will argue with that," said Henri, coming in the kitchen. "But, she does play a mean piano. Girls have you doing dishes, brother? Guess the novelty of your homecoming has worn off. Took about two days before Wyeth had me washing clothes!"

Wyeth threw a dish towel at her husband and Ethan only nodded absently.

"We were discussing Sara's romance with Tom Springer," continued Louisa, never one to let a subject like this one drop easily. "The talk is Tom has a store in Springfield and plans to take Sara with him."

"She doesn't have a ring on her finger yet," Wyeth added hastily.

"Oh, Wyeth, he follows her around like a pup! You didn't see them in town like I did last week, sitting very cozily in his buggy. I'm sure her mother wouldn't mind the match."

"I can't quite picture the two together," Henri put in.

Wyeth stood to the side of Ethan so she could observe his face.

"Well, Henri, would you have put my serious Joe and I together?" asked Louisa and they all laughed.

"Did you see Sara much in Washington, Ethan?" asked Henri. This was the only secret Wyeth had kept from him.

"Some." Ethan's mouth felt dry and he tried to think of an excuse to leave the room.

Only Wyeth could understand his sudden quiet.

Later that night he lay in bed, staring up at the ceiling. This first week at home had been such a happy one, but now a shadow had glided across the joy he had felt. A shadow cast by Sara.

Those long hours of recovery at the Chesters had given him so much time to think. He knew without any doubt that he loved Sara James. He thought of her every time they had been together— in the hospital corridors or sitting by Andy Mills' bedside, at the café or rowing on the Potomac. He smiled when he thought of the little white collar she always wore with her uniform. He thought of the lights and shadows of her beautiful hair, the smoothness of her cheek, her clear blue eyes.

As always, he would then think of the dance. Why had he behaved that way? He could not forget the feeling of her arms around him or the fullness of her lips on his. No other woman had come close to stirring him the way she had. Why had he ignored her? How deeply did she despise him now?

The days were happy, but at night, alone, he was tormented by questions, by the pain of his mistakes with her. When would he see her?

Sara stood before her bedroom mirror and studied her reflection. She wore a cream-colored dress and it pleased her, but ... She had pinned her hair up—not severely like she wore it when nursing, but loosely, in soft curls. It would be too warm, she reasoned with herself, to wear it down, and she would not wear it as she had the night of the dance.

Today was the day. He had gotten home Monday, she had heard. Then Thursday Wyeth had brought word of the picnic Saturday. Mrs. James and Sara had been putting up peach preserves all morning, their bodies damp from the kitchen heat, the whole house filled with the sweet, rich, brown smell of cooking fruit. She had given Wyeth a quick smile, not wanting to meet her eyes, then turned back to the simmering kettle on the stove. Yes, they would come, Mrs. James had enthused. Sara could feel herself trembling. It reminded her of the day, just ten days before, when Henri had burst into the ladies' quilting bee. He had bent over Wyeth and whispered in her ear. Sara could tell he brought good news, but had he brought the good news they had all been awaiting? Wyeth then spoke low to Louisa, and Louisa, who was simply not constructed to keep a confidence, sang out happily, "My little brother is coming home!"

Sara had added her voice to the chorus of pleasure from the other women, then slipped quietly into the kitchen on the pretense of getting some punch. She looked out the east window, feeling very much like she might cry. She felt breathless inside and just knew it registered on her face. She was being schoolgirlish again, she chided herself, but the reproof didn't help.

Now was the day, and here it was thirty minutes till noon and she was still in her room. She wanted to look just right, yet, a part of her didn't even want to go. They would stay a reasonable, polite time, then she would feign a headache and urge her mother and brother home.

Tom Springer would be there too. She sighed. She would have to be telling him her feelings soon. She had tried, but then, as Alice Tufts had said, he had that Springer determination. She hadn't said there was someone else she cared for, she couldn't do that. It hurt her sensitive soul deeply to cause another man pain by her rejection. She could still see in her mind the hurt eyes of the doctor.

Roy had already called up to her to hurry and now her mother's voice came from the bottom of the stairs.

"Yes, I'm coming, Ma."

Her feet moved like lead across the room. "You're being insufferably silly," she whispered to her room, casting a final look over her shoulder. "Just act normal, you goose."

She was wanting to stay . . . and wanting to see his face again . . .

Grandmother Tufts was in her element. As Baily moved in one orb of the gathering, she moved in another. It had not escaped her all-seeing eyes that Mildred Donner's hair color had changed since last week, or that the Pierce baby at six months looked altogether too chubby. They're gorging him, she decided, but held her tongue. She had sampled Carrie Miller's pound cake and knew that it had a splash of rum in it. Just a splash of course—but still, Grandmother shook her head at Carrie's irresponsibility. She kept an eagle eye on the cake to make sure no child ate too freely of it.

Will provided her a chair and she settled down to scan the picnickers from a stationary spot. It was a gorgeous day—not too warm, a fine day for celebrating Ethan's return. She fixed her gaze on him as he stood across the lawn laughing with Roy James and some other of his old chums.

Then her telescopic eyes picked up the look Ethan quickly cast in Sara James' direction. Alice Tufts, studier of looks, glances, and blatant stares, knew this was the look of someone trying very hard not to look—or be seen looking. The old lady had seen him do this no less than twice during the afternoon. No one else had seen, but Alice Tufts had. Supplementing this observation was the revelation that Sara was doing the same thing. She mentally chewed on this for a time, then smiled to herself as she came up with the truth to the situation. Well, well . . . Sara James was perfect for Ethan Alcott, she decreed. I heartily approve, she thought.

Once during the meal, Grandmother had seen Sara and Ethan lock eyes over the heads of the laughing, talking folk. No more than a split second, but there it was.

"If sparks could fly . . ." she had murmured to her plate.

Later she found Ethan at her side. He had brought her a refill of lemonade. They had chatted. Ethan enjoyed being again in the company of the old woman who was so full of ginger. When the conversation lulled momentarily, Alice Tufts decided to press her speculations. After all, wasn't that a grandmother's responsibility? In the twilight of life, pleasure comes all too infrequently, and pleasures such as this must be taken, she reasoned to herself.

"Well, Roy looks fit as a fiddle," she remarked expansively. "So glad he came back all right. Always was a good boy. Never took my plums without asking or teased the dog. What's he going to do for a living now?"

"I don't think he knows for sure. Has some ideas," said Ethan.

But of course, Grandmother did not want to talk about Roy James. He was just a lead.

"I know Mary is so relieved to have them both back."

"Yes."

"Sara was such a brave little thing to do what she did. Go all the way to Washington. I did have some reservations at first about it. Young woman with all those wounded men..."

"Hmm..."

"I imagine she was quite capable at her work."

"I'm... sure she was." Ethan was watching a hawk spiraling in the distance.

"You'd think such hard work would have blemished her. Yet she looks like a June rose."

Ethan shifted uncomfortably from foot to foot. He was tempted to look directly at Grandmother, to read in her eyes if she knew the truth in his heart. But no, how could she know?

"No lovelier girl in the county," pressed grandmother.

Grandmother waited. She had dropped her bait.

"Yes..." said Ethan. Here he was, wishing he were somewhere else again.

"War doesn't end courting of course—human nature and all that," she went on. "Now just look there! Plain to see Tom Springer's motives, hovering over Sara there like a bee in a honeysuckle vine. His intentions are plain, but I just don't know about Sara. She has a good head on those pretty shoulders."

Ethan was saved from commenting by Henri's arrival with Caleb on his shoulders. He felt a wave of relief as the conversation turned. Ethan moved off, milling through the crowd, his words saying one thing, but his mind wholly absorbed in a subject all his own. It was just as Grandmother had said—and more.

Of course she had come. He knew she would. Yet when he saw her face-to-face, it seemed all his mistakes rose up before him to accuse. He laughed, talked and enjoyed himself, but all the while he was acutely aware of Sara's presence, even across the lawn. She's like a fragrance all around me, he thought. He tried desperately not to look at her—tried to avoid her, in fact. Once, when he had been finding his place to sit down and eat, their eyes had met. It was a look no longer than any look he had given anyone else, yet a frame of time suddenly froze between them, vivid and still. Could he read anything in her look? He sat for a moment, utterly shaken that she had such an influence over him.

He watched with shy glances as Tom Springer refilled her glass, leaned over her shoulder to talk, paid her a dozen other little attentions. Ethan swallowed hard, engulfed with longing.

"Lord, help me get over her," he prayed inwardly. He had no idea she prayed the same way. His thoughts were interrupted by Baily clanging on a pot.

"Ahem! Well now, ain't this been a fine day?"

There was a cheer of agreement with the oldtimer.

"I, for one, am mighty glad Will had such a dandy idea as this picnic. Just wanted to say I'm proud and pleased that my young friend Ethan Alcott is home where he belongs. He did a fine job, workin' for Abraham as you all know, and I say 'thank you' to him."

There was clapping and smiles and everyone turned to Ethan. Roy James called out, "Speech!" and others took up the chorus.

"Say somethin' boy," prompted Baily.

Ethan wasn't sure he liked the idea of trying to make a speech, but then he looked out at their friendly faces and found he did have something to say. They had come here, a dozen or so families, to say hello and welcome home. They came to swap war stories and childhood reminiscences. God had given him a good family, this he knew. Yet as he stood looking at their expectant faces, he realized God had given him good friends as well. His loving family, friends, a home, work. That he did not have a young woman to share it with dimmed for a time in importance. Gratitude was all he could feel now. Slowly he rose to his feet.

"Well folks, I'm really not a hand for speaking up like this. Yet, I'm glad of the chance to tell all of you how much it has meant to me, your coming this afternoon. I realize I have many blessings when I look around me." He stopped a moment, pulling at the hair above his ear, trying to organize his thoughts.

One listener stood on the fringe of the crowd, under the shade of a tree, away for the moment from one who tried so to claim her heart. When she saw Ethan's familiar gesture of concentration she turned away a moment, smiling, feeling as if her heart of love would burst.

"It probably sounds strange, to most of you," Ethan went on, "that I speak of blessings. I certainly never have before. But, you see, I just couldn't get up here and open my mouth without telling you what the Lord has done for me. You see, just recently, He showed me again how His hand has been on my life. Always. If . . . I didn't tell you, it would be the worst ingratitude a man could show."

Tom Springer was a big, easygoing fellow, prone to understanding cattle and horses more than people—especially women. He had courted Sara James with all the finesse he could muster, yet still he knew she didn't belong to him. When he found she was not at his side, he scanned the crowd till he spotted her, alone and apart. He started to go to her. But her face, so honed in to that of Ethan Alcott, arrested him. He had never seen her look like that. He knew Sara and Ethan were childhood friends from way back. He knew from Roy that she had seen Alcott in Washington. The truth dawned on his slow but honest spirit. He smiled and looked down at his feet. Well, as his mother would say, "There are other fish in the creek." He turned his attention back to the speaker.

Ethan had relaxed and his voice grew stronger.

"I was always proud of what I could do, like fish and hunt, or run a foot race or fell a tree, things that pushed my body to be the best . . . But I never took the time, or wanted to look at what I was on the inside. You all thought maybe I was a good boy, a fine shot, and I was proud of what you thought. Still, what did the Lord think of me?" He stopped and thought of his mother and Rebecca.

"A little boy lived for eight years in a home with a godly mother and . . . a father that drank. A harsh man. Some days there was nothing to eat because he hadn't provided for them. The woman, she prayed, and cried and held her boy close. Then one day she prayed for him one last time, and then she died. He decided to go west. He journeyed a long time and finally ended up here, protected that long way by the hand of a Father that saw everything."

"The Lord brought him here, to this family. Will and Rebecca O'Dell, Wyeth and Louisa and Libby, Uncle Isaiah and Grandmother. They didn't treat him as a bound boy or a stranger. No, he was treated as a son and a brother from the very first. See, folks? See how good the Lord was to that boy?

"He grew up with a pa and a ma always praying for him. He went off to war. He thought maybe he could make a name for himself in it, do something in his strength. But it didn't work out that way. The Lord had other plans . . . He went down to Shiloh and was wounded, then shipped off to Washington. He was placed to work with the sixteenth president of the land. What an honor! And didn't the man know it? He . . . he grew to . . ." Ethan paused, trying to control the emotion that surged through him. He looked at the ground a moment. "He loved the President."

"One day, in all his strength and pride, a shot brought him down, took away his arm, made him . . . less. A Quaker family, a family God had picked, took care of him. His arm was well, but what about his heart? The President was gone and the man thought . . . if only he had been there."

Ethan didn't see Sara's face as he talked. In fact he focused on no particular person. He just talked from his heart. He didn't see the eyes of many of his listeners as they filled with tears. He didn't see Wyeth, who openly wept on Henri's shoulder.

"He wandered around, feeling useless and bitter. Even afraid. He felt he wasn't in control of his life anymore. A negro family took him into their home and their hearts when he had nothing. Then he finally started home. Like the prodigal son. Along the way, the Lord showed him just how much . . . just how very much He loved him and had cared for him all along."

Tears were streaming down his cheeks, but he didn't care. His voice was triumphant. He felt more at peace than he ever had in his entire life.

"Folks, I am that young man! No longer as strong as I once was. But . . . that doesn't matter anymore. I wouldn't trade what I was then or what I had for what I am today. Standing before you a new man, born into the Lord through his grace and the faithful prayers of those that loved me. I . . ." Ethan broke out in one of his very broadest smiles.

"Bet you all didn't know I was so long-winded, did ya? Well, maybe I should take up storekeepin' like Baily here, so I can tell tales all day. That's all I have to say. Thanks again for coming."

Ethan was surrounded by his friends. Will had stood and listened to his son, then with trembling steps he had slipped away, walking behind the house to the little white-fenced plot. He clutched the fence as he remembered Rebecca. He longed for her as he never had before. "Did you hear that, Rebecca?" he whispered. "Did you hear, gal?"

Wyeth noticed someone move away from the crowd when Ethan had finished. It was Sara. She disappeared into the house. Then a neighbor proposed some singing, and while a few families headed home, most stayed, reluctant to leave the good food and fellowship. A good rousing sing-along was always the perfect ending to a gathering like this. Wyeth slipped through the crowd and up to Ethan. They looked at each other, smiled, then laughed and finally hugged. There was no way she could possibly tell him what his words had meant to her.

"Henri's wrapped up with Baily and Pa is helping the Millers hitch up. Do you think you could slip into the kitchen and fetch me back that big jug of lemonade? I think we're about out, and folks will be thirsty when they're done singing."

"That may be awhile from the sounds of it," he laughed, pointing to Dan Tyler who was pulling out his harmonica. "I'll be right back."

Wyeth smiled. Not having Grandmother's cunning or Louisa's blunt skills, she was nevertheless quite capable of a little romantic sabotage.

Henri came up to her. "What are you smiling about? You look like you have a secret."

She laughed and batted her eyes. "Who, me?"

Ethan hurried to the house. He was only too glad to do the little request for his sister. He needed some time alone. A man doesn't pour out his inner heart without a certain weak feeling left inside.

He entered the kitchen and stopped in his tracks. Sara was standing at the sink, her face pale and tear-stained. They were alone in the house. Her paleness shocked him. Finally he managed to find his voice. "Sara? Are you all right?"

Besides their initial, brief greeting earlier, this was the first words he had spoken to her in over a year.

"I'm fine, Ethan. I was . . . just warm. I wanted to get out of the sun for a moment." She knew her words sounded lame.

She had spoken so softly Ethan had to strain to hear it. He glanced around the room quickly and did not see any jug of lemonade. Here he was, alone with her, and he felt terribly uncomfortable. He stood looking at the table, trying desperately to think of something to say.

Sara could think of nothing to say either. What a ridiculous situation! she thought. Ethan's words outside had made her heart swell with love for him. She had wanted to be alone, afraid someone would see her feelings mirrored on her face. It had taken courage for him to speak so openly, so honestly, and she had stood in the shade, so very proud of him.

When she had allowed herself a look in his direction throughout the picnic, she could tell, even in those covert glances, that there was something different about him. Now, she knew. So, with her symphony of love for him, there was now a chorus of praise to Him who had faithfully and patiently revealed Himself. The loss of Ethan's arm made no difference to her—he was more complete to her now than ever. The empty spot inside him had been filled.

She must think of something to say and leave quickly. Ethan finally managed his voice, though his mouth felt so dry.

"Would you—like to go for a walk? Down to the creek?"

It was the last thing she had imagined he would say and certainly closed any path to a graceful exit. She finally lifted her eyes, surprised at her own words. "Yes, Ethan. I'd like that."

Washington, D.C.

Frederick Ambrose Rufus Dilling stretched his long legs and sighed wearily. Sitting outside his front door, he felt the oppressiveness of the August humidity. Rose and the boys had gone to visit Rose's family, a trip that Ethan's money had made possible. He looked into the night sky. Stars were shaded in a thin wisp of clouds. Dilling was thinking about the young captain from Illinois, wondering how things were going for him.

Dilling's life was complete with simple pleasures. He was a happy man. His hand smoothed the rich leather cover of the book that rested on his knee. He had been reading it since Ethan had left. It was one of the books in the gift box. They had not found it immediately and it was Rufus who had spied the note stuck in the cover.

> *Of all the books in this box, I think this one must be the very best. My mother and family have always treasured it and I plan to look into it more myself. I hope it will become a treasured book for the Dilling family also.*
>
> *Ethan Alcott*

On that recommendation alone, Dilling had read it. The main character in the second half of the book fascinated him. He said such amazing things. Just this night, he had read that God is no respecter of persons. It was a heady thought. Could it possibly be true? He would have to read more...

Of course, Ethan and the Dillings would have contact in the following years, but Ethan never knew of the salvation of a generation, initiated through his simple gift. Two sons would become ministers to their people, another a schoolteacher, another an artist, all godly men. Dilling fell asleep a bit later, a blessing for the captain on his lips.

Virginia

Martha Chester rocked, though she knew she should get up and go to bed. Daniel had finally gone to sleep, despite his excitement. Dr. Jeremiah had brought the letter this evening. Ethan had made it home. His shoulder was fine. His soul was even better. They had rejoiced in his letter, and the final passage had been to Daniel.

> *When I get settled in a bit more and am on my feet better, I'd like to send you some money. I'd like you to come here to Illinois to see me. You'll be coming west! You'll not be alone, there will also be some boys near your age from Washington. We'll teach them to fish and tramp the woods. God bless you, Daniel.*
>
> *Ethan*

The letter lay in Martha's lap. She had prayed after the doctor had left and now as the clock struck ten, she knew it was time to go to bed. Still she lingered. In fact, her rocker moved with increased animation. In the quiet cabin, her smile was radiant. Dr. Jeremiah had proposed.

Peppercreek, Illinois

They passed out the back door and silently directed their steps toward the creek. The path led through a pasture where long, yellow-green grasses were moving like waves upon the land. The smell of rich warm earth hung fragrant in the air and when they came to the rise that dropped down to the creekbank, they stopped. Looking across the fields, they could see for miles. The land and the sky melted together like the dreamy, muted blue of a watercolor. They stood there, aware of the land around them, their aloneness, their connection to each other.

Then they came to the creek and Sara found a log to sit on. Ethan stood with his hand in his pocket, feeling more nervous now than when he had spoken to his neighbors earlier. Five minutes slid away in silence. Ethan looked from the corner of his eye to see Sara, apparently absorbed in watching the sparkling, clear creek.

"You see that little cropping of rocks over there?"

Sara looked up and nodded.

"That's a part of . . . my family's history."

"Really?"

"According to tradition, that's where Pepper, the dog of my adopted great-grandfather, Joshua O'Dell, ran to and started barking. Joshua was just about to give up. He'd been without water for days, and he followed the dog up here."

"And there was the water," said Sara.

"That's right. He named it Pepper Creek, then and there."

"You have a heritage to be proud of, I think," she said with a faint smile.

Ethan was pleased to see her smile. He nodded and looked out across the water. "And a heritage to be thankful for."

They were quiet again, each trying to fathom what the other was thinking. Why did he ask me to go for this walk? Sara was asking herself. I'm afraid if he says anything, I'll cry. I wish I could just slip away.

Ethan dug deeper into his pocket, as if he would come up with the right words there. How could he begin to tell her all that was in his heart? How could he express how sorry he was that he had hurt her? He took a deep breath and prayed, "Give me the words to say to her, Lord . . . then I'll leave the rest in Your hands."

He walked over to her and knelt down. The silence brought peace to him.

"Sara."

He had said her name like a caress and it made her tremble inside. She had to get up. "I need to go back. Mother is probably waiting."

"Please, wait!" He reached out and touched her arm. "Sara, I have so much I want... I need to say to you."

"What you said back at the picnic...I'm happy for you, Ethan."

She looked at her hands in her lap. He looked at them too. They were small and lovely and he longed to hold them.

"When I was talking...I wished I could have told you first. Just you, Sara."

She moved uncertainly on the log.

"There's so much—everything, really!" He laughed. "I wanted to tell you about Lincoln and how I got shot and the Chesters and the Dillings, a wonderful family in Washington. And then about my night out in the woods and...everything, Sara. All I could think of was how I wanted to talk to you. And I wanted to know about you. About the time since I last saw you at the train station a year ago," he finished softly.

Sara stood up abruptly. "I need to get back."

"Sara, won't you stay and let me finish?"

She faced him squarely.

He cleared his throat, suddenly feeling nervous again because of her direct, unemotional gaze.

"I know I hurt you in Washington. You have no idea how I've agonized over it. I...was a fool, Sara."

"Ethan, don't... It doesn't matter. It's all right."

He felt a grip of fear, but he had to know.

"Are you engaged to Tom Springer?"

He did not see the fleeting smile. "Are you engaged to Amanda Sims?" she returned.

"What? Of course not!"

"I'm not engaged to Tom." Her voice was so even Ethan didn't know how to interpret it.

"That night of the dance—"

"Don't!"

He felt deflated, uncertain. He dropped his eyes to the ground and when he looked up, he was surprised to see her still there. She was surprised to see tears in his eyes. She stepped one small step closer to him.

"I have to tell you. I need you to understand," he continued.
She said nothing, but waited.

"I didn't come back after the dance because . . . I was afraid to, Sara. I was afraid of how much I was feeling for you. I didn't know what to do about it. No one had ever made me feel . . . like you did. Sara, do you believe what I said back there, to my family and friends?"

She nodded.

"Then please believe what I say now. I ask your forgiveness for being so blind. But I'm a new man, Sara. Not a perfect one, but a new one."

She turned around and he expected her to walk off. Yet she stood still and he knew she was crying. He walked around to her.

"Please don't cry."

He didn't dare touch her because he knew if he did he would pull her close.

She ached for him to do so.

"I didn't mean to make you cry," he said. "If you want to go back . . ."

She didn't move. He felt desperate.

"Don't go! Sara, there's something . . . else I haven't said."

She looked at him now.

"I want to hold your beautiful hands to say this but if I do, then I'll want to hold all of you and—" He suddenly realized he could not hold both of her hands—the reality of his handicap washed over him again.

"I can't hold both your hands," he said slowly to himself. He felt inadequate and Sara knew it. She reached out and took his hand in hers.

"It doesn't matter, Ethan."

He looked up to find her smiling that wonderful smile he had dreamed about.

"Sara?" he asked cautiously.

"You said . . . you had something else to say," she prompted. Her head was slightly tilted and he saw her eyes sparkling.

His spirit rose in leaps. "You are so beautiful!"

She blushed furiously.

"What I said about my faith is true. And, just under that in importance, is . . . I love you, Sara! I love you very much."

She had loved him so long—she didn't know whether to laugh or cry, so she threw her arms around him, whispering over and over things for him alone. Things that had been inside her for years. Oh, to hold him close...

Cottonwood leaves trembled in the late sunshine, a bird made solitary melody on a branch nearby. A very good day had just become a very great day.

"I can only hold you with one arm, Sara, but I will hold you with all my heart—forever."

He released her reluctantly.

"I..." He smiled the smile she loved. "I want to kiss you, you know. But I won't until... we begin to court, officially."

She smiled, then they both laughed and headed back to the picnic.

It was nearly six in the evening now. The sun had begun its slow descent behind the western line of apple trees. It had been a fine picnic, but now it was time to gather up and head home to chores. Mothers were calling their scattered broods while husbands stretched and slowly made their wagons ready. Dan Taylor still sat with a few around him, coaxing tunes from the shiny little instrument in his hand.

Will glanced around, wondering what had happened to Ethan. Folks would be leaving soon and he should be there to say goodbye. Grandmother Tufts sat beside him, unable to stir in her wicker chair, for Caleb lay sprawled in sleep across her lap. Her hand rested on him in proud possession. Louisa and Joe sat there also, laughing and talking. Henri and Wyeth stood beside them, relishing the day as everyone had. Will leaned over to his daughter. "Have you seen Ethan?"

"No, but I think—" then she stopped. Ethan and Sara came walking around from the back of the house. They came, momentarily unnoticed by the rest of the neighbors, but the O'Dell family followed Wyeth's gaze. Ethan and Sara were not touching, but there was an air of possession between them. Louisa clapped her hands and laughed and Grandmother clucked her tongue approvingly. Will nodded his head and smiled.

Henri turned to Wyeth. "Didn't have any secrets from me, did you, oh wife of mine?"

She smiled up into his eyes and he kissed her.

Then someone in the group saw Ethan and called out, "You missed a mighty good singin', Ethan!"

He laughed. "No, I heard it. Roy was off-key, as usual!"

Will stepped up beside Ethan. "Folks, my family and I thank you for coming and welcoming my son home. God bless you all!"

"I can't improve on anything my father says," said Ethan. "Good evenin' to you."

But before anyone could move off, Dan Taylor called out, "Another song! A welcome-home song for the Captain!" Dan was a performer at heart and hated to give up his captive and enthusiastic audience. Someone called out a tune.

"I can play that!" said Dan, trying some notes.

"What's the matter with you, Dan? Don't you know that's a Rebel song?" a neighbor called. The popular song, known even in the North very well, was indeed a song from the South.

Will spoke up, and everyone became quiet.

"There is no Rebel or Yank anymore," he said easily. "No more blue and gray. Mothers and wives and sweethearts are welcoming their boys home all over the land. Feelings like that don't have a border. Now, Dan, go ahead and play it for us."

Ethan caught Sara's eye and they smiled. They had a future together—and nothing could be lovelier.

Dan was still trying to get the exact tune out of his little box.

Then the afternoon became even more special. Everyone stopped talking and Dan stopped playing. There was music already. Isaiah was sitting on a wagon bed, his gentle old face illuminated by a faint smile. His fiddle rested under his chin as he found the tune and played it perfectly. Isaiah was playing the fiddle again.

"...When Johnny comes marchin' home again, hurrah! hurrah."

The tapestry is finished...

Afterword

Writers of historical fiction strive to keep their work histori-
cally accurate. At the same time they maintain the liberty to use
creative license. In writing *The Tapestry*, I tried to stay within a
strict historical framework. However, on a few occasions I had to
juggle dates because of the plot line.

For those readers who are interested, it is a matter of record
that disease claimed more lives in the Civil War than bullet,
cannon, and saber wounds combined.

Journals reveal that this war was at times a "friendly" war,
with Confederate and Union soldiers fraternizing openly, sometimes sharing a canteen or even a tent.

Nearly every quote of Lincoln's is documented, from the
signing of the Emancipation Proclamation, "My signature is
weak," to "That speech [the Gettysburg Address] was a flat
failure!" to "Gloves are cruelty to animals." It is also true Lincoln
vehemently disliked security details around him, even though a
would-be sniper had placed a bullet hole neatly through his
stovepipe hat early in his first administration. Lincoln was called
"Abraham the Second" by a young admirer and could raise two
axes shoulder height.

My hope is that in reading *The Tapestry* you the reader have
received a deeper appreciation for a great American president
and a most difficult time in American history.

Thomas Carlyle wrote, "If a book comes from the heart, it
will continue to reach other hearts."

From my heart to yours,
MaryAnn Minatra

HARVEST HOUSE PUBLISHERS

For the Best in Inspirational Fiction

RUTH LIVINGSTON HILL CLASSICS

Bright Conquest
The Homecoming (mass paper)
The Jeweled Sword
This Side of Tomorrow

June Masters Bacher
PIONEER ROMANCE NOVELS

Series 1

1. Love Is a Gentle Stranger
2. Love's Silent Song
3. Diary of a Loving Heart
4. Love Leads Home
5. Love Follows the Heart
6. Love's Enduring Hope

Series 2

1. Journey to Love
2. Dreams Beyond Tomorrow
3. Seasons of Love
4. My Heart's Desire
5. The Heart Remembers
6. From This Time Forth

Series 3

1. Love's Soft Whisper
2. Love's Beautiful Dream
3. When Hearts Awaken
4. Another Spring
5. When Morning Comes Again
6. Gently Love Beckons

HEARTLAND HERITAGE SERIES

No Time for Tears
Songs in the Whirlwind
Where Lies Our Hope

ROMANCE NOVELS

The Heart that Lingers, *Bacher*
With All My Heart, *Bacher*
If Love Be Ours, *Brown*

Brenda Wilbee
SWEETBRIAR SERIES

Sweetbriar
The Sweetbriar Bride
Sweetbriar Spring

CLASSIC WOMEN OF FAITH SERIES

Shipwreck!
Lady Rebel

Lori Wick
THE CAMERON ANNALS

A Place Called Home
A Song for Silas
The Long Road Home
A Gathering of Memories

THE CALIFORNIANS

Whatever Tomorrow Brings
As Time Goes By
Sean Donovan

Ellen Traylor
BIBLICAL NOVELS

Esther
Joseph
Moses
Joshua

**Available at your
local Christian bookstore**

Dear Reader:

We would appreciate hearing from you regarding this Harvest House fiction book. It will enable us to continue to give you the best in Christian publishing.

1. What most influenced you to purchase *The Tapestry*?
   - ☐ Author
   - ☐ Subject matter
   - ☐ Backcover copy
   - ☐ Recommendations
   - ☐ Cover/Title
   - ☐ _____

2. Where did you purchase this book?
   - ☐ Christian bookstore
   - ☐ General bookstore
   - ☐ Department store
   - ☐ Grocery store
   - ☐ Other

3. Your overall rating of this book:
   - ☐ Excellent   ☐ Very good   ☐ Good   ☐ Fair   ☐ Poor

4. How likely would you be to purchase other books by this author?
   - ☐ Very likely
   - ☐ Somewhat likely
   - ☐ Not very likely
   - ☐ Not at all

5. What types of books most interest you? (Check all that apply.)
   - ☐ Women's Books
   - ☐ Marriage Books
   - ☐ Current Issues
   - ☐ Self Help/Psychology
   - ☐ Bible Studies
   - ☐ Fiction
   - ☐ Biographies
   - ☐ Children's Books
   - ☐ Youth Books
   - ☐ Other _____

6. Please check the box next to your age group.
   - ☐ Under 18
   - ☐ 18-24
   - ☐ 25-34
   - ☐ 35-44
   - ☐ 45-54
   - ☐ 55 and over

Mail to: Editorial Director
Harvest House Publishers
1075 Arrowsmith
Eugene, OR 97402

Name _____

Address _____

City _____   State _____   Zip _____

**Thank you for helping us
to help you in future publications!**